FAIR LIBERTY WAS ALL HIS CRY

Jonathan Swift
by C. Jervas

FAIR LIBERTY
WAS ALL HIS CRY

A TERCENTENARY TRIBUTE

TO JONATHAN SWIFT

1667–1745

EDITED BY

A. NORMAN JEFFARES

MACMILLAN
London · Melbourne · Toronto
ST MARTIN'S PRESS
New York
1967

© Macmillan & Co. Ltd. 1967

MACMILLAN AND COMPANY LIMITED
Little Essex Street London WC 2
also Bombay Calcutta Madras Melbourne

THE MACMILLAN COMPANY OF CANADA LIMITED
70 Bond Street Toronto 2

ST MARTIN'S PRESS INC
175 Fifth Avenue New York NY 10010

Library of Congress catalog card no. 67–12827

PRINTED IN GREAT BRITAIN

Contents

Illustrations

Jonathan Swift, by C. Jervas   *frontispiece*

Jonathan Swift, by or after C. Jervas   *facing page* 107

*Both portraits are reproduced by permission of the Trustees
of the National Portrait Gallery, London*

Acknowledgements

THE editor and publishers wish to thank the following, who have given permission for the use of copyright material: the American Folklore Society Inc., for ' "Jack and the Dane": Swift traditions in Ireland', by Mackie L. Jarrell, from the *Journal of American Folklore*; Chatto & Windus Ltd., for the extract from *Determinations: Critical Essays*, by F. R. Leavis; Mrs. J. Gray, Mrs. J. Cannon, and Mrs. J. Phipps, for 'Jonathan Swift: some observations', by D. Nichol Smith, from *Transactions of the Royal Society of Literature*; the Librarian of the John Rylands Library, for 'Jonathan Swift's Hoax of 1722 upon Ebenezor Elliston', by George P. Mayhew, from the *Bulletin of the John Rylands Library*; Johns Hopkins Press, for ' "Animal Rationis Capax." A study of certain aspects of Swift's imagery', by Kathleen M. Williams, from *Journal of English Literary History*; Professor Vivian Mercier and the Editor and publishers of *A Review of English Literature* for 'Swift and the Gaelic Tradition'; Modern Language Association of America, for 'The Origin of *Gulliver's Travels*, from *PMLA*; Frederick Muller Ltd., for 'Swift as an Ecclesiastical Statesman', by J. C. Beckett, from *Essays in British and Irish History in Honour of James Eadie Todd*; Dr. A. L. Rowse, for 'Jonathan Swift', from *The English Spirit* (Macmillan); Martin Secker & Warburg Ltd. and Harcourt, Brace & World, Inc., for 'Politics *vs.* Literature: an examination of *Gulliver's Travels*', from *Shooting an Elephant*, by George Orwell; Taylor & Francis Ltd., for 'The Scientific Background of Swift's "Voyage to Laputa" ', by Marjorie Nicolson and Nora M. Mohler, from *Annals of Science*; University of Toronto Press, for 'Swift's View of Poetry', by Herbert Davis, from *Studies in English*, ed. Malcolm Wallace; Mr. T. G. Wilson and the Editor and publishers of *A Review of English Literature* for 'Swift's Personality'; Mr. Leonard Woolf, for the extract from 'Swift's *Journal to Stella*', by Virginia Woolf; and Mr. M. B. Yeats and Crowell-Collier & Macmillan, Inc., for the extract from the Introduction to *Words upon the Window-Pane*, by W. B. Yeats.

The contributions specially commissioned for this book by Professor Bonamy Dobrée, Professor A. Norman Jeffares, Miss Claire Lamont, and Professor Ricardo Quintana are © Macmillan & Co. Ltd 1967. 'Key to the Language of the Houyhnhnms in *Gulliver's Travels*' is © Mrs. Marjorie W. Buckley 1967.

Introduction

'SWIFT haunts me,' wrote Yeats, 'he is always just around the next corner.' In writing thus in his introduction to *The Words upon the Window-Pane* Yeats was as much exploring his own Anglo-Irish heritage as contemplating the political nationalism of Ireland, which he thought Bishop Molyneux, author of *The Case of Ireland Stated* (1698), and Swift, as author of *The Drapier's Letters*, had founded, but his words still apply to the attitudes of many readers of Swift. For his is indeed a haunting presence. In Ireland he is still part of the folklore of those for whom he altered and amended the proof-sheets of Faulkner's Dublin edition of his works, which the publisher read aloud not only to him but to two men servants, whose understanding of the writings had to be clear. Not until they understood would Swift stop altering and amending and say: 'This will do; for I write to the Vulgar more than to the Learned.' Swift's place in Irish popular tradition is explored in this volume by Mackie L. Jarrell, while Vivian Mercier considers Swift's own attitude to Gaelic Ireland and its likely effect on him. His serious work for the Church of Ireland is examined by J. C. Beckett, while a discussion by George P. Mayhew of the hoax he perpetrated upon Ebenezor Elliston in Dublin reminds us that he described himself to Stella as 'not the gravest of Divines'.

Swift haunts the learned. He had the habit of writing many things which he did not intend to be printed; he concealed his authorship by having his work transcribed in an unknown hand and dropped unseen at the printers. His instructions to his friend Charles Ford about how the manuscript of *Some Free Thoughts upon the Present State of Affairs* was to reach the printer are clear:

Here it is, read it, and send it to B—— by an unknown hand . . . Do not send it by the Penny post, nor your Man, but by a Porter when you are not at your Lodgings. Get some Friend to copy out the little Paper, and send it inclosed with the rest, and let the same Hand direct it, and seal it with an unknown Seal.

Benjamin Motte, who published *Gulliver's Travels*, told Pope that
he did not know whence or from whom he had received the copy
which was 'dropped at his house in the dark, from a hackney coach'.
As a result of this desire of Swift's for anonymity, and his occasional
casualness about his own work, there has been a vast problem for
editors in determining the canon of his works. As Sir Harold
Williams remarked in the Introduction to his edition of the poems:
'During Swift's life, and after, any witty, grotesque, or indecent
piece, of Irish origin and unknown parentage, was ascribed to the
great Dean of St. Patrick's, as if by a standing affiliation order.'

This century has seen brilliant and painstaking scholarship
applied to establishing the canon and editing the texts. Textual and
bibliographical scholars — the names of Elrington Ball, Herbert
Davis, A. C. Guthkelch, D. Nichol Smith and Sir Harold Williams
spring to mind at once — have given us superbly edited texts. But
Swift himself is always just around the next corner. He has always
been.

In his own period Swift incurred the envy of lesser men: his pen
and his tongue were sharp, and he did not spare them in the service
of his religion and his political beliefs. He loathed cant and hypocrisy; his sense of satiric irony ran deep; his wit and invention were
virtually irrepressible. He was often an unhappy man, a despairing
man, and yet he could be the best and the gayest of friends. He
played a powerful part in public affairs: and was in consequence a
target for contemporary jealousy and envy — even his fellow
clergy, for instance, did not necessarily treat him with Christian
charity. And the suspicions and doubts continued after his death.
The often disapproving, sometimes even malicious *Remarks on the
Life and Writings of Dr. Jonathan Swift, Dean of St. Patrick's,
Dublin* (1752) of Lord Orrery, his first biographer, were refined
upon by Robert Shiels in Colley Cibber's *The Lives of the Poets of
Great Britain and Ireland, to the Time of Dean Swift* (1753). The
defences of his friend Dr. Delany and his relative Deane Swift did
not undo a sometimes dubious, even scandalised, view of his
character. This occurred in his own century. Johnson added to it, in
his Life, despite Thomas Sheridan's objections in his subsequent
biography, and it developed further in the nineteenth century.

Scott's generous mind, however, realised the extent of his originality and the strength of his passion, which had combined with his superb intellect to make him a great writer. It was Scott's instinct for the heroic which led him to appreciate Swift's excellence; and Hazlitt, too, with characteristic sanity, defended him as a genius who was not prompted 'to write unmeaning panegyrics on mankind'.

There were others, nevertheless, to whom Swift's mind seemed stored with images from the dunghill and the lazar house, and the raging of Jeffrey, Macaulay and Thackeray had its effect. Thackeray went so far as to think that the fourth book of *Gulliver's Travels* should not be read at all. To a certain extent some of these nineteenth-century critics failed to distinguish between Swift and his invented characters. Forster's work, so ably developed by Craik, led to a sounder view of Swift's life, for Craik did try to separate Swift and his personae.

The twentieth century has come to understand him better. The question of his madness, first treated by Sir William Wilde in an article in 1847 and more fully in a book, *The Closing Years of Dean Swift's Life* (1849), has since been more sensibly and fully discussed by Lord Brain and by Sir William Wilde's biographer, Dr. T. G. Wilson, whose article on Swift's personality is included in this volume. It puts the question of Swift's health, physical as well as mental, in perspective. But a fashion for seeing Swift as the gloomy Dean originally set in during the nineteenth century. Such critical and biographical studies seem to have prevailed unduly into our own age also, and Professor Dobrée queries these attitudes here in his essay on the jocose Dean.

Swift believed in the bagatelle: he liked teasing, and in the 'Verses on the Death of Dr. Swift' he may have been setting himself another target, of being 'cheerful to his dying day', for he had a hatred of the infirmities of age. Resilient and tough despite the giddiness and deafness which plagued him, he believed in exercise and wished his friends to do the same. There is a touching letter to Charles Ford in which he argues that life is not of much value but health worth everything: 'For my own part I labour for daily health as often and almost as many hours as a workman does for daily bread, and like a common labourer can but just earn enough to keep life and soul together.' He goes on to urge temperance and exercise on Ford, out of a solicitude for his health which reveals his gentle side and the 'true love and esteem' he had for his friends.

The range of his friendship was wide. His affection for the members of the Scriblerus Club ran deep. Harley and St. John he admired and loved and he treated them with the utmost frankness. He would not be treated with coldness or reserve; indeed St. John was warned that Swift expected that every great minister who honoured him with his acquaintance 'if he heard or saw anything to my disadvantage, would let me know in plain words, and not put me in pain to guess by the change or coldness of his countenance or behaviour; for it was what I could hardly bear from a crowned head'.

His wit and learning had earned him the right to be independent. The publication of *A Tale of a Tub* and *The Battle of the Books* in 1704 had shown his literary merits to the world. Six years later, at forty-three, he had, as Professor Herbert Davis has written, established 'his reputation as a genius and as a writer of great power both in verse and prose'. But his period as Tory pamphleteer at the centre of power was short. Once he was installed as Dean of St. Patrick's Cathedral in Dublin he felt he was living a country life in town. And at forty-six he was aware that a new age had begun: the Whigs in command in England, political dissension in the Church (indeed within the chapter of his Cathedral), and Ireland weltering in poverty and depression. He saw himself as sent to 'die like a poisoned rat in a hole'; his life had become 'a long melancholy prospect'. Eventually he recovered his energies. He made new friends in Ireland — Chetwode, Delany and Sheridan — but they, despite their loyalty and sense of fun, somehow lacked the impressive vitality of his circle of English friends, who, despite being a small minority group, were deeply involved in literature and politics in a more sophisticatedly intellectual professional way. In Dublin there was the problem of Vanessa, solved only by her death in 1723. And, always, there was Stella. 'Violent friendship', wrote Swift, 'is much more lasting, and as much engaging, as violent love.' His letters to Stella and Dingley are supremely alive: imperious and tender, instructive and teasing, scathing and gay in turns, they reflect his hopes and fears, health and finances, and convey his zest for life. They record his ideas and the ideals he pursued as well as the occasional moods of meanness that seized him in his London greatness. Virginia Woolf's essay in this volume reminds us of the extraordinary nature of this correspondence.

Again, there are letters to others which are adapted in style and tone to their different recipients: statesmanlike sometimes, chiding occasionally, jesting often, but concise always. Though Swift revealed much of himself in the poems he wrote to Stella, he seems never to have shaken off completely in his poetry what Sir Harold Williams has called self-imposed barriers, and yet, as Professor Herbert Davis (to whose equally brilliant editing of Swift we owe so much) points out in his essay, there is a power and variety in Swift's poetry to which due recognition is not always given.

His poems pursued the same aims as his prose, a purity of style which often carries great complexity of thought in 'a deceptive simplicity' — the simplicity without which, he thought, 'no human performance can arrive to any great perfection'. The learning which underpinned his work still haunts scholars. Much has been discovered of his sources. *Gulliver's Travels*, for instance, may well be more acceptable to modern readers because of this knowledge. This volume contains an example of contemporary work in this field in Professor Ehrenpreis's investigation of the origins of *Gulliver's Travels*, while Professor Kathleen M. Williams analyses the intricacy and efficiency of his imagery. Professor Marjorie Nicolson and Professor Nora M. Mohler explore the scientific background of the *Voyage to Laputa* and Mrs. Marjorie Buckley deciphers the language Swift created for the Houyhnhnms. We should remember that Swift's friends and contemporaries thought the Houyhnhms and Yahoos funny. Yet *Gulliver's Travels*, brought over to England in manuscript by Swift when he visited his friends, Pope, Arbuthnot and Gay, in 1726, despite its parody of current fashions, its literary allusions, its politics, philosophy, and science, remains his unique moral plea to man to use reason, while it is also his great satire upon man's lack of reason. 'I have finished my Travells,' he wrote to Charles Ford on 14 August 1725, 'and I am now transcribing them; they are admirable Things, and will wonderfully mend the World.'

Swift still haunts the critics. George Orwell, in the essay on politics *vs.* literature contained in this volume, argued that he was a reactionary and attempted to translate him into modern terms, seeing him as anti-democratic and inimical to intellectual curiosity. But Orwell's views may be contrasted with those of Yeats, who, in Professor Quintana's view, virtually anticipated them and answered them in advance from an Anglo-Irish viewpoint. Part of the introduction to his impressive play on Swift, *The Words upon the Window-Pane*, is included here. Swift's irony has been dealt with trenchantly by Professor F. R. Leavis, who finds in *A Tale of a Tub* the 'most remarkable expression of negative feelings that literature can offer'. These views must be taken seriously; they carry much weight, but Swift, as John Corbet, one of the characters in Yeats's play, points out, should be judged on his own terms:

His tragedy had deeper foundations. His ideal order was the Roman Senate, his ideal men Brutus and Cato. Such an order and such men had seemed possible once more but the movement passed and he foresaw the ruin to come, Democracy, Rousseau, the French Revolution; that is why he hated the common run of men, 'I hate lawyers, I hate doctors', he said, 'though I love Dr So-and-so and Judge So-and-so', that is why he wrote *Gulliver*, that is why he wore out his brain, that is why he felt *saeva indignatio*, that is why he sleeps under the greatest epitaph in history.

Great though Swift's epitaph may be, his own tribute to Stella's life and character is not less moving. He wrote it on the night of her funeral, which his sickness did not permit him to attend. Removed into another apartment that he might not see the light in the church as she was buried, he wrote hauntingly of her softness of temper, and her courage. Her readiness to learn, her goodness and friendship, her gifts of mind, her gracefulness, her wit were all described in measured terms. Just as affection had inspired the tenderness of his poem 'Stella's Birthday', written in 1727, less than a year before her death, now reason controlled his sorrow: she had been dying for six months, kept alive 'almost against nature, by the generous kindness of her physicians, and the care of her friends'. 'Never', he wrote, 'was so happy a conjunction of civility, freedom, easiness and sincerity.'

Some eight years before Stella's death Swift wrote the first of his important Irish polemics, *A Proposal for the Universal Use of Irish Manufactures* (1720). He had always wanted his preferment in England, and as Nigel Dennis has reminded us in his recent book, *Jonathan Swift: A Short Character*,[1] on Swift, the thought of being dead in Ireland was so repugnant to him 'that only at the close of his life did he remove from his will the clause that ordered that his dead body be carried to England and buried at Holyhead'. He did not wish to be one of a 'land of slaves'. But his attitude to Ireland altered as he observed the misery of the Island's economic situation. The weaving industry had collapsed and there were obvious dangers for the economy as a whole in the scheme to introduce a copper coinage, the patent for which had been granted to William Wood. Swift became a spokesman for the ordinary Irishman when he assumed the role of the Drapier in 1729. He was also attacking Walpole indirectly: by the time he wrote the third letter he had come to the crux of the problem:

Were not the People of *Ireland* born as *Free* as those of *England*? How have they forfeited their Freedom? Is not their *Parliament* as fair a *Representative* of the *People* as that of *England*? And hath not their Privy Council as great or a greater share in the Administration of Publick Affairs? Are they not Subjects of the same King? Does not the same *Sun* shine on them? And have they not the same *God* for their Protector? Am I a *Free-Man* in *England*, and do I become a *Slave* in six Hours by crossing the Channel?

It was not surprising that the fourth letter dealt with Ireland's legislative independence — and that the Irish Privy Council voted for the arrest of the printer and offered a reward of £300 for the discovery of the identity of the Drapier. Swift was responsible for the defeat of Wood's patent, but he never fully faced the inconsistencies of his own attitude to Ireland: he was for liberty, but he firmly distinguished between the ancient Irish and their English conquerors, and he maintained his distrust of Dissent, which he

[1] New York, 1964.

regarded as the only real form of treason. The complexity of his whole attitude emerges in a letter he wrote to Pope on 11 August 1729:

> As to this country, there have been three terrible years' dearth of corn, and every place strewed with beggars; but dearths are common in better climates, and our evils here lie much deeper. Imagine a nation the two thirds of whose revenues are spent out of it, and who are not permitted to trade with the other third, and where the pride of women will not suffer them to wear their own manufactures, even where they excel what come from abroad. This is the true state of Ireland in a very few words. These evils operate more every day, and the kingdom is absolutely undone, as I have been telling often in print these ten years past. What I have said requires forgiveness but I had a mind for once to let you know the state of our affairs, and my reason for being more moved than perhaps becomes a clergyman, and a piece of a philosopher, and perhaps the increase of years and disorders may hope for some allowance to complaints, especially when I may call myself a stranger in a strange land.

There followed in October the fiercest, angriest and greatest of Swift's Irish tracts, *A Modest Proposal* (1729). In this his frustration and despair at the economic situation and the economists turned to rage against Ireland.

His attitude to Ireland was always ambivalent, even paradoxical. Sympathetic to them as victims of England's arbitrary treatment of Ireland, he also despised the deluded people of Ireland for their inaction. An early unpublished allegory, 'The Story of the Injured Lady, in a Letter to her Friend, with his Answer', written in 1707, had dealt with Ireland as a ruined Lady, cast off by the Gentleman, England, who is about to marry the Lady's Rival, Scotland (then about to be united to England by the Act of Union, 1707). In this tract the ruined Lady was advised to get her tenants together and make them agree to certain resolutions; she was to act, to obtain a little quiet in order to survive. Liberty was a great blessing, but the Drapier had seen that a people long used to hardships 'lose by Degrees the very Notions of *Liberty*, they look upon themselves as Creatures at Mercy'. The Irish had themselves to remove some part at least of these evils. Swift had consistently based his own views on those of Bishop Molyneux in *The Case of Ireland Stated*, which argued that Ireland was a nation, not a colony. And Swift himself was not born to be content with the second best. He once wrote to Pope that he was ashamed to tell him that when he was very young he 'had more desire to be famous than ever since' and further told him:

All my endeavours from a boy, to distinguish myself, were only for want of a great title and fortune, that I might be used like a Lord by those who have an opinion of my parts — whether right or wrong, it is no great matter, and so the reputation of wit or great learning does the office of a blue ribbon, or of a coach and six horses.

Within Swift there raged a continuous conflict, with his reason and passion battling together, and with his dominating intellect achieving an ultimate control in the name of Liberty. For him it was the liberty 'to be used like a Lord', an ambition achieved by an absolute insistence on being himself, on pushing logic to inexorable extremes of gravity or absurdity, on satirising faults without offering hope or mercy, and, let us not forget, on forging friendships and maintaining them passionately. Apart from an appreciation of the sheer power of his intellect, the inexhaustible inventiveness of his wit, and the strength of his style, we value what his friend Arbuthnot valued in him, his being 'a sincere honest man, and speaking truth when others were afraid to speak it'. Swift's jesting imagination and sombre sensibility together recorded the dark battle between man's passion and reason with such intensity that it became titanic. Swift, genius indeed, was

beating on his breast in sibylline frenzy blind
Because the heart in his blood-sodden breast had dragged him
down into mankind.

A. NORMAN JEFFARES

B

Chronological Table

1667   30 November, born in Dublin, his father having died some months earlier.

1673   Attends Kilkenny College.

1682   Enters Trinity College, Dublin.

1686   B.A. *speciali gratia.*

1689   Joins his mother in England; later enters Sir William Temple's household at Moor Park. There meets Stella (Hester or Esther Johnson), then a girl of eight.

1690   Returns to Ireland.

1691   Travels to England (summer); later returns to Moor Park. 'Ode to the Athenian Society'.

1692   M.A. Oxford.

1694   Ordained in Ireland, appointed to prebend of Kilroot.

1696   Returns to Moor Park.

1699   Travels to Ireland after Temple's death as domestic chaplain to the Earl of Berkeley.

1700   Vicar of Laracor, Co. Meath; prebend of St. Patrick's Cathedral, Dublin.

1701   *A Discourse of the Contests and Dissentions between the Nobles and Commons in Athens and Rome etc.*

1702   D.D., Trinity College, Dublin.

1704   *A Tale of a Tub; The Battle of the Books.*

1707–9   In London: large circle of literary friends including Addison and Steele. (Congreve had been his junior at Kilkenny College and Trinity College, Dublin.) *Bickerstaff Papers.* Becomes friendly with Vanessa (Esther or Hester Vanhomrigh).

1709   *A Project for the Advancement of Religion.* Returns to Ireland (June).

1710   In London (September), acting on behalf of Church of Ireland to seek remission of First Fruits from Queen Anne. In charge of the *Examiner*; friendly with Harley. *Journal to*

Stella covers this period to 1713. Resumes old literary friendships, close to Prior and Arbuthnot.

1711   *Miscellanies in Prose and Verse.* Brothers' Club founded by Swift's Tory friends.

1712   *Conduct of the Allies.*

1713   Installed as Dean of St. Patrick's Cathedral, Dublin (June). Scriblerus Club founded (or early in following year); membership includes Gay and Parnell. Friendship with Pope established by September. Works with Pope on *Memoirs of Martinus Scriblerus* (published in 2nd volume of Pope's *Prose Works*, 1741).

1714   Returns to Ireland after death of Queen Anne (August). Works on *The History of the Last Four Years of the Queen*, begun at Windsor in 1713.

1718   Friendship with Rev. Thomas Sheridan and Rev. Patrick Delany.

1720   *A Proposal for the Universal Use of Irish Manufactures.*

1721   Works on *Gulliver's Travels.*

1722   Quarrels with Vanessa.

1723   Expects to finish *Gulliver's Travels* 'very soon' (April); Vanessa dies (June).

1724   *The Drapier's Letters.*

1725   Transcribing completed *Gulliver's Travels* (August).

1726   Travels to London, visits Pope and Arbuthnot. *Gulliver's Travels* published in London after his return to Dublin.

1727   Visits England for last time.

1728   Stella dies. Contributes to the *Intelligencer.*

1729   *A Modest Proposal.*

1731   Writes *Polite Conversation, Directions to Servants*, 'Verses on the Death of Dr. Swift', etc.

1732   Various tracts on Irish affairs and on the Test Act.

1735   *Collected Works* published in four volumes in Dublin.

1738   *Polite Conversation* published in London; fifth and sixth volumes of *Collected Works* published in Dublin.

1742   'Of unsound mind and memory.' (See pp. 19 and 41.)

1745   Dies, 19 October.

List of Abbreviations

CE	College English
CLA Journal	College Language Association Journal
EA	Études anglaises
ELH	Journal of English Literary History
ELN	English Language Notes
E&S	Essays and Studies by Members of the English Association
HLQ	Huntington Library Quarterly
JBS	Journal of British Studies
JEGP	Journal of English and Germanic Philology
JHI	Journal of the History of Ideas
MLN	Modern Language Notes
MLQ	Modern Language Quarterly
MLR	Modern Language Review
MP	Modern Philology
NRF	Nouvelle revue française
N&Q	Notes and Queries
PBSA	Papers of the Bibliographical Society of America
PMLA	Publications of the Modern Language Association of America
PQ	Philological Quarterly
QQ	Queen's Quarterly
REL	A Review of English Literature
RES	Review of English Studies
SB	Studies in Bibliography: Papers of the Bibliographical Society of the University of Virginia
SEL	Studies in English Literature, 1500–1900
SP	Studies in Philology
TLS	Times Literary Supplement
UTQ	University of Toronto Quarterly

D. NICHOL SMITH

Jonathan Swift: Some Observations

I MAKE no claim to a full understanding of Swift, nor have I sought for a clue to the problems of his character. How far do we understand our friends, and how far do they understand us? Do we always understand ourselves? How, then, can we hope to understand a man whom we know from writings in which he generally wears a mask, and from contradictory accounts by observers whom he puzzled? 'Dr. Swift', said Pope, 'has an odd blunt way, that is mistaken, by strangers, for ill-nature. — 'Tis so odd that there's no describing it but by facts.' The distance of two hundred years cannot give us a better chance of not mistaking him. But these are days of bold biography. When we find a lengthy study written round a single impression, we suspect that the old theory of the Ruling Passion has returned in a new guise:

> The clue once found, unravels all the rest,
> The prospect clears, and *each man* stands confest.

We may be driven back to say that 'there's no describing it but by facts'. From the high colours and excitements of some recent biographies we can always turn for quiet and security to the sober pages of *The Dictionary of National Biography*.

We believe in the impressions which we derive from the study of an author's life and works, but several impressions, all complementary and all just, may carry us only a short way in the study of his mind and character; and I do not know any author of whom this is more emphatically true than it is of Swift. There are many authors about whom there seems to be general agreement. I imagine that all serious admirers of Samuel Johnson think of him much in the same way. They cannot think quite alike about him; still they never seem to quarrel. I would say much the same of the serious admirers of Sir Walter Scott. I mention Johnson and Scott together the more readily because of all Swift's many biographers and critics none were better qualified to understand him; and they differ about him. There is no approach to a consensus of opinion. And what a diversity there is, from Addison, who called him 'the most agreeable companion, the truest friend, and the greatest genius of his age', to Thackeray, who spoke of him in words which I prefer not to quote, as they do not seem to me to bear that amount of likeness which is expected in a caricature. Swift had in his lifetime the power of arousing the strongest feelings either of admiration and loyalty or of dislike and active hatred, and the opposition continues to be vigorous. One day I hear his praises, and the next I hear bitter things said about him; and then I meet someone who is constrained to admire without in the least liking him. Swift has experienced every degree of imperfect sympathy. He never invites us to come to terms with him; on the contrary, he may suggest that he would prefer us to keep our distance. All his chosen friends had to make the first advances. 'Dr. Swift, upon the score of his merit and extraordinary qualities, doth claim the sole and undoubted right, that all persons whatsoever shall make such advances to him as he pleases to demand, any law, claim, custom, privilege of sex, beauty, fortune or quality to the contrary notwithstanding' — a humorous decree promulgated for the instruction of a young lady; but he acted on it all his life. The Earl of Oxford made the first advances when Swift joined the Tory party. And so it is with us.

Let me confine myself now to one or two impressions about matters usually regarded as debatable. I offer you only 'some observations'.

The question is often asked if Swift had any right to be in orders. He attained to high office in the Church as the reward of political services, but what, it is asked, could have been the convictions of the Dean who wrote about the Houyhnhnms and Yahoos? It is all very well that he improved the services in St. Patrick's Cathedral and at Laracor, and indulged bountifully in charity. A mere deist might have done all that. He did not behave like a clergyman.

His most obnoxious quality [says his friend Delany], at least that which most exposed him to censure, was his utter neglect of those appearances of religion, which he often suspected in others, and apprehended might be suspected in himself, of hypocrisy.

Here it must be owned, he was too unguarded; not sufficiently considering that it was much worse to be suspected of infidelity than hypocrisy.

Could the fear of hypocrisy be honestly carried to such lengths? Would conviction not have betrayed him into some of the outward signs expected in a clergyman? When off duty, he declined to be treated as a clergyman. He disliked the company of clergymen, as a class. In Ireland, it is true, most of his friends were in orders. The educated community from which he could there draw his friends was not so extensive as in England, and perhaps he found that orders sat more easily on Irishmen than Englishmen. But in his great days, when he was a mainstay of the government of Oxford and Boling-broke, he seems not have had a single friend who was in orders. He was, in his own words —

> A clergyman of special note
> For shunning those of his own coat.

He was a politician, waiting for ecclesiastical preferment. Where, it was wondered then, was his religious conviction? And what proof do his writings afford us of conviction? In a recent article in the *Times Literary Supplement* a sentence was quoted from one of his last letters as bearing on this question — 'I have long given up all hopes of Church or Christianity.' Taken out of its context this statement may look ominous, though I would suggest that the man who despairs of Christianity is probably a Christian, and that there is a difference between giving up hopes for Christianity and giving up Christianity itself. He calls himself a misanthrope. Are misanthropy and Christianity compatible? 'I hate and detest that animal called man,' he once said, and that, if we take it at its face value, and again away from its context, is not an accepted Christian sentiment. Doubt began with his early *Tale of a Tub*, which delayed his promotion in the Church, and was never forgotten. Certainly it is not an easy book. Gilbert Burnet, the Bishop of Salisbury, a man of vigorous common sense, declared that he could make neither head nor tail of it. Others found in it an attack on religion. In the debate on the Schism Bill in the House of Lords in 1714, the Earl of

Nottingham, a leader of the 'high church' party, went out of his way to attack Swift. He is reported to have said that the Bill was 'dangerous because though now they had the happiness of having so worthy bishops, yet it possibly might happen that a person who had wrote lewdly, nay atheistically, might by having a false undeserved character given him be promoted to a Bishopric by Her Majesty whose intentions were always good'. According to another report he said, 'I own I tremble when I think that a certain Divine who is hardly suspected of being a Christian, is in a fair way of being a bishop.'

So great was the notoriety of *A Tale of a Tub* that Swift was moved within a few years to prefix to it an apology, and there he described the *Tale* as a satire on 'the gross corruptions in Religion and Learning'. On a hasty reading it may be mistaken for a satire on religion and learning themselves.

Let us take the religious satire first. A father has three sons, whom he remembers equally in his will. They are given strict injunctions how to manage their inheritance, and they are told 'to live together in one house like brethren and friends, for then you will be sure to thrive, and not otherwise'. In course of time they all act differently and live apart. The eldest brother turns the others out of doors, and the youngest, who does not think the second brother thorough-paced enough, goes in his zeal and rage to occupy new lodgings by himself. These three brothers are Peter, Martin, and Jack — the Church of Rome, the Church of England, and the Nonconformists. Read the book carefully and we shall find no satire on Martin. He is drawn as a good fellow, patient and cautious, at times despondent and always for moderation, not given to enthusiasm, and if not clever, thoroughly honest. In many ways he has a strong resemblance to 'John Bull', whose character was first to be drawn within a few years by Swift's great friend Arbuthnot.

Swift does not spare his satire on the political pretensions and worldliness of the Church of Rome, and he makes fun of doctrines and practices which England rejected at the Reformation. He also makes fun, and very bitter fun, of the Presbyterians and other Nonconformists who have no sense of moderation and, believing in private inspiration, are a law unto themselves. If he dislikes Peter, even more does he dislike Jack — who gets his name from Calvin; Jack he despises. Elsewhere Swift has described himself as a 'high churchman', and this is borne out by the *Tale*, in which Jack, besides being more provocative of Swift's wit, is treated more seriously than Peter as a menace to Martin's peace. If politically Swift was a 'high churchman', in matters of doctrine he was perhaps not far removed from Jack, whose offence lies largely in habits and manners, in aggressiveness and lack of discipline. We may describe Swift as an Anglican of the centre. As he himself stated in reply to critics, the *Tale* celebrates the Church of England as 'the most perfect of all others in discipline and doctrine, it advances no opinion they reject, nor condemns any they receive'. But he admitted, six years after its first appearance, that there were 'several youthful sallies which from the grave and the wise may deserve a rebuke'; as in the bold passages on the sacraments, and in particular on the doctrine of transubstantiation — a difficult if not an impossible subject to handle in a spirit of satire without giving offence even to English churchmen who do not accept the doctrine. These youthful sallies were held to be irreverent, and perhaps they were; though I can imagine some English churchmen, and even some bishops, not disturbed by them. The boldest of them might have been left out without much loss; in a less 'youthful' book they would have been less crudely direct and more ironical. But once a clergyman is suspected of irreverence he will soon be accused of irreligion. That always happens in England. Swift — as we have seen — was spoken of, by one of the leaders of the 'high church' party, as 'a divine hardly suspected of being a Christian'.

At the present day there are some who hold that Swift's arguments set him on the way to the subversion of all religion. To urge that there is not a word directed against the Anglican Church is, they say, to shut one's eyes to the effect of the book as a whole. In undermining the positions of Peter and Jack, they argue, he jeopardizes the stability of Martin's. 'What Church and what creed', they ask with Taine, 'are not involved in this attack?' No one will deny that Swift's satire was a powerful weapon, which, when he wielded it freely, might do more damage than he intended. He must set us thinking about the position of Martin, as he had thought

of it himself. For years he had read widely, but had not allowed the
stores of his tenacious memory to interfere with the liberty of his
mind; and he had no fear of the conclusions to which this liberty
might lead him. Now, when he calls the Church of England the most
perfect in discipline and doctrine, he means — as in effect he says —
in comparison with others. It was not perfect; to him there was no
perfect Church any more than anything in this world could be
perfect; but it was the best of any he knew. One point that his critics
seem to ignore — and it is vital — is his treatment of the will. The
good father leaves a simple but a great inheritance. Were these three
sons worthy of it? To Swift, Christianity was greater than any of the
Churches. He always, I believe, draws this distinction. He does not
say whether Christianity could be comprehended in the Church,
as some must hold; but it was not comprehended in any Church that
he knew. It was a divine gift, but it had passed into human management, and what man had made of it — that was the subject of his
satire.

That Swift should be supposed to satirize learning, either in the
Tale of a Tub or *Gulliver's Travels*, is no less unfortunate. Again we
have to remember his own words: 'the gross corruptions in Religion
and Learning'. These corruptions are seen in pretence and pedantry,
in the ostentation of learning and the pursuit of learning for its own
sake. Much of what passes for learning is easily acquired by the use
of indexes and abstracts, and other short cuts to knowledge; but real
learning is shown when a man's mind is enriched or tinctured by
what he has read, when the acquired information has been mastered
and turned into blood and nourishment. If pretence is intellectual
dishonesty, pedantry is a form of intellectual indigestion. In 'the art
of being deep-learned and shallow-read' modern scholarship seemed
to him to be too proficient. The satire on the use of summaries,
extracts, lexicons, prefaces, title-pages, indexes is recurrent:

The whole Course of Things being thus entirely changed between *Us* and the *Antients*; and the *Moderns* wisely sensible of it,
we of this Age have discovered a shorter, and more prudent
Method, to become *Scholars* and *Wits*, without the Fatigue of
Reading or of *Thinking*. The most accomplisht Way of using Books
at present, is twofold: Either first, to serve them as some Men do

Lords, learn their *Titles* exactly, and then brag of their Acquaintance. Or Secondly, which is indeed the choicer, the profounder, and politer Method, to get a thorough Insight into the *Index*, by which the whole Book is governed and turned, like *Fishes* by the *Tail*. For, to enter the Palace of Learning at the *great Gate*, requires an Expence of Time and Forms; therefore Men of much Haste and little Ceremony, are content to get in by the *Back-Door*.

Admirable satire. And do any of us escape? He was thinking chiefly of Bentley, in whom he discovered a mass of unassimilated information, bad manners, and little taste. In so far as he could understand Bentley's scholarship, he doubted it. But let us not be misled by his failure to recognize the greatness of that pugnacious and provocative scholar. Because he satirizes what he believes to be pretence in scholarship, let us not jump to the conclusion that he satirized scholarship itself. Reduced to its simplest form his view is only the common view that learning ought to be carried lightly, that the truly learned man makes no parade of his acquirements. It is the typically English view, somewhat disguised by the manner of its expression. Pope suggested it in his 'Essay on Criticism', and illustrated it in the fourth book of *The Dunciad*. Learning that is dissociated from the business of living is suspect; it has to justify itself. When Johnson visited Pembroke College, he commiserated the lot of a fellow who was 'lost in a convent's solitary gloom'; he himself was to be regarded as a man first, and not first as an author. And you will remember what Voltaire tells us of his visit to Congreve:

He spoke of his works as trifles that were beneath him, and told me in our first conversation to regard him as a gentleman who led a very simple life. I answered that if he had had the misfortune to be only a gentleman like any other I should never have come to see him.

Voltaire adds that he was shocked at this misplaced vanity. But Congreve spoke as an Englishman. I suggest to you that Swift, Johnson, Pope and Congreve shared the same view, and that Swift's satire on the abuses of learning is based on it, though the foundations may be concealed by the remarkable superstructure. Swift himself was a learned man, as every reader of the *Tale of a Tub* must know.

His treatment of mathematics corresponds to his treatment of classical scholarship, though there was this difference that Swift was not a mathematician. His one mention of Sir Isaac Newton in the *Tale* is respectful and unquestionable. We are told by his friend Delany that when he was settling down in Dublin as Dean of St. Patrick's 'he could so ill bear to be considered as a cypher in any *scientific* society, that he applied himself even to mathematics in that period, and made some progress in them'. His proficiency probably did not extend beyond the ordinary arithmetic of daily life; and how proficient he was in that is suggested by his capacity as a man of business. Some of his critics say that he had a hatred of mathematics; but, again, we must not jump to that conclusion because he satirizes certain types of mathematicians. *Gulliver's Travels* should keep us from that error. The mathematicians in Lilliput are eminently practical people. In Brobdingnag they are great public servants. Let me quote:

The Learning of this People is very defective; consisting only in Morality, History, Poetry and Mathematicks; wherein they must be allowed to excel. But the last of these is wholly applied to what may be useful in Life; to the Improvement of Agriculture and all mechanical Arts; so that among us it would be little esteemed. And as to Ideas, Entities, Abstractions and Transcendentals, I could never drive the least Conception into their Heads.

Contrast with this what he says of the inhabitants of Laputa:

Their Houses are very ill built, the Walls bevil, without one right Angle in any Apartment; and this Defect ariseth from the Contempt they bear for practical Geometry; which they despise as vulgar and mechanick, those Instructions they give being too refined for the Intellectuals of their Workmen; which occasions perpetual Mistakes.

Put these two quotations together and Swift's position is clear. In mathematics, in all branches of science, he looked for the practical purpose, the social purpose. He knew as well as we do that Wren could not have built St. Paul's without the aid of mathematics, and that science could reveal the exact ingredients in Wood's halfpence. But when he sought in vain for a social purpose in the investigations of learned bodies, or for any directions they might find out by indirections, they seemed to him to be engaged in beating the air. And for our part we must say that when we look at the transactions of the

Royal Society in those days, we get the impression that there is a large proportion of chaff to wheat.

Swift's most honoured friend was Arbuthnot, the friend also of Pope. He was a physician — he was doctor to Queen Anne — and he was a learned man. He wrote an 'Essay on the Usefulness of Mathematical Learning', and he translated a treatise 'Of the Hazards of Game', or dicing — which obviously had a social purpose. These three friends brought out their longest works in three consecutive years — *Gulliver's Travels* in 1726, *The Dunciad* in 1728. What did Arbuthnot publish in 1727? 'Tables of Ancient Coins, Weights and Measures' — a standard work. He ended his preface with these words: 'I propose no reputation by it, and I hope I shall lose none.' We may be certain that he lost none with Swift for this remarkable volume, the fruit of the leisure hours of a busy and fashionable doctor. Arbuthnot approached nearer than any other man to Swift's ideal of what a learned man should be. 'Oh ! if the world had but a dozen Arbuthnots in it, I would burn my Travels,' he wrote on hearing that Arbuthnot had been ill; and he added, 'I pray God protect him, for he is an excellent Christian, though not a Catholic, and as fit a man either to live or die as ever I knew.'

Gulliver's Travels is sometimes spoken of as if it were the bitter fruit of his disappointment, but his satire never varied in kind. Writing to Pope when the *Travels* were finished but not published, he said: 'I desire you and all my friends will take a special care that my disaffection to the world may not be imputed to my age, for I have credible witnesses ready to depose that it has never varied from the twenty-first to the fifty-eighth year of my life.' The witnesses whom we have to call are his writings. We could easily make a selection of passages which it would not be possible to date, or even to place in chronological order, by the test of substance or purpose. Take this passage on political parties:

Man is so apt to *imitate*, so much of the Nature of *Sheep* (*Imitatores, servum pecus*) that whoever is so bold to give the first *great Leap over the Heads of those about him* (tho' he be the worst of the Flock), shall be quickly followed by the rest. Besides, when Parties are once formed, the Stragglers look so ridiculous, and become so insignificant, that they have no other way but to run into the Herd, which at least will hide and protect them; and where to be much considered, requires only to be very violent.

In the same pamphlet he calls the parliamentary recess the 'lucid interval'. It was his first pamphlet, published three years before the *Tale of a Tub*. But many years before that he had proclaimed:

> My hate, whose lash just heaven has long decreed
> Shall on a day make sin and folly bleed . . .

and he had spoken of

> . . . what oft I vainly strive to hide,
> That scorn of fools, by fools mistook for pride.

Later, in his great London days, he says: 'I never expect sincerity from any man, and am no more angry at the breach of it than at the colour of his hair.' It was the *Tale* which caused the stir in his own time. Now his great offence seems to be the Yahoos. They did not greatly disturb the equanimity of the first eager readers. I sometimes wonder what we should have heard about Swift's misanthropy had he not written that fourth book.

There is some evidence that Swift liked that book best, and there are some readers — shall I say a select few? — who like it best. I cannot think that the critics who hold, in the words of one of them, that 'the Yahoo is the embodiment of the bestial element in man, and Swift in his wrath takes the bestial for the predominating element' — I cannot think that they have tried to see the book as Swift saw it. In Lilliput we are in a land where the inhabitants are twelve times smaller than we are, in Brobdingnag twelve times greater, and we engage in what a later poet called a willing suspension of disbelief; but the suspension appears to be less willingly granted when we are taken to a land where the relation of man to one of the so-called lower animals is not as we know it. All four books are based on an abnormal experience. Most satirists deal with things directly. Pope is direct enough. Jane Austen, in her kinder way, is direct enough. If there is an allegory, as in 'Absalom and Achitophel', still the persons play their part in an ordinary human drama. But Swift asks us to look at ourselves under strange conditions, on the chance that we shall see some things in ourselves a little more clearly.

He asks us to imagine a land where the horse is in power. Not to put too great a strain on our imagination he chooses the animal which we agree in calling the noblest. He does not choose the dog, or the fox, or the sheep, or the worm; he chooses the horse. Our complacency may be insulted by our dethronement from the lordship of creation; but so much the better. Is not the horse in some respects our superior? He does not commit murder, or cheat, or wage war, or lord it over his neighbours. Does he not lead a moral life? Does he not lead a better life, by all standards of morality, than many professing Christians?

Let me remind you how Sir Philip Sidney began his *Apologie for Poetrie*. He tells us that when in Italy he was instructed in riding by a teacher who grew lyrical about the horse:

> Then would he add certain praises by telling what a peerless beast a horse was; the only serviceable courtier without flattery, the beast of most beauty, faithfulness, courage, and such more, that if I had not been a piece of a logician before I came to him, I think he would have persuaded me to have wished myself a horse.

Now Swift never wished himself a horse, such as he knew in either England or Ireland. All the horses that he ever knew — and he knew many, for he was a great rider — were degenerate Houyhnhnms. When Gulliver returns to England, he proceeds to apply those excellent lessons of virtue which he had learned among the Houyhnhnms, and —

> ... to lament the Brutality of *Houyhnhnms* in my own Country, but always treat their Persons with Respect, for the Sake of my noble Master, his Family, his Friends, and the whole *Houyhnhnm* Race, whom these of ours have the Honour to resemble in all their Lineaments, however their Intellectuals came to degenerate.

The Houyhnhnms were not horses as we know them. Similarly the Yahoos, who were their slaves, were not men such as we are. Gulliver was taken by the Houyhnhnms to be a superior kind of Yahoo, 'a perfect Yahoo', and as such he surprised them. They had never seen an animal quite like him.

We are led to think of a prehistoric time before the mastery of man or of the horse had been established. Swift says nothing about

c

that; but he certainly asks us to assume that in the course of years animal life, or rather the intellectual and moral life, has passed on to what Keats calls 'a fresh perfection', or has receded. In our world man has got the better of the horse; but in this imaginary land the horse has been at liberty to develop his virtues, and man, living in a state of subjection, has degenerated. The idea ought not to be difficult to us. The doctrine of evolution may be a commonplace now, but something of it is implicit in the fourth book of *Gulliver's Travels*.

Gulliver is a Yahoo; the Brobdingnagians, the great people whose cultured and beneficent king thought that the natives of Gulliver's country must be 'the most pernicious race of little odious vermin that nature ever suffered to crawl upon the surface of the earth' — they were Yahoos. They were the 'least corrupted' of Yahoos, but they were Yahoos none the less. All this we are too apt to forget. In ordinary usage nowadays the word has a much narrower meaning than Swift gave it.

Grant the simple fiction, and the rest follows. Swift never gave himself a better opportunity for exhibiting the sin, and the folly, and the unpleasantness of man. His attack is levelled at pride, the deadliest of the seven deadly sins — pride intellectual, moral, political, personal, physical. Towards the conclusion he says so in so many words:

When I behold a Lump of Deformity, and Diseases both in Body and Mind, smitten with *Pride*, it immediately breaks all the Measures of my Patience; neither shall I be ever able to comprehend how such an Animal and such a Vice could tally together.

There are no signs of impatience in the writing of the book, which is all of a piece, all directed to the same end and unflinching. If he wrote in his wrath, as has been said, his wrath was wonderfully well controlled. This book was his greatest sermon on humility.

When the four books were finished he said to the friend with whom he corresponded most intimately, in a letter which has only recently been published:

I have finished my Travells, and I am now transcribing them; they are admirable Things, and will wonderfully mend the World.

These words sound the top note of exaltation in all his writings. Had he suspected that the letter was to be printed, he would have been ironically grave. But for this once we catch him unawares and are given a glimpse of his conviction that *Gulliver's Travels*, these 'admirable Things', would shake man into seeing what a knave or a fool he generally is, and so put him on the fair way to mend. The book was written to 'mend the World'. His satire was

> with a moral view designed
> To cure the Vices of Mankind.

'I wrote for their amendment, and not their approbation.'

I believe — and I give this only as an impression, though if it is wrong I do not know how to account for the persistent quality of his satire — I believe (and here I revert) that Swift was a definitely religious man with an overmastering sense of the weakness of human nature. His admiration of his friends, such as Arbuthnot, served only to strengthen his aversion from what he despised. With hypocrisy and selfishness and knavery in any form he would not come to terms, and he bludgeoned them. Who will say that he bludgeoned them from the mere joy of destruction? If I find misanthropy in *Gulliver's Travels*, it is a misanthropy that is bent on defeating itself. But to find hopelessness is to make the book incomprehensible.

I have said nothing about Stella. Today is her birthday, 13 March. Latterly, and perhaps from an earlier year than we know, Swift celebrated it with a poem. I should like to quote from the last of the series. Her health had long been declining, and he knew what was at hand:

> This Day, whate'er the Fates decree,
> Shall still be kept with Joy by me:
> This Day then, let us not be told,
> That you are sick, and I grown old,
> Nor think on our approaching Ills,
> And talk of Spectacles and Pills;
> Tomorrow will be Time enough
> To hear such mortifying Stuff.

Hitherto he had been playful in his birthday verses, but on this occasion he says:

> From not the gravest of Divines,
> Accept for once some serious Lines.

He argues, simply, that just as our bodies are built up by food, so past actions, which we may have forgotten, have contributed to make our minds what they are; and thus he comes to this conclusion:

> Believe me *Stella*, when you show
> That true Contempt for Things below,
> Nor prize your Life for other Ends
> Than merely to oblige your Friends,
> Your former Actions claim their Part,
> And join to fortify your Heart.
> For Virtue in her daily Race,
> Like *Janus*, bears a double Face;
> Looks back with Joy where she has gone,
> And therefore goes with Courage on.
> She at your sickly Couch will wait,
> And guide you to a better State.
>
> O then, whatever Heav'n intends,
> Take Pity on your pitying Friends;
> Nor let your Ills affect your Mind,
> To fancy they can be unkind.
> Me, surely me, you ought to spare,
> Who gladly would your Suff'rings share;
> Or give my Scrap of Life to you,
> And think it far beneath your Due;
> You, to whose Care so oft I owe,
> That I'm alive to tell you so.

In this poem, which was intended only for the eyes of Stella, Swift speaks from the heart, and reveals a side of his character which he was at pains to disguise in his prose for the public. It was written a few months after the appearance of *Gulliver's Travels*, and is the next piece, with the exception of some letters, to which we can give a definite date. A strange epilogue to that bitter satire, you may think; but there is no disagreement. Swift wore a mask in print; and what he said in print we understand the better by knowing what he said intimately to his friends.

T. G. WILSON
Swift's Personality

THERE can be few historical or literary figures who have aroused more controversy or who have had more nonsense written about them than Jonathan Swift. Since his death more than two hundred years ago the comment about him has grown steadily more abusive. Dr. Johnson started the process and it has continued ever since. Thackeray's vilification of his character in *English Humourists* is quite absurd. Robert Louis Stevenson likened him to 'a kind of human goat, leaping and wagging [his] scut on mountains of offence'.[1] Sir Harold Nicolson calls him '. . . a turncoat, a place seeker, and a most untruthful journalist' and speaks of 'his cruelty' and of 'the envy that turned his soul a putrid green'.[2] These are hard words, but they can at least be supported by a superficial knowledge of Swift's career. But Malcolm Muggeridge's statement in the same national Sunday newspaper that he suffered from general paralysis of the insane, better known as G.P.I. which is a late effect of syphilis, is quite unjustifiable.[3]

During Swift's lifetime no such violent attacks were made on him, and while his outspoken views made him many bitter enemies equally he had many faithful friends, not only amongst the greatest men of his age but also amongst the humblest. In his later days he was adulated and venerated by the people of Dublin, who celebrated his birthday every year with bonfires and scenes of rejoicing. His friend the Rev. Dr. Delany called him:

A steady persevering, inflexible friend; a wise, a watchful and a faithful counsellor, under many severe trials and bitter persecutions, to the manifest hazard both of his liberty and fortunes. He lived a

---

[1] *The Works of Robert Louis Stevenson* (Tusitala Edition: XVIII: London, 1924), p. 112.
[2] *Observer*, 24 November, 1957.   [3]*Observer*, 28 March 1965.

bles ing, died a benefactor, and his name will ever live in honour to Ireland.[1]

Much of the more modern comment is, of course, due to lack of understanding of the nature and purport of his writings, but it is true to say that he was a most enigmatic and contradictory person, one whose public life abounds with puzzles and paradoxes and whose private life, particularly his relationship with women, seems equally peculiar.

Swift was indeed a most mysterious person, and, as Denis Johnston has pointed out,[2] the mystery surrounding him seems to be very largely of his own making. Most authors delight in recounting the experiences of their youth and adolescence, but Swift seldom does this, openly at least. He tells us very little of his origins and early upbringing, of which his knowledge may indeed have been scanty. In the short autobiographical fragment, written in his later years, as Johnston says, we get the feeling that he is telling us what he would like us to think and that what he is telling us may not necessarily be the truth.[3] We are driven to the conclusion that he does not want the world to know too much about him. This secretiveness is all the more remarkable because he was a very personal writer and also both introspective and a valetudinarian. His medical history in contrast is fully documented, particularly in his letters. One gains the impression that for some reason he could not unburden himself of the intimate matters of his tangled private life and was compelled to relieve his inner tensions by writing about his health.

Swift's Medical History

Nevertheless there is still a great deal of ignorance about Swift's medical history. Much of this is due to the fact that Sir William Wilde's book, *The Closing Years of Dean Swift's Life*,[4] is still

[1] Patrick Delany, *Observations upon Lord Orrery's Remarks on the Life and Writings of Dr. Jonathan Swift* (1754), p. 197.

[2] *In Search of Swift* (Dublin, 1959), pp. 10 ff.

[3] Denis Johnston, 'The Mysterious Origin of Dean Swift', *Dublin Historical Record*, June–August 1941, p. 89.

[4] 2nd ed., Dublin, 1849.

regarded by many lay authors as the leading authority on the subject. It is now quite out of date, and in any case it is often wrong
both in fact and deduction. It is, in fact, quite unworthy of either
Swift or Wilde. Another cause of error is the curiously persistent
and quite erroneous idea, denied by Wilde, that Swift became a
lunatic in his later years and died insane. To this day the man in the
street is firmly convinced that he ended his life a raving lunatic in
the asylum he himself founded. If we exclude, as we should, his
three final years, when he suffered from senile decay, or senile
dementia as we now call it, Swift was never in any sense of the word
insane. Louis Bredvold's recent statement that 'his final insanity . . .
as far as modern medical authorities can determine was . . . the last
stage of a lifelong disease of the inner ear'[1] is absolute nonsense,
neither more nor less.

It is, of course, now well established that Swift suffered from his
youth onwards from bilateral Ménière's disease, the internal ear
ailment to which Bredvold is referring, but this condition never
leads to insanity. Ménière's disease is a most distressing complaint in
which the patient suffers from periodic and sometimes completely
incapacitating attacks of giddiness and vomiting, accompanied by
head-noises and increasing deafness. There is every excuse for the
earlier writers who failed to recognise it, for its aetiology was not
properly ascertained until 1861. Giddiness, deafness and vomiting
are apparently unrelated symptoms, and in the state of knowledge
of the time there was no obvious reason to connect them with a
single disease of the internal ear. Nevertheless, although Wilde and
the physicians of the middle of the nineteenth century thought Swift's
symptoms were of separate origin, the doctors of the previous
century realised that they were related symptoms. Since Wilde's
time Swift's letters to Charles Ford have come to light. In his letter
of 20 November 1733 he says:

And although in the London Dispensatory approved by the
Physicians there are Remedyes named both for Giddyness and
deafness, none of them that I can find, were prescribed to me. . . .
The Doctors here think that both these Aylments in me are united

---

[1] Louis I. Bredvold, *Pope and his Contemporaries* (New York, 1949), p. 2.

in their Causes, but they were not always so; for one has often left me when the other stayd.[1]

Swift's habitual vagueness about dates makes it difficult to say exactly when he first suffered an attack of Ménière's disease, but it was apparently in his early twenties. He continued to suffer from it for the rest of his life. In the letter to Stella dated 31 October 1710 he says:

. . . this morning, sitting in my bed, I had a fit of giddiness: the room turned round for about a minute, and then it went off, leaving me sickish, but not very. . . . I saw Dr. Cockburn to-day, and he promises to send me the pills that did me good last year; and like-wise has promised to send me an oil for my ear, that he has been making for that ailment for somebody else.[2]

Later, in 1724, he complained: 'I have been this month past so pestered with a return of the *noise and deafness* in my ears that I had not the spirit to perform the common offices of life.' Writing to Charles Ford on 9 October 1733 he says:

It is very long since I writ to you, or heard from you; and indeed it is long since I writ to any body else, For I have been some months in a bad dispirited way with Deafness, and giddyness, and Fluxes. I am now and have been a month confined to the house, by the two former aylment[s], though the last hath left me at present. I let no Company see me except Mr. Worrall and his Wife, who is a Chear-full woman with a clear voice.[3]

It is clear that although he became more gloomy and depressed as he grew older, at no time until his terminal illness was he in any way incapable. When in 1737, after the Bettesworth affair, an address of gratitude and support was presented to him, it is on record that

when this paper was delivered Swift was in bed, giddy and deaf, having been some time before seized with one of his fits; but he

---

[1] Harold Williams (ed.), *The Correspondence of Jonathan Swift* (Oxford, 1963–5), vol. IV, p. 210. Hereafter cited as Williams (ed.), *Correspondence*.

[2] Harold Williams (ed.), *Journal to Stella* (Oxford, 1948), vol. I, p. 77.

[3] Williams (ed.), *Correspondence*, vol. IV, p. 197.

dictated an answer in which there is all the dignity of habitual pre-eminence and all the resignation of humble piety.[1]

The popular idea that Swift was mad seems to originate from biographies written by Dr. Johnson and by Sir Walter Scott. Both these Lives contain phrases such as 'madness . . . compounded of rage and fatuity' and 'Frantic fits of passion', but neither bring forward any real evidence to show that Swift's mind was diseased. The idea may have arisen in the first instance from Swift's habit of referring to his attacks of giddiness, deafness and sickness as 'fitts', 'fitts of deafness', 'a small giddy fitt and swimming in head'. This constant talk of 'fitts' also led to the theory being put forward that he suffered from epilepsy, but Swift was not an epileptic. It is quite obvious from reading his journals that he used the word 'fit' when we would say 'attack'.

His Psychological Make-up

Swift was, therefore, a lifelong sufferer from Ménière's disease, and he was far from being insane. But he was undoubtedly a psychopath. He was, of course, a genius; and geniuses cannot be judged by the standards applied to ordinary mortals.

It is not altogether easy to arrive at an exact definition of genius. It is certainly not 'an infinite capacity for taking pains' as was said, I think, by Dickens. It has been described as the highest conceivable form of original ability, something beyond supreme educational prowess. It differs from talent in that the latter does not possess the essential spark of productive originality. Perhaps the best definition of genius in writing has been supplied by Swift himself when he said that an author was a genius if, when writing about a deserving subject, he was 'able to open new scenes, and discover a vein of true and noble thinking, which never entered into any imagination before'. He said of such a writer that every stroke of his pen was worth all the paper blotted by hundreds of others in the course of their lives.

One interesting feature about genius is the frequency with which it is associated with disease, real or imaginary. Beethoven was stone

[1] Wilde, *The Closing Years of Dean Swift's Life*, 2nd ed., p. 37.

deaf when he composed his later works, Schumann eventually
became insane, Paganini was a consumptive epileptic. Purcell,
Weber, Chopin, Schubert and many others were also tuberculous.
Of the great soldiers in history — and we cannot withhold the
attribution of genius from them — Julius Caesar is commonly
supposed to have been an epileptic, and so also was Mohammed,
who is recorded on one occasion as 'falling heavily to the ground
and snorting like a camel'. Isaac Newton, a great contemporary of
Swift's, suffered from periodic attacks of insanity. He was born
prematurely and was so small that it was said he could have been
fitted into a quart pot.

Authors, particularly perhaps poets, seem to be more than
ordinarily hypochondriacal. It has been said that when they are not
worrying about their bodies they are worrying about their minds.
Shelley, for instance, was for ever worrying about his health. He
was introspective to a degree, and on one occasion became firmly
convinced that he had contracted elephantiasis by sitting beside a fat
old lady in a stage coach. On another occasion he had the startling
experience of meeting himself face to face when out walking. One
could multiply instances of the illnesses and eccentricities of authors,
but it is only necessary to mention three more: Byron, Pope, and
Swift himself, who have it in common that they have all been
accused of misanthropy and they all suffered from a severe physical
disability. Pope, who was of course a great friend of Swift's, was a
hunch-backed dwarf, Byron had a congenital deformity of the foot,
and as we have seen Swift suffered from bilateral Ménière's disease
from the time of his early manhood.

This relatively uncommon ailment is now becoming almost as
fashionable a complaint as allergy, and any person who suffers to
even a minor extent from giddiness and nausea is liable to be told
he has Ménière's disease. But true Ménière's disease is far from being
a minor ailment. Anybody who has suffered from really severe sea-
sickness can imagine what it is like. The patient suffers without
warning, at irregular intervals of weeks, months or years from
violent and perhaps completely incapacitating episodes of giddiness
and vomiting. The deafness increases with each attack and may
eventually be almost total, as in Swift's case. It is no wonder there-

fore that he was on the borderline of being a psychopath. Dr. Johnson wrote:

The greatest difficulty that occurs, in analysing his character, is to discover by what depravity of intellect he took delight in revolving ideas from which almost every other mind shrinks with disgust. The ideas of pleasure, even when criminal, may solicit the imagination; but what has disease, deformity, and filth upon which the mind can be allured to dwell? [1]

The answer, of course, is that Swift like John Donne, Charles Dickens, and *par excellence* Johnson himself, was what psychiatrists call an obsessional personality, a compulsive obsessive in fact, and this was one of the forms his obsession took.

To be a compulsive obsessional may at first sight appear to be a serious matter. But probably all reasonably intelligent people are or have been compulsive obsessives to some extent. It is particularly common in childhood, so much so as to be almost a natural part of children's behaviour. Many of us remember from our own childhood the way in which we felt we had, for instance, to step on every third paving-stone, touch our fingertips together before entering a house, or jump over cracks in the pavement — a compulsion which is interpreted as the symbolic avoidance of chasms leading to the infernal regions. To the imaginative child these rituals serve to ward off unknown evils. They tend to become submerged in adult life, except perhaps for occasionally 'touching wood', but then the average adult is not an imaginative author.

Nevertheless, obsessive-compulsive features of varying extent do occur in normal healthy adults. They are apt to become exaggerated in times of illness or mental stress, when they may be associated with mental depression. Such individuals are perfectionists who aspire to very high standards of performance, which once attained may be re-set even higher so that they come to act 'like the carrot before the donkey'. Their lives show an exaggerated orderliness, their library is neatly arranged, so much so that the books tend never to be read; their handwriting is neat and tidy and they delight in making lists.

[1] Samuel Johnson, *Lives of the English Poets* (ed. G. B. Hill: London, 1905), vol. III, p. 62.

All these activities are accompanied to some extent by a feeling of compulsion.

The normal obsessive-compulsive traits of the individual shade almost imperceptibly into neurotic disease. It is impossible to define the boundary between normal, if exaggerated, obsessional traits of the personality and the minor forms of the corresponding neurosis. It is true to say that severe forms of the latter may incapacitate the patient to the extent of making his life a hell on earth. One form it takes is *folie de doute*: 'Have I turned off the gas?' 'Have I left the front door open?' 'Have I forgotten to stamp the letters?' Another concerns numbers, the compulsive obsession to count the flowers on the wallpaper, or to add up the numbers on a bus ticket. If interrupted one must start counting all over again.

People afflicted in this way are usually more than ordinarily intelligent. Heredity plays an important part in the aetiology of the condition, as also does environment, as for instance a more than ordinarily puritan upbringing. In psychoanalytical theory, obsessive-compulsive symptoms are viewed as mechanisms of ego-defence. The insistent thoughts or acts are symbolic of disguised self-reproach. Sexual transgressions during life's initial phase of infantile immorality are postulated to later evoke feelings of shame and guilt in the course of subsequent maturation. The repression of these memories occurs but promotes their disguised re-emergence in the form of obsessional thoughts or compulsive acts. Freud drew attention to a relationship between obsessional symptomatology and the 'anal-erotic character' with its features of orderliness, parsimony and obstinacy.[1]

It must be stressed that while Swift had a compulsive-obsessive personality, it amounted to an exaggeration of the normal but certainly not to a definite neurosis. It is interesting to note how clearly the characteristics of the obsessional can be recognised in his make-up. Nobody can deny his intelligence. He was tidy to a degree, and cleanliness of person, for himself and others, was almost an article of religion to him. So also was a passion for physical exercise. He was rigid in his habits, somewhat inflexible in thought,

[1] *Aspects of Psychiatry for General Practice*, Roche Products Ltd. (London), June 1966.

and very careful with his money. He was subject to moods of intense depression. The urge to write, the *cacoethes scribendi* as Middleton Murry called it, which seized him at times also comes under this head, and with it is linked his apparent coprophilia, which has always been, and remains, a source of uneasiness to his biographers.

His Scatological Obsession

It is interesting, and most important, that this scatological element in his published work does not appear in his personal writings, such as the *Journal to Stella* and other private letters not intended for publication. Risky remarks are there in plenty, but not of this type. In the Journal there are several jokes of a 'sexy' nature, but the scatological vituperation, which has so scandalised his readers in the past, is reserved for his published work.

Let us, however, try to put the matter in perspective. We are today still feeling the effects of the Victorian era, when an extreme prudery demanded reticence, and exaggerated squeamishness forced the physiology of the human, even the mammalian body in general, into the background. Had it not been for this reticence Dickens might have been a much greater man, perhaps almost another Shakespeare.

In the seventeenth and eighteenth centuries a different set of conventions prevailed. There is nothing in Swift's writing so startlingly crude as the description in *Humphry Clinker* of the man who bottled the effluvia of a close-stool for future delectation. Even Celia Fiennes, writing in the late 1690s about the wonders of Derbyshire, has this to say:

The 6th Wonder is at Casleton . . . its a town lyes at the foote of an exceeding steep hill . . . this is what they call the Devills Arse . . . the hill on one end jutting out in two parts and joyns in one at the top, this part or cleft between you enter a great Cave which is very large . . . .[1]

Daniel Defoe could see no great wonder in this somewhat

[1] Christopher Morris (ed.), *The Journeys of Celia Fiennes*, 2nd ed. (London, 1949).

peculiarly shaped hill. He said the only wonder lay in the coarseness of our ancestors in thinking of 'so homely a sirname' for it, but he adds, 'it seems they talked broader in those days than we do now'. The process of refinement had already started.

It is interesting to observe that Celia Fiennes could be outspoken in this way, but nevertheless took exception to those paintings of the female nude which Antonio Verrio had just completed for the Earl of Exeter at Burghley House. She commented on 'the immodesty of the Pictures especially in my Lords appartment', and she noted with disapproval that 'they were all without garments or very little'.

We are now suffering from a reaction to the prudery of the latter half of the last century, a reaction in which the pendulum seems to have swung too much the other way. Much modern writing appears to be obscene just for the sake of obscenity. In Joyce's *Ulysses* the characters seem to be contemplating their own sexual lives to no particular end or purpose, and the same applies to D. H. Lawrence's work. Swift in his more scatological and horrifying moments is at least attacking some human weakness or abuse, recognised with disgust but with great perceptive vision. His mind may have been 'richly stored with images from the dunghill and the lazar-house' as Macaulay said, but at least he used these images to some purpose. What purpose is there in W. H. Auden's verse:

> Revelation came to
> Luther in a privy
> (Crosswords have been solved there):
> Rodin was no fool
> When he cast his Thinker,
> Cogitating deeply,
> Crouched in the position
> Of a man at stool.

This may be realism, but what is the point of it?

Swift therefore uses his great powers of horrifying invective to what he considered to be a good end. Auden is down to earth presumably for the sake of realism, and Smollett and, for example, Chaucer in *The Miller's Tale*, are bawdy in the cause of ribald humour. One feels that Swift's elevation of his scatological writings to a serious plane shows a certain lack of a sense of humour (apart from a lack of a sense of the ridiculous, of which nobody could accuse him), and when all the arguments for the defence are marshalled this unpleasant obsession about excrement remains difficult to explain.

Lord Brain tries to do so by saying that Swift was 'emotionally arrested' at an immature state of development. He reminds us that jokes about excretion are normal in boys below the age of puberty, after which their place is taken by jokes about sex. He states that sexual immaturity is not incompatible with great intellectual development, or even with intellectual development amounting to genius.

Such a man as Swift [he says] cannot be regarded as merely emotionally immature. He is exposed by the very combination of his intellectual genius with his emotional immaturity to mental stresses and strains greater than those to which ordinary men are subject, and which themselves contribute to his emotional instability.[1]

He goes on to quote the well-known passage from *Gulliver's Voyage to the Houyhnhnms*:

As soon as I entered the House, my Wife took me in her Arms and kissed me at which, having not been used to the Touch of that odious Animal for so many Years, I fell in a Swoon for almost an Hour. At the Time I am writing it is five Years since my last Return to England: during the first Year I could not endure my Wife or Children in my Presence, the very Smell of them was intolerable, much less could I suffer them to eat in the same Room. To this Hour they dare not presume to touch my Bread, or drink out of the same Cup, neither was I ever able to let one of them take me by the Hand.[2]

No author, says Lord Brain, would project these feelings upon one of his characters if he had not experienced them himself, and no man so revolted by the flesh could achieve a normal married life.

At first sight this argument seems plausible, but surely the nature and actions of an imaginative writer's characters need not necessarily

[1] In *Irish Journal of Medical Science*, Sixth Series, pp. 337–45.
[2] Herbert Davis (ed.), *Gulliver's Travels* (Oxford, 1941), p. 273.

be autobiographical? If they were, one must conclude that most of the present generation of Englishmen were conceived either amongst gorse bushes or in the backs of motor cars.

Gulliver continues:

The first Money I laid out was to buy two young Stone-Horses, which I keep in a good Stable, and next to them the Groom is my greatest Favourite; for I feel my spirits revived by the Smell he contracts in the Stable. My Horses understand me tolerably well; I converse with them at least four Hours every Day. They are strangers to Bridle or Saddle; they live in great Amity with me, and Friendship to each other.[1]

If we agree with Lord Brain in equating the author with his character, it now follows that Gulliver and therefore Swift preferred men and horses to women. In other words, he is open to charges of homosexuality and — shall we be squeamish and say hippophilia? Gulliver's sentiments in this respect are underlined by a curious poem printed among the preliminary pages of some of the early editions of *Gulliver*. This poem is said to have been written by Pope. It is entitled 'Mary Gulliver to Capt. Lemuel Gulliver, an Epistle', and part of it goes as follows:

> Welcome, thrice welcome to thy native Place!
> — What, touch me not? what, shun a Wife's Embrace?
> Have I for this thy tedious Absence born,
> And wak'd and wish'd whole Nights for thy Return?
> In five long Years I took no second Spouse:
> What *Redriff* Wife so long has kept her vows?
>
> Not touch me! never Neighbour call'd me Slut?
> Was *Flimnap's* Dame more sweet in *Lilliput*?
> I've no red Hair to breath an odious Fume;
> At least thy Consort's cleaner than thy *Groom*.
> Why then that dirty Stable-boy thy Care?
> What mean those Visits to the Sorrel Mare?
> Say, by what Witchcraft, or what Daemon led,
> Preferr'st thou Litter to the Marriage Bed?

[1] Davis (ed.), *Gulliver's Travels*, p. 274.

My Bed, (the Scene of all our former Joys,
Witness two lovely Girls, two lovely Boys)
Alone I press: in Dreams I call my Dear,
I stretch my Hand; no *Gulliver* is there:
I wake, I rise, and shiv'ring with the Frost,
Search all the House; my *Gulliver* is lost!
Forth in the Street I rush with frantick Cries;
The Windows open; all the neighbours rise;
Where sleeps my Gulliver? O tell me where?
The Neighbours answer '*With the Sorrel Mare*'.[1]

This is all very odd, and indeed builds up to a formidable indictment if, as Lord Brain suggests, we read 'Swift' for 'Gulliver'. But when examined more closely, it all falls to the ground, and with it Brain's suggestion of sexual immaturity, for the simple reason that Swift's relations with women were normal, perhaps indeed to a fault. The only reason for suspecting otherwise is that as far as we know he never married Stella, and for this he probably had a good reason.

Early loves: Betty Jones and Varina

He was, in fact, attracted to many women during his life. His first serious flame may have been his cousin Betty Jones whom he met when staying with his mother in Leicestershire in the autumn of 1691. Mrs. Swift did not approve of this flirtation, and removed him from the temptress by sending him away. Writing some months later from Moor Park, Sir William Temple's place in Surrey, he expressed his somewhat chastened views on marriage:

... the very ordinary observations I made with going Half a mile beyond the University, have taught me experience enough not to think of marriage, till I settle my fortune in the world, wch I am sure, will not be in some years, and even then my self I am so hard to please that I suppose I shall put it off to the other world.[2]

These sentiments have been held to express his permanent views

[1] Quoted in W. A. Eddy, *Gulliver's Travels: A Critical Study* (Princeton and London, 1923).

[2] 11 Feb. 1691/2. Williams (ed.), *Correspondence*, vol. I, p. 3.

on marriage, but they are not more than any prudent young man
might express.

He goes on to say:

How all this suits with my behaviour to the woman in hand, you
may easily imagine; when you know, that there is something in me
which must be employ'd, & when I am alone, turns all, for want of
practice, into speculation & thought . . . . [1]

Who 'the woman in hand' was we do not know. Elrington Ball
says that she 'seems to have been a substitute' whom he found to
amuse him during his stay at Leicester.[2]

Betty Jones disappears from the scene, but we hear of her again
long afterwards in a letter Swift wrote in 1728/9 to the Rev. John
Worrall, the Dean's Vicar and the husband of the 'Chearfull woman
with a clear voice'. Swift says, referring to Betty:

My prudent mother was afraid I should be in love with her; but
when I went to *London* she married an inn-keeper in *Loughborow* . . .
This woman (my mistress with a pox) left several children, who are
all dead but one daughter, *Ann* by name.

There is no suggestion that Anne was Betty's daughter by Swift,
and indeed no reason to think she was. The somewhat unclerical
reference to Betty as 'my mistress with a pox' is, of course, merely a
disclaimer couched in the slang of the period.

The next affair of Swift's which we know of is the celebrated
episode with Miss Jane Waring, or Varina, as he called her. This
took place during Swift's first incumbency, as Vicar of Kilroot,
near Carrickfergus, County Antrim. He has been severely taken to
task for his treatment of poor Varina, but probably without just
cause. It is a simple story. He fell in love with her and proposed to
her; she refused him, but some years later, after he had left Kilroot,
she changed her mind and wrote to him saying so. In the meanwhile
Swift had also changed his mind, as any other young man might
have done. But Swift was not an ordinary young man. The letter
he wrote back to her was very characteristic, and it is on the score of
this letter that criticism lies. Varina may have been fortunate, for

[1] Williams (ed.), *Correspondence*, vol. I, pp. 3–4.
[2] Williams (ed.), *Correspondence*, vol. III, p. 309.

she does not appear to have been likely to make a suitable wife for Swift. She died unmarried about the year 1720 and cannot have been a very hot-blooded creature.

Vanessa

Next we must consider Vanessa, to whom this comment certainly does not apply. Swift's liaison with Vanessa took place between the years 1709 and 1723. Before, during and after this period he was also closely concerned with Stella, and this is the key to the whole affair.

Esther Vanhomrigh was the daughter of a Dutch merchant who had risen to eminence in Dublin. He died in 1703, and in 1707 his widow and her four children moved to London, where Swift found them when he himself went to London about the same time.

In 1710 he had lodgings in St. Albans Street, only five doors away from the Vanhomrighs, and although he changed his residence to Chelsea in 1711, they obviously remained on close terms for he kept his 'best wig and gown' with them and changed there twice daily on his visits to town. His acquaintance with Vanessa rapidly ripened into something much stronger. The letters which passed between Swift and Vanessa at this period are cryptic enough, but clearly their meaning had no mystery for either party. This was the period of the *Journal to Stella*, and it is noteworthy that although the Vanhomrighs are mentioned in it many times, Vanessa is referred to indefinitely and cursorily on three occasions only.

It was at Windsor in 1713 that Swift wrote the famous verses 'Cadenus and Vanessa'. This is a remarkable work in many ways. It tells of two people, a youthful pupil and her elderly teacher, who become embroiled in a secret love affair. Cadenus is at times remorseful, and would like to withdraw when he realises that Vanessa has fallen in love with him, but the final outcome is left indefinite.

The story is told in the form of an allegory about Venus and the Court of Love:

> The *Shepherds* and the *Nymphs* were seen
> Pleading before the *Cyprian* Queen.
> The Council for the Fair began,
> Accusing that false Creature, *Man*.

> The Brief with weighty Crimes was charg'd,
> On which the Pleader much enlarg'd;
> That *Cupid* now has lost his Art,
> Or blunts the Point of ev'ry Dart: —
> His Altar now no longer smokes
> His Mother's Aid no Youth invokes . . .[1]

Cupid, to avenge his mother, Venus, determines that Vanessa shall fall in love with her teacher. He shoots an arrow to her heart, and leaves the pair to work out their destiny. Cadenus does not at first realise that she is in love with him, but when he does so he feels that they must part. Vanessa, however, thinks otherwise:

> Had he employ'd his Time so long,
> To teach her what was Right or Wrong,
> Yet cou'd such Notions entertain,
> That all his Lectures were in vain?
> She own'd the wand'ring of her Thoughts,
> But he must answer for her Faults.

Both parties now realise their exact position, and much heart-searching ensues. Cadenus is alternately shamed, surprised, and guilty, and he is worried about what people may think. Surely Vanessa is not serious? Of course she is, she replies, and it is his own fault for teaching her so much reason and learning, wit and wisdom. Cadenus acknowledges to himself that this is so, and now his shame turns to pride that such a creature should love him. And, indeed, why should she not do so? But what can he give her in return? He can at least offer friendship:

> A constant, rational Delight,
> On Virtue's Basis fix'd to last,
> When Love's Allurements long are past . . .

Vanessa listens to this, but she is not satisfied:

> While thus *Cadenus* entertains
> *Vanessa* in exalted Strains,

---

[1] Quotations of Swift's verse in this essay are from Harold Williams (ed.), *The Poems of Jonathan Swift*, 2nd ed. (Oxford, 1958).

> The Nymph in sober Words intreats
> A Truce with all sublime Conceits

> He has a Forfeiture incurr'd,
> She vows to take him at his Word,
> And hopes he will not think it strange
> If both shou'd now their Stations change.
> The Nymph will have her Turn, to be
> The Tutor; and the Pupil, he.

The roles are now reversed. The pupil has become the teacher and Vanessa will instruct Cadenus in the matters of the heart, but with what result we are not told:

> But what success *Vanessa* met,
> Is to the World a Secret yet:
> Whether the Nymph, to please her Swain,
> Talks in a high Romantick Strain;
> Or whether he at last descends
> To like with less Seraphick Ends;
> Or, to compound the Business, whether
> They temper Love and Books together;
> Must never to Mankind be told,
> Nor shall the conscious Muse unfold.

'Cadenus and Vanessa' is a long and quite extraordinary poem. Its full meaning is obviously concealed from the casual reader and intended for Swift and Vanessa alone. In taking extracts from it one is reminded of the saying that the devil can quote the Bible for his own purpose, and in fact different meanings have been taken from it. But surely no man would address such a long and carefully composed poem to a female friend unless he were in love with her. Nowhere does it imply that Cadenus is incapable of physical love.

After 1712 the correspondence between Swift and Vanessa is on increasingly intimate terms. From reading it the conclusion is inevitable that Vanessa was not only in love with Swift, but that she was his mistress. What else can be the meaning of the various references in Swift's letters to 'Coffee', first referred to by Horace Walpole, and again recently by Middleton Murry and by Denis Johnston? Here are a few extracts:

I wish I were to walk with you fifty times about yr Garden, and then — drink your Coffee. [15 October 1720]

Cad — assures me he continues to esteem and love and value you above all things, and so will do to the End of his Life, but at the same time entreats that you would not make your self or him unhappy by Imaginations.... Without Health you will lose all desire of drinking your Coffee... I can say no more being called away, mais soyez assurè que jamais personne du monde a etè aimèe honorèe estimèe adorèe par votre amie [*sic*] que vous, I drank no Coffee since I left you, nor intend till I see you again, there is none worth drinking but yours, if my *self* may be the judge — adieu. [5 July 1721]

... remembr, that Riches are nine parts in ten of all that is good in Life, and Health is the tenth, drinking Coffee comes long after, and yet it is the eleventh; but without the two former you cannot drink it right... [1 June 1722]

The best Maxim I know in this life is, to drink your Coffee when you can, and when you cannot, to be easy without it.... Thus much I sympathise with you that I am not chearfull enough to write, for I believe Coffee once a week is necessary to that. [13 July 1722][1]

These references to coffee and coffee-drinking seem to mean one thing only. It is true that on one occasion Swift referred to coffee in connection with Vanessa when writing to her mother. Writing from Chester on 6 June 1713 he says: 'I could not see any marks in the Chimn[ey] at Dunstable, of the Coffee Hessy spilt there.'[2]

But this letter was written some seven years earlier and the code may not then have been invented.

If these passages mean what one imagines they must, and Swift was on these terms with Vanessa, why did he not marry her? She was a personable young lady and quite a suitable *parti*. Swift's nephew, Deane Swift, wrote that:

I have been assured that Miss Vanhomrigh was in her general converse with the world, as far from encouraging any stile or address, inconsistent with the rules of honour and good-breeding; as any woman alive. Neither can it be said ... that she was either a

---

[1] Williams (ed.), *Correspondence*, vol. II, pp. 361, 392–3, 427, 430.
[2] Williams (ed.), *Correspondence*, vol. I, p. 366.

vain woman, or fond of dress; although she was extremely nice and delicate, as well in the cleanliness of her person, as in everything she wrote. Her only misfortune was that she had a passion for Dr. Swift...[1]

The reason Swift did not marry Vanessa was that his loyalty, and probably his true affection also, was engaged elsewhere — with Stella, in fact. There can be little doubt that he and Stella shared a deep and lasting affection. Whether he was married to her or not is of small consequence. His affair with Vanessa was like the temporary aberration of a married man, with the important difference that he and Stella probably were not married.

Stella

Esther, or Hester, Johnson was born on 13 March 1681. She was reputedly the daughter of Edward Johnson (who according to Lord Orrery was steward to Sir William Temple) and his wife, who was in the service of Temple's sister Lady Giffard. It appears probable, however, that Stella was in fact Temple's illegitimate daughter. Among the reasons adduced for this allegation are the strong resemblance she bore to him and to his niece, Lady Portland, her similarity in taste and temperament, and the high quality of her intelligence:

... Miss Hetty's eyes and hair were of a most beautiful black; and all the rest of her features bore so strong a resemblance to those of Sir William Temple that no one could be at a loss to determine what relation she bore to that gentleman. And could the striking likeness have been overlooked, Sir William's uncommon regard for her and his attention to her education, must have convinced every unprejudiced person that Miss Hetty Johnson was the daughter of one who moved in a higher sphere than a Dutch trader.[2]

In addition to this, Stella had as a companion Miss Rebecca Dingley, who was a near cousin of Sir William himself, and it is difficult to explain this if Stella was only his housekeeper's daughter. Again, Temple left her fairly comfortably provided for in his will.

[1] Deane Swift, *An Essay on the Life, Writings and Character of Dr. Jonathan Swift* (1755 ed., London and Dublin), p. 277.

[2] *Gentleman's Magazine*, November 1757.

And, finally, in the year 1693 one de Cros, a diplomatic official employed by the Duke of Holstein, published a letter attacking Sir William Temple. In it he said:

I shall enlarge no further, that I may not engage myself to publish the misfortune of Sir William's family, which I suppose would not be like a gentleman. I have no reason that I know of to complain, neither of his lady, nor of his son, nor of his *daughters*.

Sir William had only one legitimate daughter, Diana, who died in 1684; and the italics were in the original pamphlet. The inference is obvious.

When Swift entered Temple's household at Moor Park in 1689 Stella was about eight years of age. In her early years, he tells us, 'he had some share in her education, by directing her in the principles of honour and virtue; from which she never swerved in any one action or moment of her life'. He goes on to say:

She was sickly from her childhood until about the age of fifteen; but then grew into perfect health, and was looked upon as one of the most beautiful, graceful and agreeable young women in London, only a little too fat. Her hair was blacker than a raven, and every feature of her face in perfection.[1]

Temple seems to have entrusted the care of Stella to Swift. He died when Swift was vicar of Laracor in County Meath, and 'the ladies' then came to live near by at Trim. Except for one visit to England in either 1705 or 1708 Stella never went to England again. She and Swift lived in ever-increasing intimacy, with Dingley as chaperone and companion. It was obvious that the move from England would excite gossip — as Swift said 'a secret history in such a removal' was suspected, but Stella's 'excellent conduct' put a stop to it. They did in fact take great care to observe the proprieties. Stella and Dingley often stayed in the vicarage at Laracor and later in Swift's Dublin lodgings or at the Deanery, but never when he himself was in residence. On these occasions the ladies moved out — to a cottage in the vicinity, to a house in Trim, or later to their own lodgings in Dublin. Many people, including

[1] Temple Scott (ed.), *The Prose Works of Jonathan Swift, D.D.* (London, 1897–1908), vol. XI, p 127.

Swift's cousin, the Rev. Thomas Swift, and Archbishop King expected them to get married, but whether they did so or not this curious method of existence was never altered.

Whatever her position would have been in England, Stella's gaiety, her ready wit and high intelligence soon gained her an accepted place in Dublin society. She liked an evening out, was fond of a game of cards and frequently went to stay with friends in the country. Her life seems to have been happy and equable. Her means were fairly adequate and any financial shortcomings were met by Swift, who made her a regular and not inconsiderable allowance. To his credit there is reason to believe that he did not let her realise that this addition to her income came out of his own pocket.

There can be little doubt that Swift and Stella were in love with each other, and in a deep and lasting manner. The tender and intimate *Journal to Stella* with its 'little language' is proof enough of this. There are also the various poems he wrote to her on her birthday and other occasions. They are enigmatic, it is true, and capable of differing interpretations. He constantly draws attention to the changes wrought by time in her appearance, but never fails to praise her qualities of mind and heart:

> Stella this Day is thirty four,
> (We won't dispute a Year or more)
> However Stella, be not troubled,
> Although thy Size and Years are doubled,
> Since first I saw Thee at Sixteen
> The brightest Virgin of the Green,
> So little is thy Form declin'd
> Made up so largly in thy Mind.

In the verses for 1721 he wrote:

> Now, this is Stella's Case in Fact;
> An Angel's Face, a little crack't;
> (Could Poets or could Painters fix
> How Angels look at thirty six)
> This drew us in at first to find
> In such a Form an Angel's Mind
> And ev'ry Virtue now supplyes
> The fainting Rays of Stella's Eyes . . .

Quite why he dwells so insistently on her physical deterioration is hard to understand; possibly it is to console her for the obvious ravages of phthisis from which she suffered, like Vanessa and so many of Swift's other women friends. She herself refers to this change in her appearance in her poem, 'St. Patrick's Dean, Your Country's Pride'. In any case, raillery of some sort is necessary in verses of this kind to prevent them from becoming too extravagantly sentimental. Swift also repeatedly reminds her that he too is growing old. Here is what he says about Stella as a nurse:

> When on my sickly Couch I lay,
> Impatient both of Night and Day,
> Lamenting in unmanly Strains,
> Call'd every Pow'r to ease my Pains,
> Then *Stella* ran to my Relief
> With chearful Face, and inward Grief;
> And, though by Heaven's severe Decree
> She suffers hourly more than me,
> No cruel Master could require
> From Slaves employ'd for daily Hire
> What *Stella* by her friendship warm'd,
> With Vigour and Delight perform'd.
> My sinking Spirits now supplies
> With Cordials in her Hands and Eyes.
> Now with a soft and silent Tread,
> Unheard she moves about my Bed.
> I see her taste each nauseous Draught,
> And so obligingly am caught:
> I bless the Hand from whence they came,
> Nor dare distort my Face for shame.

If further proof of Swift's devotion is required, one only has to read his essay *On the Death of Mrs. Johnson*, written just after she died; a tribute charged with emotion in every line.

There can be no doubt that Swift's estimate of Stella was true. As W. A. Eddy says, one can read history for a very long time without encountering another woman who surpassed Stella in gentleness and heroism.

And what did Stella think of Swift? She tells us herself in verses as good as Swift ever wrote:

> St. Patrick's dean, your country's pride,
> My early and my only guide,
> Let me among the rest attend,
> Your pupil and your humble friend,
> To celebrate in female strains
> The day that paid your mother's pains;
> Descend to take that tribute due
> In gratitude alone to you.
>
> .   .   .
>
> Long be the day that gave you birth
> Sacred to friendship, wit, and mirth;
> Late dying may you cast a shred
> Of your rich mantle o'er my head;
> To bear with dignity my sorrow,
> One day *alone, then die to-morrow.*

Why, then, did Swift and Stella never live together as man and wife? One explanation is that put forward by Denis Johnston.[1] This, in brief, is that Swift was the son of Sir John Temple, Sir William Temple's father, and therefore Stella's doubly illegitimate uncle. If true, this was an effective barrier to their marriage, for marriage or intercourse between uncle and niece was, and is, contrary to Canon Law and is also an indictable offence under Criminal Law. This theory receives some support from the fact that it was widely rumoured in Swift's time that he, as well as Stella, was Sir William's child, but this was later proved to be impossible as at the operative time Sir William was Ambassador to the Low Countries.

The Temples were a distinguished Leicestershire family. The first to come to Ireland was the William Temple in whose arms Sir Philip Sidney died at Zutphen. This William Temple became the fourth Provost of Trinity College, Dublin. His son, Sir John, became Master of the Rolls in Ireland and may have been instrumental in obtaining the Stewardship of King's Inns for Swift's father. Swift's mother was Abigail Erick, or Herrick, of Leicestershire. She was ten years older than the elder Jonathan Swift, and Denis Johnston suggests that she was in fact Sir John Temple's farmed-out mistress. Swift's father died before his son was born, which event took place at least nine or ten months after his death,

[1] In *Dublin Historical Record,* June–Aug. 1941.

according to Johnston. What is more natural, he says, than that when widowed she should turn for consolation to her former protector? Possibly, but to have a child by him at this late stage is another matter, although by no means beyond the bounds of possibility. However, the argument is plausible, and the reader is recommended to Denis Johnston's work for further details. The Temples are certainly a brilliant family. Since Swift's time it has produced three First Lords of the Treasury, two Secretaries of State, two Keepers of the Privy Seal, four First Lords of the Admiralty, the famous Lord Palmerston and two recent Archbishops. The Swift family has no such record.

The theory that Swift was an illegitimate Temple explains the facts of Swift's life very well. It is easy to imagine the shock which would be suffered by a gifted young man like Swift when he discovered such a tragic and irreversible fact. He was conscious of his great intellectual endowment and knew that he had the ability to reach great heights, but here was an effectual barrier in his path. When he found that the same reason prevented him from living openly with Stella as man and wife his cup of bitterness was filled to overflowing. 'You have just seen the most unhappy man on earth, but on the subject of his wretchedness you must never ask a question,' said Archbishop King to the Rev. Patrick Delany.

Denis Johnston's theory, while incapable of definite proof unless further facts come to light, is undoubtedly engaging, but somehow it fails to carry complete conviction. One reason for this is the disparate ages of Sir John, Abigail and the elder Jonathan. About the time of Swift's birth Sir John was some thirty-five years older than Abigail, and, if she was indeed the butcher's daughter from Wigston Magna, her husband was her junior by ten years. But there is some doubt as to whether this worthy was in fact her father.

According to Denis Johnston, his name was Thomas Erick or Herrick (there was considerable latitude in the spelling of surnames in the early seventeenth century). Although his vocation was humble he laid claim to a distinguished ancestry. His son, Thomas, was Vicar of Frisby in Shropshire, whose daughter married the Rev. John Kendall, Vicar of Thornton, near Leicester. Swift corresponded with Kendall, subscribing himself on one occasion at least 'I am, good cousin, your very friend and servant'.

However, according to Ehrenpreis, Abigail was the daughter, not of Thomas Erick, the butcher of Wigston Magna, but of the Rev. James Ericke, Vicar of Thornton in Leicestershire from 1627 to 1634.[1] After 1634 the Rev. Mr. Ericke and his wife moved to Dublin where Abigail was born in 1640.

At this point the two stories come together, for Abigail's brother Thomas Errick was Vicar of Frisby-on-the-Wreake, Leicestershire, from 1664 to 1681, and his daughter married the Rev. John Kendall, Vicar of Thornton, Leicestershire, from 1684 to 1717.

If the second version is the true one, Abigail was ten years younger than Denis Johnston supposes, in fact the same age as her husband; and the gap between her age and that of Sir John Temple so much greater. Forty-five years, more or less, is a very considerable difference in age between a mistress and her lover. But stranger things have happened.

Physically Swift was of medium height and full figure. Dr. Johnson said that:

> The person of Swift had not many recommendations. He had a kind of muddy complexion, which, though he washed himself with oriental scrupulosity, did not look clear. He had a countenance sour and severe, which he seldom softened by any appearance of gaiety. He stubbornly resisted any tendency to laughter.[2]

This description does not correspond with the earlier portraits of Swift, particularly that by Jervas in the National Portrait Gallery, London. Here we see a confident, cheerful-looking individual with strong well-cut features and the light-blue eyes so frequently commented upon — 'quite as azure as the Heavens', as Pope said. His complexion as rendered by Jervas is certainly clear enough, if the painter is to be depended upon.

In spite of Dr. Johnson's statement he seems to have had a considerable streak of gaiety in his character, and he certainly had a

---

[1] Irvin Ehrenpreis, *Swift the Man, his Works and the Age:* vol. I. *Mr. Swift and his Contemporaries* (London, 1962).
[2] *Lives of the English Poets*, ed. G. B. Hill, vol. III, pp. 55–56.

most unusual and unpredictable sense of humour. Its manifestations
were sometimes subtle, sometimes almost childish, amounting to
buffoonery. He was not above making what we would consider
most deplorable puns or carrying out practical jokes on his friends.
He has been accused of parsimony, but it is not easy to be over-
generous on a limited income, and we know that the income of his
deanery never exceeded £700 a year. Nevertheless he subscribed
liberally to charity and always kept his pockets full of coins of
varying value to give to the poor. As we have seen he augmented
Stella's private income on many occasions without her knowledge
and he did the same for Dingley. Many other attributes went to form
his complex personality. Morally he was not very courageous, for he
was always inclined to take cover in times of crisis. On the credit
side is his loyalty to his friends, high and low, and the somewhat
surprising fact that he respected his opponents' views if he thought
they held them genuinely. He was not particularly interested in
either art or music, for all his creative and critical faculties were
directed to literature. In religion he was a devout and convinced
member of the Church of Ireland, a communion which more or less
equates with Episcopalians in the United States and Anglicans in
England. He disliked Roman Catholics but abhorred Nonconformists, as may easily be recognised from *A Tale of a Tub*. In
religion he was certainly no mystic, but he was active, conscientious
and successful as Dean of St. Patrick's.

After the death of Stella in 1728 Swift still led an active life
politically and socially. The 'Drapier' was idolised in Dublin and
wielded great power, and he continued to have many friends, both
male and female: Sheridan, Ford, the Rev. Doctor and Mrs. Delany,
Mrs. Pilkington, Mrs. Howard and Lady Betty Germaine. In spite
of this he grew steadily more gloomy and depressed: '*Vertiginosus,
inops, surdus, male gratus amicis*', while his writings became more
mordant and obsessed.

> See, how the Dean begins to break:
> Poor Gentleman, he droops apace,
> You plainly find it in his Face.
> That old Vertigo in his Head,
> Will never leave him, till he's dead:

> Besides, his Memory decays,
> He recollects not what he says . . .

As he grew older his mind turned again and again to a matter which had interested him in his younger days. Wandering through the Liberties of St. Patrick's he must have seen many of the mentally afflicted roaming the streets, accepted by the common man as part of the social order of the day. To Swift their plight was a challenge. He worked and saved for fifteen years to establish a hospital for their care. That hospital still flourishes, still largely governed by the enlightened constitution which he devised. It is a sad postscript that so many people should still believe that he founded his hospital because he was afraid that he himself might become insane, and that he died as one of its inmates. This, of course, is far from the truth. He died in his Deanery of that saddest of diseases, senile decay.

About this time he suffered from a series of boils on the arms and body and he also developed a large and painful swelling of the left eye. Subsequently he had considerable difficulty in expressing himself, and as Lord Brain has pointed out, the utterances which he did achieve were of an emotional nature, which is a characteristic of aphasia. Lord Brain suggests that this may have been due to thrombophlebitis spreading from a small venous sinus in the orbit to the superior petrosal sinus and thence to the cortical veins, which drain the lower part of the frontal lobe of the brain, including, on the left side, Broca's area, which is concerned with speech.

About the year 1741 or 1742 when he was about seventy-five years of age he began to lose his memory and to act irrationally. It was evident to those about him that his brain had failed, and that he had lapsed into a state of

> Second childishness and mere oblivion
> Sans teeth, sans eyes, sans taste, sans everything.

He was, in fact, suffering from the disease which Dr. Oliver Gogarty once described somewhat cynically as 'delayed burial'. He remained in this pathetic condition for three years before he died.

BONAMY DOBRÉE

The Jocose Dean

NORMALLY, when Swift comes into our minds, we think of him as a man filled with a savage indignation that never ceased to lacerate his heart; as a man who throughout his life wrote the most withering, even bitter, satires; and to think of him dying is to think of an empire falling. Or we consider him to have lived as an unhappy being, suffering one gruelling disappointment after another and, for some reason, or reasons, inhibited in his loves. We are inclined to forget that when St. John was most politically harried, nothing would refresh him more than 'to walk in the Park with the jocose Dean': that Swift could be seen to 'laugh and shake in Rab'lais' easy Chair'; and we may not remember that Ford could write to him as one of 'those who are formed for mirth and society'. (8 July 1736.) After all, a man cannot live wrathfully all the time; a balance is needed, and it would seem that Swift's *saeva indignatio* was offset, even perhaps sustained, by his enormous gaiety. It is this aspect that I should like to try to consider here.

Try; because, of course, it is almost, if not quite, impossible to catch the tone. How can we tell by what japes and jests, what puns and preposterous propositions he was notoriously the life and soul of any party or gathering? Why was he so indispensable at meetings of the Brothers' Club, or later with the Scriblerians? — who, incidentally, in their turn produced three classics of our literature, *The Beggar's Opera*, *The Dunciad*, and *Gulliver's Travels*, born of their conversations. So much for London. And then in Ireland, where at one time he felt that he had gone 'to die like a poisoned rat in a hole', why was he welcome for long periods at Quilca with the Sheridans, at Loughgall with the Copes, at Market Hill with the Achesons; or why were people eager for invitations to dine at the Deanery? We cannot hear the jokes, or share the gay spirit of his discourse. And are we to suppose that he was not greeted by Stella in Dublin or by Vanessa at Celbridge as much for his fun as for his tenderer communications? All we can do is to guess at this gay spirit from what he wrote, especially in his letters, for these, naturally, are the closest to conversation. We can begin with these.

We find his conversational tone, for instance, when he writes from Laracor on 17 April 1710 to Stearne, the then Dean of St. Patrick's:

. . . I am this minute very busy, being to preach to-day to an audience of at least fifteen people, most of them gentle, and all simple.

I can send you no news; only the employment of my parishioners may, for memory-sake, be reduced under these heads: Mr. Percival is ditching; Mrs. Percival in her kitchen; Mr. Wesley switching; Mrs. Wesley stitching; Sir Arthur Langford riching, which is a new word for heaping up riches. I know no other rhyme but bitching, and that I hope we are all past.

or when on 11 May 1711 he writes to St. John, and one catches a flavour of the walks in the Park:

Pray, Sir, find an expedient. Finding expedients is the business of Secretaries of State. I will yield to any reasonable conditions not below my dignity. I will not find fault with the victuals; I will restore the water-glass that I stole, and solicit for my Lord Keeper's salary. And, Sir, to show you I am not a person to be safely injured, if you dare refuse me justice in this point, I will appear before you in a pudding-sleeve gown, I will disparage your snuff, write a lampoon upon Nably Car,[1] dine with you upon a foreign post-day; nay, I will read verses in your presence, until you snatch them out of my hands.

Again, there is a letter he wrote to John Hill, Lady Masham's brother-in-law, on 12 August 1712 about a snuff-box he had been given by, as she then was, Mrs. Hill:

My Lord Treasurer, who is the most malicious person in the world, says, you ordered a goose to be drawn at the bottom of my box, as a reflection upon the clergy; and that I ought to resent it. But I am not angry at all, and his Lordship observes by halves; for the goose is there drawn pecking at a snail, just as I do at him, to make him mend his pace in relation to the public, although it be hitherto in vain.

[1] Probably Billy Carr, apparently a sort of hanger on, who in Sept. 1714 was appointed a Groom of the Bedchamber to George I.

And besides, Dr. Arbuthnot, who is a scholar, says, you meant it as a compliment for us both: that I am the goose who saved the Capitol by my cackling, and that his Lordship is represented by the snail, because he preserves his country by delays.

One senses there something of the bantering spirit Swift would indulge in when conversing with his friends; and there is, too, a touch of satire on Harley's dilatoriness, or, as we, free from Swift's impatience, might see it, his wise holding back from precipitate action.

One can tell something of the sort of interchange in jesting between Swift and his friends from some of the letters they wrote to him. Thus on 8 December 1713 Pope writes from Binfield:

> Not to trouble you at present with a recital of all my obligations to you, I shall mention only two things, which I take particularly kind of you — your desire that I should write to you, and your proposal of giving me twenty guineas to change my religion, which last you must give me leave to make the subject of this letter.
> Sure no clergyman ever offered so much out of his own purse for the sake of any religion . . .

Pope develops the subject entertainingly, arguing that far more money is needed for that sort of transaction. Especially when you come to consider prayers for the dead (a matter that Pope is reluctant to give up), since masses are expensive:

> Old Dryden, though a Roman Catholic, was a poet; and it is revealed in the visions of some ancient saints, that no poet was ever saved under some hundreds of masses. I cannot set his delivery from purgatory at less than fifty pounds sterling.

He goes on to say that there is one person especially whom he would wish the Ministry concerned with these matters to see to:

> The person I mean is Dr. Swift, a dignified clergyman, but one who, by his own confession, has composed more libels than sermons. If it be true, what I have heard often affirmed by innocent people, that too much wit is dangerous to salvation, this unfortunate gentleman must certainly be damned to all eternity.

Swift will have chuckled over the neat way of turning a compliment,

and still more perhaps at the way Pope goes on with a little joke
about their important political friends:

But I hope his long experience in the world, and frequent conversation with great men, will cause him, as it has some others, to have
less and less wit every day.

Bolingbroke, of course, was recognised as a stimulating intellectual,
while Harley, now Lord Oxford, known among the group as 'the
Dragon', was a by no means dull or unperforming member of the
Brothers' Club. In private conversation, Swift told Archbishop
King, Harley was 'wholly disengaged and very facetious'.

On 25 July 1714 Swift writes to another Brother, namely John
Arbuthnot, who had offered him a loan:

The mischief is, I never borrow money of a friend. You are mightily
mistaken; all your honour, generosity, good nature, good sense,
wit, and every other quality, will never make me think one jot the
better of you. That time is now some years past, and you will never
mend in my opinion. But really, Brother, you have a sort of shuffle
in your gait; and now I have said the worst that your most mortal
enemy could say of you with truth.

As good a jocose way as could be imagined of paying a handsome
tribute to an affectionate friend.

He tends always to be amusing in his private letters, and Bolingbroke could write to him (12 August 1714): 'I swear I did not
imagine, that you could have held out through two pages, even of
small paper, in so grave a style.' The 'style', needless to say, varies
enormously. The letters to Stella abound with gaiety; they are
jocular in the sense that they are full of affectionate raillery, what
one might call teasing, with puns and jingles and April-fooling,
these being in a way extensions of the 'little language'. In the
Journal to Stella we hear too of what he was doing by way of conversational amusement: thus in October 1710: 'Then I visited Lord
Pembroke, who is just come to town, and we were very merry
talking of old things, and I hit him with one pun.' And in November
1711: 'I designed a jaunt into the city to-day to be merry, but was
disappointed.' Among letters too might be placed *A Decree for*

Concluding the Treaty between Dr. Swift and Mrs. Long, a kind of epistle to Vanessa, heightening what was evidently a joke in the Vanhomrigh circle.

His letters immediately after his departure into 'exile' are not so lively; but he gradually overcame his depression, being able to write to Archdeacon Walls on 16 December 1716: 'I'm sorry you disturbed yourself so early this morning as four o'clock. I doubt you were ready to sleep at your own sermon.' On 29 May 1718 Prior writes to him: 'I have nothing more to tell you, but that you are the happiest man in the world; and if you are once got into *la bagatelle*, you may despise the world.' On 28 September 1721 Swift writes to Archbishop King:

I have a receipt [against melancholy] to which you are a stranger; my Lord Oxford and Mr. Prior used to join with me in taking it, to whom I often said, when we were two hours diverting ourselves with trifles, *vive la bagatelle*.

He really recovered himself completely after the success of *The Drapier's Letters*, which brought him so much fame in Ireland and the love of the Dublin populace. But we do not find him joking much with his English friends, though he writes happily, and to Pope occasionally mentions *vive la bagatelle*. With Gay also he can be a little jesting, as when the latter's *Wife of Bath*, originally a failure, was being successfully revived: he writes on 20 November 1729:

I have heard of the Wife of Bath; I think Shakespeare. If you wrote one it is out of my head. I had not the cant word damned in my head; but if it were acted and damned and printed, I should not now be your counsellor to new lick it.

His 'mistake' is obviously intentional: he knew his Chaucer. But on the whole he talks more seriously to those in far-away England.

To make up for this, he gives rein to all his jocoseness with his Irish acquaintance, especially Thomas Sheridan, largely in the matter of word play. In June 1735 he has a long letter devoted to chat, and the suffix -ling:

I suppose you are now angle ling with your tack ling in a purr ling stream, or pad ling and say ling in a boat, or sad ling your stum ling horse with a sap ling in your hands, and snare ling at your groom, or set ling your affairs, or tick ling your cat, or tat ling with your neighbour Price; not always toy ling with your school. . . .

A lady whose understanding was sing ling me out as a wit ling or rather a suck ling, as if she were tick ling my fancy, tang ling me with question, tell ling me many stories, her tongue toe ling like a clapper; says she, an old man's dar ling is better than a young man's war ling.

It is as though in his old age, feeling his general wit no longer as active as it used to be, he is finding refuge in word games with Sheridan, as when he plays with their *Latino-Anglicus*, for instance in a letter of 30 September 1735:

. . . I shall describe a certain female of your acquaintance whose name shall be Dorothy; it is in the following manner: Dolies astra per, astra mel, a sus, a quoque et, atra pes, an id lar, alas i bo nes, a præ ter, at at lar, avi si ter, age ipsi, astro lar . . .

meaning 'Doll is a strapper, a trammel, a souse, a coquette, a trapes, an idler, a lazy-bones, a prater, a tattler, a visitor, a gipsy, a stroller . . .' He concludes the first of two long paragraphs:

Sir, I entreat you will please to observe, since I must speak in the vulgar language, that in the above forty-three denominations for females, many of them end with the domestic deity Lar, to show that women were chiefly created for family affairs; and yet I cannot hear that any other author hath made the same remark.

It all seems rather desperate, though the last sentence is a release into slightly acid wit from the drudgery, as it must to some extent have been, of composing a letter in *Latino-Anglicus*, or the separate *Consultation of Four Physicians* in the same manner.

But we get a more bantering tone when he and Sheridan together write to Mrs. Whiteway, Swift's housekeeper at the Deanery. Swift had been ailing, and gone away to recuperate at Cavan with Sheridan. Swift begins with a more or less normal letter about practical matters, the document being taken over by Sheridan, who goes on:

I can assure you, dear Madam, with pleasure, that the Dean begins to look healthier and plumper already; and I hope will mend every day. But, to deal plainly with you, I am a little afraid of his good stomach, though victuals are cheap, because it improves every day, and I do not know how far this may increase my family expenses. He pays me but two crowns a week for his ordinary, and I own, that I am a little too modest to grumble at it; but if you would give him a hint about wear and tear of goods, I make no doubt but his own discretion would make him raise his price. I am, to you and yours, as much yours as the Dean aforesaid.

Then Swift:

I desire you will hint to the Doctor that he would please to abate four shillings a week from the ten, which he most exorbitantly makes me pay him; but tell him you got this hint from another hand, and that all Dublin cries shame at him for it.

As a final example from the correspondence I would give a letter he wrote to Mrs. Whiteway on 30 October 1738, after having been given a box of soap and a shaving-brush by Deane Swift:

Mr. Swift's gimcracks of cups and balls, in order to my convenient shaving with ease and dispatch, together with the prescription on half a sheet of paper, was exactly followed, but some inconveniences attended; for I cut my face once or twice, was just twice as long in the performance, and left twice as much hair behind as I have done this twelvemonth past. I return him therefore all his implements, and my own compliments, with abundance of thanks, because he has fixed me during life in my old humdrum way.

Something of the old jocosity is still there. But is there also just a touch of irritation? Why can't they leave me alone!

We can also gather what he was like in company from occasional lines in a poem, as, for instance, in 'My Lady's Lamentation and Complaint against the Dean', supposedly written by Lady Acheson, whom he called 'Skinny' and 'Snipe', and who complains that he is always chipping her habits, her appearance and so on; and then:

> He's all the day saunt'ring,
> With labourers bant'ring,
> Among his colleagues,
> A parcel of Teagues

(Whom he brings in among us
And bribes with mundungus.)

And then in another poem 'written' by Lady Acheson, 'A Panegy-
rick on the Dean', she says at one point:

> Now, as a Jester, I accost you;
> Which never yet one Friend has lost you.
> You judge so nicely to a Hair,
> How far to go, and when to spare:
> By long Experience grown so wise,
> Of ev'ry Taste to know the Size;
> There's none so ignorant or weak
> To take Offence at what you speak.

Or he writes to Sheridan in answer to a poem by the latter, who next
refers to Swift's 'Billingsgate Muse' —

> Hum — excellent good — your anger was stirr'd:
> Well, punners and rhymers must have the last word . . .

— the whole going on in the jocose manner Swift usually employs
with Sheridan, as in the epistle dated 14 December 1719, *at Night*,
about the muddle Sheridan seems to have made about bottling the
wine he has sent. And again we have the riddles in verse he con-
cocted for Sheridan, or the 'circular' letters, that is, verse written in
circles. This appears to be something other than jocoseness; it
would involve too great and sustained an effort; it is not impulsive,
and would seem to be done as a relief from more troublesome
thoughts. Certainly much of all this — including the George
Nim-Dan-Dean letters, and those pretended to be written by somebody else, Delany or others — strikes us as very boring.

We can get some idea, then, of why everybody found Swift such
good company, some notion of his response to others and the
effusion of high spirits that seemed always to accompany him. Yet
there is one very strange aspect of his personality in company.
Edward Young told Spence that 'Swift had a mixture of insolence
in his conversation', an insolence which, however, must have been
largely humorous, as we gather from the Lady Acheson poems. Yet
Pope told Spence, 'Dr. Swift has an odd blunt way, that is mistaken,

by strangers, for ill-nature. — 'Tis so odd that there's no describing it but by facts.' And he goes on:

One evening Gay and I went to see him: you know how intimately we were all acquainted. On our coming in: 'Hey-day, gentlemen,' says the Doctor, 'what's the meaning of this visit? How come you to leave all the great lords, that you are so fond of, to come hither to see a poor Dean?' — Because we would rather see you than any of them. — 'Ay, any one that did not know you so well as I do, might believe you. But since you are come, I must get some supper for you, I suppose?' — No, Doctor, we have supped already. — 'Supped already! that's impossible: why, 'tis not eight o'clock yet.' — Indeed we have. — 'That's very strange: but if you had not supped, I must have got something for you. — Let me see, what should I have had? a couple of lobsters? ay, that would have done very well; two shillings: tarts; a shilling. But you will drink a glass of wine with me, though you supped before your time, only to spare my pocket?' — No, we had rather talk with you than drink with you. — 'But if you had supped with me, as in all reason you ought to have done, you must have drank with me. — A bottle of wine; two shillings. — Two and two is four; and one is five: just two and sixpence a piece. There, Pope, there's half a crown for you; and there's another for you, sir: for I won't save anything by you I am determined.' This was all said and done with his usual seriousness on such occasions: and in spite of every thing we could say to the contrary, he actually obliged us to take the money.[1]

It is all rather puzzling. How far was it a joke? How far behind it all was there a feeling of unease, a sense of insult, even? Had they indeed supped before their time on purpose to save his pocket? Was he aware that some people thought him over-careful, mean even, in casual expenditure, and he suspected that they were taking this rather ungenerous view of him? And again, 'his usual seriousness _on such occasions_'. One feels that very often Swift's humour was deliberate, rather than a spontaneous bubbling-up of mirth.

With a few notable exceptions, especially 'Cadenus and Vanessa', and the verses on Stella's birthdays, Swift's poetry, after the dismal pindarics, is for the most part laughter-provoking. Dryden was well inspired when he said: 'Cousin Swift, turn your thoughts another

---

[1] Joseph Spence, _Anecdotes, Observations, and Characters of Books and Men_ (London, 1820), pp. 19–20.

way [that is, express yourself differently, choose other subjects],
for nature never intended you for a Pindaric poet.' Nearly always,
however, an element of satire intrudes, even though it is light-
heartedly humorous as in 'Helter-Skelter':

> Now the active young Attorneys
> Briskly travel on their Journies,
> Looking big as any Gyants,
> On the horses of their Clients;

and there are, notoriously, the bitingly satiric ones, such as the
rather vicious 'The Salamander', or the virulent 'The Legion Club',
compared with which 'Sid Hamet's Rod' is genial. It is as though he
felt that, generally speaking, satire in itself, if too heavily taken, was
something rather ridiculous. Ordinary humour, rather than jocoseness, pervades such a masterpiece as 'Verses on the Death of Dr.
Swift', to which I shall return. One senses about so many of Swift's
autobiographical verses that he is saying, 'You may sometimes think
me a dreadful bore with my moralisings, but all the same I'm rather
fun!' Then again it may be the other way round: fun might change
to seriousness; there would be too much point in the drollery of
'A Dialogue between an Eminent Lawyer and Dr. Swift Dean of
St. Patrick's, being an allusion to the first Satire of the second book
of Horace':

> ... there are persons who complain
> There's too much satire in my vein,
> That I am often found exceeding
> The rules of raillery and breeding ...

for Swift's mind appears to have been exceptionally unified in its
complexity; he could bind together a medley of emotions. Suddenly,
in the middle of a light conversation, he would break out, making
Lady Acheson expostulate:

> DEUCE is in you, Mr. DEAN;
> What can all this Passion mean?
> Mention Courts, you'll ne'er be quiet;
> On Corruptions running Riot.

He had been generously given the gift to see himself as others saw
him, perhaps too generously, as might be suggested by the odd

encounter with Pope and Gay referred to above. But at least detachment went with the gift, permitting him to be humorous about
himself.

There is some difficulty in distinguishing between jocoseness and
humour, the former being of a more vigorous social sort, perhaps
deliberately provoking a retort in kind. Quiet humour is apparent
in Swift's verse from the moment that he turned his thoughts
another way, and produced 'The Lady's Ivory Table-Book', which,
however, turns to mild satire at the end. Where we meet humour,
especially, is in the fairly early 'Mrs. Harris's Petition' and the much
later 'Mary the Cook-maid's Letter', from each of which a little may
be quoted. 'The Humble Petition of Frances Harris' humbly
sheweth:

> That I went to warm my self in Lady *Betty*'s Chamber, because I
>   was cold,
> And I had in a Purse, seven Pound, four Shillings and six Pence,
>   besides Farthings, in Money, and Gold;
> So because I had been buying things for my *Lady* last Night,
> I was resolved to tell my Money, to see if it was right;
> Now you must know, because my Trunk has a very bad Lock,
> Therefore all the Money, I have, which, *God* knows, is a very small
>   Stock,
> I keep in a Pocket ty'd about my Middle, next my Smock . . .

That is a story, told simply as such, Swift jokingly, but with some
sympathy, putting himself into Mrs. Harris's self: in 'Mary the
Cook-Maid's Letter to Dr. Sheridan' Swift carries on a humorous
rally of name-calling with his friend:

> Well; if I ever saw such another Man since my Mother bound my
>   Head,
> You a Gentleman! marry come up, I wonder where you were bred?
> I am sure such Words does not become a Man of your Cloth,
> I would not give such Language to a Dog, faith and troth.
> Yes; you call'd my Master a Knave: Fie Mr. *Sheridan*, 'tis a Shame
> For a Parson, who shou'd know better Things, to come out with
>   such a Name.
> Knave in your Teeth, Mr. *Sheridan*, 'tis both a Shame and a Sin,
> And the Dean my Master is an honester Man than you and all your
>   kin:

He has more Goodness in his little Finger, than you have in your
    whole Body,
My Master is a parsonable Man, not a spindle-shank'd hoddy doddy.
And now whereby I find you would fain make an Excuse,
Because my Master one Day in anger call'd you Goose....

    You say you will eat Grass on his Grave: a Christian eat Grass!
Whereby you now confess your self to be a Goose or an Ass...

Here we get a glimpse of the sort of conversation, if that kind of
schoolboy interchange can be called such, carried on in the intervals
of more serious talk, from which Swift possibly sought the easing
of mirth. We find him achieving the same species of relief in his more
deeply felt autobiographical verses, as in those 'On the Death of
Dr. Swift'. For that poem is not by any means altogether joking.
Here and there it has touches of light humour, but it seems characterised for the most part by a humour that is slightly sardonic —
unless this be the wise detachment of a man sixty-four years old.
He worked over this poem tremendously hard, telling Gay on
1 December 1731:

I have been several months writing near five hundred lines on a
pleasant subject, only to tell what my friends and enemies will say
on me after I am dead. I shall finish it soon, for I add two lines every
week, and blot out four and alter eight.

He repudiated having composed what has been considered as a draft
of the poem, namely 'The Life and Character of Dean Swift', but it
seems likely that it was really his. The final complex 'Verses on the
Death of Dr. Swift' reads in some parts as a mollifying, rather
touching, affectionate tribute to his friends, especially when we
remember that for several days he was to leave unopened a letter
from Pope, having a premonition that it contained the news of Gay
having died. But one passage at least has a certain jocoseness, as
though he were digging his friends in the ribs, while at the same
time paying them his tribute:

> Why must I be outdone by Gay,
> In my own hum'rous biting Way?
>   ARBUTHNOT is no more my Friend,
> Who dares to Irony pretend;

> Which I was born to introduce,
> Refin'd it first, and shew'd its Use.

a tone repeated with sad overtones, the result of experience reflected upon in:

> Poor POPE will grieve a Month; and GAY
> A Week; and ARBUTHNOTT a Day.
> St. JOHN himself will scarce forbear
> To bite his Pen, and drop a Tear.

And here the tone changes to one of detachment:

> The rest will give a Shrug and cry
> I'm sorry; but we all must dye . . .

A common remark, which we may have made ourselves about people whom we have scarcely met or only heard of: 'Oh, well. We've all got to die some time.' Earlier we have read — and this is mirth overcoming the justifiable annoyance about the matter to which it refers:

> Kind Lady *Suffolk* in the Spleen,
> Runs laughing up to tell the Queen.
> The Queen, so Gracious, Mild, and Good,
> Cries, 'Is he gone?' 'tis time he shou'd . . . .'

But we get a more central view of him as the genial companion at the end of the poem, where the generality of people say:

> 'He knew an hundred pleasant Stories,
> With all the Turns of *Whigs* and *Tories*:
> Was chearful to his dying Day,
> And Friends would let him have his Way.'

There is no need to pursue Swift's jocoseness in the poems, most of them being intentionally humorous or light. It is more revealing to see how it would keep breaking in even with the serious — often deadly serious — prose pieces. This, too, from the very beginning. There is no doubt that he felt he had something important to say in *A Tale of a Tub*, and also that to write a dull theological treatise would be quite ineffectual. Ordinary satire, again, would be too blunt; and besides, to write a fable, an absurdly exaggerated story, would be such enormous fun! And with him the sense of fun was almost irrepressible. As he says in 'The Author upon Himself':

> S——had the Sin of Wit no venial Crime;
> Nay, 'twas affirm'd, he sometimes dealt in Rhime:
> Humour, and Mirth, had Place in all he writ:
> He reconcil'd Divinity and Wit.

Nevertheless we may be allowed to think that this, his first book, is rather fumbling; it is, in a way, too full: 'What a genius I had when I writ that book.' Yes; but it is the genius of overfulness, of too great exuberance. But how amusing it must have been to write, near the end of the Preface:

But I forget that I am expatiating on a Subject, wherein I have no concern, having neither a Talent nor an Inclination for Satyr; On the other side, I am so entirely satisfied with the whole present Procedure of Human Things, that I have been for some Years preparing a *Panegyric upon the World* . . . but finding my Common-Place-Book fill much slower than I had reason to expect, I have chosen to defer them to another Occasion.

And, as a contrast to this bland 'satyr', in section XI he describes how Jack (the Dissenters) treats the Will, that is, the New Testament:

He had a Way of working it into any Shape he pleased; so that it served him for a Night-cap when he went to Bed, and for an Umbrello in rainy Weather. He would lap a Piece of it about a sore Toe, or when he had Fits, burn two Inches under his Nose; or if any Thing lay heavy on his Stomach, scrape off and swallow as much of the Powder as would lie on a silver Penny, they were all infallible Remedies.

And so on. This, surely, is not satire, so much as sheer inventive, though pointedly critical, fun.

And, obviously, it was ingenious sense of fun that made him write *A Meditation upon a Broom-Stick*, to be solemnly read to the Countess of Berkeley as one of Robert Boyle's pietistic effusions. There was double amusement in this; that of taking off Boyle, and that of taking in Lady Berkeley, who, at first gulled into believing it authentic, took it in good part when the truth was told her. Swift must have enormously relished the doing of it, quite apart from the reading of it:

This single Stick, which you now behold ingloriously lying in that neglected Corner, I once knew in a flourishing State in a Forest. It was full of Sap, full of Leaves, and full of Boughs: But now, in vain does the busy Art of Man pretend to vie with Nature, by tying that withered Bundle of Twigs to its sapless Trunk.... When I beheld this, I sighed, and said within my self, SURELY MORTAL MAN IS A BROOMSTICK....

But a Broom-stick, perhaps you will say, is an Emblem of a Tree standing on its Head; and pray what is Man but a topsy-turvy Creature?

In the same vein, though unlike it, is *A Tritical Essay upon the Faculties of the Mind*, in which Swift gathered together all the trite sayings that occurred to him, and aped a serious essay, not, it must be confessed, very brilliantly.

A great deal must be left out in an article on a subject that it would take a book to deal with adequately; but one cannot omit the essay against the abolition of Christianity. The full title is wonderful, and one can imagine it arising out of a conversation in which Pope, perhaps, or Gay, or Arbuthnot said: 'Mightn't it be rather inconvenient if Christianity were to be abolished?' And then Swift, immensely entertained by the mild epithet, devising the heading: *An Argument to prove, That the Abolishing of CHRISTIANITY IN ENGLAND, May, as Things now Stand, be attended with some Inconveniences, and, perhaps, not produce those many good Effects proposed thereby.* And how he must have chuckled to himself as he discovered certain things to say which, otherwise phrased, would be directly satirical or devastatingly withering. After all, Swift was profoundly serious in this matter. So we read:

I hope, no Reader imagines me so weak to stand up in the Defence of *real* Christianity; such as used in primitive Times (if we may believe the Authors of those Ages) to have an Influence upon Mens Belief and Actions: To offer at the Restoring of that, would indeed be a wild Project; it would be to dig up Foundations; to destroy at one Blow *all* the Wit and *half* the Learning of the Kingdom; to break the entire Frame and Constitution of Things; to ruin Trade, extinguish Arts and Sciences with the Professors of them; in short, to turn our Courts, Exchanges and Shops into Desarts: . . .

How too he must have enjoyed his beautiful double-shafted joke: 'Nor do I think it wholly groundless, or my Fear altogether imaginary: that the Abolishing of Christianity may perhaps bring the Church in Danger; or at least put the Senate to the trouble of another Securing Vote.' Swift, of course, was passionately for the Church; but what effect would it have to answer the attackers of Christianity, the Tolands and Asgills, in their own dull language?

> . . . my method of Reforming
> Is by Laughing, not by Storming,

not only because it was more telling — 'ridicule is the test of truth' — but because it was infinitely more enlivening to oneself.

A proportion of what he wrote is obviously fun, as in the *Bickerstaff Papers*, especially in making play with the astrologer Partridge. Here, besides the obvious need to explode silly nonsense, there was his desire to reduce Partridge as a man who favoured the abolition of the Test Act. The churchman, as well as the common-sense man, came into play once more. But suppose that Bickerstaff were to foretell the death of Partridge, then declare that he had died on the predicted day, and then scoff at him when he declared that he most certainly was alive! If Partridge had had only a tithe of Swift's sense of humour, how entertaining he might have found it to write from the grave!

To make a jump, take *The Drapier's Letters*, in which Swift was fighting hard against what he regarded as an intolerable imposition on the people of Ireland. Certainly, indignation was behind it all, but it is as though he were always, not searching for, but overtaken by the ridiculous through the sheer make-up of his nature. Here, for instance, is one of the passages in which he supposes that Wood's half-pence have been imposed upon Ireland:

They say that Squire Connolly has Sixteen Thousand Pounds a Year; now if he sends for his *Rent* to Town, *as it is likely he does,* he must have *Two Hundred and Fifty Horses* to bring up his *Half Year's Rent*, and two or three great *Cellars* in his House for Stowage . . .

That sort of thing was amusing enough; but what probably tickled him most was the finding of terms in which to describe the unfortunate Wood: we get in Letter I: 'Mr. Wood, *a mean ordinary Man, a Hard-Ware Dealer*', and almost immediately '*an ordinary Fellow*', to be followed soon by '*this sorry Fellow*, Wood': and in the next, 'this Honest Liberal Hard-Ware-Man Wood'; and soon after, 'this little impudent *Hard-Ware-Man*' at the beginning of a paragraph which ends with 'one single, diminutive, insignificant Mechanick'. He revels through Letter III in variations on the theme: 'one *Single, Rapacious, Obscure, Ignominious* PROJECTOR', or 'a *poor, private obscure Mechanick*', or 'one obscure *Ironmonger*'. Not very dignified, nor perhaps very honest; but what good popular pamphleteering! And what opportunities for entertaining oneself in devising such variants!

Gulliver's Travels does not, on the whole, offer much scope for adventitious fooling. The first two books and the last embody too serious a philosophical pondering on the nature of man to permit of much jocularity, though there is plenty of humour throughout. Occasionally, however, there is the more light-hearted note, as when he describes the handwriting of the Lilliputians, in the spirit, one imagines, that characterised his converse with his friends:

> ... their Manner of writing is very peculiar; being neither from the Left to the Right, like the *Europeans*; nor from the Right to the Left, like the *Arabians*; nor from up to down, like the *Chinese*; nor from down to up like the *Cascagians*; but aslant from one Corner of the Paper to the other, like Ladies in *England*.

It is, rather, in the interpolated third book that he gives a loose to his sense of the ridiculous, especially in a favourite amusement of driving ideas to their logical conclusion. So taking Sprat's dictum in the *History of the Royal Society* that the ideal of prose was to deliver 'so many "Things", almost in an equal number of "Words" ', Swift propels this to:

> ... a Scheme for entirely abolishing all Words whatsoever: And this was urged as a great Advantage in Point of Health as well as Brevity. For, it is plain, that every Word we speak is in some Degree a Diminution of our Lungs by Corrosion; and consequently

contributes to the shortning of our Lives. An Expedient was therefore offered, that since Words are only Names for *Things*, it would be more convenient for all Men to carry about them, such *Things* as were necessary to express the particular Business they are to discourse on . . .

The objections being that women and the vulgar and illiterate were determined to be allowed to speak with their tongues, after the manner of their forefathers; and that it would be impossible for the learned and wise to carry about with them as many objects as they wished to talk about.

It is easy to guess that as Swift lost contact with his friends in England, or they died, he found most of the society in which he had to pass his time in Dublin more than tiresome; and perforce subjected to the sort of talk current in drawing-rooms, he got his amusement — and his revenge — out of it by composing *A Complete Collection of Genteel and Ingenious Conversation*, etc., appropriately written by Simon Wagstaff (he seems to have made early jottings in 1704), with a beautifully mocking Introduction, from which a passage, totally irrelevant, may be taken. He has been talking about fame, and how, after all that he, Simon Wagstaff, has accomplished, he would consider himself most inhumanly treated, and 'would resent it as the highest indignity, to be put upon the Level, in Point of Fame, in after Ages, with *Charles* XII late King of *Sweden*'. He goes on:

And yet, so incurable is the Love of Detraction, perhaps, beyond what the charitable Reader will easily believe, that I have been assured by more than one credible Person, how some of my Enemies have industriously whispered about, that one *Isaac Newton*, an Instrument-Maker, formerly living near *Leicester* Fields, and afterwards a Workman in the Mint, at the Tower, might possibly pretend to vye with me for Fame in future Times. The Man, it seems, was knighted for making Sun-Dyals better than others of his Trade, and was thought to be a Conjurer, because he knew how to draw Lines and Circles upon a Slate, which no Body could understand. But, adieu to all noble Attempts for endless Renown, if the Ghost of an obscure Mechanick [he seems to have been fond of that phrase], shall be raised up, to enter into Competition with me, only for skill in making Pothooks and Hangers, with a Pencil; which many thousand accomplished Gentlemen and Ladies can perform as well, with a Pen and Ink, upon a Piece of Paper, and in a Manner as little intelligible as those of Sir *Isaac*.

It were to be wished that the three dialogues of genteel conversation were a tithe so amusing. It is a little depressing to think that all these repartees, rejoinders, and so on, he had 'with infinite Labour and close Application, during the Space of thirty six Years been collecting'. The labour may not have been infinite, nor the application very close, but even so the result seems incommensurate with the care and time the writing must have taken. Yet it is well to remind ourselves that it was all part of a serious campaign for preserving the language, including the foundation of an English Academy, on the lines of the French one, as set out in *A Proposal for Correcting . . . the English Tongue*, and *Hints towards an Essay on Conversation* of many years earlier. But no doubt Swift derived a good deal of amusement from noting the idiocies of small-talk.

Naturally an element of satire enters into such things, just as most satire implies a certain amount of fun, as we find in the more clearly satirical *Directions to Servants*, which evidences a good deal of irritation. This piece again he may have been making jottings for as early as 1704, to return to it in 1731, and tinker with until 1739. It is better reading than 'Genteel Conversation', and, as he said, might prove 'very useful as well as humorous'. It certainly shows that he was well aware of what went on below stairs, whether he is considering the footman, the coachman, the waiting-maid, or any of the others. The cook may provide us with a brief group of directions:

Scrape the Bottoms of your Pots and Kettles with a Silver Spoon, for fear of giving them a Taste of Copper.

When you send up Butter for Sauce, be so thrifty as to let it be half Water; which is also much wholesomer.

Never make use of a Spoon in any thing that you can do with your Hands, for fear of wearing out your Master's Plate.

Some is jocose, but much evidences disgust:

You are to look upon your Kitchen as your Dressing-room; but, you are not to wash your Hands till you have gone to the Necessary-house, and spitted your Meat, trussed your Pullets, pickt your

Sallad, nor indeed till after you have sent up the second Course; for your Hands will be ten times fouled with the many Things you are forced to handle; but when your Work is over, one Washing will serve for all.

All that, we may think, is gruff humour rather than exuberant amusement.

But what really, we begin to ask ourselves, was the basis of Swift's jocoseness, which persisted to almost the end of his life? Was it an attempt to throw off the savage indignation which never ceased to lacerate his heart? — an evident over-statement. It would seem that in his early days it was what one would call exuberance, given, of course, that he had a natural sense of humour. There is no indignation in *A Tale of a Tub*, only a sharp critical spirit making its point in this way. *A Meditation upon a Broom-Stick*, and its use, is a sheer lark. Later, it might be conjectured, his passionate rebellion against the folly, meanness, injustice and dishonesty of mankind often relieved itself by an overwhelming sense of the ridiculous, or a more coolly directed sense of what would tell. The bitter jokes in *A Modest Proposal* cannot be classed as jocose. As to jesting, much of this, as already suggested, especially as regards the Sheridan 'exercises', as one may call them, must have been an attempt to break the tedium of his Dublin existence, the boredom of genteel conversation, finding something to do — especially after the deaths of Vanessa and Stella. As he aged, feeling some of his old super-abundant energy, physical as well as mental, beginning to fail, he indulged more and more in horse exercise, and took to walking faster than anyone else, so that those who walked with him panted behind. Even while expiring 'a driv'ller and a show', he satisfied his need both for exercise and for convincing himself that he needed it, by walking endlessly up and down stairs. So what was there left for him in the intellectual sphere but to force himself to fantastic humour? Laughter is the release that men such as Swift are granted for combating the evils of existence.

HERBERT DAVIS
Swift's View of Poetry

IT is strange that Swift has not been given more attention both on account of what he has written in verse and of what he has written about poetry. For although he did not profess to be either a poet or a critic of poetry, he is nevertheless in his casual and contemptuous manner the most extreme example that we have ever had in England of reaction against the heroic or romantic view of the poet's function and art.

Dryden, of course, is rightly regarded as in theory and practice the great champion of the new poetry of his day, the character of which had been sketched so admirably — as we are reminded in Dr. Mark van Doren's study, *John Dryden*[1] — in the introductory matter contributed by Waller, Denham, Hobbes, and D'Avenant to the latter's *Gondibert*, published in 1651. Yet Dryden never accepted fully the logical conclusion of these theories. 'He spoke often, in common with his contemporaries, of the *furor poeticus*; he championed poetic license; and he tried to write like Shakespeare.' Indeed, throughout his whole career Dryden continued constantly to use the traditional language whenever he spoke of the art of poetry. He remained essentially a heroic poet, and loved to flaunt the pomp and colours of his cause:

> O gracious God! how far have we
> Profan'd thy heav'nly gift of poesy!
> Made prostitute and profligate the Muse,
> Debas'd to each obscene and impious use,
> Whose harmony was first ordain'd above
> For tongues of angels, and for hymns of love!   [56–61]

This 'Ode to Mrs. Anne Killigrew' was probably written in 1685, but

[1] New York, 1920.

again in the epistle prefixed to 'Beauty in Distress' (1698), 'To my
Friend Mr. Motteux' he speaks of

> That sacred art, by heav'n itself infus'd
> Which Moses, David, Salomon have us'd ...   [3–4]

And however little Dryden may have really believed in thus ascrib-
ing to the art of poetry all the sacredness that Milton had claimed for
it — at least in its finest manifestations — he would probably have
readily accepted that noble claim made by Sir William Temple in his
'Essay on Heroick Virtue' (1690):

Among all the Endowments of Nature, or Improvements of Art
wherein Men have excelled and distinguished themselves most in the
World, there are Two only that have had the Honour of being called
Divine, and of giving that Esteem or Appellation to such as
possessed them in very eminent Degrees; which are, Heroick
Virtue, and Poetry: For Prophecy cannot be esteemed any Excel-
lency of Nature or of Art, but, wherever it is true, is an immediate
Gift of God, and bestowed according to his Pleasure, and upon
Subjects of the meanest Capacity; upon Women or Children, or
even Things inanimate....[1]

The careful distinction here made in the use of the word 'divine'
as applied to the inspiration of the poet and the prophet respec-
tively should be remarked. It seems to have been preserved in the
eighteenth century, so that, while the deists and the sceptics were
making an increasingly violent attack upon the idea of the supernatural revelation of the prophet, there was on the other hand an
almost dogmatic insistence on the true faith and the efficacy of the
canonical books, i.e. the classics, in the tradition of poetry.

This is exactly the attitude of Pope. In his attempt to 'trace for
English readers the just boundaries of taste in literature' in his
'Essay on Criticism', he shows the mentality of a young priest of the
strictest orthodoxy, bold, proud, dogmatic, with nothing but scorn
for those who are not of the true faith. He looks upon poetry as the
special activity of a privileged and well-trained hierarchy, which
professes and believes literally in a creed that has been handed down
by the great founders and leaders of the order. They alone have the

[1] Sir William Temple, *Works* (London, 1740), vol. I, p. 191.

true faith — to them the revelation has been made of Nature, 'the source, and end, and test of art'.

> Those Rules of old discovered, not devis'd
> Are Nature still, but Nature methodiz'd . . .

Virgil found that 'Nature and Homer were the same':

> Learn hence for ancient rules a just esteem;
> To copy Nature is to copy them.   [139–40]

He knows himself to be a faithful member of this true Church, devoted to the work to which he has been called, delighting to do honour to the great fathers of the Church, who are infallible:

> Nor is it Homer nods, but we that dream.

With fine rhetoric, and not without a flash of pride, he breaks out into a great hymn in honour of the temple of poetry, and the altars of the dead still green with bays:

> Still green with bays each ancient Altar stands,
> Above the reach of sacrilegious hands;
> Secure from Flames, from Envy's fiercer rage,
> Destructive War, and all-involving Age.
> See, from each clime the learn'd their incense bring!
> Hear, in all tongues consenting Pæans ring!
> In praise so just let ev'ry voice be join'd,
> And fill the gen'ral chorus of mankind.   [180–8]

Finally he approaches humbly to take of the fire from the altar, that he may go forth to speak a word to the people, and declare to them the glories they can admire but not share.

> Oh may some spark of your celestial fire,
> The last, the meanest of your sons inspire,
> (That on weak wings, from far, pursues your flights;
> Glows while he reads, but trembles as he writes)
> To teach vain Wits a science little known,
> T' admire superior sense, and doubt their own!   [195–200]

He has all the rigour and the sternness of the true priest; he would proscribe all field-preachers and Nonconformists, and he would stamp out every heresy. He is careful to show that he is no sectarian, but a member of the true Church, which is limited to no small corner of the earth, nor to a single generation, and he protests against those who would apply 'wit'

> To one small sect, and all are damn'd beside.
> Meanly they seek the blessing to confine
> And force the sun but on a part to shine,
> Which not alone the southern wit sublimes
> But ripens spirits in cold northern climes. [397–401]

It is important to notice, too, his claim that so long as the poet belongs to the true lineage he may receive inspiration in many diverse ways. He does not receive his great gifts by any mechanical operation — by a mere following of Rules:

> Some beauties yet no Precepts can declare,
> For there's a happiness as well as care. [141–2]

> Thus Pegasus, a nearer way to take,
> May boldly deviate from the common track; [150–1]

> And snatch a grace beyond the reach of art,
> Which without passing thro' the judgment, gains
> The heart, and all its end at once attains. [155–7]

Thus confidently, in spite of his youth and inexperience, did Pope come forward, clothed already in the dignity and authority of his high calling, to preach to his generation, to saints and sinners alike, to noble lords like Lansdowne and the Duke of Buckingham as well as outsiders like Dennis, what he believed to be the true nature and function of poetry.

Swift had none of this professional pride, and never showed the least inclination to set much value on the business of writing poetry. He was willing to use it either to gain a reputation and establish his influence or to force his views upon the public. He wrote always not as an artist, but as a man of action, or else he wrote as a gentleman writes, to amuse himself and his friends. He refused to be considered as a writer or a poet professionally, and he emphasized the difference contemptuously in *Thoughts on Various Subjects continued*, 1726: 'A copy of verses kept in the cabinet, and only shewn to a few friends, is like a virgin much sought after and admired; but when printed and published, is like a common whore, whom anybody may purchase for half-a-crown.'

This may sound like the common affectation of an eighteenth-century gentleman, who was rather expected to sneer at those who fiddle for pay, or write a prologue or a dedication for ten pound. But yet it would be a greater affectation still for the author of *A Tale of a Tub* to allow himself to be impressed by such idle fancies as the poet's claim to divine honours. Is it likely that the satirist of kings and courts, politicians and lawyers, scholars and scientists, will show respect before the less tangible dignity of a poet, however magnificently he may wrap his singing robes around him? In Bedlam he had found the poets so numerous and in such poor company, that they were not worth special mention: 'I shall not descend so minutely, as to insist upon the vast number of beaux, fiddlers, poets and politicians, that the world might recover...'

One of the main themes of *A Tale of a Tub* is, of course, an analysis of 'enthusiasm', which is defined as a 'lifting-up of the soul, or its faculties, above matter'. And in the *Discourse on the Mechanical Operation of the Spirit* he adds a fantastic travesty of a mechanistic theory of the activity of the brain, which purports to be an explanation of the way in which poetry is written. The brain is to be considered as a crowd of little animals clinging together like bees in a perpetual swarm upon a tree:

That all Invention is formed by the Morsure of two or more of these Animals, upon certain capillary Nerves, which proceed from thence, whereof three Branches spread into the Tongue, and two into the right Hand.... Farther, that nothing less than a violent Heat, can disentangle these Creatures from their hamated Station of Life, or give them Vigor and Humor, to imprint the Marks of their little Teeth. That if the Morsure be Hexagonal, it produces Poetry...[1]

But perhaps the most fundamental attack upon 'inspiration', which may be equally applied to the prophetical or poetical variety, is found in the preceding paragraph:

[1] H. Davis (ed.), *The Prose Works of Jonathan Swift* (Oxford, 1939–   ), vol. I, pp. 181–2.

For, I think, it is in *Life* as in *Tragedy*, where, it is held, a Convic-
tion of great Defect, both in Order and Invention, to interpose the
Assistance of preternatural Power, without an absolute and last
Necessity. However, it is a Sketch of Human Vanity, for every
Individual, to imagine the whole Universe is interess'd in his meanest
Concern. . . . Who, that sees a little paultry Mortal, droning, and
dreaming, and drivelling to a Multitude, can think it agreeable to
common good Sense, that either Heaven or Hell should be put to the
Trouble of Influence or Inspection upon what he is about? Therefore, I am resolved immediately, to weed this Error out of Mankind,
by making it clear, that this Mystery, of vending spiritual Gifts is
nothing but a *Trade*, acquired by as much instruction, and mastered
by equal Practice and Application as others are.[1]

If he had needed support in thus challenging the notion of divine
inspiration Swift might well have quoted Hobbes, who in his
Answer to Sr Will. D'Avenant's Preface Before Gondibert (1650) had
approved of his innovation in omitting 'to invoke a Muse or some
other Deity', for though he refuses to condemn that Heathen
custom in them, yet

why a Christian should think it an ornament to his Poem, either to
profane the true God or invoke a false one, I can imagin no cause
but a reasonless imitation of Custom, of a foolish custome, by which
a man, enabled to speak wisely from the principles of nature and his
own meditation, loves rather to be thought to speak by inspiration,
like a Bagpipe.
  Time and Education begets experience; Experience begets
memory; Memory begets Judgment and Fancy: Judgment begets
the strength and structure, and Fancy begets the ornaments of a
Poem.[2]

There, at any rate, is an intelligent explanation of the phenomenon
of poetry, which Swift may well have accepted; he would at least
have approved of Hobbes's point of view. It might even be said that
with all its limitations it is nevertheless sufficient to account for that
kind of poetry which Swift himself produced.
  Swift amused himself in similar fashion in verse, by laughing at

[1] Davis (ed.), *The Prose Works*, vol. I, pp. 180-1.
[2] J. E. Spingarn (ed.), *Critical Essays of the Seventeenth Century*
(London and Danville, Ill., 1957), vol. II, p. 59.

the exalted flights of Grub-Street wits, when sufficiently freed from
the 'Incumbrances of Food and Clothes', but whose inspiration immediately flags as soon as they have received their pay. It is a short
poem in very colloquial octosyllabic lines, called 'The Progress of
Poetry'. But it was followed much later by one of Swift's most vigorous and sustained efforts in verse, which he is said to have regarded as
one of his best pieces, 'On Poetry: A Rapsody', which was published
anonymously in London on 31 December 1733.

Swift begins by looking over the whole commonwealth of letters,
and ridiculing the strange ambition of the human race, which drives
every fool to try to be a wit and a poet:

> But *Man* we find the only Creature
> Who, led by *Folly*, fights with *Nature*;
> Who, when *she* loudly cries, *Forbear*,
> With Obstinacy fixes there;
> And, where his *Genius* least inclines,
> Absurdly bends his whole Designs.[1]

It is a strange and inexplicable malady, for nothing is more certain
to ruin a man's chance of success than a career which offers only one
single prize — the Laureate's pittance of just 'one annual hundred
pound'.

> Not Beggar's Brat, on Bulk begot;
> Nor Bastard of a Pedlar *Scot*;
> Nor Boy brought up to cleaning Shoes,
> The Spawn of *Bridewell*, or the Stews;
> Nor Infants dropt, the spurious Pledges
> Of *Gipsies* littering under Hedges,
> Are so disqualified by Fate
> To rise in *Church*, or *Law*, or *State*,
> As he, whom Phebus in his Ire
> Hath *blasted* with poetick Fire.

In an earlier and happier time perhaps a Congreve or an Addison
could win his way to fame and success with a poem, but now the
only profitable game is to sell yourself to a corrupt and venal Court:

[1] Quotations of Swift's poetry in this essay are taken from Harold
Williams (ed.), *The Poems of Jonathan Swift* (1st ed., Oxford, 1937;
2nd ed., Oxford, 1958).

> From Party-Merit seek Support;
> The vilest Verse thrives best at Court.
> A Pamphlet in Sir Rob's Defence
> Will never fail to bring in Pence:
> Nor be concern'd about the Sale,
> He pays his Workmen on the Nail.

Such then is the poet's fate: neither profit, nor dignity, nor pleasure can be found in the pursuit of poetical fame. In the world of letters, as everywhere else in life, Hobbes's view is justified that every creature lives in a state of war by nature, only here it is the lesser who prey upon the greater — a condition of things found in nature only among vermin.

> So, Nat'ralists observe, a Flea
> Hath smaller Fleas that on him prey,
> And these have smaller Fleas to bite 'em,
> And so proceed *ad infinitum*.

Swift is, of course, not concerned in this poem with any poetic ideal; he is satirizing directly the inhabitants of Grub-Street, and the conditions of society which make such a Grub-Street possible.

> In Bulk there are not more Degrees
> From *Elephants* to *Mites* in Cheese,
> Than what a curious Eye may trace
> In Creatures of the rhiming Race.
> From bad to worse, and worse they fall,
> But, who can reach the Worst of all?
> For, tho' in Nature Depth and Height
> Are equally held infinite . . .
> In Poetry the Height we know;
> 'Tis only infinite below.

In such a world what room is there for the sublime and the pathetic? There is nothing left to do but to rail, or simply to amuse oneself and one's friends. Swift was not one of those who could build a little private palace of art for himself, or find consolation in dreams of a better existence than the present; he was never willing to buy happiness at the price of being well deceived, nor would he allow himself to be lulled into contentment by the soothing incantations or divine raptures of romantic poetry.

It would be easy of course to suggest that just as Swift's satire on politicians was largely due to his bitter hatred of Walpole and the Whigs, and his fall with the Tories from power and influence, so his satire on poets was due to his early disappointments and failures, and especially to Dryden's emphatic and rather brutal judgement on his attempts to gain attention by writing pindaric odes after the manner of Cowley. But Swift, however unable to forget such a remark, was hardly one to be crippled by it, and we have evidence enough to show how he came to scorn the poetic Muse, scoff at her claims for devotion, and turn his technical skill as a verse-writer to account in the service of a less romantic mistress.

Perhaps too much has been made of Swift's confession that he was devoted to Cowley's poetry while he was still at school, for he seems to have begun to write verse himself in a very different vein — crude satirical doggerel intended to satisfy the taste of his fellow undergraduates at Trinity College. In Dr. Elrington Ball's study, *Swift's Verse*,[1] reference is made to all the early verses attributed to Swift by Vice-Provost Barrett in his *Essay on the earlier part of the Life of Swift* (1808), and later by Sir William Wilde on the evidence of the Christie volume — a sort of commonplace book of Swift's which dates from his undergraduate years. Whether we regard any of these verses as the work of Swift or not, perhaps more importance should be attached to the fact that here at any rate are verses which Swift copied out in his own hand, which show already that his taste was entirely for satire and buffoonery and for occasional poems concerned with public affairs and political and religious controversy. Here is an early indication of Swift's natural bent; and this is very significant in showing that it was only after settling at Moor Park — and I suggest under the direct influence of Sir William Temple — that he turned aside and was persuaded to try to imitate Cowley, and indulge in what Dr. Ball very rightly calls a period of 'Pindaric and Heroic Aberration'. And a careful study of these pieces, which are not by any means as uninteresting or as weak as is often suggested, show Swift struggling with an unsuitable medium, and forced into an attitude, a pose which he soon recognized as an affectation, and then contemptuously abandoned. It is perhaps

[1] London, 1929.

worth remarking that only the 'Ode to the Athenian Society' was published in his lifetime. Dunton had printed it as the work of a country gentleman in the Supplement to the *Fifth Volume of the Athenian Gazette* (1691), and it was printed again in pamphlet form in 1725 with the title 'Sphinx: A Poem ascrib'd to certain Anonymous Authors: By the Revd. Dean S—t'. The rest of these Moor Park poems were not printed in Swift's lifetime.

They are interesting because here we see Swift for the only time trying seriously to be a poet. His letters indicate that he set himself industriously to try for fame in the conventional manner, following the example of Dryden and Cowley. He comes to pay his court to the accepted Muse, with panegyrics in pindaric form. And the result is exactly what we should expect. What had he to do with writing the praise of great men, giving honour to noble deeds? Was the world that he knew, even at that time, a place for compliments and the praise of beauty and virtue?

But it was while he was making these experiments that he began to realize how much cant there is in all this talk of the divine inspiration of the poet.

> Thus the *deluding Muse* oft blinds me to her Ways,
> And ev'n my very Thoughts transfers
> And changes all to Beauty, and the Praise
>   Of that proud Tyrant Sex of Hers.
> The *Rebel Muse*, alas, takes part,
> But with my own Rebellious Heart. . .

And in the 'Ode to Dr. William Sancroft', written probably two years later, panegyric turns already into scepticism and satire:

> No wonder, then, we talk amiss
> Of truth, and what, or where it is:
> Say, Muse, for thou, if any, know'st,
> Since the bright essence fled, where haunts the reverend ghost?

This appeal to the Muse for guidance, with that little qualification, 'thou, if any, know'st', is very like Swift.

And again:

> Forgive (Original Mildness) this ill-govern'd zeal,
> 'Tis all the angry slighted Muse can do

> In the pollution of these days;
> No province now is left her but to rail,
> And poetry has lost the art to praise,
> Alas, the occasions are so few . . .

Nevertheless in the 'Ode to Sir William Temple', written about the same time, he seems determined to put aside all doubts and try what he can do. Here, after an outburst in Temple's own manner against 'philosophy, the lumber of the schools' and the 'ill-manner'd pedantry' of those who

> purchase Knowledge at the Expence
> Of common Breeding, common Sense,
> And at once grow Scholars and Fools . . .

he devotes himself to limitless adulation of his patron, and of that quiet life in a country retreat which he has chosen, and launched in full career boasts at last of his own slavery to the poetic Muse, and even refers to the hopes and encouragements that have bound him to her service.

> Nature the hidden Spark did at my Birth infuse,
> And kindled first with Indolence and Ease,
> And since too oft debauch'd by Praise,
> 'Tis now grown an incurable Disease:
> In vain to quench this foolish Fire I try
> In Wisdom and Philosophy;
> In vain all wholesome Herbs I sow,
> Where nought but Weeds will grow.
> Whate'er I plant (like Corn on barren Earth)
> By an equivocal Birth
> Seeds and runs up to Poetry.

This was the end of the pindarics, though not of complimentary verse. It is almost as though Swift realized that this was in every way the least sincere piece he ever wrote. And in the two poems that follow, 'To Mr. Congreve' and 'Occasioned by Sir William Temple's late Illness and Recovery', he is too much concerned with his own disillusionment to have much thought for his subjects. It is true that he talks of disappointment and despair, but I do not feel with Dr. Elrington Ball that he was despondent 'because of his

failure to succeed in the Cowleyan School'. It is true, too, that for
the next five years, from 1693 to 1698, he wrote no more verses — or
at least none survive — but that may equally well be due to the fact
that he had discovered, not that he could not write like Cowley or
Dryden, but that he did not want to. There was no sign of lack of
confidence surely in the famous lines:

> *My hate, whose lash just heaven has long decreed*
> *Shall on a day make sin and folly bleed* . . .

nor in the lines quoted from a lost ode, inscribed 'The Poet':

> *Beat not the dirty paths where vulgar feet have trod,*
> > *But give the vigorous fancy room.*
> *For when like stupid alchymists you try*
> > *To fix this nimble god,*
> > > *This volatile mercury,*
> *The subtil spirit all flies up in fume;*
> *Nor shall the bubbl'd virtuoso find*
> *More than a fade insipid mixture left behind* . . .

It is hardly the voice of the disappointed worshipper, rejected by
the muse that he had patiently courted, but of one who is thoroughly
disillusioned, and anxious to expose the cheat that he had detected,
that we hear in such lines as these:

> Malignant goddess! bane to my repose,
> Thou universal cause of all my woes;
> Say, whence it comes that thou art grown of late
> A poor amusement for my scorn and hate;

> . . .

> Ah, should I tell a secret yet unknown,
> That thou ne'er hadst a being of thy own,
> But a wild form dependent on the brain,
> Scatt'ring loose features o'er the optic vein;
> Troubling the chrystal fountain of the sight,
> Which darts on poets eyes a trembling light;
> Kindled while reason sleeps, but quickly flies,
> Like antic shapes in dreams, from waking eyes:
> In sum, a glitt'ring voice, a painted name,
> A walking vapor, like thy sister fame.

And, finally, with a triumphant cry he breaks away, turning his **back**

upon visionary dreams and fancies, eager only to gaze with un-
troubled sight upon a world of reality:

> There thy enchantment broke, and from this hour
> I here renounce thy visionary pow'r;
> And since thy essence on my breath depends,
> Thus with a puff the whole delusion ends.

Instead of poetry Swift turned to prose satire, and in the following
years, until the death of Sir William Temple, was probably mainly
occupied with the *Tale of a Tub*. When that finally appeared in 1704,
its author must have felt that he had successfully evaded the power
of the malignant goddess who troubles the crystal fountain of the
sight and fills the brain with antic shapes while reason sleeps. And if
further proof was required of his emancipation, it could scarcely
have been better provided than in the volume of *Miscellanies*,
published in 1711, in which he included thirteen poems, chosen out
of a considerable amount of political and satirical verse, some already
published as broadsides. It seems almost as if he wished to flout the
votaries of the heroic and romantic muse by ostentatiously placing
at the very beginning of this little group the lines 'Written in a
Lady's Ivory Table-book, 1698'. Here, instead of compliment or a
lover's devotion, he makes a collection of some of the stupidest of
the senseless trifles it contains, and exposes them as a revelation of
its owner's heart:

> Here you may read (*Dear Charming Saint*)
> Beneath (*A new Receit for Paint*)
> Here, in Beau-spelling (*tru tel deth*)
> There in her own (*far an el breth*)
>
> . . .
>
> Who that had Wit would place it here,
> For every peeping Fop to Jear.

And this is followed by the delightfully absurd chatter of 'The
Humble Petition of Frances Harris', with its vigorous caricatures of
the servants in the Earl of Berkeley's household. It almost seems as
if immediately Swift escaped from the restrained and dignified
atmosphere of Sir William Temple's household, where he had tried
to produce conventional poetry, and returned to Dublin in the train

of the Earl of Berkeley, he found encouragement to indulge his own taste for ridicule and burlesque. Temple had particularly disapproved of this in his essay on 'Ancient and Modern Learning':

I wish the Vein of Ridiculing all that is Serious and Good, all Honour and Virtue, as well as Learning and Piety, may have no worse Effects on any other States: 'Tis the Itch of our Age and Climate, and has over-run both the Court and the Stage; enters a House of Lords and Commons, as boldly as a *Coffee*-House, Debates of Council as well as private Conversation; and I have known, in my Life, more than one or two Ministers of State, that would rather have said a Witty Thing, than done a Wise One; and made the Company laugh, rather than the Kingdom rejoice.[1]

And Swift himself in *The Battle of the Books* had upheld Temple in this, and gone on further to scoff at the characteristically modern claim for originality.

For any Thing else of Genuine, that the *Moderns* may pretend to, I cannot recollect; unless it be a large Vein of Wrangling and Satyr, much of a Nature and Substance with the *Spider*'s Poison; which, however they pretend to spit wholly out of themselves, is improved by the same arts, by feeding upon the *Insects* and *Vermin* of the age.[2]

This was probably written in the latter part of 1697, and this scornful attitude towards even the genuine productions of the Moderns was doubtless intended to win the approval of his dignified patron. It is strange that none of Swift's critics, so far as I know, have turned this to account, by quoting it as a good description of a great deal of his own writing, which is certainly — as Swift liked himself to think — 'spit wholly out of himself' and often improved 'by feeding upon the insects and vermin of the age'.

Few of Swift's biographers and critics have indeed troubled much with his poetry; like Dr. Johnson, they find little upon which to exercise their powers, and are content to compliment him on his facility and ease, or protest against his outspokenness, without indicating very clearly the character and significance of his work as a

---

[1] Sir William Temple, *Works*, p. 169.
[2] Davis (ed.), *Prose Works*, vol. 1, p. 151.

whole. They often give the impression that, like Lord Orrery, they would have been better pleased if his editors had not been so active in bringing together every trifle that may have come from his pen. 'Many of them', he says, 'are spurious, and many more are trifling, and in every respect improper for the public view'; an attitude which is, of course, in accord with his pompous conventionality shown in his remarks on the 'low humour' of the *Directions to Servants*:

Superior talents seem to have been intended by Providence as public benefits, and the person, who possesses such blessings, is certainly answerable to Heaven for those endowments, which he enjoys above the rest of mankind. Let him jest with dignity, and let him be ironical upon useful subjects: leaving poor slaves to *heat their porridge* or *drink their small beer*, in such vessels as they shall find proper. The Dean, it seems, had not this way of thinking.[1]

He certainly had not; and it was with very different standards from those of his lordship that Swift chose out of all the infinite variety of circumstance the particular occasion for poetry; and when the occasion demanded, he never refused the challenge, and often answered with surprising readiness and quickness. Most frequently his poetry was prompted entirely from without, as was all the political verse, and a great deal that belongs to his friendships and enmities. There is no more struggle, as in his early attempts, at heroic verse. He never courts the Muse, but turns instead to the laughing and irrepressible demon of satire, always ready at his elbow to use anything or anybody for its own disreputable purpose. It may be a mere Partridge — shoemaker, quack, and astrologer, who is given an elegy exalting him to a place among the heavenly bodies, where he may still follow his calling. Or it may be Lord Cutts — who, while acting temporarily as a Lord Justice in Ireland in 1705, was the first of many who held that office to attract Swift's violent dislike — whose character and appearance are made to fit so admirably Pliny's description of a Salamander. Or it may be a more pleasant joke, delightfully elaborated on the subject of the tiny house

[1] John Boyle, *Earl of Orrery, Remarks on the Life and Writings of Jonathan Swift* (2nd ed. 1752), p. 180.

that Vanbrugh, the architect and dramatist, had built out of the profits of a play. Or even a street scene in the City in the early morning, or when it is raining — the two perfect sketches in heroic couplets which Swift contributed to the *Tatler*.

It is interesting to note that the second of these — the 'Description of a City Shower' — had, as Dr. Elrington Ball points out, 'an ulterior motive, namely, to make the use of the triplet and alexandrine ridiculous', in these concluding lines:

Sweepings from Butchers Stalls, Dung, Guts, and Blood
Drown'd Puppies, stinking Sprats, all drench'd in Mud,
Dead Cats and Turnip-Tops come tumbling down the Flood.

It has perhaps not been clearly enough recognized that a good number of Swift's pieces owe their existence entirely to such purely literary motives. However true it may be that much of his writing is the work of a man of action rather than a man of letters, yet Swift was always very closely associated with the literary world, and keenly interested in the work of his contemporaries. He was concerned, moreover, to influence their taste, and to do that he employed his usual method of satirizing what seemed to him to be the affectations and absurdities of poetical fashions. He scorned above all the artificial conventions, the outworn ornaments and false sentimentality, which are perhaps at all times the marks of minor poetry. His attitude towards such poetry is shown in a parody, written probably in 1733, 'A Love Song in the modern Taste'. All the usual tricks are here exposed — the ornamental epithet, the classical references, the personification, the alliteration, the sing-song lilt, the unreal language, the sentimental commonplaces, and all the dreary staleness of these false, imitated, poetical devices:

> *Cynthia*, tune harmonious Numbers;
>   Fair Discretion string the Lyre;
> Sooth my ever-waking Slumbers:
> Bright *Apollo* lend thy Choir.

>   .   .   .

> Melancholly smooth *Meander*,
>   Swiftly purling in a Round,

> On thy Margin Lovers wander,
> With thy flow'ry Chaplets crown'd.

Again, in a reply to some complimentary verses by Dr. Delany, 'News from Parnassus' — which reports that at a session of the poets on Parnassus, convened by Apollo on 27 February 1720, Swift was appointed his vicegerent on earth — Swift, assuming this new dignity, issues what he called 'Apollo's Edict', and in a very easy pleasant manner proclaims therein what may and what may not be done by his vassals. Swift's own methods are of course to be imitated:

> Let his Success our Subjects sway
> Our Inspirations to obey,
> And follow where *he* leads the Way:
> Then study to correct your Taste,
> Nor *beaten* Paths be longer trac'd.

Then follows a list of things to be avoided — all the worn-out tags of poetic finery:

> No Simile shall be begun,
> With *rising* or with *setting* Sun:...
> No Son of mine shall dare to say,
> *Aurora usher'd in the Day*,
> Or ever name the *milky Way*....
> Your tragick Heroes shall not rant,
> Nor Shepherds use *poetick Cant*:

Even Denham's famous line so often quoted and so much admired is forbidden:

> Nor let my Votaries show their Skill
> In apeing Lines from *Cooper's Hill*;
> For know I cannot bear to hear,
> The Mimickry of *deep yet clear*.

And especially of course he proscribes all the nonsense of love poetry:

> When you describe a lovely Girl,
> No Lips of *Coral* Teeth or *Pearl*.

> *Cupid* shall ne'er mistake another,
> However beauteous for his Mother:
> Nor shall his Darts at random fly
> From Magazeen in *Cælia's* Eye.

A more violent attack on poetic cant is made in a little group of poems, which were included in the *Miscellanies* by Pope in 1727. The first of these — 'Phillis; or, The Progress of Love, 1716'— which gives the past history of the landlord and hostess of the Old Blue Boar, at Staines, which Swift used to pass on his journeys to Windsor, is possibly a version of some story he has heard; but even if that is so, it is certainly at the same time a satire upon the popular notions of romantic love and such attendant follies as a girl's elopement with a servant to escape from a reasonable match properly arranged by her parents. She leaves behind, of course, a note of explanation and an appeal to her father for forgiveness:

> ('Tis always done, Romances tell us,
> When Daughters run away with Fellows)
>
> .   .   .
>
> It was her Fate; must be forgiven;
> For Marriages are made in Heaven:
> His Pardon begg'd, but, to be plain,
> She'd do't if 'twere to do again.
> Thank God, 'twas neither Shame nor Sin,
> For John was come of honest Kin:
> Love never thinks of Rich and Poor,
> She'd beg with John from Door to Door:

The adventures which befell them are very rapidly sketched, until at last

> Fate put a Period to the Farce;
> And with exact Poetick Justice:
> For John is Landlord, Phillis Hostess;
> They keep at Stains the old blue Boar,
> Are Cat and Dog, and Rogue and Whore.

It is worth while to compare with this poem a letter that Swift wrote to Mrs. Swanton, a distant relative, on 12 July 1733, giving her advice how to deal with her daughter who had left her home in order to be free to marry according to her own wishes.

Although such an action in a daughter whom you have used so well can deserve no pardon, yet I would have you leave her without excuse. Send to her to come home; if she refuse, send a second and third time, and if she still refuseth, let her know in plain terms, that you will never have the least correspondence with her, and when she is ruined, as will certainly be the case, that you will never see her, nor give or leave her or her children, if she have any, a morsel of bread. Let her know you have given her fair warning, and if she will run into destruction with her eyes open, against common sense and the opinion of all rational people, she hath none to blame but herself; And that she must not expect to move your compassion some years hence with the cries of half a dozen children at your door for want of bread. . . . [1]

In life and in literature Swift never ceased to protest against ideas and conduct, which he considered 'against common sense and the opinion of rational people'.

'The Progress of Beauty, 1720' shows how Swift is prepared to deal himself with subjects which have been sicklied o'er with the sentimentality of romantic poets. And I would suggest that some of the unpleasant qualities of these poems, which have caused his admirers so much difficulty, may have been due as much to his impatience with poetic cant as to any unspeakable perversions in his mind. 'No lips of coral, teeth of pearl' he had already demanded; now he goes a little further, and substitutes for the usual flatteries such lines as these. Is it the beauty of the moon that the poets celebrate, then let them look more closely:

> When first Diana leaves her Bed,
> Vapors and Streams her Looks disgrace,
> A frouzy dirty colour'd red
> Sits on her cloudy wrinckled Face.

And there is an exact parallel between earthly females and the moon:

> To see her from her Pillow rise
> All reeking in a cloudy Steam,
> Crackt Lips, foul Teeth, and gummy Eyes,
> Poor Strephon! how would he blaspheme!

[1] F. E. Ball (ed.), *The Correspondence of Jonathan Swift* (London, 1910–14), vol. v, p. 11.

It is only a matter of shifting the colours round, as he proceeds very innocently to explain:

> Three Colours, Black, and Red, and White,
> So gracefull in their proper Place,
> Remove them to a diff'rent Light,
> They form a frightfull hideous Face:
>
> For instance; when the Lilly slipps
> Into the Precincts of the Rose,
> And takes Possession of the Lips,
> Leaving the Purple to the Nose.
>
> So Celia went entire to bed,
> All her Complexions safe and sound;
> But, when she rose, the black and red,
> Though still in Sight, had chang'd their Ground.

The comparison is continued throughout, and Celia's fading beauties given no longer date than the waning moon; the last stanza closes the story with a gay little note, unusual in Swift.

> Ye Pow'rs who over Love preside,
> Since mortal Beautyes drop so soon,
> If you would have us well supply'd,
> Send us new Nymphs with each new Moon.

It may be said, of course, that these are all very slight productions, and that it is not of much real significance that Swift amuses himself thus in attacking the romantic attitude. The test comes only when he is actually confronted by those experiences in life which have inspired the poets with their most sublime utterances. Is there any evidence that at such moments Swift turned to poetry? Does he succeed then in still maintaining his complete control of himself? Is it true that he never touches 'the sublime or the pathetic'? Is he never betrayed into sentimentality, or stirred to emotional fervour?

We should expect to find an answer in 'Cadenus and Vanessa' and in the 'Stella' poems, which Swift allowed Pope to include in the *Miscellanies* in 1727. Fortunately we do not need here to repeat all the stories that have been written about the two women whom Swift loved. We are concerned only with the way in which he treats these personal experiences of love and friendship in his verse. We are concerned with the poems as literature, not as a clue to certain biographical problems, however intriguing. And 'Cadenus and Vanessa' is as literary as anything that Swift ever produced. Apart from the title, which alone removes it just outside the world of plain happenings, Swift has carefully framed it in a fantasy, in which gods and goddesses play their part, endowing Vanessa with graces and gifts rarely combined in women. And when this prodigy is finally introduced into the world, Swift indulges his usual banter at the expense of the 'fashionable fops' and 'glittering dames From around the purlieus of St. James':

> Both Sexes, arm'd with Guilt and Spite,
> Against *Vanessa's* Pow'r unite;
> To copy her, few Nymphs aspir'd;
> Her Virtues fewer Swains admir'd . . .

But a few had better taste, whom she entertained with pleasing arts. Among these was Cadenus; and Cupid — piqued at his lack of success with her — determines to take revenge, by making her fall in love with him.

> *Cadenus* is a Subject fit,
> Grown old in Politicks and Wit;
> Caress'd by Ministers of State,
> Of half Mankind the Dread and Hate.

It is curious that Vanessa is represented as being particularly affected by some lines in a poem of Swift's:

> *Cadenus* many things had writ;
> *Vanessa* much esteem'd his Wit,
> And call'd for his Poetick Works;
> Mean time the Boy in secret lurks,
> And while the Book was in her Hand,
> The Urchin from his private Stand
> Took Aim, and shot with all his Strength
> A Dart of such prodigious Length,
> It pierc'd the feeble Volume thro',
> And deep transfix'd her Bosom too.
> Some Lines, more moving than the rest,
> Stuck to the Point that pierc'd her Breast;

> And, born directly to the Heart,
> With Pains unknown increased her Smart.

As the episode referred to must have taken place in 1712 or 1713, when Swift's published verses were still very slight in bulk, it is tempting to speculate what these lines could have been — unless this specific detail is merely a little joke. Most of Swift's biographers agree that it probably happened sometime after his return to London, on 9 September 1713, on one of his visits to the court at Windsor, which continued until the end of December 1713. On 31 October Swift had addressed some lines 'To Lord Harley, on his Marriage', and in this poem there is at least a passage which might very well have served as an introduction to Vanessa's declaration of love. For there Swift, in an unusual vein of happy compliment, praises Harley's young bride, the daughter of the Duke of Newcastle, for her sensible choice of the virtuous and the learned Harley, in preference to the glittering crowd of fortunes and titles that had aspired to her. How aptly, if Vanessa had been reading this poem, could she have turned the argument to her own purpose. She too had been taught by Swift to despise the ordinary ways of the world:

> Terrestrial nymphs, by formal arts,
> Display their various nets for hearts:
> Their looks are all by method set,
> When to be prude, and when coquette;
> Yet, wanting skill and pow'r to chuse,
> Their only pride is to refuse.
> But, when a Goddess would bestow
> Her love on some bright youth below,
> Round all the earth she casts her eyes;
> And then, descending from the skies,
> Makes choice of him she fancies best . . .

Her taste was surely even more exalted, leading her to choose before all the Court a Dean twice her age. The latter part of the poem has always been regarded as a reliable account of what happened. Naturally when the poem was published in 1726 Swift, wishing to dismiss it lightly, referred to it in a letter to Knightley Chetwode, 19 April 1726, as 'a task performed on a frolic among some ladies at

Windsor ... for my own part, I forget what is in it, but believe it to be only a cavalier business ... a private humorsome thing, which, by an accident inevitable, and the baseness of particular malice, is made public'.[1]

That is perhaps hardly fair, and yet the phrases 'a cavalier business' — 'a private humorsome thing' are not inaccurate descriptions of the poem. Whatever the episode itself was — however charged with passion and pity, however difficult and dangerous — Swift treats it with as little emotion as possible; he is neither cynical nor sentimental, he detaches himself gently from it, and places it a little way off, and sees it as something separate, a private affair of Cadenus and Vanessa, a delicate subject to be touched carefully with wit and fancy and humour.

Nothing that Swift ever wrote shows more perfectly his mastery of himself and his art than these lines, describing at length the dispute between Cadenus and Vanessa. He recognizes the force of her argument, he is fairly caught, it is a 'bite'. But he may well be proud at her confession:

> Constr'ing the Passion she had shown,
> Much to her Praise, more to his Own.
> Nature in him had Merit plac'd,
> In her, a most judicious Taste.

In return he gladly offers her 'friendship in its greatest height'.

> His Want of Passion will redeem,
> With Gratitude, Respect, Esteem:
> With what Devotion we bestow,
> When Goddesses appear below.

But Vanessa has been taught too well by him; she knows the proper value of such 'exalted strains':

> The Nymph in sober Words intreats
> A Truce with all sublime Conceits.
> For why such Raptures, Flights, and Fancies,
> To her, who durst not read Romances;
> In lofty Style to make Replies,
> Which he had taught her to despise.

[1] Ball (ed.), *Correspondence*, vol. III, p. 306.

She will have her turn to be tutor, and will teach him the science

> Wherein his Genius was below
> The Skill of ev'ry common Beau ...

And now in this extremely delicate situation, Swift must avoid either the bathos of a happy ending, or a hint perhaps of the tragedy that was to follow. He preserves instead the 'humorsome' tone perfectly, by ending in cavalier fashion:

> But what Success *Vanessa* met,
> Is to the World a Secret yet:
> Whether the Nymph, to please her Swain,
> Talks in a high Romantick Strain;
> Or whether he at last descends
> To like with less Seraphick Ends;
> Or, to compound the Business, whether
> They temper Love and Books together;
> Must never to Mankind be told,
> Nor shall the conscious Muse unfold.

The poems to Stella are, if possible, both in subject and in style an even more complete triumph over any temptation to indulge in sentiment or romance; and it is surprising, as Dr. Elrington Ball remarks, 'that Swift could have borne the publication of these verses, especially when he believed her to be dying and was writing to Sheridan in an agony of affliction'. And he can only offer the not very convincing explanation that it was due to Swift's infatuation for Pope and his wish to leave the arrangement of the *Miscellanies* entirely in his hands. It may well be that Pope was anxious to have as much new material as possible in order to give some justification for the publisher's advertisement, which described the *Last Volume* as 'consisting of several Copies of Verses, most of them never before printed'. But it is perhaps equally reasonable to suppose that Swift definitely wished to include, and set over against the 'Cadenus and Vanessa', these plain records of his friendship with Stella.

The birthday verses belong to the last years of her life, 1719–27, and are perfectly described by a phrase which Swift uses to describe the character of his poetry in some lines written 'To Mr. Delany, Nov. 10, 1718'.

> To you the Muse this Verse bestows,
> Which might as well have been in Prose;
> No Thought, no Fancy, no Sublime,
> But simple Topicks told in Rime.

He might perhaps have gone further and said that he sometimes wrote verse because it was easier than to write prose. The doggerel trifles that he and Sheridan tossed off together were, of course, very much easier, as Sheridan admits in his verses 'To the Dean, when in England, in 1726':

> Because hot weather makes me lazy
> To write in metre is more easy.

Sometimes Swift wrote down his verses with his left hand, while the other hand was at the same time writing letters of business, or (if we may believe his time-keeping) at the tremendous speed of thirty-eight rhyming lines 'Written, sign'd, and seal'd, five minutes and eleven seconds after the receipt of yours, allowing seven seconds for sealing and superscribing, from my bed-side, just eleven minutes after eleven, Sept. 15, 1718'. But in his best work too, Swift forces the rhymed octosyllabic couplet to serve him as a means of obtaining an effect of perfect spontaneity and ease, a medium of expression even less formal than prose. Most poets use verse where prose would not be good enough for their particular purpose. Swift seems almost to have used it as a more familiar, more intimate way of communication. He could do anything he liked with prose, except, I think, that he was not a master of the familiar style; even in the *Journal to Stella* he is obliged to fall back upon 'little language'.

And so, just as in dealing with his enemies in political controversy he used verse for his roughest and least considered outbursts, tossing off ballads and broadsides shaped to popular tunes, so in his friend-ships his most familiar manner of address was always in verse. What could be more familiar — and at the same time an excellent parody on the usual complimentary birthday odes — than the first of the poems written for 'Stella's Birthday, March 13, 1718–19'.

> Stella this Day is thirty four,
> (We won't dispute a Year or more)
> However Stella, be not troubled,

> Although thy Size and Years are doubled,
> Since first I saw Thee at Sixteen . . .

He delights always to emphasize that she is no longer either young or beautiful:

> An Angel's face, a little crack't . . .

he boasts that in all his addresses to her there had been only sincerity — 'To Stella, who collected and transcribed his Poems, 1720':

> Thou *Stella*, wert no longer young,
> When first for thee my Harp I strung:
> Without one Word of *Cupid's* Darts,
> Of killing Eyes, or bleeding Hearts:
> With Friendship and Esteem possesst,
> I ne'er admitted Love a Guest.
>
> .   .   .
>
> Your Virtues safely I commend,
> They on no Accidents depend:
> Let Malice look with all her Eyes,
> She dares not say the Poet lyes.

There are a good many commonplaces, and too many repetitions on the birthday theme, which Swift himself seems to have tired of, for in 1724–5 he complains that he can no longer dance in rhyme:

> Adieu bright Wit, and radiant Eyes;
> You must be grave, and I be wise.
> Our Fate in vain we would oppose,
> But I'll be still your Friend in Prose:
> Esteem and Friendship to express,
> Will not require Poetick Dress;
> And if the Muse deny her Aid
> To have them *sung*, they may be *said*.

Yet two years later, on Stella's last birthday, he offers her a splendid final poem, where without any change of tone these plain prosaic octosyllables take on real force and dignity.

In such verses we can perhaps best feel the limitations of Swift's poetry; for here in a line or two we can see them as it were just giving way. That severe plainness of speech, that unwillingness to allow words to become emotional or musical, the flat tonelessness of many of the serious poems almost disappears, and we are half persuaded that we can distinguish tones from another kind of poetry in that last couplet:

> To morrow will be time enough
> To hear such mortifying Stuff.

But still he limits himself to his particular theme, and allows nothing fanciful or extraneous to enter. It was doubtless Swift himself who chose the title for the volume of poems which Faulkner included in the first collected edition of the *Works*, 1735 — *Poems on several Occasions*. It is a most accurate description — for all his verse is in the strictest sense occasional, and when the occasion is private, he rarely allows it to expand into general significance. This is partly because verses like these to Stella were written primarily for her and for their friends, without any consideration of a wider audience. When the occasion is public, the poetry is often more powerful, for then it is generally aimed with a definite purpose at the larger public; with the result that it takes on a character which Scott has well described:

Sometimes, however, the intensity of the satire gives to his poetry a character of emphatic violence, which borders upon grandeur. . . . [It] indicates rather ardour of temper than power of imagination. *Facit indignatio versus*. The elevation of tone arises from the strong mood of passion rather than from poetical fancy.

There was one great occasion which Swift took full advantage of — the death of the Duke of Marlborough. The poem was 'A Satyrical Elegy on the death of a late famous General, 1722':

> His Grace! impossible! what dead!
> Of old age too, and in his bed!
>
> .   .   .
>
> Behold his funeral appears,
> Nor widow's sighs, nor orphans' tears,
> Wont at such times each heart to pierce,
> Attend the progress of his herse.
> But what of that, his friends may say,
> He had those honours in his day.

True to his profit and his pride,
He made them weep before he dy'd.

Come hither, all ye empty things,
Ye bubbles rais'd by breath of Kings;
Who float upon the tide of state,
Come hither, and behold your fate.
Let pride be taught by this rebuke,
How very mean a thing's a Duke;
From all his ill-got honours flung,
Turn'd to that dirt from whence he sprung.

Is truth, or prejudice, too nakedly exposed? Must we therefore say that this cannot be poetry? If the imagination may trace the noble dust of Alexander till it is found stopping a bung-hole, may it not also triumph in the return of the ignoble to 'that dirt from whence he sprung'?

Swift seems to delight to go through the whole realm of poetry, turning everything upside down. If we look for elegies, fitting a solemn moment, this is what we find; if we want sentiment and the delicate play of fancy, we are offered a parody of Cowley's 'Clad all in White' — one of the love verses from *The Mistress*. Swift changes the title to 'Clad all in Brown', and proceeds to cover with filth his detested and despised enemy Richard Tighe. This is again a poem which can be regarded either as the product of a diseased imagination or as a contemptuous revolt against poetic sentiment. Here are a few lines of the original and the parody:

Fairest thing that shines below . . .	Foulest Brute that stinks below . . .
So *clouds* themselves like *Suns* appear,	Not one Jot better looks the Sun
When the *Sun* pierces them with Light:	Seen from behind a dirty Clout:
So *Lillies* in a glass enclose,	So T - - ds within a Glass enclose,
The *Glass* will seem as white as those. . . .	The Glass will seem as brown as those. . . .
Such robes the *Saints* departed wear,	Old carted Bawds such Garments wear,

Woven all with *Light* divine. . . .   When pelted all with Dirt they
                                                 shine . . .

It is little to be wondered at that some of his contemporaries declared that there was no traditional name for such a writer as this. In
Gulliveriana (1728) Dean Smedley describes Swift's verse as follows:

Low, groveling Poetry all of it; and I challenge all the World, to
show one good *Epic*, *Elegiac* or *Lyric* Poem of his; one *Eclogue*,
Pastoral, or anything like the Antients; and as he can't write like
them, so they had no name for such a Writer as he is: And his
Doggerel and *Burlesque* had Banish'd him *Rome*, notwithstanding he
is so often huzza'd in *Dublin*.

In 1733 Swift wrote an admirable reply to this criticism of his
practice of poetry; it is a long piece, entitled 'An Epistle to a Lady,
who desired the Author to make Verses on Her, in the Heroick
Style'. She asks him to

> suspend a While
> That same paultry, *Burlesque* Stile;
> Drop, for once, your constant Rule,
> Turning all to Ridicule . . .

She will provide him with material, and he is to try instead to sing
her praise in strain sublime. But the attempt is vain; he allows her
due praise, but instinctively turns to give her advice, and then offers
this apology:

> To conclude this long Essay;
> Pardon if I disobey:
> Nor, against my nat'ral Vein,
> Treat you in Heroick Strain.
> I, as all the Parish knows,
> Hardly can be grave in Prose:
>
> .   .   .
>
> From the Planet of my Birth
> I encounter Vice with Mirth.

Then he turns to have a fling at kings and courts, and corrupt
ministers, but here too constantly insists that his only method of
treating all such things is ridicule.

> Safe within my little Wherry,
> All their Madness makes me merry:
> Like the Watermen of *Thames*,
> I row by, and call them Names.
> Like the ever-laughing Sage,
> In a Jest I spend my Rage:
> (Tho' it must be understood,
> I would hang them if I cou'd;)

And he concludes:

> For your Sake, as well as mine,
> I the lofty Stile decline.
> I shou'd make a Figure scurvy,
> And your Head turn Topsy-turvy.

When Faulkner published the volume of collected poems, it was prefaced by an 'Advertisement', dated Dublin 1734, which must have been approved if not written by Swift. The collection is said to consist chiefly 'of Humour or Satyr, and very often of both together'. And the one claim that is made for the poems is that at any rate they do not follow the old well-trodden paths: 'the Author never was known either in Verse or Prose to borrow any Thought, Simile, Epithet, or particular Manner of Style: but whatever he writ, whether good, bad, or indifferent, is an Original in itself'.

Twenty years later, it was pointed out in the *Connoisseur* (no. 67) that a great age in literature is always marked by variety and originality, and its authors are distinguished by cultivating different branches of poetry from each other. 'We admire Swift, Pope, Gay, Bolingbroke, Addison, etc., but we admire each for his particular beauties separate and distinguished from the rest.' At least during the eighteenth century it was not forgotten that the poetry of the Augustans was both original and varied; the differences were never merged together under some stupid generalization, merely for the convenience of the historian in contrasting them with something else. Even Dr. Elrington Ball is inclined, I think, to give too much importance to Swift's association with Addison and Prior, though strangely enough he makes no reference whatever to Samuel Butler. If we wish to account for the particular quality of Swift's verse, if we wish to place him in a tradition, we shall have to investigate first of all what he owed to *Hudibras*, and to the popular verse-satire of the seventeenth century.

Swift was, however, like his contemporaries in claiming that all his satire, whether concerning public affairs or the manners of society, 'hath no other Aim than to reform the Errors of both Sexes'. Many of his critics, as well in the eighteenth century as in the twentieth, have not been satisfied with this explanation of such poems as 'The Lady's Dressing Room', 'A beautiful young Nymph going to Bed', and 'Strephon and Chloe'. I will pass over the usual objections, and consider only an attack from an unexpected quarter; for it is particularly interesting to find that Aldous Huxley and D. H. Lawrence were distressed by these poems.

The latter objects, in an essay entitled 'Apropos of Lady Chatterley's Lover' (1930), that Swift in 'The Lady's Dressing Room' (which he refers to in a very misleading fashion as a poem 'to his mistress Celia') gives evidence of a mind diseased by 'terror of the body'.

A great wit like Swift could not see how ridiculous he made himself. ... Think of poor Celia, made to feel iniquitous about her proper natural function, by her lover. It is monstrous. And it comes from having taboo words, and from not keeping the mind sufficiently developed in physical and sexual consciousness.

And yet of course Swift had no taboo words, and shocked even some of his eighteenth-century readers because he manifests that so clearly in this very poem, and because he was willing to bring so much of the physical into consciousness. The whole significance of these poems lies in the fact that Swift hated the sentimentality of the ordinary romantic love-stuff. He is repeating here — even more drastically — what he had done in the poems already referred to, 'The Progress of Beauty', and 'Clad all in Brown'. Instead of rapturously describing the beauty of the body, or the poetry of dress, and all that stimulates desire, he is as usual turning things upside down, and with complete lack of restraint exposing the ugliness and unpleasantness of certain physical functions, and of certain aspects of private life in English fashionable society of the time, which were usually kept hidden. What squeamish people really object to is that in such poems Swift, as he readily admits, mingles humour with satire. They cannot forgive him because, in the very act of uncovering these unsavoury things, instead of making a horrified grimace, he is able to grin; it is in accordance with his experience:

> Thus, I find it by Experiment,
> Scolding moves you less than Merriment.
> I may storm and rage in vain;
> It but stupefies your Brain.
> But with Raillery to nettle,
> Set your Thoughts upon their Mettle . . .

Aldous Huxley's essay on Swift[1] is a brilliant elaboration of the same point. It is suspicious, however, in the first place because of the violence of his language. He quotes a casual remark of Swift's from a letter to Stella ('I hate the word bowels') and then continues excitedly:

Yes, how he hated it! And not the word only — the things too, the harmless necessary tripes — he loathed and detested them with an intensity of hatred such as few men have ever been capable of. It was unbearable to him that men should go through life with guts and sweetbreads, with liver and lights, spleens and kidneys. . . . All this was 'a source of excruciating suffering' . . . his resentment was incredibly bitter.

Did it ever occur to Mr. Huxley in the first place that the word 'bowels' had been used (in its metaphorical and sentimental sense) throughout the seventeenth century by all the canting preachers whom Swift most detested, till the very sound of it must have been unendurable in his ears? Even the few references given in the *New English Dictionary* are significant enough. There is a Parliamentary Proclamation for 1651, which refers to 'Want of bowels in preaching towards them who are in hazard to perish.' Fuller could not resist quoting a horrible pun in 1655: 'Bloody Bonner . . . full (as one said) of guts, and empty of bowels.' And this continued into the eighteenth century, as for instance in this delightful phrase from the

---

[1] In *What You Will* (New York, 1929).

London Gazette just a little earlier than Swift's protest: 'To shew their bowels for their country.'

I doubt very much Mr. Huxley's remark that Swift loathed 'the things too, the harmless necessary tripes'. It seems to me only a proof of the extreme sensitiveness of the twentieth-century humorist that accounts for his abhorrent disgust at Swift's unsavoury jokes. And, I am sure, a little further acquaintance with Swift would have prevented Mr. Huxley from writing such a sentence as: 'Swift's greatness lies in the intensity, the almost insane violence of that "hatred of bowels" which is the essence of his misanthropy and which underlies the whole of his work.' Is this not to forget a little too obviously that the Dean of St. Patrick's was in the first place a wit and a humorist?

But, to return to the poems, is it fantastic to suggest that 'Strephon and Chloe' can be most fairly judged, if it is regarded as a burlesque Epithalamium? At least it is a satire on a subject which always drove Swift to violent ridicule — romantic nonsense about marriage, a poison which he always feared as a great menace to human happiness. Whenever he speaks of marriage it is with almost incredible detachment and cold reasonableness. In one of his earliest letters it will be remembered that he had written to Varina to make a proposal of marriage. After a long list of questions, which he had always resolved to put to her with whom he meant to pass his life, he concludes: 'whenever you can heartily answer them in the affirmative, I shall be blessed to have you in my arms, without regarding whether your person be beautiful, or your fortune large. Cleanliness in the first, and competency in the other, is all I look for.'[1] Again when asked for advice about getting married by his friend Knightley Chetwode, Swift replied (12 February 1729–30):

As to changing your single life, it is impossible to advise without knowing all circumstances both of you and the person. Archbishop Sheldon advised a young Lord to be sure to get money with a wife, because he would then be at least possessed of one good thing.[2]

At any rate Swift always felt that it was a dangerous business, and he endeavours repeatedly in his poem 'Strephon and Chloe' to make

---

[1] Ball (ed.), *Correspondence*, vol. I, p. 35.
[2] Ball (ed.), *Correspondence*, vol. IV, p. 123.

his moral purpose clear. He allows full play to his satirical wit in picturing Strephon's fall out of the clouds of romance, but constantly interrupts his story to give advice of the plainest kind:

> Since Husbands get behind the Scene,
> The Wife should study to be clean;
>
>   .   .   .
>
> Authorities both old and recent,
> Direct that Women must be decent;
> And, from the Spouse each Blemish hide
> More than from all the World beside.

And the concluding moral is almost too commonplace and serious:

> On Sense and Wit your Passion found,
> By Decency cemented round;
> Let Prudence with Good Nature strive,
> To keep Esteem and Love alive.
> Then come old Age whene'er it will,
> Your Friendship shall continue still;
> And thus a mutual gentle Fire,
> Shall never but with Life expire.

We are reminded of a splendid tribute to Swift, in one of Arbuthnot's letters, written on 20 September 1726:

I had a great deal of discourse with your friend, her Royal Highness. She insisted upon your wit, and good conversation. I told her Royal Highness, that was not what I valued you for, but for being a sincere honest man, and speaking truth when others were afraid to speak it.[1]

But it was that indeed which was the very source of Swift's wit; he needed only to say with his perfect simplicity and directness what he saw to be true, and to those of his readers who lived perpetually in a world of romance and sentiment, it seemed the most biting irony. To them he appeared a mad fellow indeed, turning everything to wit and foolery — friendship and hate, love and marriage, and, at last, death and judgement.

Even Lucretius, in his argument against the fear of death, allows that death brings grief for those who are left behind:

[1] Ball (ed.), *Correspondence*, vol. III, p. 343.

But we, thy friends, shall all those sorrows find,
Which in forgetful death thou leav'st behind;
No time shall dry our tears, nor drive them from our mind.[1]

But Swift turns even this to scorn, with his motto from La Roche-foucald, which he takes as his theme for the 'Verses on the Death of Dr. Swift', published in 1739:

In all Distresses of our Friends
We first consult our private Ends,
While Nature kindly bent to ease us,
Points out some Circumstance to please us.

The poem is an *apologia pro vita sua*, and characteristically concerned more with what he was and did, than with what he wrote. He does, however, repeat once more his favourite boast that 'what he writ was all his own' and

. . . with a moral View design'd
To cure the Vices of Mankind . . .

but he finally admits

Perhaps I may allow, the Dean
Had too much Satyr in his Vein;
And seem'd determin'd not to starve it,
Because no Age could more deserve it.

But that does not restrain him from one last stroke — beautifully expressive of the way in which so often he mingled generosity and contempt.

He gave the little Wealth he had
To build a House for Fools and Mad:
And shew'd by one satyric Touch,
No Nation wanted it so much . . .

There is not much further scope left for wit and satire. But after his death there was found among his papers, in his own handwriting, a poem on 'The Day of Judgment'. It was very fitting that it was first

[1] Dryden's translation of the latter part of the Third Book, included in *Sylvae* (1685), lines 92–94.

printed as quoted by Lord Chesterfield, in a letter to Voltaire, dated 27 August 1752.

It describes the Last Day, with the world standing trembling before Jove's throne, and then gives very shortly the epilogue to the whole comedy of life:

> Offending Race of Human Kind,
> By Nature, Reason, Learning, blind;
> You who thro' Frailty step'd aside,
> And you who never fell — *thro' Pride*;
> You who in different Sects have shamm'd,
> And come to see each other damn'd;
> (So some Folks told you, but they knew
> No more of Jove's Designs than you)
> The World's mad Business now is o'er,
> And I resent these Pranks no more.
> I to such Blockheads set my Wit!
> I damn such Fools! — Go, go, you're bit.

Here is the complete triumph of the Comic Spirit, unabashed and unafraid, delighting to overthrow all mankind's claims to dignity and importance, and 'ending with a puff' the whole heroic and romantic delusion.

A. L. ROWSE

Swift as Poet

I

O F ALL the books that have come out in late years about Swift, there are few that are up to the subject. Middleton Murry's biography was, surprisingly, the best; but then Murry had a remarkable critical intelligence and even finer understanding, when away from his hobbies. Professor Louis Landa gave us an excellent specialist book on Swift and the Church. Professor Quintana limited himself to a study of Swift's mind and art as a writer.[1] This provides a careful survey of Swift's work, connects it up with the large body of research that has accumulated on the subject, and gives us enough of Swift's life to make it intelligible.

It is the background to Swift's thought, the various elements that entered into it from other thinkers, where they came from and how they affected him, that now need more study. There is this excuse, that there is no history of English thought in the seventeenth century, as there is of the eighteenth century, by Sir Leslie Stephen. One notices this lack most in regard to the problem of Swift's belief — or unbelief; for there was a strain of deism, or of definite unbelief, among English thinkers of that age, which must surely have left its mark on Swift's mind. Professor Quintana notices the influence of Hobbes's materialism upon Swift's view of the imagination and his aesthetics generally; but it may be that that influence went further, to affect the whole of Swift's intellectual position, to instil scepticism into a mind not naturally sceptical, to denude him of any vestige of idealism in his view of the world and experience. There is a considerable body of deistic writing contemporaneous

[1] Ricardo Quintana, *The Mind and Art of Jonathan Swift* (London and New York, 1936: 2nd ed., London, 1953).

with Swift, which is part of his intellectual background: such writers as Shaftesbury, Toland, Mandeville. Professor Quintana says that 'when the great Dean of St. Patrick's died in 1745, he had already ceased to be understood by the eighteenth century'. All the more reason to consider him historically in relation to his environment.

The question of Swift's religious convictions is central. On this point neither defence nor excuse is necessary; it is enough to understand him. 'It is not that Swift wavered in belief, nor that in conduct he failed to be guided by it,' says Professor Quintana. 'In all these matters he was rigorously consistent, rigorously in accord with his theoretical premises.' But the point is whether these premises were in accordance with orthodox Christianity. I cannot but think that Archbishop Sharp, Queen Anne, the instinct of religious believers (typified by Dr. Johnson, who knew very well), were right about Swift. They scented that there was no religious belief in him. As for getting a bishopric, he was lucky to become a dean. Only an age when patronage was in the ascendant would have been so broadminded; any other age would have expected a dean to believe.

Such conception of religion as he had was of an external and institutional character; there is no sign of personal belief. Even in the 'Prayers for Stella', the nearest in expression he achieved, there is more evidence of doubt than of faith or hope; whereas he frequently gives expression to the Manichee view that life is in itself an evil to be endured. Perhaps, however, one need not take him so seriously as he took himself on this point; he clearly enjoyed some parts of his own life — the years 1709–14, for example, the exercise of power, his many friendships, writing.

Professor Quintana is at pains to rebut the charge that Swift was a misanthrope. Why shouldn't Swift be a misanthrope? Hatred of human beings is as legitimate a subject of art as love of them, and its possibilities more rarely explored. Nor need one be prudish about the scatological poems with their 'disgusting' imagery. They are often artistic successes, and are as much part of Swift's mind as the 'fine, satiric touch' — indeed more intimately part of his mind, all the more revealing of what kind of mind that was. The self-laceration of these poems may represent an excessive sensibility, turned back upon itself, turned inside out. 'I was to see Lady ——,' he wrote to Stella, 'who is just up after lying-in; and the ugliest sight I have seen, pale, dead, old and yellow, for want of her paint. *She has turned my stomach.* But she will soon be painted, and a beauty again.' In this one perceives the type of all those poems of physical disgust he wrote: they are due to a morbid degree of sensitiveness, acting upon a disillusioned temperament, to make him torture himself and others.

There was certainly an acute tension between defeatism in his view of human nature and an active temperament in himself, between reason and the emotions, in Swift's mind. He had no illusions about human nature, yet he did — perhaps unreasonably — expect men to be better than they are. He insisted always upon the moral responsibility of the person. In his outlook there was too great a dichotomy between reason and the emotions; he thought of them as simply and necessarily in conflict and this increased the strain in his inner life. The tension bore fruit in his art, but it made for unhappiness in the man. Swift believed, in accordance with the materialism of Hobbes, that 'self-love, as it is the motive to all our actions, so it is the sole cause of our grief'. It is a forbidding view to hold, repressive of the emotional life, especially with a man so self-conscious as Swift: he at any rate was not under the illusions that most people are as to their motives. He girded at *la condition humaine*, but might he not have been a little happier if, realising how little disinterestedness there was in the world or in himself, he had made it more his aim?

As it was, his intellectual position was at every point that which his interests demanded and with which his person was identified. A churchman, he saw only the interests of his own sect; a Tory, of his own party; an Irish Protestant, he stood up for the Irish Church against both Catholics and Dissenters. If he had happened to be a Dissenter, or had remained a Whig, he would have been as vehement on the other side. Professor Quintana comments, 'however ignoble his actuating impulses may have been, the ends which he achieved cannot be judged solely in terms of motive'. What is odd is Swift's consciousness of the situation and his acceptance of it. It is like his denial of any place to idealism in life, or to imagination in poetry: an abnegation springing from his fear of disillusionment. He realised all too clearly the discomfort of the latter, but did not allow for the necessity for a certain amount of illusion or even humbug to make life tolerable. As T. S. Eliot constantly enforced, human beings can bear very little reality. Swift stripped life to the bare bones.

Professor Quintana insists upon the richness and fertility of Swift's later phase. 'Nothing is further from the truth than the idea commonly entertained regarding Swift's latter years of activity. He was still the great artist, producing verse and prose of undiminished brilliance and intensity, and he remained an imperious public figure.' So often this period is treated merely as an aftermath. Yet it is in this period that he produced *Gulliver's Travels* and much o the best of his poetry. All the more reason for not agreeing that *Gulliver* is inferior to *A Tale of a Tub*. There is a universality and a range in *Gulliver* which the earlier work does not compass; it has, too, a depth of experience and conviction, where *A Tale of a Tub* is more intellectual, cold and academic. *Gulliver* is the work that the world has chosen; that kind of universal consensus is not likely to be wrong.

II

The poetry of Swift is an esoteric taste. There is hardly anyone in our literary history who has had a liking for it since his own time. Yeats is a notable exception, perhaps the only poet whose verse was directly influenced by Swift, and that is partly owing to their common Irish background, Swift's living tradition there and the cult of him in Dublin. However, contemplating and brooding over Swift was an element in making the later verse of Yeats what it became, in content and temper. But apart from Yeats, nobody. This lack of appreciation springs from the dominance of the romantic tradition in our literature — the line that runs from Spenser, Shakespeare, the Caroline poets, to the great Romantics, Words-worth, Coleridge, Shelley and the later. But for some time such poets as Skelton, Donne, Dryden, Byron have been coming back into their own. Perhaps this definitive edition may have the effect of enabling Swift to do so too.[1]

[1] Harold Williams (ed.), *The Poems of Jonathan Swift* (1st ed., Oxford, 1937; 2nd ed., Oxford, 1958).

There is so much in his poetry that should appeal to this age: its realism and ruthlessness, its exposure of the human condition, without pity or illusion, its stripping away of all pretences, its very nudity, its terse force, concentration and clarity.

Hitherto, Swift has been universally underestimated as a poet. To some extent he is himself to blame; for it has been partly due to that pride which made him careless, where Pope was so careful, about the publishing of his poems. It was Swift's foible to care more for the reputation of a gentleman than of a poet: 'I do not call him a poet that writes for his diversion,' he said, 'any more than that gentleman, a fiddler, who amuses himself with a violin.' Swift left his verse publications in indescribable confusion until Sir Harold Williams came along to bring order out of chaos, as nobody had done previously. 'No part of his writing has been so neglected and mishandled by editors,' Sir Harold says. Partly the neglect of Swift's poetry may be put down to the rapid change of fashion that came about after his death, in the latter half of the eighteenth century; and in part, too, to his consistent, half-humorous depreciation of his own verse:

> In Pope, I cannot read a Line,
> But with a Sigh I wish it Mine . . .

But it does not say much for later generations of critics that they have been so ready to take a master of irony *au pied de la lettre*. Sir Harold says that to the unhappiness of Swift's life there was added 'the misfortune of falling short of his friends, Pope, Prior and Gay, in the poetic content of his work. . . . In verse Pope was his superior. Gay and Prior had a more lyrical gift. Swift's genius lay in the succession of Samuel Butler.' Swift was a less accomplished poet than Pope, and he had altogether less charm — though he was a more astonishing apparition, a stranger genius, and this appears in his verse no less than in his prose. But fall short of Prior? or Gay? Surely not.

The truth is in force, range, persistence, he is a great poet. Swift expressed himself more fully and more continuously in his verse than in his prose. Sir Harold Williams allows that 'he was constantly turning verse as a common part of his everyday life, so much so that

no part of his writing is as complete an autobiography'. He concludes: 'We are closer to Swift in his verse, and in his letters, than
in his prose-writings'; and he quotes Dr. Elrington Ball's summing-
up, 'Without knowledge of his verse a true picture of Swift cannot
be drawn. In his verse he sets forth his life as in a panorama, he
shows more clearly than in his prose his peculiar turn of thought,
and he reveals his character in all its phases.' He took earlier to the
writing of poetry, and in an early poem, the 'Ode to Sir William
Temple', describes how everything that he writes turns to verse:

> In vain all wholesome Herbs I sow,
>   Where nought but Weeds will grow.
> Whate'er I plant (like Corn on barren Earth)
>   By an equivocal Birth
> Seeds and runs up to Poetry.

That in itself is evidence of his early bent; and though there comes a
break after these early poems, six years in which he is not known to
have written any verse, the characteristic traits of Swift appear early.
It is usual to mark a complete contrast between this first group of
pindaric odes and the later poems. Yet in these first poems there is
the declared intention of the satirist to lash mankind for its folly:

> *My hate, whose lash just heaven has long decreed*
> *Shall on a day make sin and folly bleed.*

There is 'that scorn of fools, by fools mistook for pride', the
authentic note of contempt for mankind, the incapacity for contentment which such thoughts, in the human condition, must induce:

> Madness like this no fancy ever seiz'd,
> Still to be cheated, never to be pleas'd.

There is the inhibiting doctrine that all knowledge comes only from
memory, enshrined in a remarkable passage to which Yeats drew
Sir Harold Williams' attention:

> But what does our proud Ign'rance Learning call,
>   We oddly *Plato's* Paradox make good,
> Our Knowledge is but mere Remembrance all,
>   Remembrance is our Treasure and our Food;

> Nature's fair Table-book our tender Souls
> We scrawl all o'er with odd and empty Rules,
> Stale Memorandums of the Schools;
> For Learning's mighty Treasures look
> In that deep Grave a Book.

All this in those first few poems, the neglected odes: the poems on which Dryden is said to have commented: 'Cousin Swift, you will never be a poet.' Evidently Dryden said something of the sort; for Swift underwent some kind of crisis, was silent for six years, and then emerged with a totally different style, fully formed, from which he never afterwards departed. But the themes were continuous and received their full development in the mature poetry.

There is a good case for holding that the more complete Swift is the Swift of the poems. There is nothing he said in prose that he did not say as well in verse; only the reputation of the author of *Gulliver* and of *A Tale of a Tub* has overshadowed the fact. There is all the savagery of the last book of *Gulliver* in 'The Legion Club'; and there are a good many things among the poems which are hardly paralleled in the prose. The good-humoured, below-stairs fun of the remarkable early poem 'Mrs. Harris's Petition' is paralleled in the late prose work, the *Directions to Servants*, but with the added note of bitterness his experience of life had induced. It is revealing that it was in verse only that Swift expressed the precarious ambiguity of his relations with Vanessa; nothing like it in his prose. And how well that complex, poised state of mind, neither wholly one thing nor the other, is described:

> But what Success Vanessa met,
> Is to the World a Secret yet:
> Whether the Nymph, to please her Swain,
> Talks in a high Romantic Strain;
> Or whether he at last descends
> To like with less Seraphick Ends;
> Or, to compound the Business, whether
> They temper Love and Books together;
> Must never to Mankind be told,
> Nor shall the conscious Muse unfold.

As to form, Swift's verse was a perfect instrument for the expression of what he intended; it too has greater variety than is usually realised. Even Dr. Johnson, whose criticism of Swift's poems was casual and unsympathetic, allowed this: 'They [the poetical works] are, for the most part, what their author intended. . . . All his verses exemplify his own definition of a good style, they consist of "proper words in proper places".'

The ends Swift set himself were too restricted or, at a deeper level, inhibited by his fear of giving himself away, of giving hostages to fortune in the realm of the emotions. One can appreciate the motives that made him repress his hopes and desires — his determination to have his life as far as possible under his own control, a rational control; the realisation of the insentience of the universe to the sufferings of men; his refusal to lay himself open to experience, especially in regard to sex. The paradox is that it is just those persons who go out of their way to reject experience for fear of the suffering it may entail, who suffer most. The searing irony of Swift's life is that the man who imposed so rational a control upon his emotions should have ended by losing his reason. Sir Harold Williams concludes that if Swift had been prepared to let himself go, he would have been a greater poet, that 'he had something to give to English poetry that he never wholly gave'. On the other hand, it is that very sense of restraint that gives the impression of such power in reserve. And it is present, perfectly and precisely expressed, in all the metres and verse-forms he chose to write in.

The real criticism against Swift's poetry is not, then, on the score of lack of variety either of subject, or of metre, but rather a lack of variety in *tone*. But may not the same be said of many other poets whom the poetic tradition recognises without demur — Spenser, Shelley, Keats — though with them the tone is a different one? It may be agreed that Swift, for a poet, wrote too much from the head, and not enough from the heart; and it is not a good thing for a poet to write wholly from the head, never to allow himself freedom from the limits consciously imposed by the intellect. That is what Swift set himself to do, and the result we have to take for what it is. It is hardly just to demand that it should be something other than it is, as so many have done, and say, 'This is not poetry.' They start from a carefully selective view of what poetry should be — one moreover which is not sanctioned by the practice of the poets — and then impose that standard upon poetry like Swift's.

Naturally, with a dominantly intellectual approach and with his experience of the world what it was, Swift's creative impulse turned mainly to satire. He might have said with his so much admired model, Juvenal: 'Difficile est non satiram scribere.' And he was well aware of the criticism that might be pointed against him:

> Perhaps I may allow, the Dean
> Had too much Satyr in his Vein;
> And seem'd determin'd not to starve it,
> Because no Age could more deserve it.

It is clear that this was the frame of mind which with him released the aesthetic impulse, that this was the psychological groove along which his inspiration and its expression ran most easily. There is a strong case for Swift's classicism, that controlled and deliberately directed emotion, as opposed to the romantic inspiration. For one thing his chief emotion was intellectual passion, a rare thing in an Englishman; which is perhaps why the English have never properly understood him or his poetry.

Jonathan Swift
by or after C. Jervas

VIRGINIA WOOLF

Swift's Journal to Stella

IN any highly civilised society disguise plays so large a part politeness is so essential, that to throw off the ceremonies and conventions and talk a 'little language' for one or two to understand, is as much a necessity as a breath of air in a hot room. The reserved, the powerful, the admired, have the most need of such a refuge. Swift himself found it so. The proudest of men coming home from the company of great men who praised him, of lovely women who flattered him, from intrigue and politics, put all that aside, settled himself comfortably in bed, pursed his severe lips into baby language and prattled to his 'two monkies', his 'dear Sirrahs', his 'naughty rogues' on the other side of the Irish Channel.

Well, let me see you now again. My wax candle's almost out, but however I'll begin. Well then don't be so tedious, Mr. Presto; what can you say to MD's letter? Make haste, have done with your preambles — why, I say, I am glad you are so often abroad.

So long as Swift wrote to Stella in that strain, carelessly, illegibly, for 'methinks when I write plain, I do not know how, but we are not alone, all the world can see us. A bad scrawl is so snug . . .', Stella had no need to be jealous. It was true that she was wearing away the flower of her youth in Ireland with Rebecca Dingley, who wore hinged spectacles, consumed large quantities of Brazil tobacco, and stumbled over her petticoats as she walked. Further, the conditions in which the two ladies lived, for ever in Swift's company when he was at home, occupying his house when he was absent, gave rise to gossip; so that though Stella never saw him except in Mrs. Dingley's presence, she was one of those ambiguous women who live chiefly in the society of the other sex. But surely it was well worth while. The packets kept coming from England, each sheet written to the rim in Swift's crabbed little hand, which she imitated to perfection, full of nonsense words, and capital letters, and hints which no one but Stella could understand, and secrets which Stella was to keep, and little commissions which Stella was to execute. Tobacco came for Dingley, and chocolate and silk aprons for Stella. Whatever people might say, surely it was well worth while.

Of this Presto, who was so different from that formidable character 't'other I', the world knew nothing. The world knew only that Swift was over in England again, soliciting the new Tory government on behalf of the Irish Church for those First Fruits which he had begged the Whigs in vain to restore. The business was soon accomplished; nothing indeed could exceed the cordiality and affection with which Harley and St. John greeted him; and now the world saw what even in those days of small societies and individual pre-eminence must have been a sight to startle and amaze — the 'mad parson', who had marched up and down the coffee-houses in silence and unknown a few years ago, admitted to the inmost councils of State; the penniless boy who was not allowed to sit down at table with Sir William Temple dining with the highest ministers of the Crown, making dukes do his bidding, and so run after for his good offices that his servant's chief duty was to know how to keep people out. Addison himself forced his way up only by pretending that he was a gentleman come to pay a bill. For the time being Swift was omnipotent. Nobody could buy his services; everybody feared his pen. He went to Court, and 'am so proud I make all the lords come up to me'. The Queen wished to hear him preach; Harley and St. John added their entreaties; but he refused. When Mr. Secretary one night dared show his temper, Swift called upon him and warned him

never to appear cold to me, for I would not be treated like a school-boy. . . . He took all right; said I had reason . . . would have had me dine with him at Mrs. Masham's brother, to make up matters; but I would not. I don't know, but I would not.

He scribbled all this down to Stella without exultation or vanity. That he should command and dictate, prove himself the peer of great men and make rank abase itself before him, called for no comment on his part or on hers. Had she not known him years ago at Moor Park and seen him lose his temper with Sir William Temple, and guessed his greatness and heard from his own lips what he planned and hoped? Did she not know better than anyone how strangely good and bad were blent in him and all his foibles and eccentricities of temper? He scandalised the lords with whom he dined by his stinginess, picked the coals off his fire, saved halfpence on coaches; and yet by the help of these very economies he practised, she knew, the most considerate and secret of charities — he gave poor Patty Rolt 'a pistole to help her a little forward against she goes to board in the country'; he took twenty guineas to young Harrison, the sick poet, in his garret. She alone knew how he could be coarse in his speech and yet delicate in his behaviour; how he could be cynical superficially and yet cherish a depth of feeling which she had never met with in any other human being. They knew each other in and out; the good and the bad, the deep and the trivial; so that without effort or concealment he could use those precious moments late at night or the first thing on waking to pour out upon her the whole story of his day, with its charities and meannesses, its affections and ambitions and despairs, as though he were thinking aloud.

With such proof of his affection, admitted to intimacy with this Presto whom no one else in the world knew, Stella had no cause to be jealous. It was perhaps the opposite that happened. As she read the crowded pages, she could see him and hear him and imagine so exactly the impression that he must be making on all these fine people that she fell more deeply in love with him than ever. Not only was he courted and flattered by the great; everybody seemed to call upon him when they were in trouble. There was 'young Harrison'; he worried to find him ill and penniless; carried him off to Knightsbridge; took him a hundred pounds only to find that he was dead an hour before. 'Think what grief this is to me! . . . I could not dine with Lord Treasurer, nor anywhere else; but got a bit of meat toward evening.' She could imagine the strange scene, that November morning, when the Duke of Hamilton was killed in Hyde Park, and Swift went at once to the Duchess and sat with her for two hours and heard her rage and storm and rail; and took her affairs, too, on his shoulders as if it were his natural office, and none could dispute his place in the house of mourning. 'She has moved my very soul', he said. When young Lady Ashburnham died he burst out, 'I hate life when I think it exposed to such accidents; and to see so many thousand wretches burdening the earth, while such as her die, makes me think God did never intend life for a blessing.' And then, with that instinct to rend and tear his own emotions which made him angry in the midst of his pity, he would round upon the mourners, even the mother and sister of the dead woman, and part them as they cried together and complain how 'people will pretend to grieve more than they really do, and that takes off from their true grief'.

All this was poured forth freely to Stella; the gloom and the anger, the kindness and the coarseness and the genial love of little ordinary human things. To her he showed himself fatherly and brotherly; he laughed at her spelling; he scolded her about her health; he directed her business affairs. He gossiped and chatted with her. They had a fund of memories in common. They had spent many happy hours together. 'Do not you remember I used to come into your chamber and turn Stella out of her chair, and rake up the fire in a cold morning and cry *uth, uth, uth*!' She was often in his mind; he wondered if she was out walking when he was; when Prior abused one of his puns he remembered Stella's puns and how vile they were; he compared his life in London with hers in Ireland and wondered when they would be together again. And if this was the influence of Stella upon Swift in town among all the wits, the influence of Swift upon Stella marooned in an Irish village alone with Dingley was far greater. He had taught her all the little learning she had when she was a child and he a young man years ago at Moor Park. His influence was everywhere — upon her mind, upon her affections, upon the books she read and the hand she wrote, upon the friends she made and the suitors she rejected. Indeed, he was half responsible for her being.

But the woman he had chosen was no insipid slave. She had a character of her own. She was capable of thinking for herself. She was aloof, a severe critic for all her grace and sympathy, a little formidable perhaps with her love of plain speaking and her fiery temper and her fearlessness in saying what she thought. But with all her gifts she was little known. Her slender means and feeble health and dubious social standing made her way of life very modest. The society which gathered round her came for the simple pleasure of talking to a woman who listened and understood and said very little herself, but in the most agreeable of voices and generally 'the best thing that was said in the company'. For the rest she was not learned. Her health had prevented her from serious study, and though she had run over a great variety of subjects and had a fine severe taste in letters, what she did read did not stick in her mind. She had been extravagant as a girl, and flung her money about until her good sense took control of her, and now she lived with the utmost frugality. 'Five nothings on five plates of delf' made her supper. Attractive, if not beautiful, with her fine dark eyes and her raven black hair, she dressed very plainly, and thus contrived to lay by enough to help the poor and to bestow upon her friends (it was an extravagance that she could not resist) 'the most agreeable presents in the world'. Swift never knew her equal in that art, 'although it be an affair of as delicate a nature as most in the course of life'. She had in addition that sincerity which Swift called 'honour', and in spite of the weakness of her body 'the personal courage of a hero'. Once when a robber came to her window, she had shot him through the body with her own hand. Such, then, was the influence which worked on Swift as he wrote; such the presence that mingled with the thought of his fruit-trees and the willows and the trout stream at Laracor when he saw the trees budding in St. James's Park and heard the politicians wrangle at Westminster. Unknown to all of them, he had his retreat; and if the ministers again played him false, and once more, after making his friends' fortunes, he went empty-handed away, then after all he could retire to Ireland and to Stella and have 'no shuddering at all' at the thought.

But Stella was the last woman in the world to press her claims. None knew better than she that Swift loved power and the company of men: that though he had his moods of tenderness and his fierce spasms of disgust at society, still for the most part he infinitely preferred the dust and bustle of London to all the trout streams and cherry-trees in the world. Above all, he hated interference. If anyone laid a finger upon his liberty or hinted the least threat to his independence, were they men or women, queens or kitchen-maids, he turned upon them with a ferocity which made a savage of him on the spot. Harley once dared to offer him a bank-note; Miss Waring dared hint that the obstacles to their marriage were now removed. Both were chastised, the woman brutally. But Stella knew better than to invite such treatment. Stella had learnt patience; Stella had learnt discretion. Even in a matter like this of staying in London or coming back to Ireland she allowed him every latitude. She asked nothing for herself and therefore got more than she asked. Swift was half annoyed:

... your generosity makes me mad; I know you repine inwardly at Presto's absence; you think he has broken his word, of coming in three months, and that this is always his trick: and now Stella says, she does not see possibly how I can come away in haste, and that MD is satisfied, etc. An't you a rogue to overpower me thus?

But it was thus that she kept him. Again and again he burst into language of intense affection:

Farewell dear Sirrahs, dearest lives: there is peace and quiet with MD, and nowhere else.... Farewell again, dearest rogues: I am never happy, but when I write or think of MD.... You are as welcome as my blood to every farthing I have in the world: and all that grieves me is, I am not richer, for MD's sake.

One thing alone dashed the pleasure that such words gave her. It was always in the plural that he spoke of her; it was always 'dearest Sirrahs, dearest lives'; MD stood for Stella and Mrs. Dingley together. Swift and Stella were never alone. Grant that this was for form's sake merely, grant that the presence of Mrs. Dingley, busy with her keys and her lap-dog and never listening to a word that was said to her, was a form too. But why should such forms be necessary? Why impose a strain that wasted her health and half spoilt her pleasure and kept 'perfect friends' who were happy only in each other's company apart? Why indeed? There was a reason; a secret that Stella knew; a secret that Stella did not impart. Divided they had to be. Since, then, no bond bound them, since she was afraid to lay the least claim upon her friend, all the more jealously must she have searched into his words and analysed his conduct to ascertain the temper of his mood and acquaint herself instantly with the least change in it. So long as he told her frankly of his 'favourites' and showed himself the bluff tyrant who required every woman to make advances to him, who lectured fine ladies and let them tease him, all was well. There was nothing in that to rouse her suspicions. Lady Berkeley might steal his hat; the Duchess of Hamilton might lay bare her agony; and Stella, who was kind to her sex, laughed with the one and grieved with the other.

But were there traces in the *Journal* of a different sort of influence — something far more dangerous because more equal and more intimate? Suppose that there were some woman of Swift's own station, a girl, like the girl that Stella herself had been when Swift first knew her, dissatisfied with the ordinary way of life, eager, as Stella put it, to know right from wrong, gifted, witty, and untaught — she indeed, if she existed, might be a rival to be feared. But was there such a rival? If so, it was plain that there would be no mention of her in the *Journal*. Instead, there would be hesitations, excuses, an occasional uneasiness and embarrassment when, in the midst of writing freely and fully, Swift was brought to a stop by something that he could not say. Indeed, he had been only a month or two in England when some such silence roused Stella's suspicions. Who was it, she asked, that boarded near him, that he dined with now and then? 'I know no such person,' Swift replied; 'I do not dine with boarders. What the pox! You know whom I have dined with every day since I left you, better than I do. What do you mean, Sirrah?' But he knew what she meant: she meant Mrs. Vanhomrigh, the widow who lived near him; she meant her daughter Esther. 'The Vans' kept coming again and again after that in the *Journal*. Swift was too proud to conceal the fact that he saw them, but he sought nine times out of ten to excuse it. When he was in Suffolk Street the Vanhomrighs were in St. James's Street and thus saved him a walk. When he was in Chelsea they were in London, and it was convenient to keep his best gown and periwig there. Sometimes the heat kept him there and sometimes the rain; now they were playing cards, and young Lady Ashburnham reminded him so much of Stella that he stayed on to help her. Sometimes he stayed out of listlessness; again he stayed because he was very busy and they were simple people who did not stand on ceremony. At the same time Stella had only to hint that these Vanhomrighs were people of no consequence for him to retort, 'Why, they keep as good female company as I do male. . . . I saw two lady Bettys there this afternoon.' In short, to tell the whole truth, to write whatever came into his head in the old free way, was no longer easy.

Indeed, the whole situation was full of difficulty. No man detested falsehood more than Swift or loved truth more whole-heartedly. Yet here he was compelled to hedge, to hide, and to prevaricate. Again, it had become essential to him to have some 'sluttery' or private chamber where he could relax and unbend and be Presto and not 't'other I'. Stella satisfied this need as no one else could. But then Stella was in Ireland; Vanessa was on the spot. She was younger and fresher; she too had her charms. She too could be taught and improved and scolded into maturity as Stella had been. Obviously Swift's influence upon her was all to the good. And so with Stella in Ireland and Vanessa in London, why should it not be possible to enjoy what each could give him, confer benefits on both and do no serious harm to either? It seemed possible; at any rate he allowed himself to make the experiment. Stella, after all, had contrived for many years to make shift with her portion; Stella had never complained of her lot.

But Vanessa was not Stella. She was younger, more vehement, less disciplined, less wise. She had no Mrs. Dingley to restrain her. She had no memories of the past to solace her. She had no journals coming day by day to comfort her. She loved Swift and she knew no reason why she should not say so. Had he not himself taught her 'to act what was right, and not to mind what the world said'? Thus when some obstacle impeded her, when some mysterious secret came between them, she had the unwisdom to question him. 'Pray what can be wrong in seeing and advising an unhappy young woman? I can't imagine.' 'You have taught me to distinguish,' she burst out, 'and then you leave me miserable.' Finally in her anguish and her bewilderment she had the temerity to force herself upon Stella. She wrote and demanded to be told the truth — what was Stella's connection with Swift? But it was Swift himself who enlightened her. And when the full force of those bright blue eyes blazed upon her, when he flung her letter on the table and glared at her and said nothing and rode off, her life was ended. It was no figure of speech when she said that 'his killing, killing words' were worse than the rack to her; when she cried out that there was 'something in your look so awful that it strikes me dumb'. Within a few weeks of that interview she was dead; she had vanished, to become one of those uneasy ghosts who haunted the troubled background of Stella's life, peopling its solitude with fears.

Stella was left to enjoy her intimacy alone. She lived on to practise those sad arts by which she kept her friend at her side until, worn out with the strain and the concealment, with Mrs. Dingley and her lap-dogs, with the perpetual fears and frustrations, she too died. As they buried her, Swift sat in a back room away from the lights in the churchyard and wrote an account of the character of 'the truest, most virtuous, and valuable friend, that I, or perhaps any other person, was ever blessed with'. Years passed; insanity overcame him; he exploded in violent outbursts of mad rage. Then by degrees he fell silent. Once they caught him murmuring. 'I am what I am', they heard him say.

F. R. LEAVIS

The Irony of Swift

SWIFT is a great English writer. For opening with this truism I have a reason: I wish to discuss Swift's writings — to examine what they are; and they are (as the extant commentary bears witness) of such a kind that it is peculiarly difficult to discuss them without shifting the focus of discussion to the kind of man that Swift was. What is most interesting in them does not so clearly belong to the realm of things made and detached that literary criticism, which has certainly not the less its duties towards Swift, can easily avoid turning — unawares, and that is, degenerating — into something else. In the attempt to say what makes these writings so remarkable, reference to the man who wrote is indeed necessary; but there are distinctions. For instance, one may (it appears), having offered to discuss the nature and import of Swift's satire, find oneself countering imputations of misanthropy with the argument that Swift earned the love of Pope, Arbuthnot, Gay, several other men and two women: this should not be found necessary by the literary critic. But the irrelevancies of Thackeray and of his castigator, the late Charles Whibley — irrelevancies not merely from the point of view of literary criticism — are too gross to need placarding; more insidious deviations are possible.

The reason for the opening truism is also the reason for the choice of title. To direct the attention upon Swift's irony gives, I think, the best chance of dealing adequately, without deviation or confusion, with what is essential in his work. But it involves also (to anticipate an objection) a slight to the classical status of *Gulliver's Travels*, a book which, though it may represent Swift's most impressive achievement in the way of complete creation — the thing achieved and detached — does not give the best opportunities for examining his irony. And *Gulliver's Travels*, one readily agrees, hasn't its classical status for nothing. But neither is it for nothing that, suitably abbreviated, it has become a classic for children. What for the adult reader constitutes its peculiar force — what puts it in so different a class from *Robinson Crusoe* — resides for the most part in the fourth book (to a less extent in the third). The adult may re-read the first two parts, as he may *Robinson Crusoe*, with great interest, but his interest, apart from being more critically conscious, will not be of a different order from the child's. He will, of course, be aware of an ingenuity of political satire in 'Lilliput', but the political satire is, unless for historians, not very much alive today. And even the more general satire characteristic of the second book will not strike him as very subtle. His main satisfaction, a great deal enhanced, no doubt, by the ironic seasoning, will be that which Swift, the student of the *Mariner's Magazine* and of travellers' relations, aimed to supply in the bare precision and the matter-of-fact realness of his narrative.

But what in Swift is most important, the disturbing characteristic of his genius, is a peculiar emotional intensity; that which, in *Gulliver*, confronts us in the Struldbrugs and the Yahoos. It is what we find ourselves contemplating when elsewhere we examine his irony. To lay the stress upon an emotional intensity should be matter of commonplace: actually, in routine usage, the accepted word for Swift is 'intellectual'. We are told, for instance, that his is pre-eminently 'intellectual satire' (though we are not told what satire is). For this formula the best reason some commentators can allege is the elaboration of analogies — their 'exact and elaborate propriety'[1] — in *Gulliver*. But a muddled perception can hardly be expected to give a clear account of itself; the stress on Swift's 'intellect' (Sir Herbert Read alludes to his 'mighty intelligence'[2]) registers, it would appear, a confused sense, not only of the mental exercise involved in his irony, but of the habitually critical attitude he maintains towards the world, and of the negative emotions he specializes in.

From 'critical' to 'negative' in this last sentence is, it will be observed, a shift of stress. There are writings of Swift where 'critical'

[1] Churton Collins, *Jonathan Swift, A Biographical and Critical Study* (London, 1893), p. 202.
[2] *English Prose Style* (1928; new revised ed. 1952).

is the more obvious word (and where 'intellectual' may seem correspondingly apt) — notably, the pamphlets or pamphleteering essays in which the irony is instrumental, directed and limited to a given end. The *Argument Against Abolishing Christianity* and the *Modest Proposal*, for instance, are discussible in the terms in which satire is commonly discussed: as the criticism of vice, folly, or other aberration, by some kind of reference to positive standards. But even here, even in the *Argument*, where Swift's ironic intensity undeniably directs itself to the defence of something that he is intensely concerned to defend, the effect is essentially negative. The positive itself appears only negatively — a kind of skeletal presence, rigid enough, but without life or body; a necessary pre-condition, as it were, of directed negation. The intensity is purely destructive.

The point may be enforced by the obvious contrast with Gibbon — except that between Swift's irony and Gibbon's the contrast is so complete that any one point is difficult to isolate. Gibbon's irony, in the fifteenth chapter, may be aimed against, instead of for, Christianity, but contrasted with Swift's it is an assertion of faith. The decorously insistent pattern of Gibbonian prose insinuates a solidarity with the reader (the implied solidarity in Swift is itself ironical — a means to betrayal), establishes an understanding and habituates to certain assumptions. The reader, it is implied, is an eighteenth-century gentleman ('rational', 'candid', 'polite', 'elegant', 'humane'); eighteen hundred years ago he would have been a pagan gentleman, living by these same standards (those of absolute civilization); by these standards (present everywhere in the stylized prose and adroitly emphasized at keypoints in such phrases as 'the polite Augustus', 'the elegant mythology of the Greeks') the Jews and early Christians are seen to have been ignorant fanatics, uncouth and probably dirty. Gibbon as a historian of Christianity had, we know, limitations; but the positive standards by reference to which his irony works represent something impressively realized in eighteenth-century civilization; impressively 'there' too in the grandiose, assured and ordered elegance of his history. (When, on the other hand, Lytton Strachey, with a Gibbonian period or phrase or word, a 'remarkable', 'oddly', or 'curious', assures us that he feels an amused superiority to these Victorian puppets, he succeeds only in conveying his personal conviction that he feels amused and superior.)

Gibbon's irony, then, habituates and reassures, ministering to a kind of judicial certitude or complacency. Swift's is essentially a matter of surprise and negation; its function is to defeat habit, to intimidate and to demoralize. What he assumes in the *Argument* is not so much a common acceptance of Christianity as that the reader will be ashamed to have to recognize how fundamentally unchristian his actual assumptions, motives and attitudes are. And in general the implication is that it would shame people if they were made to recognize themselves unequivocally. If one had to justify this irony according to the conventional notion of satire, then its satiric efficacy would be to make comfortable non-recognition, the un-consciousness of habit, impossible.

A method of surprise does not admit of description in an easy formula. Surprise is a perpetually varied accompaniment of the grave, dispassionate, matter-of-fact tone in which Swift delivers his intensities. The dissociation of emotional intensity from its usual accompaniments inhibits the automatic defence-reaction:

He is a Presbyterian in politics, and an atheist in religion; but he chooses at present to whore with a Papist.

What bailiff would venture to arrest Mr Steele, now he has the honour to be your representative? and what bailiff ever scrupled it before?

— Or inhibits, let us say, the normal response; since 'defence' suggests that it is the 'victim' whose surprise we should be con-templating, whereas it is our own, whether Swift's butt is Wharton or the atheist or mankind in general. 'But satire, being levelled at all, is never resented for an offence by any, since every individual makes bold to understand it of others, and very wisely removes his par-ticular part of the burden upon the shoulders of the World, which are broad enough and able to bear it.'[1] There is, of course, no contradiction here; a complete statement would be complex. But, actually, the discussion of satire in terms of offence and castigation, victim and castigator, is unprofitable, though the idea of these has

[1] *A Tale of a Tub*: the Preface.

to be taken into account. What we are concerned with (the reminder
is especially opportune) is an arrangement of words on the page
and their effects — the emotions, attitudes and ideas that they
organize.

Our reaction, as Swift says, is not that of the butt or victim;
nevertheless, it necessarily entails some measure of sympathetic
self-projection. We more often, probably, feel the effect of the
words as an intensity in the castigator than as an effect upon a victim:
the dissociation of animus from the usual signs defines for our
contemplation a peculiarly intense contempt or disgust. When, as
sometimes we have to do, we talk in terms of effect on the victim,
then 'surprise' becomes an obviously apt word; he is to be betrayed,
again and again, into an incipient acquiescence:

Sixthly, This would be a great Inducement to Marriage, which all
wise Nations have either encouraged by Rewards, or enforced by
Laws and Penalties. It would increase the Care and Tenderness of
Mothers towards their Children, when they were sure of a Settle-
ment for Life, to the poor Babes, provided in some Sort by the
Publick, to their annual Profit instead of Expence; we should soon
see an honest Emulation among the married Women, *which of them
could bring the fattest Child to the Market.* Men would become as *fond*
of their Wives, during the Time of their Pregnancy, as they are now
of their *Mares* in Foal, their *Cows* in Calf, or *Sows* when they are
ready to farrow, nor offer to beat or kick them (as is too *frequent* a
Practice) for fear of a Miscarriage.

The implication is: 'This, as you so obligingly demonstrate, is the
only kind of argument that appeals to you; here are your actual faith
and morals. How, on consideration, do you like the smell of them?'

But when in reading the *Modest Proposal* we are most engaged,
it is an effect directly upon ourselves that we are most disturbingly
aware of. The dispassionate, matter-of-fact tone induces a feeling
and a motion of assent, while the burden, at the same time, compels
the feelings appropriate to rejection, and in the contrast — the
tension — a remarkably disturbing energy is generated. A sense of
an extraordinary energy is the general effect of Swift's irony. The
intensive means just indicated are reinforced extensively in the
continuous and unpredictable movement of the attack, which turns

this way and that, comes now from one quarter and now from another, inexhaustibly surprising — making again an odd contrast with the sustained and level gravity of the tone. If Swift does for a moment appear to settle down to a formula it is only in order to betray; to induce a trust in the solid ground before opening the pitfall.

His *Tale of a Tub* has little resemblance to his other pieces. It exhibits a vehemence and rapidity of mind, a copiousness of images, a vivacity of diction, such as he afterwards never possessed, or never exerted. It is of a mode so distinct and peculiar, that it must be considered by itself; what is true of that, is not true of anything else he has written.

What Johnson is really testifying to here is the degree in which the *Tale of a Tub* is characteristic and presents the qualities of Swift's genius in concentrated form. 'That he has in his works no meta-phors, as has been said, is not true,' says Johnson a sentence or two later, 'but his few metaphors seem to be received rather by necessity than choice'. This last judgement may at any rate serve to enforce Johnson's earlier observation that in the *Tale of a Tub* Swift's powers function with unusual freedom. For the 'copiousness of images' that Johnson constates is, as the phrase indicates, not a matter of choice but of essential genius. And, as a matter of fact, in this 'copiousness of images' the characteristics that we noted in discussing Swift's pamphleteering irony have their supreme expression.

It is as if the gift applied in *Gulliver* to a very limiting task — directed and confined by a scheme uniting a certain consistency in analogical elaboration with verisimilitude — were here enjoying free play. For the bent expressing itself in this 'copiousness' is clearly fundamental. It shows itself in the spontaneous metaphorical energy of Swift's prose — in the image, action or blow that, leaping out of the prosaic manner, continually surprises and disconcerts the reader: 'such a man, truly wise, creams off Nature, leaving the sour and the dregs for philosophy and reason to lap up'. It appears with as convincing a spontaneity in the sardonic vivacity of comic vision that characterizes the narrative, the presentment of action and actor.

If, then, the continual elaborate play of analogy is a matter of cultivated habit, it is a matter also of cultivated natural bent, a congenial
development. It is a development that would seem to bear a relation
to the Metaphysical fashion in verse (Swift was born in 1667). The
spirit of it is that of a fierce and insolent game, but a game to which
Swift devotes himself with a creative intensity.

And whereas the mind of man, when he gives the spur and bridle
to his thoughts, does never stop, but naturally sallies out into both
extremes of high and low, of good and evil, his first flight of fancy
commonly transports him to ideas of what is most perfect, finished,
and exalted, till, having soared out of his own reach and sight, not
well perceiving how near the frontiers of height and depth border
upon each other, with the same course and wing he falls down plump
into the lowest bottom of things, like one who travels the east into
the west, or like a straight line drawn by its own length into a circle.
Whether a tincture of malice in our natures makes us fond of
furnishing every bright idea with its reverse, or whether reason,
reflecting upon the sum of things, can, like the sun, serve only to
enlighten one half of the globe, leaving the other half by necessity
under shade and darkness, or whether fancy, flying up to the
imagination of what is highest and best, becomes over-short, and
spent, and weary, and suddenly falls, like a dead bird of paradise, to
the ground . . .

One may (without difficulty) resist the temptation to make the
point by saying that this is poetry; one is still tempted to say that
the use to which so exuberant an energy is put is a poet's. 'Exuberant'
seems, no doubt, a paradoxical word to apply to an energy used as
Swift uses his; but the case is essentially one for paradoxical
descriptions.

In his use of negative materials — negative emotions and
attitudes — there is something that it is difficult not to call creative,
though the aim always is destructive. Not all the materials, of
course, are negative: the 'bird of paradise' in the passage above is
alive as well as dead. Effects of this kind, often much more intense,
are characteristic of the *Tale of a Tub*, where surprise and contrast
operate in modes that there is some point in calling poetic. 'The most
heterogeneous ideas are yoked by violence together' — and in the
juxtaposition intensity is generated.

'Paracelsus brought a squadron of stink-pot-flingers from the snowy mountains of Rhætia' — this (which comes actually from *The Battle of the Books*) does not represent what I have in mind; it is at once too simple and too little charged with animus. Swift's intensities are intensities of rejection and negation; his poetic juxtapositions are, characteristically, destructive in intention, and when they most seem creative of energy are most successful in spoiling, reducing, and destroying. Sustained 'copiousness', continually varying, and concentrating surprise in sudden local foci, cannot be represented in short extracts; it must suffice here to say that this kind of thing may be found at a glance on almost any page:

Meantime it is my earnest request that so useful an undertaking may be entered upon (if their Majesties please) with all convenient speed, because I have a strong inclination before I leave the world to taste a blessing which we mysterious writers can seldom reach till we have got into our graves, whether it is that fame, being a fruit grafted on the body, can hardly grow and much less ripen till the stock is in the earth, or whether she be a bird of prey, and is lured among the rest to pursue after the scent of a carcass, or whether she conceives her trumpet sounds best and farthest when she stands on a tomb, by the advantage of a rising ground and the echo of a hollow vault.

It is, of course, possible to adduce Swift's authority for finding that his negations carry with them a complementary positive — an implicit assertion. But (*pace* Charles Whibley) the only thing in the nature of a positive that most readers will find convincingly present is self-assertion — *superbia*. Swift's way of demonstrating his superiority is to destroy, but he takes a positive delight in his power. And that the reader's sense of the negativeness of the *Tale of a Tub* is really qualified comes out when we refer to the Yahoos and the Struldbrugs for a test. The ironic detachment is of such a kind as to reassure us that this savage exhibition is mainly a game, played because it is the insolent pleasure of the author: 'demonstration of superiority' is as good a formula as any for its prevailing spirit. Nevertheless, about a superiority that asserts itself in this way there is something disturbingly odd, and again and again in the *Tale of a Tub* we come on intensities that shift the stress decisively and

K   J.F.L.

remind us how different from Voltaire Swift is, even in his most complacent detachment.

I propose to examine in illustration a passage from the *Digression Concerning the Original, the Use, and Improvement of Madness in a Commonwealth* (i.e. section IX). It will have, in the nature of the case, to be a long one, but since it exemplifies at the same time all Swift's essential characteristics, its length will perhaps be tolerated. I shall break up the passage for convenience of comment, but, except for the omission of nine or ten lines in the second instalment, quotation will be continuous:

For the brain in its natural position and state of serenity disposeth its owner to pass his life in the common forms, without any thought of subduing multitudes to his own power, his reasons, or his visions, and the more he shapes his understanding by the pattern of human learning, the less he is inclined to form parties after his particular notions, because that instructs him in his private infirmities, as well as in the stubborn ignorance of the people. But when a man's fancy gets astride on his reason, when imagination is at cuffs with the senses, and common understanding as well as common sense is kicked out of doors, the first proselyte he makes is himself; and when that is once compassed, the difficulty is not so great in bringing over others, a strong delusion always operating from without as vigorously as from within. For cant and vision are to the ear and the eye the same that tickling is to the touch. Those entertainments and pleasures we most value in life are such as dupe and play the wag with the senses. For if we take an examination of what is generally understood by happiness, as it has respect either to the understanding or to the senses, we shall find all its properties and adjuncts will herd under this short definition, that it is a perpetual possession of being well deceived.

Swift's ant-like energy — the businesslike air, obsessed intentness and unpredictable movement — have already had an effect. We are not, at the end of this instalment, as sure that we know just what his irony is doing as we were at the opening. Satiric criticism of sectarian 'enthusiasm' by reference to the 'common forms' — the Augustan standards — is something that, in Swift, we can take as very seriously meant. But in the incessant patter of the argument we have (helped by such things as, at the end, the suggestion of animus in that oddly concrete 'herd') a sense that direction and tone are changing. Nevertheless, the change of tone for which the next passage is most remarkable comes as a disconcerting surprise:

And first, with relation to the mind or understanding, it is manifest what mighty advantages fiction has over truth, and the reason is just at our elbow; because imagination can build nobler scenes and produce more wonderful revolutions than fortune or Nature will be at the expense to furnish. . . . Again, if we take this definition of happiness and examine it with reference to the senses, it will be acknowledged wonderfully adapt. How sad and insipid do all objects accost us that are not conveyed in the vehicle of delusion! How shrunk is everything as it appears in the glass of Nature, so that if it were not for the assistance of artificial mediums, false lights, refracted angles, varnish, and tinsel, there would be a mighty level in the felicity and enjoyments of mortal men. If this were seriously considered by the world, as I have a certain reason to suspect it hardly will, men would no longer reckon among their high points of wisdom the art of exposing weak sides and publishing infirmities — an employment, in my opinion, neither better nor worse than that of unmasking, which, I think, has never been allowed fair usage, either in the world or the playhouse.

The suggestion of changing direction does not, in the first part of this passage, bring with it anything unsettling: from ridicule of 'enthusiasm' to ridicule of human capacity for self-deception is an easy transition. The reader, as a matter of fact, begins to settle down to the habit, the steady drift of this irony, and is completely unprepared for the sudden change of tone and reversal of attitude in the two sentences beginning: 'How sad and insipid do all objects', etc. Exactly what the change means or is, it is difficult to be certain (and that is of the essence of the effect). But the tone has certainly a personal intensity and the ironic detachment seems suddenly to disappear. It is as if one found Swift in the place — at the point of view — where one expected to find his butt. But the ambiguously mocking sentence with which the paragraph ends reinforces the uncertainty.

The next paragraph keeps the reader for some time in uneasy doubt. The irony has clearly shifted its plane, but in which direction is the attack going to develop? Which, to be safe, must one dissociate oneself from, 'credulity' or 'curiosity'?

In the proportion that credulity is a more peaceful possession of the mind than curiosity, so far preferable is that wisdom which converses about the surface to that pretended philosophy which enters into the depths of things and then comes gravely back with informations and discoveries, that in the inside they are good for nothing. The two senses to which all objects first address themselves are the sight and the touch; these never examine further than the colour, the shape, the size, and whatever other qualities dwell or are drawn by art upon the outward of bodies; and then comes reason officiously, with tools for cutting, and opening, and mangling, and piercing, offering to demonstrate that they are not of the same consistence quite through. Now I take all this to be the last degree of perverting Nature, one of whose eternal laws is to put her best furniture forward. And therefore, in order to save the charges of all such expensive anatomy for the time to come, I do here think fit to inform the reader that in such conclusions as these reason is certainly in the right; and that in most corporeal beings which have fallen under my cognisance the outside hath been infinitely preferable to the in, whereof I have been further convinced from some late experiments. Last week I saw a woman flayed, and you will hardly believe how much it altered her person for the worse.

The peculiar intensity of that last sentence is, in its own way, so decisive that it has for the reader the effect of resolving uncertainty in general. The disturbing force of the sentence is a notable instance of a kind already touched on: repulsion is intensified by the momentary co-presence, induced by the tone, of incipient and incompatible feelings (or motions) of acceptance. And that Swift feels the strongest animus against 'curiosity' is now beyond all doubt. The natural corollary would seem to be that 'credulity', standing ironically for the 'common forms' — the sane, socially sustained, common-sense illusions — is the positive that the reader must associate himself with and rest on for safety. The next half-page steadily and (to all appearances) unequivocally confirms this assumption:

Yesterday I ordered the carcass of a beau to be stripped in my presence, when we were all amazed to find so many unsuspected faults under one suit of clothes. Then I laid open his brain, his heart, and his spleen, but I plainly perceived at every operation that the farther we proceeded, we found the defects increase upon us in number and bulk; from all of which I justly formed this conclusion to myself, that whatever philosopher or projector can find out an art to sodder and patch up the flaws and imperfections of Nature, will deserve much better of mankind and teach us a much more useful science than that, so much in present esteem, of widening and exposing them (like him who held anatomy to be the ultimate end of physic). And he whose fortunes and dispositions have placed him in a convenient station to enjoy the fruits of this noble art, he that can with Epicurus content his ideas with the films and images that fly off upon his senses from the superficies of things, such a man, truly wise, creams off Nature, leaving the sour and the dregs for philosophy and reason to lap up.

Assumption has become habit, and has been so nourished that few readers note anything equivocal to trouble them in that last sentence: the concrete force of 'creams off', 'sour', 'dregs' and 'lap up' seems unmistakably to identify Swift with an intense animus against 'philosophy and reason' (understood implicitly to stand for 'curiosity' the anatomist). The reader's place, of course, is with Swift.

The trap is sprung in the last sentence of the paragraph:

This is the sublime and refined point of felicity called the possession of being well-deceived, the serene peaceful state of being a fool among knaves.

What is left? The next paragraph begins significantly: 'But to return to madness'. This irony may be critical, but 'critical' turns out, in no very long run, to be indistinguishable from 'negative'. The positives disappear. Even when, as in the Houyhnhnms, they seem to be more substantially present, they disappear under our 'curiosity'. The Houyhnhnms, of course, stand for Reason, Truth and Nature, the Augustan positives, and it was in deadly earnest that Swift appealed to these; but how little at best they were anything solidly realized comparison with Pope brings out. Swift did his best for the Houyhnhnms, and they may have all the reason, but the Yahoos have all the life. Gulliver's master 'thought Nature and reason were sufficient guides for a reasonable animal', but nature and reason as Gulliver exhibits them are curiously negative, and the reasonable animals appear to have nothing in them to guide. 'They have no fondness for their colts or foals, but the care they take in educating them proceeds entirely from the dictates of reason.' This freedom from irrational feelings and impulses simplifies other matters too: 'their language doth not abound in variety of words, because their wants and passions are fewer than among us'. And so conversation, in this model society, is simplified: 'nothing passed but what was useful, expressed in the fewest and most significant words . . .'

Courtship, love, presents, jointures, settlements, have no place in their thoughts, or terms whereby to express them in their language. The young couple meet and are joined, merely because it is the determination of their parents and friends: it is what they see done every day, and they look upon it as one of the necessary actions of a reasonable being.

The injunction of 'temperance, industry, exercise, and cleanliness . . . the lessons enjoined to the young ones of both sexes', seems unnecessary; except possibly for exercise, the usefulness of which would not, perhaps, be immediately apparent to the reasonable young.

The clean skin of the Houyhnhnms, in short, is stretched over a void; instincts, emotions and life, which complicate the problem of cleanliness and decency, are left for the Yahoos with the dirt and the indecorum. Reason, truth and nature serve instead; the Houyhnhnms (who scorn metaphysics) find them adequate. Swift too scorned metaphysics, and never found anything better to contend for than a skin, a surface, an outward show. An outward show is, explicitly, all he contends for in the quite unironical *Project for the Advancement of Religion*, and the difference between the reality of religion and the show is, for the author of the *Tale of a Tub*, hardly substantial. Of Jack we are told, 'nor could all the world persuade him, as the common phrase is, to eat his victuals like a Christian'. It is characteristic of Swift that he should put in these terms, showing a complete incapacity even to guess what religious feeling might be, a genuine conviction that Jack should be made to kneel when receiving the Sacrament.

Of the intensity of this conviction there can be no doubt. The Church of England was the established 'common form', and, moreover, was Swift's Church: his insane egotism reinforced the savagery with which he fought to maintain this cover over the void, this decent surface. But what the savagery of the passage from the *Digression* shows mainly is Swift's sense of insecurity and of the undisguisable flimsiness of any surface that offered.

The case, of course, is more complex. In the passage examined the 'surface' becomes, at the most savage moment, a human skin. Swift's negative horror, at its most disturbing, becomes one with his disgust-obsession: he cannot bear to be reminded that under the skin there is blood, mess and entrails; and the skin itself, as we know from *Gulliver*, must not be seen from too close. Hypertrophy of the sense of uncleanness, of the instinct of repulsion, is not uncommon; nor is its association with what accompanies it in Swift. What is uncommon is Swift's genius, and the paradoxical vitality with which this self-defeat of life — life turned against itself — is manifested. In the *Tale of a Tub* the defeat is also a triumph; the genius delights in its mastery, in its power to destroy, and negation is felt as self-assertion. It is only when time has confirmed Swift in disappointment and brought him to more intimate contemplation of physical decay that we get the Yahoos and the Struldbrugs.

Here, well on this side of pathology, literary criticism stops. To attempt encroachments would be absurd, and, even if one were qualified, unprofitable. No doubt psychopathology and medicine have an interesting commentary to offer, but their help is not necessary. Swift's genius belongs to literature, and its appreciation to literary criticism.

We have, then, in his writings probably the most remarkable expression of negative feelings and attitudes that literature can offer — the spectacle of creative powers (the paradoxical description seems right) exhibited consistently in negation and rejection. His verse demands an essay to itself, but fits in readily with what has been said. 'In poetry', he reports of the Houyhnhnms, 'they must be allowed to excel all other mortals; wherein the justness of their similes and the minuteness as well as exactness of their descriptions are, indeed, inimitable. Their verses abound very much in both of these. . . .' The actuality of presentment for which Swift is notable, in prose as well as verse, seems always to owe its convincing 'justness' to, at his least actively malicious, a coldly intense scrutiny, a potentially hostile attention. 'To his domesticks', says Johnson, 'he was naturally rough; and a man of rigorous temper, with that vigilance of minute attention which his works discover, must have been a master that few could bear.' *Directions to Servants* and the *Polite Conversation* enforce obviously the critical bearing and felicity of Johnson's remark.

A great writer — yes; that account still imposes itself as fitting, though his greatness is no matter of moral grandeur or human centrality; our sense of it is merely a sense of great force. And this force, as we feel it, is conditioned by frustration and constriction; the channels of life have been blocked and perverted. That we should be so often invited to regard him as a moralist and an idealist would seem to be mainly a witness to the power of vanity, and the part that vanity can play in literary appreciation: *saeva indignatio* is an indulgence that solicits us all, and the use of literature by readers and critics for the projection of nobly suffering selves is familiar. No doubt, too, it is pleasant to believe that unusual capacity for egotistic animus means unusual distinction of intellect; but, as we have seen, there is no reason to lay stress on intellect in Swift. His work does indeed exhibit an extraordinary play of mind; but it is not great intellectual force that is exhibited in his indifference to the problems raised — in, for instance, the 'Voyage to the Houyhnhnms' — by his use of the concept, or the word, 'Nature'. It is not merely that he had an Augustan contempt for metaphysics; he shared the shallowest complacencies of Augustan common sense: his irony might destroy these, but there is no conscious criticism.

He was, in various ways, curiously unaware — the reverse of clairvoyant. He is distinguished by the intensity of his feelings, not by insight into them, and he certainly does not impress us as a mind in possession of its experience.

We shall not find Swift remarkable for intelligence if we think of Blake.

KATHLEEN M. WILLIAMS

'*Animal Rationis Capax.*' *A study of certain aspects of Swift's imagery*

I

S WIFT has given offence to his readers, from his day to our own, through his habit of referring to the physical qualities — and, since his purpose is usually satiric, often the more unpleasant physical qualities — of human beings or of animals. So frequently does he use allegory or incidental imagery of this nature that one may wonder whether it had some particular significance for him, for it is generally used to convey meaning; even poems like 'The Lady's Dressing Room' or 'Strephon and Chloe' cannot be dismissed as examples of a merely pathological insistence on physical functions. Sometimes, of course, the meaning is quite plain, as in the straight-forward allegory of the spider and the bee in *The Battle of the Books*, where the context makes it clear that the physical habits of the insects are the equivalents of the methods of modern and ancient learning. But even this allegorical use can be misinterpreted in less simple and unambiguous contexts, and some of the attacks made by Swift's contemporaries upon his character and opinions seem to have been based on an over-literal interpretation of those satires in which he presents the moral in terms of the physical. Swift was himself conscious of being misunderstood, as he shows in the Apology for *A Tale of a Tub*, and in certain of the poems. His 'Panegyric on the Reverend Dean Swift', for instance, was written as a parody of the attacks made on him, and in this poem, he tells Lord Bathurst, he attributes to himself qualities in the direct reverse of his character.[1] Here he reproduces the familiar charge of atheism, repeated ever

[1] F. E. Ball (ed.) *The Correspondence of Jonathan Swift* (London, 1910–14), vol. IV, p. 167.

since his exuberant physical satire in *A Tale of a Tub*, and the charge
of malicious misanthropy, supported by a too literal reading of the
fourth book of *Gulliver's Travels*:

> Since you alone of all the Race
> Disclaim the *Human Name*, and Face,
> And with the *Virtues* pant to wear
> (May Heav'n Indulgent hear your Pray'r!)
> The *Proof* of your high *Origine*,
> The *Horse's Countenance Divine*.
>
>   ('A Panegyric on Dean Swift', 171–6)

We are nowadays on our guard against such literalism, and aware
of Swift's frequent use of the human or animal body to represent
something else, as the spider represents modern barbarism, or as the
passionless Houyhnhnms represent, by their un-human shape, their
un-human quality as beings guided by 'reason alone'. But in some
instances our awareness of the allegorical intention is less sharp
because the physical so exactly and inevitably embodies the moral,
and there is no longer any question of an arbitrary choice of
allegorical figures on Swift's part, or of an arbitrary separation of
figure and meaning on ours. The Yahoos, with their brutish parodies
of human appearance and behaviour, do not simply represent, but
are, that part of our nature which arises from the physical; they
embody in visible shape the animal passions of man, and it is because
of this unity of expression and meaning that they achieve such
haunting conviction.

In such cases, it is only too easy to be so overwhelmed by the
physical impact that we look no further; and this is true also of
several of the poems, in which physical characteristics are used in a
different way, not allegorically but as particular illustrations of a
general truth about mankind. Often Swift's intention in such poems
as these is to ridicule the unreal elegance of contemporary poetry of
compliment and love. 'The Progress of Beauty', for example, is a
literary *jeu d'esprit*, an extended conceit of the 'diminishing' kind, in
which the conventional comparison of the chaste lady with the pure
Diana is reversed and as many comparisons as possible are found
between the unchaste Celia and the consequently unchaste moon, for

> 'Twixt earthly Femals and the Moon
> All parallells exactly run.
>> ('The Progress of Beauty', 9–10)

The impulse behind the poem is akin to that of Gay's *The Shepherd's Week*, though Swift's precise reversal of a conventional compliment has the sharper wit; in each case, the charming unreality of a poetic convention is being neatly broken. More typically, ridicule of a literary form is combined with a more explicit disapproval of the attitude of mind behind it, as in 'Strephon and Chloe' and the related 'Cassinus and Peter'. Strephon, the romantic and idealising lover, seeing his Chloe in terms of pastoral love poetry, feels himself too gross to approach 'so high a Nymph'

> For, as he view'd his Person round,
> Meer mortal Flesh was all he found.
>> ('Strephon and Chloe', 75–6)

The result of this refusal to recognise that Chloe, like himself, is 'meer mortal Flesh' is exaggerated disillusionment; like the spiritual intriguers of *A Discourse concerning the Mechanical Operation of the Spirit*, Strephon falls into matter.[1] Chloe too has a lesson to learn, but what is stressed is the absurdity of Strephon's expectations:

> What Edifice can long endure
> Rais'd on a Basis unsecure?
>> ('Strephon and Chloe', 299–300)

The melancholy heroes of 'Cassinus and Peter' and 'The Lady's Dressing Room' go through a similar experience, and are left with their imaginations sickened by the sudden realisation that their lovely Celias or Chloes are, after all, as subject as they are themselves to bodily limitations.

It would seem then that Swift saw, in conventional love poetry and the attitude of mind that it fostered, one aspect of that remoteness from real experience and blindness to inescapable fact which he so constantly attacked. Deception, especially self-deception, is a

---

[1] A. C. Guthkelch and D. Nichol Smith (eds.), *A Tale of a Tub*, 2nd ed. (Oxford, 1958), pp. 259 ff.

recurring theme in his work; in 'Day of Judgment' it is not humanity's wickedness but its blindness of which Jove complains. Other eighteenth-century satirists — Fielding, for example — have concerned themselves with self-deception, but with Swift it takes on a particular and dominating form. Man deceives himself most by not recognising the limitations of his nature, and so setting himself and his fellows an impossible standard of intellect, morality, rarefied beauty. When this standard is not achieved, man can only 'let go his hold' and fall back into disillusionment as Strephon does or as Gulliver does in his indiscriminate loathing for his fellow-men, good and bad alike, after his voyage to the Houyhnhnms. Gulliver and Strephon in their different ways expect more than mankind can give, and in their disappointment lose something of their own proper humanity. Swift frequently comments on man's strange inability, shared with no other animal, to know his own capacities (e.g. 'On Poetry: A Rhapsody', lines 17–20), and the form which this inability most often takes, in *A Tale of a Tub* and *Gulliver's Travels* as well as in poems like 'Strephon and Chloe', is a refusal to realise how narrowly we are bounded by our bodies, by senses and passions and by all the accidents of our physical presence in a material world. To come to terms with the facts of physical existence is essential if we are to live a sensible life in touch with reality, and Swift is continually trying to bring us back to earth. His stress on the physical is part of that attempt.

II

Strephon's is not the only way in which we can deceive ourselves into forgetfulness of our physical predicament. The people of Laputa, in the third book of *Gulliver's Travels*, live significantly above 'the firm earth' on their flying island, and in their case remoteness from reality takes the form of an excessive reliance on abstract speculation and a complete disregard for the body. They have no conception of physical or sensuous beauty, for they see beauty only in mathematical abstractions:

If they would, for example, praise the beauty of a woman, or any other animal, they describe it by rhombs, circles, parallelograms, ellipses, and other geometric terms.

Their music is strange to Gulliver, for the Laputians claim to have their ears adapted to the music of the spheres and so, presumably, to have escaped from the tyranny of the senses. The result is disastrous: suits made according to mathematical formulae do not fit, the agricultural land on Balnibarbi is ruined by theory, and the Laputians are in constant danger of violent death through their lack of any normal contact with physical reality and their scorn for 'the common actions and behaviour of life'. But Gulliver himself, in this book, falls victim to self-deception, though of a more generous and sympathetic kind, when he forgets that in man moral qualities, no less than intellectual ones, can be considered only in relation to the body; that even the longest life will be affected by the senses and passions, by diseases and despairs, and that the noble plans he has laid down for the immortal Struldbrugs can no more be attained by them than by us. Here again, it is by physical description that Swift brings home to us the full pathos of man's predicament as Gulliver feels it when he sees these lost creatures of whom he had hoped so much.

This is a lesson to be repeated, at greater length though not more painfully, in the fourth book; but already in the first and second books a similar impression has been made by a steady accumulation of slight hints and pressures, preparing us gradually for the devastating experiences which we, with the optimistic Gulliver, are to undergo among the Struldbrugs and the Yahoos. Gulliver's adventures in Lilliput and Brobdingnag leave us with the impression that man's intellectual and moral achievement is to some extent dependent on his physical situation. The 'device of relative size' is of course one way of ensuring the detached vision which the satirist requires, but a secondary point is made by Swift's continual stressing of the effect on the mind of such physical accidents as size, and his care in drawing attention to them. For example, he ends the first chapter of the second book, which recounts Gulliver's difficulties in the land of the giants, by remarking that particulars of this nature, 'however they may appear to grovelling minds, yet will certainly help a philosopher to enlarge his thoughts and imagination'.

All the characters in the first and second books are subject to this influence of bodily circumstance on mental qualities. The Lilliputian mind is precise, but petty and limited, just as their vision is: 'Nature hath adapted the eyes of the Lilliputians to all objects proper for their view: they see with great exactness, but at no great distance.'

In their narrow, insect-like way they are well enough adapted to their environment, but the arrival of the giant Gulliver brings out their most cruel and treacherous qualities in their efforts to assert themselves. Gulliver for his part is here at his most attractive, behaving towards the Lilliputians with great generosity and kindness, but this same Gulliver in the second book becomes very like a Lilliputian himself, for in his new situation magnanimity is impossible and he feels a constant need to insist on 'the dignity of human kind' by behaviour which he later recognises as absurd. After being ignominiously carried off by a pet monkey, he tells the king:

if my fears had suffered me to think so far as to make use of my hanger (looking fiercely and clapping my hand upon the hilt as I spoke) when he poked his paw into my chamber, perhaps I should have given him such a wound, as would have made him glad to withdraw it with more haste than he put it in.

This conceited posturing little creature is scarcely recognisable as the kindly and humble Gulliver of the first book, so much has his character changed with his physical situation. In Brobdingnag he is constantly subjected to great dangers, both to life and to character, from causes in themselves trifling, and the resulting sense of the precariousness of human life and virtue is reinforced by his account of an old Brobdingnagian treatise which complains that the giants themselves are 'liable to destruction from every little accident of a tile falling from a house, or a stone cast from the hand of a boy, or of being drowned in a little brook'.

Gulliver's comment suggests that it is useless to draw matter of discontent 'from the quarrels we have with nature', our natural limitations must be accepted.

The same effect is gained by the use of insect and animal comparisons, which are especially frequent in the second book. Gulliver is, to the giants, a 'small dangerous animal', as alarming as a toad or a spider: he fears that the children may torment him as ours do 'sparrows, rabbits, young kittens, and puppy dogs'. At best he is a pet, at worst a representative of a race of 'little odious vermin', and the giants find it difficult to recognise him as a rational creature, hampered as he is by his diminutive size. The most extended use of the insect image occurs in the giant king's description of European houses and cities as 'little nests and burrows'; the king, from his vantage point of size, can see human activities as essentially elaborations of necessities which man shares with the animal creation. This idea, suggested in the second book, is far more powerfully stressed later in the description of the Yahoos.

Throughout the second book the physical or animal aspects of humanity, whether innocent or vicious, are constantly thrust upon our attention. Apart from the animal comparison, and the suggestion that Gulliver and the giants are alike influenced by accidents of physical size and surroundings, there is the deliberate insistence on the enormous bodies of the giants, descriptions of their skin and beards and gestures, and more unpleasantly of the horrors of disease and dirt. These accounts are often related to ourselves by a reference to the magnifying glass which would make the fine skin of English ladies look as coarse as that of the Brobdingnagians, or to the sight of European insects through a microscope. Everywhere in the second book is a sense of overwhelming physical presence, forcing upon us the realisation of man's nature as in part animal; he is the 'animal rationis capax' in whom mind and body must somehow come to terms. The giants seem to have achieved, as well as human beings can, a proper relationship between the two forces in man. Their reasoning powers are used for practical and benevolent purposes, they attempt only what they are capable of, and they allow the claims of feeling as well as of reason in guiding their behaviour. For good and ill, the animal side of man's nature is accepted, with its senses, passions, instinctive affections as well as its brutishness, and the giant king's benevolence has behind it not only reason, but human warmth and sympathy. Even the Gulliver of the fourth book, obsessed as he is by the pure reason of the alien Houyhnhnm race, grudgingly admits that the giants are 'the least corrupted' of the Yahoo peoples — as direct a commendation as Swift's ironical method and habit of mind will allow him to make.[1]

III

Swift's stress on the physical, then, cannot be dismissed as a morbid preoccupation. He has certainly a strong, perhaps an abnormally strong, dislike of what is unclean or diseased, and this gives added emotional force to some of the poems or, more importantly, to the descriptions of the Struldbrugs and the beggars of Brobdingnag; but both these descriptions are there for a clear purpose, they contribute to meaning and are not merely expressions of personal loathing. Swift recognises the strength of the physical, and the consequent danger of ignoring it, and so he brings it to ou notice. What we ignore we cannot control, and some degree of control was, in Swift's view, both possible and necessary.[2] He did not suppose that man was at the mercy of the animal part of his nature, or of the chances of the material world. *A Tale of a Tub* shows his strong disapproval of any philosophical system, ancient or modern, which tended towards materialism or mechanism, and his early poems express more directly the same dislike of the merely physical, the mindless, whether in man or in the cosmos. Like Dryden, he is here concerned with 'the providence of wit', the shaping mind in both spheres, and refuses to see the universe as the result of 'Atoms casually together hurl'd' or, in his own phrase, 'A Crowd of atoms justling in a heap'. Swift shares with Dryden and with Pope the desire for an intelligent purposeful order, and the 'Ode to the Athenian Society' in particular is full of clashing contrasts, mind, life, order, against chaos and death. He is again reminiscent of Dryden and, of course, of earlier poets in his acceptance of the unity and changelessness of truth; addressing eternal truth as 'First of God's darling attributes' he continues:

> Nor does thy essence fix'd depend on giddy circumstance
>   Of time or place,

[1] Temple Scott (ed.), *The Prose Works of Jonathan Swift, D.D.* (London, 1897–1908), vol. VIII, p. 303. Compare Gulliver's comment on the admirable Don Pedro in the previous chapter, that he had 'very good *human* understanding'. The italics are Swift's.

[2] See, for example, the last entry in *Thoughts on Religion*, in T. Scott (ed.), *Prose Works*, vol. III, p. 309.

Two foolish guides in ev'ry sublunary dance.
('Ode to Dr. William Sancroft', 7–9)

But with Swift's love of, and belief in, the single light of truth goes a deepening conviction that man's search for that light is hampered by 'giddy circumstance'. The images in these early poems are often variations on the theme of the one steady light unseen or broken by mortal frailty. In the 'Ode to Dr. William Sancroft' the world is represented, in traditional and perhaps conventional Platonic fashion, as an imperfect copy of the heaven where alone truth resides, but this sense of limitation is given greater urgency by a reference to the inescapable distortions (presented in terms of the 'Cartesian artists') which accompany man's efforts to reach that truth. In fact the old contrast between the world of eternal certainty and that of sublunary change and 'giddy circumstance' is intensified by the disturbing suggestions of contemporary science. Our own limitations are such that it is difficult for us to recognise even the imperfect copies of truth which surround us; we are caught in uncertainties, in 'the fairy-land of dreams'. In the same poem Swift again makes use of an image which blends the old and the new, in his own version of an example which the philosophers of the seventeenth and eighteenth centuries adopted to illustrate the deceptiveness of the senses — the example of the sun which to our sense perceptions appears smaller and closer than it is.[1] Swift uses, instead of the sun, the fixed stars, and thus gives a familiar illustration deeper significance by linking it with an old symbol[2] of certainty and eternal truth:

> Nothing is fix'd that mortals see or know,
> Unless, perhaps, some stars above be so;
> And those, alas, do show
> Like all transcendent excellence below;
> In both, false mediums cheat our sight,
> And far exalted objects lessen by their height.
> ('Ode to Dr. William Sancroft', 143–8)

[1] A familiar variant is the stick which looks crooked when seen through water, an example also known to the ancient sceptics.

[2] e.g. Spenser, *Faerie Queene*, III, i, 57, lines 6–7.

L

The odes, then, suggest an attitude rooted in the conceptions of the Renaissance, but affected by contemporary developments. There is no question that Swift valued the ordering mind which gives meaning to the confusion of existence, but he seems to have been deeply conscious of the difficulties which in man, limited as he is by physical accident, attend the proper functioning of mind. The sense of being cut off from the single truth is deepened by the uncertainties of the age, the arguments of philosophers and the experiments of scientists. The theme of deception, found everywhere in Swift's later work, has its beginnings here. Man is cheated by 'false mediums' and necessarily to some degree in a state of deception.

For the difficulties which Swift saw, there could be only a tentative, partial solution; he is concerned to hold the precarious balance of a traditional view in an increasingly hostile world. To know that truth exists, but to acknowledge the difficulty of attaining it; to weigh the claims of mind and body, of eternal truth and inescapable 'circumstance' was, in this period, to be assailed from all sides. Extreme rationalism and enthusiasm, the determined optimism of Shaftesbury and the cynicism of Mandeville, all these divergent attitudes were in some way upsetting the balance, over-simplifying the complex and difficult reality of life and so moving further into the dangers of deception. Swift's satire, consequently, is of a particularly complicated kind, for the extremes which he attacks are aberrations from a norm, which is in itself a compromise difficult to express in positive terms and existing in avoidance of error, the error of stressing one aspect of the human situation to the detriment of the rest.

It is perhaps this difficulty, as much as personal idiosyncrasy, which produces Swift's noticeable habit of withdrawal, of qualifying an apparent conclusion, sometimes with its opposite. As one of his critics has said, 'simplicity was never one of Swift's failings'. He must refuse to be fully committed to a single point of view, for dogmatism would destroy the exact knife-edge balance. If he seems at times to insist overmuch on the animal nature of man he is careful to indicate why — because extreme rationalism, romantic idealising, and other contemporary errors must be corrected, and the balance restored. Balance and compromise are of the essence of Swift's

satiric method, with the result, of course, that the angry or contemptuous vigour of the attack on extremes makes a stronger
impression than the values so indirectly suggested. His most typical
satire is built up on an elaborate system of checks and counter-
weights, by means of which we may guess at his positive intention
and so by indirections find directions out. Where this intention
can be pinned down, we find it to be generally a careful balancing of
extremes, a realistic compromise. In Swift's thinking it is the
compromise that gives life, for it includes all that is essential and
inescapable, whether good or bad. So in *Gulliver's Travels* he
presents the giants of Brobdingnag, as he had earlier presented the
Anglican Church, as not necessarily the best conceivable, but
certainly the best achievable in the circumstances. The fourth book
of the *Travels* can be seen as a summing-up of the themes of the
preceding books; in its meticulous balance of figures it gives shape
to the more discursive methods of the earlier voyages. The two
extremes are the Yahoos and the Houyhnhnms, each an isolated
part of human nature; the Yahoos are unreasoning, animal, passionate, the Houyhnhnms passionless and therefore able to be guided
entirely by reason. Between these extremes of brute passion and un-
mixed reason stands man, of whose possible excellence the Portu-
guese sea-captain and the giant king (here again pointedly brought
to our notice) are good examples. Admiration of Houyhnhnm
reason is carefully qualified; for example, we can scarcely help
contrasting the warm kindliness of the giant king, Glumdalclitch,
and Don Pedro, to say nothing of the early Gulliver, with the
results of 'reason alone' when the Houyhnhnms are able calmly to
send Gulliver to almost certain death on conclusions reached by the
purest logical reason. Gulliver finds it impossible to refute these
conclusions, but even he uneasily feels that they lack something of
the humane, and that reason might be tempered by pity. He knows
that he, 'a miserable Yahoo', cannot overcome the 'solid reasons' of
the Houyhnhnms, 'yet, in my weak and corrupt judgment, I thought
it might consist with reason to have been less rigorous'. Again,
Gulliver's inhuman and unrealistic attitude to his fellow-men, when
once his imagination is filled with 'the virtues and ideas of those
exalted Houyhnhnms', is emphasised by the Letter from Captain

Gulliver to his Cousin Sympson, which has a heavily ironical tone
hardly to be missed when we are accustomed to Swift's handling of
his various satirical mouthpieces. The giants on the other hand are
like ourselves and unlike the Houyhnhnms. They are creatures
whose reason is easily swayed by passion, but they make good use
of their mixed abilities within those necessary limits. The 'Voyage to
the Houyhnhnms', the most powerful of Swift's presentations of the
nature and habits of man, is arranged in a pattern which itself suggests his characteristic solution of balance and compromise and
gives as do the preceding books a strong sense of our mixed nature
and of the difficulties and rewards it involves. A cancelled passage
from one of Swift's later poems sums up with a similar neatness this
traditional view:

> 'Tis sung Prometheus forming Man
> Thro' all the brutal Species ran,
> Each proper Quality to find
> Adapted to a human Mind,
> A mingled Mass of Good & Bad,
> The worst & best that could be had.
>
> ('On Poetry: A Rhapsody', 21–26)

IV

Swift's fight against deception, then, is conditioned by his feeling
that only by compromise can we find place for the whole of our
complicated reality. The fight is one that must be conducted with
the greatest care, for some of our aberrations from truth and reason
are part of our very nature and condition, and we must not strip
away too much in our search. There are matters in which our
passions inevitably control our reason,[1] and even self-love, love of
fame, and such irrational affections, can be an incitement to virtue.[2]
So Jack in *A Tale of a Tub* strips away some of the necessary fabric
of the Church in his enthusiastic reformation, and Swift emphasises
the point in his 'Apology', where he tells us that he has 'endeavour'd
to Strip himself of as many real Prejudices as he could: I say real

---

[1] *Thoughts on Religion*, in T. Scott (ed.), *Prose Works*, vol. III, p. 309.
[2] *Thoughts on Various Subjects*, in T. Scott (ed.), *Prose Works*, vol. I,
p. 278.

ones, because under the Notion of Prejudices he knew to what dangerous Heights some Men have proceeded'.

'Prejudices', in the usual philosophical terminology of the day, meant those notions which are based on 'opinion'; that is, the mistaken impressions we pick up in the haphazard irrational business of daily life — in 'giddy circumstance' — as opposed to the conceptions of 'right ratiocination'.[1] Malebranche, whose work Swift possessed, makes more explicit than Hobbes the connection between prejudices and the impressions made upon us by our senses, passions, and instincts; all that comes to us through the body — 'par le corps, ou à l'occasion du corps' — obscures the eternal truth of reason.

Le principe général de nos préjugés c'est que nous ne distinguons pas entre *connaître* et *sentir*, et qu'au lieu de juger des choses par les *idées* qui les représentent, nous en jugeons par les *sentiments* que nous en avons.[2]

The *Discourse concerning the Mechanical Operation of the Spirit* makes a similar distinction between mind and body, but Swift considers that these prejudices must be handled with the greatest circumspection, since what at first appears to be prejudice, hiding the fabric of truth, may prove to be removable only at the cost of the fabric itself. We may indeed come to regard our proper humane feelings as prejudice, as in Gulliver's comment on the 'prejudices' shown by the King of Brobdingnag's horror at the effects of gunpowder.[3] Again: 'Some men, under the notion of weeding out prejudices eradicate virtue, honesty, and religion.'[4]

The metaphor of weeding out, or stripping away, those things that hide the truth is a favourite one in Swift's attacks on deception found in the early poems and developed later. It takes several forms, but frequently the image is that of the human body disguised by

---

[1] Hobbes, *Human Nature*, ch. x, para. 8.

[2] 'Entretiens sur la Métaphysique', Cinquième Entretien, xiii. The sharp distinction between mind and bodily 'prejudice' is stressed throughout the 5th, 6th and 7th dialogues.

[3] T. Scott (ed.), *Prose Works*, vol. viii, p. 138.

[4] *Thoughts on Various Subjects*, in T. Scott (ed.), *Prose Works*, vol. i, p. 275.

elaborate clothes or by paint. In the 'Ode to the Athenian Society' philosophy is represented as a woman whose beauty, obscured by the fashions of 'Modern Pedantry', is now being restored to its former simplicity, and in the 'Ode to Dr. William Sancroft' a similar metaphor is applied to religion, but here with a further turn to the thought: the 'wild reformers' have contrived

> To tear Religion's lovely face;
> Strip her of ev'ry ornament and grace,
> In striving to wash off th' imaginary paint.
> ('Ode to Dr. William Sancroft', 248–50)

Here we approach the theme of *A Tale of a Tub*: even in striving to eradicate prejudices, we are still in their power, for the paint we see may be imaginary. The metaphor of the human body was developed by Swift into an image of considerable subtlety and complexity of suggestion, for it could indicate at one and the same time the necessity and the hazards of the search for truth. We may go beyond removing the clothes and the paint to rend the flesh itself. The modern author whose identity Swift adopts in *A Tale of a Tub* writes, in *A Digression in the Modern Kind*:

To this End, I have some Time since, with a World of Pains and Art, dissected the Carcass of Humane Nature, and read many useful Lectures upon the several Parts, both Containing and Contained: till at last it smelt so strong, I could preserve it no longer. Upon which, I have been at a great Expence to fit up all the Bones with exact Contexture, and in due Symmetry; so that I am ready to shew a very compleat Anatomy thereof to all curious Gentlemen and others.

This 'modern' philosopher has so anatomised human nature that everything has been stripped away but the skeleton; his attempt to reach the truth has ended in the substitution of dead bones for the flesh and blood of reality. Similarly the famous metaphor of the flayed woman is placed near the close of a long passage which brilliantly sets against one another 'that Wisdom, which converses about the Surface' and 'that pretended Philosophy which enters into the Depth of things'. Here Swift's irony is at its most dazzling, and his characteristic method, of suddenly undermining previous praise or blame, at its most agile. A delicate balance is maintained between the pleasures of the deluding senses and the misery of reason's 'opening, and mangling, and piercing'. Of course it is reason that is preferred: nature is not to be known only by the 'false Lights, refracted, Angles, Varnish, and Tinsel' which make up the happiness of the senses, but by the mind which investigates and interprets. It is the task of the imagery, however, to supply a counterweight: reason must observe its proper limits and not lay bare what nature herself has hidden:

Last week I saw a woman flay'd, and you will hardly believe, how much it altered her Person for the worse.

Throughout *A Tale of a Tub* and *A Discourse concerning the Mechanical Operation of the Spirit* Swift uses his imagery of the human body with the greatest conciseness and economy. By means of it he can sum up his theme of the intermingling of man's intellectual powers and spiritual aspirations with his senses and passions, and can suggest that though reason must be pre-eminent the search for eternal and rational truth must not involve too radical a weeding-out of the other parts of man's nature. In this way Swift's two important themes, the nature of deceit and the nature of man, can be brought together and a vital compromise put forward. Whether in the form of single images or in the extended symbols of the Brobdingnagians or the Yahoos, it is in terms of the human body that Swift communicates most powerfully with his readers, because these are the terms in which his ideas can be most fully explored and conveyed.

J. C. BECKETT

Swift as an Ecclesiastical Statesman

THE sincerity of Swift's religion has been a matter of controversy from his own day to ours. The gibe of his contemporary, Smedley, that he

> ... might a bishop be in time
> Did he believe in God

echoes the tradition that it was Queen Anne's pious horror of *A Tale of a Tub* which prevented Swift's elevation to the episcopal bench. This interpretation of Swift's religious position has been elaborated by later writers and as elaborately confuted. But final decision in such a dispute is impossible. The evidence of what a man really believed is bound to be of such a nature that our interpretation of it will depend upon our estimate of the man himself; and in fact all the writers on Swift's personal religion have, consciously, or unconsciously, approached the subject with their minds made up.[1]

This essay is not an attempt to refight an old battle with modern weapons. But there is an aspect of Swift's religious life which (so

---

[1] Professor C. Looten (*La Pensée religieuse de Swift et ses antinomies*, Lille, Facultés catholiques, 1935) presents a detailed and carefully written study of Swift's religion, based on his career, his books, and his correspondence. But he puts Swift in the dock and then searches (not very sympathetically) for evidence for the defence; his knowledge of English Church history is inadequate, so that he treats Swift in isolation; and he has no sense of humour. Professor G. V. Jourdan ('The Religion of Dean Swift' in *Church Quarterly Review*, June–Sept. 1938) and Dr. R. Wyse Jackson (*Jonathan Swift: Dean and Pastor*, S.P.C.K., 1939) attempt, from different viewpoints, to refute Professor Looten's conclusions (for a review of these two, see *I.H.S.* vol. II (March 1940) pp. 97–99). E. Pons (*Swift: les années de jeunesse et le Conte du Tonneau*, Strasbourg, 1925) is only slightly concerned with the question of Swift's personal religion. Unlike Professor Looten he does not find the teaching of the *Tale of a Tub* irreconcilable with Swift's position as an Anglican priest.

far as the present writer is aware) has never been clearly set out, and which, while it may serve to illuminate his personal religious convictions, can be treated independently of them. As an Anglican priest Swift was not only a minister of religion, he was also an official of a large and influential organisation. How did Swift regard this organisation? What part did he take in its life? What connections can be traced between his life as a churchman and his life as a politician and a man of letters? These are some of the questions to which an answer must now be attempted.[1]

Swift took orders in 1694, but a very brief experience of parochial life in the north of Ireland sent him back to Moor Park. He still had literary ambitions; he might hope to combine his clerical calling with some political or diplomatic office; Temple or some other patron might provide for him in England.[2] The death of Temple in 1699 and Swift's acceptance of the vicarage of Laracor, in the diocese of Meath, early in the following year[3] may be taken to mark the temporary abandonment of any scheme of promotion outside the regular routine of Church preferment. Such preferment, if it was to equal Swift's hopes and his value of himself, could come only from the government. The circumstances of the time compelled him to look to the favour of a political party and, in the uneasy coalition which ruled England during the early years of Queen Anne, Swift's chief friends were the Whigs, to whom his *Discourse of the Contests and Dissensions between the Nobles and the Commons in Athens and Rome* (published in 1701) had commended him.[4] But though the

[1] Ricardo Quintana (*The Mind and Art of Jonathan Swift*, London and New York, 1936) gives a useful commentary on Swift's theory of the relations of Church and State, but he does not pay sufficient attention to unfinished *Remarks* on Tindal's *Right of the Christian Church*, and his interpretation of Anglican political theory of the period, though fuller than Professor Looten's, is still inadequate. The introduction to the second volume of *The Prose Works of Jonathan Swift* (ed. Herbert Davis, Oxford, 1939) deals with Swift's writings on the Church and with the connection between his politics and his religion; it is valuable as far as it goes, but its purpose is strictly limited.

[2] F. E. Ball (ed.), *The Correspondence of Jonathan Swift* (London, 1910–1914), vol. I, Introduction, pp. xxi, xxxv (by J. H. Bernard).

[3] Ball (ed.), *Correspondence*, vol. I, p. 32 n.

[4] Ball (ed.), *Correspondence*, vol. I, p. 39 n.

Whigs were in office they were not in power,[1] and after a visit to England in 1703–4 Swift remained in Ireland for three and a half years.[2] His return to London at the end of 1707, primarily on a mission for the Irish Church, was probably connected with the change in the balance of parties, which in the following year brought the Whigs completely into power.[3]

It was now that Swift might hope to gain something from his friendship with Whig leaders. But that prospect made it necessary for him to consider carefully his attitude to Whig policy. Promotion would come only at the price of political support. Swift wanted to make it clear that the extent of that support must be determined by a stronger duty to the Church. To set out the limits within which he was willing to serve a party cause, and perhaps also to warn his Whig friends of the danger of arousing church opposition, he published, in 1708, *The Sentiments of a Church of England Man with Respect to Religion and Government*.[4] In this we have the basic expression of Swift's views on the relations of Church and State, but it must be read in relation to its context and it must be supplemented from his other writings. Its main purpose, like that of all Swift's works, was an immediate one. As Sir Herbert Read says: 'All that Swift wrote is empirical, experimental, *actuel*. It is impossible to detach it from circumstances; we must consider each book or pamphlet in relation to its political intention.'[5] Swift contended that though there were two political parties there was only one Church, which was not tied to either of them.[6] She had certain political

---

[1] K. Feiling, *History of the Tory Party, 1640–1714* (Oxford, 1951), pp. 360 ff.

[2] R. Quintana, *Mind and Art of Jonathan Swift*, p. 113.

[3] Swift to King, 6 Dec. 1707 (Ball (ed.), *Correspondence*, vol. I, pp. 60–63). For details of Swift's mission see below, p. 156.

[4] Herbert Davis (ed.), *The Prose Works of Jonathan Swift* (Oxford, 1939–), vol. II, Introduction, p. xvi.

[5] *Collected Essays in Literary Criticism* (London, 1938), p. 196.

[6] 'A church of England man may with prudence and a good conscience, approve the professed principles of one party more than the other, according as he thinks they best promote the good of church and state.' (*The Sentiments of a Church of England Man*, in Davis (ed.), *Prose Works*, vol. II, p. 24.)

principles of her own, by which to test competing policies, and on one of the most urgent questions of the day — the treatment of Protestant Dissenters — *The Sentiments of a Church of England Man* gives a clear and consistent opinion. In doing this it was impossible to avoid raising the fundamental question of the relations of Church and State; and though it is pretty clear that Swift disliked arguing about abstract principles, he did not hesitate to answer the question as far as the occasion required. It is because this answer was not the main purpose of the pamphlet, and because, in giving it, Swift had in mind that he was writing an eirenicon and not a challenge, that we must expand and supplement the scheme of Church–State relationship here expressed.

Such an investigation is the more necessary because some of the statements in *The Sentiments of a Church of England Man*, taken in isolation, can be easily misunderstood. Thus, Professor Looten writes, 'Sa volonté de conjuguer les deux pouvoirs est si arêtée que jamais pour légitimer l'existence et la mission de l'église il n'invoque son droit divin ou son origine surnaturelle. On dirait qu'il ne la conçoit qu'en marge et en fonction de l'état.'[1] Not only is the general trend of this contrary to explicit statements in the *Remarks* upon Tindal's *Rights of the Christian Church*, but the last sentence attributes to Swift a conception of the Church and State directly contrary to that which he laboured to establish. For Swift held clearly, though carefully, the doctrine that the Church's power was derived directly from Christ and his Apostles.[2] But he made no attempt to consider this in its wider applications. He barely mentions the possible state of affairs under a heathen government. He thinks it necessary to enter some defence of the conception of the

---

[1] C. Looten, *La Pensée religieuse de Swift*, p. 121.

[2] 'But as the supreme power can certainly do ten thousand things more than it ought, so there are several things which some people may think it can do, although it really cannot . . . because the law of God [i.e. of the Church] hath otherwise decreed; which law, although a nation may refuse to receive it, cannot alter in its own nature. But the Church of England is no creature of the civil power, either as to its polity or its doctrines. The fundamentals of both were deduced from Christ and his apostles . . .' (*Remarks*, in Davis (ed.), *Prose Works*, vol. II, pp. 75, 79.)

Church as a world-wide corporation.[1] He is satisfied to deal with the particular case immediately present — that of the Church of England.

The line of argument used is significant. Swift was, and always remained, essentially a Whig in politics, tied to the principles of the revolution and opposed to absolute rule, either by one or by many.[2] But the traditional 'high church' scheme did not fit easily into this pattern. That scheme had developed during the seventeenth century. By the end of Elizabeth's reign the Church of England was free from the immediate danger of a papal restoration imposed from without; but papal propaganda in England continued, and the pressure of the Puritans, whether avowed Dissenters or nominally within the Church, grew stronger. Against this double attack it was necessary to build up a moral defence not only of doctrine, but also, and urgently, of jurisdiction. A solid basis had been laid in Hooker's *Laws of Ecclesiastical Polity*, but his arguments required expansion and particular application. The great problem was to show on what authority the jurisdiction of the Church rested. The circumstances of the English Reformation, the Act of Supremacy, and the thirty-seventh Article of Religion all pointed to the crown; but any doctrine of royal supremacy required to be justified, not only against Rome but against Geneva, both ever ready to detect and condemn Erastianism. To avoid secularising the Church the Anglican theologians had to sanctify the monarchy and to claim that the Church and the State were but different aspects of the same commonwealth. To maintain such a position after the Restoration, when the Dissenters formed a considerable section of the population, was difficult. The 1689 revolution made it impossible: the Church had to choose between the king and the nation. In this dilemma, the Non-jurors, who stuck to the letter of their theory,

[1] 'Here we must show the necessity of the Church being a corporation all over the world: to avoid heresies and preserve fundamentals, and hinder corrupting of scripture, etc.' (*Remarks*, in Davis (ed.), *Prose Works*, vol. II, p. 105.)

[2] 'As to the abdication of King James. . . . I think a man may observe every article of the English Church without being in much pain about it.' (*The Sentiments of a Church of England Man*, in Davis (ed.), *Prose Works*, vol. II, p. 29.)

were compelled to experience its logical result in their extrusion from their benefices; for Church and nation could not represent the same commonwealth if they had different kings. Not unnaturally, the Non-jurors saw in this exercise of state authority that Erastianism round which they and their predecessors had been steering so careful a course for over a century.[1]

The witness of the Non-jurors made it necessary for those churchmen who had accepted the revolution to reconsider the basis of the Church's authority. It was the need to do this which sharpened the demand that Convocation should be allowed to function.[2] Bishop King of Derry, who wanted the Irish Church to enjoy the same privileges as the English, put the matter succinctly:[3]

> The first article in magna carta is that the church of England shall be free, and that freedom can consist in nothing but in choosing the ecclesiastical constitutions by which she is governed in convocations. . . . If the church once come to have her constitutions altered without convocations, which are her legal representatives, she is no more free but an absolute slave, and our religion would in earnest be what the papists call it, a parliamentary religion.

But the meeting of Convocation could not settle the question, for it met by royal authority, and could transact business only by royal licence. Yet the 1689 revolution had shown that if the Church possessed any divine right it must be separable from that of hereditary monarchy; or else the Non-jurors were, as they claimed to be, the true Church of England. Swift's common sense revolted from a conclusion which would have branded the bulk of the nation

---

[1] The more moderate Non-jurors came to regard the dispute as one over the authority of the Church rather than over divine right. 'As for the schism, I believe I can propose a way to end it, but it is not practicable till the convocation meets, and then, if the face of affairs alter not, I make no question but erastianism will be condemned, which by some of us has been proposed as a means of reunion.' Bishop Ken to Bishop Lloyd, 7 April 1702 (E. H. Plumptre, *Life of Thomas Ken* (1888), vol. II, p. 122).

[2] [F. Atterbury], *A Letter to a Convocation Man, 1697*; H. Beeching, *Francis Atterbury* (London, 1909), pp. 53 ff.

[3] Bishop King to Southwell, 21 Dec. 1697 (T.C.D., MS.N3. 1, p. 149).

as schismatics.[1] But he was equally unwilling to accept the opposite
extreme, that the Church had no divine right at all. His task was to
reconcile such a divine right in the Church with his own Whig
principles in politics. As in his political theory he goes back to a
social contract by which power passed from the many to the few, so
here he goes back to the period at which the State embraced
Christianity. Characteristically, he is concerned not with individual
conversions, but with an official transaction between the rulers of the
State and the rulers of the Church, by which the former received the
doctrines and practices of the Church 'as a divine law . . . and consequently, what they could not justly alter, any more than the
common laws of nature'.[2] Clearly, the relations of Church and State
in England were based on such a contract. The supreme power
(which for Swift was the Legislature)[3] was morally bound to support
the doctrine and discipline of the Church; but this doctrine and
discipline, being part of the law of God, were, unlike the law of the
State, immutable.

Up to this point, Swift's argument seems to make directly for that
kind of ecclesiastical independence, that *imperium in imperio*, which
has provided one of the recurring problems of political life for
many centuries. Of one obvious solution, later epitomised in the
phrase 'a free Church in a free State', he speaks with contempt; the
idea of a clergy supported by the alms of the people was repugnant
to him.[4] On the other hand, he could not logically quarrel with the
existing constitution of the Established Church in England and
Ireland, to the defence of which all his efforts were directed. He
finds a way out of the difficulty by distinguishing between the
Church's power, and liberty to use that power. The former comes

[1] The attempt to continue the schism by consecrating new non-juring
bishops aroused Swift's contempt, '. . . a parcel of obscure zealots in
London, who, as we hear, are setting up a new church of England by
themselves' (Swift to Archbishop King, 13 Nov. 1716, in Ball (ed.),
Correspondence, vol. II, p. 337).

[2] *Remarks* on Tindal's *Rights of the Christian Church*, in Davis (ed.),
Prose Works, vol. II, p. 77.

[3] *Sentiments of a Church of England Man*, in Davis (ed.), *Prose Works*,
vol. II, p. 23.

[4] *Remarks*, in Davis (ed.), *Prose Works*, vol. II, p. 96.

directly from God, the latter from the civil authority.

And, therefore, although the supreme power can hinder the clergy or church from making any new canons, or executing the old; from consecrating bishops, or refusing those they do consecrate; or, in short, from performing any ecclesiastical office, as they may from eating, drinking, and sleeping; yet they cannot themselves perform those offices, which are assigned to the clergy by our saviour and his apostles; or, if they do, it is not according to the divine institution, and consequently null and void.[1]

This theory of Church–State relationship was designed to fit existing circumstances, to salve the divine right of the Church, without challenging too openly the power of the state or reflecting upon the principles of the 1689 revolution. To adapt the phrase which Swift applied to his *Modest Proposal*, it was 'calculated' for England and Ireland in the reign of Queen Anne. The expression of it in *The Sentiments of a Church of England Man* is modified by the immediate political problem, but the enlargements in Swift's other

[1] *Remarks*, in Davis (ed.), *Prose Works*, vol. II, p. 77. Swift's younger contemporary, Charles Wheatley (1686–1742), puts forward the complementary view that the State legislates in ecclesiastical matters only to give civil force to the decisions of the Church: 'For it appears by the proceedings observed in the reformation of the service of the church, that this reformation was regularly made by the bishops and clergy in their provincial synods; the king and parliament only establishing by the civil sanction what was there done by ecclesiastical authority.' 'Our liturgy was therefore first established by the convocations or provincial synods of the realm, and thereby became obligatory *in foro conscientiae*; and was then confirmed and ratified by the supreme magistrate in parliament, and so also became obligatory *in foro civili*. It has therefore all authority, ecclesiastical and civil.' Wheatley goes on to make the logical deduction that no Act of Parliament can alter ecclesiastical authority. Dissenters may be tolerated by civil law; but they remain schismatics 'and so guilty of a damnable sin, which no toleration granted by the civil magistrate can authorise or justify' (*A Rational Illustration of the Book of Common Prayer* (ed. 1880), pp. 30–31, 33). For further elaboration of this point of view see G. W. O. Addleshaw, *The High Church Tradition* (London, 1941), pp. 36–38. Swift would probably have accepted Wheatley's historical statement. But his common sense showed him that toleration of existing sects was inevitable. (*Sentiments of a Church of England Man*, in Davis (ed.), *Prose Works*, vol. II, p. 6.)

writings on the church, in the *Examiner*, and in his correspondence, follow logically from the principles there laid down.

One part of Swift's theorizing on Church and State was of immediate practical importance. He agreed with Hobbes that there must be an absolute authority in the State; but unlike Hobbes he placed this absolute authority in the legislature and not in the executive part of the government.[1] The legislature could do no wrong. It was by its authority that the Church of England was established[2] and the legislature could at will establish paganism or popery or Presbyterianism instead. The safety of the church, therefore, required that her enemies should be excluded from the legislature and from all places of political influence. This was the essential basis of Swift's opposition to the Protestant Dissenters, both in England and in Ireland. He was ready to ridicule their religious peculiarities, but his arguments against them did not arise from a theological horror of schism. He had no objection to toleration, provided the Dissenters were not left free to proselytise or to acquire political power.[3] It is significant that he was much less alarmed about possible danger from the Roman Catholics, even in Ireland where they formed the vast majority of the population, because their political power was so completely gone that they could not be a danger to the Established Church.[4]

Swift's determination to exclude Protestant Dissenters from political influence brought him into opposition with the Whigs almost as soon as they had secured control of the government. The great grievance of the Dissenters was the sacramental test, and they looked to their political allies to remove it. But the test had stood in

[1] Hobbes 'perpetually confounds the executive with the legislative power'. (*Sentiments of a Church of England Man*, in Davis (ed.), *Prose Works*, vol. II, p. 16.)

[2] But Swift carefully distinguishes between 'established' and 'founded': '. . . what is contained in the idea of established? Surely not existence. Doth establishment give being to a thing?' (*Remarks*, in Davis (ed.), *Prose Works*, vol. II, p. 78).

[3] *Sentiments of a Church of England Man*, in Davis (ed.), *Prose Works*, vol. II, p. 6.

[4] *A Letter from a Member of the House of Commons in Ireland . . . concerning the Sacramental Test*, in Davis (ed.), *Prose Works*, vol. II, p. 120.

England since 1673 and was regarded by the Church party as their main security; a direct attack upon it would be unpopular and probably unsuccessful. In the meantime, its full rigour was somewhat modified by the practice of occasional conformity, which the Tories had vainly attempted to suppress in 1703. But in Ireland the sacramental test was a new thing, imposed for the first time in 1704 by the action of the English government; and though the Church party had welcomed it as a protection against the powerful Presbyterian population in Ulster, the latter were naturally hopeful that a Whig ministry would remove it. Swift, like many other churchmen, was convinced that the attack upon the sacramental test in Ireland would be merely a preparation for a similar attack in England.[1]

As early as 1707 there had been some sort of move in the Irish Commons to repeal the test, a move which had been inspired, or at least encouraged, by the English ministry. It met with strong opposition, and Archbishop King's account shows how readily the government gave in for the sake of securing peace: 'You can hardly imagine what a healing measure this has proved, and how far it has prevailed to oblige those that were in great animosities against one another, to comply in all reasonable proposals; whereas, if the repeal of the test had been insisted on, it would have broken all in pieces, and made them form parties on principles which before were founded only on personal quarrels.'[2] In the following year the situation was different. The English government was now clearly committed to an effort at repealing the test in Ireland, even before the choice of Lord Wharton as the new lord-lieutenant advertised the fact to the world.[3] All this was matter of the greatest importance

---

[1] 'I hope you are prepared to take off the sacramental test, because that will be a means to have it taken off here among us', Swift to Archbishop King, London, 30 Nov. 1708 (Ball (ed.), *Correspondence*, vol. I, pp. 126–7). According to Swift, the English Dissenters had subscribed £100,000 to promote the repeal of the test in Ireland. For the imposition of the sacramental test in Ireland and the early attempts to secure its repeal, see J. C. Beckett, *Protestant Dissent in Ireland*, 1687–1750 (London, 1948), pp. 40 ff.

[2] Archbishop King to Annesley, 16 Aug. 1707 (R. Mant, *History of the Church of Ireland* (1840), vol. II, p. 186).

[3] *Liber munerum public Hiberniae*, part II, p. 10; Archbishop King to Southwell, 16 Feb. 1709 (King correspondence, T.C.D. transcript).

to Swift. As a Whig, he might now hope to secure preferment, but he could not conceal his anxiety about the ministry's ecclesiastical policy; especially since he was a sort of ambassador from the Irish Church and so must be drawn into the government's policy for Ireland. In the opening paragraph of *The Sentiments of a Church of England Man* he had expressed his attitude to party loyalty: 'A wise and a good man may indeed be sometimes induced to comply with a number, whose opinion he generally approves, although it be perhaps against his own. But this liberty should be made use of upon very few occasions, and those of small importance, and then only with a view of bringing over his own side another time to something of greater and more public moment.'[1] But the first occasion on which he had to test the strength of his own influence with the Whig leaders provided a disappointment. Swift's journey to England in 1707 had been undertaken with the approval of Archbishop King of Dublin for the purpose of soliciting for the Irish Church a grant of the first fruits and twentieth parts similar to the grant made by the Queen to the English Church some years earlier.[2] He was coldly received by the treasurer (Godolphin), put off with vague assurances, puzzled by obscure hints, and finally made to understand that the government was prepared to make the grant provided the Irish Church would accept the removal of the sacramental test.[3]

Once more Swift felt it necessary to make his position clear and to warn his Whig friends of the dangers involved in their ecclesiastical policy. The *Letter from a Member of Parliament in Ireland to a Member of Parliament in England concerning the Sacramental Test* was published in December 1708, shortly after Wharton's appointment as lord-lieutenant.[4] It is a natural corollary to *The Sentiments of a Church of England Man*, for the scheme of Church–State relationship described in the latter would be valid only so long as

[1] *Sentiments of a Church of England Man*, in Davis (ed.), *Prose Works*, vol. II, p. 1.

[2] 2 & 3 Anne, c. 11 (Queen Anne's Bounty Act, 1703).

[3] Swift to Archbishop King, 1 Jan. 1708, 10 June 1708, 28 Aug. 1708 (Ball (ed.), *Correspondence*, vol. I, pp. 67, 92–93, 105).

[4] Davis (ed.), *Prose Works*, vol. II, p. 109. The date on the title-page is 1709, but it was published in Dec. 1708 (Swift to Archbishop King, 6 Jan. 1709 (Ball (ed.), *Correspondence*, vol. I, p. 130 and n.).

establishment was a reality. The core of the argument in the *Letter concerning the Sacramental Test* is that the removal of the test would virtually establish Presbyterianism in Ireland as a rival Church; and there is a clear hint that the government has in mind a similar policy for England.[1] Another pamphlet, the *Letter to a Member of Parliament in Ireland upon the choosing a New Speaker there*,[2] also published in 1708, went over much the same ground. But already the Whigs were beginning to waver in their determination. When Swift first informed Archbishop King of the appointment of Wharton as lord-lieutenant, he added a character of the man who was generally expected to go as his secretary: 'One, Mr Shute ... a young man, but reckoned the shrewdest head in Europe; and the person in whom the presbyterians chiefly confide ... As to his principles, he is truly a moderate man, frequenting the church and the meeting indifferently.'[3] But before Wharton set out, a change in the government's attitude was reflected in the substitution of Addison for Shute.

Mr. Addison, who goes over as first secretary, is a most excellent person; and being my most intimate friend, I shall use all my credit to set him right in his notions of persons and things. I spoke to him with great plainness upon the subject of the test; and he says he is confident my Lord Wharton will not attempt it, if he finds the bent of the nation against it.[4]

And the archbishop himself soon received similar assurances from the lord-lieutenant's friends of his intention to keep the 'government of state and church on the same foot as they are'.[5] So although Wharton repeatedly urged upon the Irish Parliament the need for

[1] 'We at this distance, who see nothing of the springs of action, are forced by mere conjecture to assign two reasons for your desiring us to repeal the sacramental test. One is, because you are said to imagine it will be a step towards the like good work in England.' (*Letter concerning the Sacramental Test*, in Davis (ed.), *Prose Works*, vol. II, p. 113.)

[2] Davis (ed.), *Prose Works*, vol. II, p. 127.

[3] Swift to Archbishop King, 30 Nov. 1708 (Ball (ed.), *Correspondence*, vol. I, pp. 127–8).

[4] Swift to Archbishop King 6 Jan. 1709 (Ball (ed.), *Correspondence*, vol. I, p. 131).

[5] Archbishop King to Southwell, 16 Feb. 1709 (King corr., T.C.D., transcript).

unity among Protestants, he made no open attack upon the sacramental test.[1] By the end of 1710 the Tories were once more in
power in England and Wharton had been replaced by Ormonde. For
the next four years the Dissenters, both in England and in Ireland,
were on the defensive.

Swift had maintained in *The Sentiments of a Church of England
Man* that he was in favour of toleration for existing sects, provided
that they were excluded from political power and prevented from
proselytising; and he seems to have himself acted on this principle.
He took no part in the repressive measures against the Protestant
Dissenters which were planned and carried out during the last years
of Queen Anne. In Ireland, the great aim of the high church party,
the suspension of the *regium donum* of £1200 a year paid to the
Ulster Presbyterians, was achieved in 1714.[2] In England, controversy centred round the occasional conformity Bill, which eventually
became law in 1711. On the *regium donum* question Swift says
nothing; and though he mentions the occasional conformity Bill
from time to time, and must certainly have known what was going
on, there is nothing to show that he supported it.[3] He may have been
partly influenced by the recollection of his noncommittal attitude to
the same question in 1703; but it is more reasonable to see here a
logical carrying out of the principles laid down in *The Sentiments of
a Church of England Man*.[4] His attitude to the Dissenters was not an
aggressive one, and while their expansion seemed to be effectively

[1] *Commons' jn. Ire.*, vol. III, pp. 414–15, 502, 514, 507–8.
[2] *Records of the General Synod of Ulster* (Belfast, 1890–8), vol. I, pp. 335,
341.
[3] 15 Dec., 22 Dec. 1711 (Harold Williams (ed.), *Journal to Stella*
(Oxford, 1948), vol. II, pp. 438, 443–4); Swift to Bishop Stearne, 29 Dec.
1711; Swift to Archbishop King, 8 Jan. 1712 (Ball (ed.), *Correspondence*,
vol. I, pp. 310, 314). In these letters Swift shows no more than a casual
interest. He may have assisted Harley in replying to the complaints of a
dissenting minister, after the Bill had passed (Ball (ed.), *Correspondence*,
vol. I, app. VII, pp. 390–2).
[4] In 1703 Swift professed to have been persuaded by Peterborough,
Somers, and Bishop Burnet that the Bill against occasional conformity
could be rejected without danger to the Church. But although he prepared
a pamphlet against it, he did not publish it. (Swift to Wm. Tisdall, 16 Dec.
1703, 3 Feb. 1704, in Ball (ed.), *Correspondence*, vol. I, pp. 38–39, 44.)

checked and their political power curbed he was content to leave them in peace.

Swift's transfer of his allegiance from the Whigs to the Tories in 1710 arose largely from his dissatisfaction with the Whigs' ecclesiastical policy. It was not merely their failure to carry through the grant of the first-fruits to the Irish church which had alienated him, but also their attempt to remove the sacramental test, first in Ireland and then in England, and their tolerant attitude towards writers whom Swift regarded as deistical or atheistical. Naturally he expected preferment from his new allies, the professed patrons of the church; but after many disappointments in England he had to accept the deanery of St. Patrick's, Dublin.[1] Here he retired in 1714, when the Whigs returned to power; and such political influence as he retained was confined almost exclusively to Ireland. But his policy in ecclesiastical matters was unchanged. Whether in England or in Ireland, the Established Church stood in the same relation to the State and had to face the same threat from the Protestant Dissenters. The changes of 1714 necessarily diminished the political influence of the Church, and Swift was not prepared to challenge the new government.[2] The Presbyterians naturally rejoiced, the *regium donum* was restored, the occasional conformity Act, which was on the point of being extended to Ireland, was repealed, and in 1719 the Irish Parliament at last granted a legal toleration to Protestant Dissenters. To all this Swift said nothing. Even a visit to Ulster in 1722 did not draw from him any public comment on the activities of the Presbyterians. But once the question of repealing the sacramental test was raised again, he came forward to defend it.

[1] In 1711 Peterborough expressed surprise that Harley had not yet provided Swift with 'a lean bishopric or a fat deanery' (Peterborough to Swift, Vienna, 18/6 April 1711, in Ball (ed.), *Correspondence*, vol. I, p. 245). Swift's anxiety about his position appears in his reply to Peterborough (4 May 1711) and in a letter to Archbishop King (1 Oct. 1711, in Ball (ed.), *Correspondence*, vol. I, pp. 254, 291–2). A year later he writes to Stella almost in despair (15 Sept., 29 Dec. 1712, Williams (ed.), *Journal to Stella*, vol. II, pp. 556, 590).

[2] The attitude of some of the Irish clergy was defiant (Mant, *Church of Ireland*, vol. II, p. 275).

The new struggle was fought out in the Irish Parliament and the Irish Council in 1732 and 1733. At one stage Swift regarded the cause as lost. On November 1733 he wrote to Ford:

It is reckoned that the test will be repealed. It is said that £30,000 have been returned from England; and £20,000 raised here from servants, labourers, farmers, squires, whigs, etc., to promote the good work. Half the bishops will be on their side. Pamphlets pro and con fly about . . . but we all conclude the affair desperate. For the money is sufficient among us to abolish Christianity itself. All the people in power are determined for the repeal . . .[1]

But he had over-estimated the danger; the Irish government — directed by Primate Boulter rather than by the lord-lieutenant — hesitated to force on a policy so distasteful to the bulk of the House of Commons. By the end of the year the repeal project had been shelved.[2] It is hard to estimate the importance of Swift's contribution to this result. His pamphlets simply go over the old ground once again,[3] and the country gentlemen who refused to be cajoled or frightened by Boulter or Dorset did not need to have their opinions and their prejudices expressed for them. Swift was arguing for a cause which would have triumphed without him. But his vigour may have made the government's surrender more speedy and probably helps to account for its completeness. He was on the alert from the beginning. The first signs of danger arose in England[4] and Swift discussed with his printer, Motte, the idea of reprinting his *Letter concerning the Sacramental Test*, announcing at the same time

[1] Swift to Ford, 20 Nov. 1732 (D. Nichol Smith (ed.), *Letters of Swift to Ford* (Oxford, 1935), pp. 160–1).
[2] Boulter to Newcastle, 18 Dec. 1733; same to Bishop Gibson of London, 20 Dec. 1733 (*Boulter Letters* (ed. 1769–70), vol. II, pp. 108 ff., 112 ff.))
[3] *Queries wrote by Dr. J. Swift in the year 1732* (1732); *The Advantages Proposed by Repealing the Sacramental Test impartially considered* (1732); *The Presbyterian Plea of Merit in order to take off the Test, impartially examined* (1733), in *Prose Works* (ed. Temple Scott, London, 1897–1908), vol. IV. 'On the Words — Brother Protestants, and Fellow Christians, so familiarly used by the Advocates for the Repeal of the Test Act in Ireland, 1733' in Harold Williams (ed.), *The Poems of Jonathan Swift*, 1st ed. (Oxford, 1937), vol. III, pp. 809–13.
[4] Swift to Ford, 9 Dec. 1732 (*Letters of Swift to Ford*, p. 144).

that 'if the same wicked project [of repealing the test] shall be attempted here, I shall so far suspend my laziness as to oppose it to the utmost'.[1] Though the pamphlets which this 'suspension of laziness' produced show no development of thought on the question of Protestant Dissenters, one of them does lay stress on an aspect of the matter which Swift was usually content to pass over very lightly. One of the *Queries wrote by Dr J. Swift in the year 1732* is this: 'Whether any clergyman ... if he think his own profession most agreeable to holy scriptures, and this primitive church, can really wish in his heart, that all sectaries should be put on an equal foot with the churchmen, in point of civil power and employments?'[2] The emphasis on theological differences and the direct appeal to the clergy probably arose from the fear that the clergy themselves were no longer solidly against repealing the test. Probably, too, it was this which he had in mind when he complained that 'those who by their function, their conscience, their honour, their oaths, and the interest of their community are most bound to obstruct such a ruin to the church, will be the great advocates for it'.[3]

Though the project for repealing the sacramental test in Ireland was dropped, and not renewed during Swift's lifetime, his fear of the Dissenters remained. In 1736 he complained of 'the insolence of the dissenters, who, with their pupils the atheists, are now wholly employed in ruining the church and have entered into public associations subscribed and handed about publicly for that purpose'.[4] But his alarm for the Church during these years did not arise exclusively from the Dissenters. The gentlemen of the Irish House of Commons, though they had consistently defended the sacramental test, were not inclined to allow their support of the Church to

[1] Swift to B. Motte, 9 Dec. 1732, 9 Jan. 1733 (Ball (ed.), *Correspondence* vol. IV, pp. 362, 367).

[2] T. Scott (ed.), *Prose Works*, vol. IV, p. 70.

[3] Swift to B. Motte, 9 Dec. 1732 (Ball (ed.), *Correspondence*, vol. IV, p. 367).

[4] This linking together of Dissenters and atheists or freethinkers was usual with Swift. After he joined the Tories he added the Whigs. In 1711 he writes of the Dissenters and 'their comrades, the whigs and freethinkers' (*Examiner*, no. 36, 12 April 1711, in Davis (ed.), *Prose Works*, vol. III, p. 130). The alliance was a natural one, but Swift undoubtedly hoped to damn the Dissenters and Whigs by their company.

interfere with their incomes. They considered tithes a heavy burden, and found a welcome prospect of relief in the argument that no tithe was due from grazing land (tithe of agistment). The question was hotly debated, and in 1735 the Commons passed a resolution against the collection of the tithe of agistment. Though this had no legal force it was, in fact, acted upon, and clerical incomes suffered accordingly.[1] Such a move touched Swift on one of his tenderest points. The rights of his order were to him even dearer than his own, or rather, he could not consider them apart; and this attack seemed to him to threaten the ruin of the Church:

I have given up all hopes of church or Christianity. A certain author, I forget his name, hath writ a book, I wish I could see it, that the Christian religion will not last above three hundred and odd years. He means there will always be Christians, as there are Jews; but it will be no longer a national religion; and there is enough to justify the scripture, that the gates of hell shall not prevail against it. As to the church, it is equally the aversion of both kingdoms: you for the quakers' tithes, we for grass, or agistment as the term of art is.[2]

Swift's loyalty to his order appears at every stage of his ecclesiastical activity. Of humanity in general he wrote, in a famous passage, that he despised and hated it in the mass, while loving individuals. His attitude to the clergy was almost the reverse: there were few of them with whom he was on consistently friendly terms, but he never lost an opportunity of supporting their cause. In seeking the grant of the first-fruits for the Irish Church he was concerned chiefly with the benefit to the poorer clergy;[3] and slackness on the part of the officials who might be expected to forward the affair he interpreted as indifference towards clerical interests. Of one such he wrote, in a letter to Archbishop King, that he 'would not give threepence to save all the established clergy in both kingdoms from the gallows'.[4] He was concerned about the material welfare of the

[1] Mant, *Church of Ireland*, vol. II, pp. 308–9.

[2] Swift to Ford, 22 June 1736 (Ball (ed.), *Correspondence*, vol. v, p. 351).

[3] Swift to Archbishop King, 31 Dec. 1704; Swift to Harley, 1710 (Ball (ed.), *Correspondence*, vol. I, pp. 50, 201).

[4] Swift to Archbishop King, 28 Aug. 1708 (Ball (ed.), *Correspondence*, vol. I, p. 104).

clergy both as an end in itself, and because he was convinced that their poverty reduced them to contempt, and deprived them of their proper place in society.[1] It is not unreasonable to see here a close connection between Swift's personal character and his ecclesiastical policy. Few men were quicker to take offence or to detect an insult, and he was inclined to regard himself as open to attack in the person of each individual clergyman or in the clergy as a body. His opinion on the position of the clergy is temperately expressed in *The Sentiments of a Church of England Man*: '... he does not see how that mighty passion for the church, which some men pretend, can well consist with those indignities, and that contempt they bestow on the persons of the clergy....'[2] Later, in the *Examiner*, he speaks more strongly: 'For several years past there hath not, I think, in Europe, been any society of men upon so unhappy a foot, as the clergy of England.'[3] Swift was thinking of the lower clergy. In spite of his support of episcopacy as a form of Church government, his love of independence made it difficult for him to accept episcopal authority. With Bishop Evans of Meath, who was his diocesan as vicar of Laracor, he quarrelled bitterly; and even with Archbishop King his relations were sometimes strained. But in his vigorous support of the lower houses of the English Convocations against the upper, he was careful to point out that 'a dislike to the proceedings of any of their lordships, even to the number of a majority, will be purely personal, and not turned to the disadvantage of the order'.[4] After his retirement to Ireland in 1714 he had stronger grounds of opposition to the bishops, for they were often Englishmen and almost always Whigs: 'It is happy for me that I know the persons of very few bishops, and it is my constant rule, never to look into a coach; by which I avoid the terror that such a sight would strike me with.'[5]

[1] In *A project for the advancement of religion* Swift advocated the 'lay-conversation' of the clergy (Davis (ed.), *Prose Works*, vol. II, p. 54).

[2] Davis (ed.), *Prose Works*, vol. II, p. 8.

[3] *Examiner*, no. 21, 28 Dec. 1710 (Davis (ed.), *Prose Works*, vol. III, p. 46).

[4] *Examiner*, no. 21, 28 Dec. 1710 (Davis (ed.), *Prose Works*, vol. III, p. 51).

[5] Swift to Bishop Stearne, July 1733 (Ball (ed.), *Correspondence*, vol. V, p. 18).

When, in 1733, two Bills, one for compelling incumbents to reside and build houses on their glebes, the other for the division of large benefices, passed the Irish House of Lords, with the support of almost all the bishops, Swift wrote bitterly of 'those two abominable bills, for enslaving and beggaring the clergy, which took their birth from hell'; and asserted that the bishops who supported them had mostly done so 'with no other view, bating farther promotion, than a premeditated design, from the spirit of ambition and love of arbitrary power, to make the whole body of the clergy their slaves and vassals, until the day of judgement, under the load of poverty and contempt'.[1] This furious sensitiveness touching his order seems to have grown on him in later years, and was probably increased by his feeling of powerlessness.

Swift's work as an ecclesiastical statesman cannot be easily summarised or accurately estimated. His career was made up of broken patches. He entered late upon the political world, and was thrown in with a party which, on grounds both personal and of principle, he could not long stand by. Later he won favour and influence in a party which he could honourably serve, but which, in spite of his efforts, was ruined by internal dissension. He was exiled to Ireland, where he could exercise only indirect influence on the course of government, through his powerful friends or through the mob. So Swift's work for the Church was neither that of a scholar nor that of an experienced administrator. He was essentially a man of action, but his hopes of taking an effective part in directing the affairs of the Church and of the nation were constantly thwarted, and he was forced to find an outlet in the vigorous administration of his little kingdom of the liberties of St. Patrick's and in defending its independence against the archbishop's seneschal.[2] The same love of action appears in his writings on Church and State, every one of which is related to some immediate problem. More than this, he wrote for power and place. It would probably be possible to find some personal motive behind every pamphlet; and though Swift

[1] Swift to Bishop Stearne, July 1733 (Ball (ed.), *Correspondence*, vol. v, p. 17); Mant, *Church of Ireland*, vol. ii, pp. 544 ff.
[2] Swift to ———, 15 April 1737 (Ball (ed.), *Correspondence*, vol. vi, pp. 9–10).

never allowed such motives to pervert his principle, the bitterness of his attacks upon the Whigs for their ill-treatment of the church owed something to political expediency and, in his later life, to disappointed ambition.

This element of partisanship is the ruling factor in Swift's achievement as an ecclesiastical statesman. On the one hand it weakened his influence within the Church. Those who already suspected his orthodoxy were not reconciled by the violence and apparent instability of his party attachment. Thus, though the grant of the first-fruits and twentieth parts to the Irish Church in 1711 was largely due to Swift's patient negotiation, the bishops felt it wiser to give the credit to the Duke of Ormonde, or to the queen herself.[1] On the other hand, it was just because he was both a clergyman and an active member of a political party that Swift was compelled to face the problem of an Established Church in a parliamentary state. It was not in his nature to produce a complete system; he solved problems and answered difficulties as they arose. But in doing so he laid down principles, briefly examined in this paper, which form an important contribution to Anglican thought on the relations of Church and State, and might have guided the Church into a middle way between the fantastic unrealities of the Non-jurors and the blank erastianism of the Hanoverian bishops.

[1] Mant, *Church of Ireland*, vol. II, pp. 234 ff.; R. Wyse Jackson, *Jonathan Swift: Dean and Pastor*, pp. 58 ff.

GEORGE ORWELL

Politics vs. Literature: an examination of Gulliver's Travels

IN *Gulliver's Travels* humanity is attacked, or criticized, from at least three different angles, and the implied character of Gulliver himself necessarily changes somewhat in the process. In part I he is the typical eighteenth-century voyager, bold, practical and unromantic, his homely outlook skilfully impressed on the reader by the biographical details at the beginning, by his age (he is a man of forty, with two children, when his adventures start), and by the inventory of the things in his pockets, especially his spectacles, which make several appearances. In part II he has in general the same character, but at moments when the story demands it he has a tendency to develop into an imbecile who is capable of boasting of 'our noble Country, the Mistress of Arts and Arms, the Scourge of France', etc., etc., and at the same time of betraying every available scandalous fact about the country which he professes to love. In part III he is much as he was in part I, though, as he is consorting chiefly with courtiers and men of learning, one has the impression that he has risen in the social scale. In part IV he conceives a horror of the human race which is not apparent, or only intermittently apparent, in the earlier books, and changes into a sort of unreligious anchorite whose one desire is to live in some desolate spot where he can devote himself to meditating on the goodness of the Houyhnhnms. However, these inconsistencies are forced upon Swift by the fact that Gulliver is there chiefly to provide a contrast. It is necessary, for instance, that he should appear sensible in part I and at least intermittently silly in part II, because in both books the essential manœuvre is the same, i.e. to make the human being look ridiculous by imagining him as a creature six inches high. Whenever Gulliver is not acting as a stooge there is a sort of continuity in his character, which comes out especially in his resourcefulness and his observation of physical detail. He is much the same kind of person, with the same prose style, when he bears off the warships of Blefuscu, when he rips open the belly of the monstrous rat, and when he sails away upon the ocean in his frail coracle made from the skins of Yahoos. Moreover, it is difficult not to feel that in his shrewder moments Gulliver is simply Swift himself, and there is at least one incident in which Swift seems to be venting his private grievance against contemporary Society. It will be remembered that when the Emperor of Lilliput's palace catches fire, Gulliver puts it out by urinating on it. Instead of being congratulated on his presence of mind, he finds that he has committed a capital offence by making water in the precincts of the palace, and

I was privately assured, that the Empress, conceiving the greatest Abhorrence of what I had done, removed to the most distant Side of the Court, firmly resolved that those buildings should never be repaired for her Use; and, in the Presence of her chief Confidents, could not forbear vowing Revenge.

According to Professor G. M. Trevelyan (*England under Queen Anne*), part of the reason for Swift's failure to get preferment was that the Queen was scandalized by the *Tale of a Tub* — a pamphlet in which Swift probably felt that he had done a great service to the English Crown, since it scarifies the Dissenters and still more the Catholics, while leaving the Established Church alone. In any case no one would deny that *Gulliver's Travels* is a rancorous as well as a pessimistic book, and that especially in parts I and III it often descends into political partisanship of a narrow kind. Pettiness and magnanimity, republicanism and authoritarianism, love of reason and lack of curiosity, are all mixed up in it. The hatred of the human body with which Swift is especially associated is only dominant in part IV, but somehow this new preoccupation does not come as a surprise. One feels that all these adventures, and all these changes of mood, could have happened to the same person, and the inter-connection between Swift's political loyalties and his ultimate despair is one of the most interesting features of the book.

Politically, Swift was one of those people who are driven into a sort of perverse Toryism by the follies of the progressive party of the moment. Part I of *Gulliver's Travels*, ostensibly a satire on human greatness, can be seen, if one looks a little deeper, to be simply an attack on England, on the dominant Whig party, and on the war with France, which — however bad the motives of the Allies may have been — did save Europe from being tyrannized over by a single reactionary power. Swift was not a Jacobite or strictly speaking a Tory, and his declared aim in the war was merely a moderate peace treaty and not the outright defeat of England. Nevertheless there is a tinge of quislingism in his attitude, which comes out in the ending of part I and slightly interferes with the allegory. When Gulliver flees from Lilliput (England) to Blefuscu (France) the assumption that a human being six inches high is inherently contemptible seems to be dropped. Whereas the people of Lilliput have behaved towards Gulliver with the utmost treachery and meanness, those of Blefuscu behave generously and straight-forwardly, and indeed this section of the book ends on a different note from the all-round disillusionment of the earlier chapters. Evidently Swift's animus is, in the first place, against *England*. It is 'your Natives' (i.e. Gulliver's fellow-countrymen) whom the King of Brobdingnag considers to be 'the most pernicious Race of little odious vermin that Nature ever suffered to crawl upon the surface of the Earth', and the long passage at the end, denouncing coloniza-tion and foreign conquest, is plainly aimed at England, although the contrary is elaborately stated. The Dutch, England's allies and target of one of Swift's most famous pamphlets, are also more or less wantonly attacked in part III. There is even what sounds like a personal note in the passage in which Gulliver records his satis-faction that the various countries he has discovered cannot be made colonies of the British Crown:

The *Houyhnhnms*, indeed, appear not to be so well prepared for War, a Science to which they are perfect Strangers, and especially against missive Weapons. However, supposing myself to be a Minister of State, I could never give my advice for invading them. . . . Imagine twenty thousand of them breaking into the midst of an *European* army, confounding the Ranks, overturning the Carriages, battering the Warriors' Faces into Mummy, by terrible Yerks from their hinder hoofs . . .

Considering that Swift does not waste words, that phrase, 'battering the warriors' faces into mummy', probably indicates a secret wish to see the invincible armies of the Duke of Marlborough treated in a like manner. There are similar touches elsewhere. Even the country mentioned in part III, where 'the Bulk of the People consist, in a Manner, wholly of Discoverers, Witnesses, Informers, Accusers, Prosecutors, Evidences, Swearers, together with their several subservient and subaltern Instruments, all under the Colours, the Conduct, and Pay of Ministers of State', is called Langdon, which is within one letter of being an anagram of England. (As the early editions of the book contain misprints, it may perhaps have been intended as a complete anagram.) Swift's *physical* repulsion from humanity is certainly real enough, but one has the feeling that his debunking of human grandeur, his diatribes against lords, politicians, court favourites, etc., has mainly a local application and springs from the fact that he belonged to the unsuccessful party. He denounces injustice and oppression, but he gives no evidence of liking democracy. In spite of his enormously greater powers, his implied position is very similar to that of the innumerable silly-clever Conservatives of our own day — people like Sir Alan Herbert, Professor G. M. Young, Lord Elton, the Tory Reform Committee or the long line of Catholic apologists from W. H. Mallock onwards: people who specialize in cracking neat jokes at the expense of whatever is 'modern' and 'progressive', and whose opinions are often all the more extreme because they know that they cannot influence the actual drift of events. After all, such a pamphlet as *An Argument to prove that the Abolishing of Christianity*, etc., is very like 'Timothy Shy' having a bit of clean fun with the Brains Trust, or Father Ronald Knox exposing the errors of Bertrand Russell. And the ease with which Swift has been forgiven — and forgiven, sometimes, by devout believers — for the blasphemies of *A Tale of a Tub* demonstrates clearly enough the feebleness of religious sentiments as compared with political ones.

However, the reactionary cast of Swift's mind does not show

itself chiefly in his political affiliations. The important thing is his attitude towards science, and, more broadly, towards intellectual curiosity. The famous Academy of Lagado, described in part III of *Gulliver's Travels*, is, no doubt, a justified satire on most of the so-called scientists of Swift's own day. Significantly, the people at work in it are described as 'Projectors', that is, people not engaged in disinterested research but merely on the look-out for gadgets which will save labour and bring in money. But there is no sign — indeed, all through the book there are many signs to the contrary — that 'pure' science would have struck Swift as a worth-while activity. The more serious kind of scientist has already had a kick in the pants in part II, when the 'scholars' patronized by the King of Brobdingnag try to account for Gulliver's small stature:

After much Debate, they concluded unanimously that I was only *Relplum Scalcath*, which is interpreted literally, *Lusus Naturae*; a Determination exactly agreeable to the modern philosophy of *Europe*, whose Professors, disdaining the old Evasion of *Occult Causes*, whereby the followers of *Aristotle* endeavoured in vain to disguise their Ignorance, have invented this wonderful Solution of All Difficulties, to the unspeakable Advancement of human Knowledge.

If this stood by itself one might assume that Swift is merely the enemy of *sham* science. In a number of places, however, he goes out of his way to proclaim the uselessness of all learning or speculation not directed towards some practical end:

The learning of (the Brobdingnagians) is very defective, consisting only in Morality, History, Poetry, and Mathematics, wherein they must be allowed to excel. But, the last of these is wholly applied to what may be useful in Life, to the improvement of Agriculture, and all mechanical Arts so that among us it would be little esteemed. And as to Ideas, Entities, Abstractions, and Transcendentals, I could never drive the least Conception into their Heads.

The Houyhnhnms, Swift's ideal beings, are backward even in a mechanical sense. They are unacquainted with metals, have never heard of boats, do not, properly speaking, practise agriculture (we are told that the oats which they live upon 'grow naturally'), and appear not to have invented wheels.[1] They have no alphabet, and evidently have not much curiosity about the physical world. They do not believe that any inhabited country exists beside their own, and though they understand the motions of the sun and moon, and the nature of eclipses, 'this is the utmost progress of their *Astronomy*'. By contrast, the philosophers of the flying island of Laputa are so continuously absorbed in mathematical speculations that before speaking to them one has to attract their attention by flapping them on the ear with a bladder. They have catalogued ten thousand fixed stars, have settled the periods of ninety-three comets, and have discovered in advance of the astronomers of Europe, that Mars has two moons — all of which information Swift evidently regards as ridiculous, useless and uninteresting. As one might expect, he believes that the scientist's place, if he has a place, is in the laboratory, and that scientific knowledge has no bearing on political matters:

What I . . . thought altogether unaccountable, was the strong Disposition I observed in them towards News and Politics, perpetually enquiring into Public Affairs, giving their judgments in Matters of State, and passionately disputing every inch of a Party Opinion. I have, indeed, observed the same Disposition among most of the Mathematicians I have known in *Europe*, though I could never discover the least Analogy between the two Sciences; unless those people suppose, that, because the smallest Circle hath as many Degrees as the largest, therefore the Regulation and Management of the World require no more Abilities, than the Handling and Turning of a Globe.

Is there not something familiar in that phrase 'I could never discover the least analogy between the two sciences'? It has precisely the note of the popular Catholic apologists who profess to be astonished when a scientist utters an opinion on such questions as the existence of God or the immortality of the soul. The scientist, we are told, is an expert only in one restricted field: why should his opinions be of value in any other? The implication is that theology is just as much an exact science as, for instance, chemistry, and that the priest is also

---

[1] Houyhnhnms too old to walk are described as being carried in 'sledges' or in 'a kind of vehicle, drawn like a sledge'. Presumably these had no wheels.

an expert whose conclusions on certain subjects must be accepted. Swift, in effect, makes the same claim for the politician, but he goes one better in that he will not allow the scientist — either the 'pure' scientist or the *ad hoc* investigator — to be a useful person in his own line. Even if he had not written part III of *Gulliver's Travels*, one could infer from the rest of the book that, like Tolstoy and like Blake, he hates the very idea of studying the processes of Nature. The 'reason' which he so admires in the Houyhnhnms does not primarily mean the power of drawing logical inferences from observed facts. Although he never defines it, it appears in most contexts to mean either common sense — i.e. acceptance of the obvious and contempt for quibbles and abstractions — or absence of passion and superstition. In general he assumes that we know all that we need to know already, and merely use our knowledge incorrectly. Medicine, for instance, is a useless science, because if we lived in a more natural way, there would be no diseases. Swift, however, is not a simple-lifer or an admirer of the Noble Savage. He is in favour of civilization and the arts of civilization. Not only does he see the value of good manners, good conversation, and even learning of a literary and historical kind, he also sees that agriculture, navigation and architecture need to be studied and could with advantages be improved. But his implied aim is a static, incurious civilization — the world of his own day, a little cleaner, a little saner, with no radical change and no poking into the unknowable. More than one would expect in anyone so free from accepted fallacies, he reveres the past, especially classical antiquity, and believes that modern man has degenerated sharply during the past hundred years.[1] In the island of sorcerers, where the spirits of the dead can be called up at will:

I desired that the Senate of *Rome* might appear before me in one large chamber, and a modern Representative in Counterview, in another. The first seemed to be an Assembly of Heroes and Demy-

---

[1] The physical decadence which Swift claims to have observed may have been a reality at that date. He attributes it to syphilis, which was a new disease in Europe and may have been more virulent than it is now. Distilled liquors, also, were a novelty in the seventeenth century and must have led at first to a great increase in drunkenness.

Gods, the other a Knot of Pedlars, Pick-pockets, Highwaymen and Bullies.

Although Swift uses this section of part III to attack the truthfulness of recorded history, his critical spirit deserts him as soon as he is dealing with Greeks and Romans. He remarks, of course, upon the corruption of imperial Rome, but he has an almost unreasoning admiration for some of the leading figures of the ancient world:

I was struck with profound Veneration at the sight of *Brutus*, and could easily discover the most consummate Virtue, the greatest Intrepidity and Firmness of Mind, the truest Love of his Country, and general Benevolence for Mankind, in every Lineament of his Countenance.... I had the honour to have much Conversation with *Brutus*, and was told, that his Ancestors *Junius, Socrates, Epaminondas, Cato* the younger, *Sir Thomas More*, and himself, were perpetually together: a *Sextumvirate*, to which all the Ages of the World cannot add a seventh.

It will be noticed that of these six people, only one is a Christian. This is an important point. If one adds together Swift's pessimism, his reverence for the past, his incuriosity and his horror of the human body, one arrives at an attitude common among religious reactionaries — that is, people who defend an unjust order of society by claiming that this world cannot be substantially improved and only the 'next world' matters. However, Swift shows no sign of having any religious beliefs, at least in an ordinary sense of the words. He does not appear to believe seriously in life after death, and his idea of goodness is bound up with republicanism, love of liberty, courage, 'benevolence' (meaning, in effect, public spirit), 'reason' and other pagan qualities. This reminds one that there is another strain in Swift, not quite congruous with his disbelief in progress and his general hatred of humanity.

To begin with, he has moments when he is 'constructive' and even 'advanced'. To be occasionally inconsistent is almost a mark of vitality in Utopia books, and Swift sometimes inserts a word of praise into a passage that ought to be purely satirical. Thus, his ideas about the education of the young are fathered on to the Lilliputians, who have much the same views on this subject as the

Houyhnhnms. The Lilliputians also have various social and legal institutions (for instance, there are old-age pensions, and people are rewarded for keeping the law as well as punished for breaking it) which Swift would have liked to see prevailing in his own country. In the middle of this passage Swift remembers his satirical intention and adds: 'In relating these and the following Laws, I would only be understood to mean the original Institutions, and not the most scandalous Corruptions into which these people are fallen by the degenerate Nature of Man': but as Lilliput is supposed to represent England, and the laws he is speaking of have never had their parallel in England, it is clear that the impulse to make constructive suggestions has been too much for him. But Swift's greatest contribution to political thought in the narrower sense of the words, is his attack, especially in part III, on what would now be called totalitarianism. He has an extraordinarily clear prevision of the spy-haunted 'police State', with its endless heresy-hunts and treason trials, all really designed to neutralize popular discontent by changing it into war hysteria. And one must remember that Swift is here inferring the whole from a quite small part, for the feeble governments of his own day did not give him illustrations ready-made. For example, there is the professor at the School of Political Projectors who 'shewed me a large Paper of Instructions for discovering Plots and Conspiracies', and who claimed that one can find people's secret thoughts by examining their excrement:

Because Men are never so serious, thoughtful, and intent, as when they are at Stool, which he found by frequent Experiment: for in such Conjunctures, when he used meerly as a trial to consider what was the best Way of murdering the King, his Ordure would have a tincture of Green; but quite different when he thought only of raising an Insurrection, or burning the Metropolis.

The professor and his theory are said to have been suggested to Swift by the — from our point of view — not particularly astonishing or disgusting fact that in a recent State trial some letters found in somebody's privy had been put in evidence. Later in the same chapter we seem to be positively in the middle of the Russian purges:

In the Kingdom of Tribnia, by the Natives called Langdon . . . the Bulk of the People consist, in a Manner, wholly of Discoverers, Witnesses, Informers, Accusers, Prosecutors, Evidences, Swearers. . . . It is first agreed, and settled among them, what suspected Persons shall be accused of a Plot: Then, effectual Care is taken to secure all their Letters and Papers, and put the Owners in Chains. These papers are delivered to a Sett of Artists, very dexterous in finding out the mysterious Meanings of Words, Syllables, and Letters. . . . Where this method fails, they have two others more effectual, which the Learned among them call *Acrostics* and *Anagrams*. *First*, they can decypher all initial Letters into political Meanings: Thus: N shall signify a Plot, B a Regiment of Horse, L a Fleet at Sea: Or, *Secondly*, by transposing the Letters of the Alphabet in any suspected Paper, they can lay open the deepest Designs of a discontented Party. So, for Example if I should say in a Letter to a Friend, *Our Brother Tom has just got the Piles*, a skilful Decypherer would discover that the same Letters, which compose that Sentence, may be analysed in the following Words: *Resist — a Plot is brought Home — The Tour*.[1] And this is the anagrammatic method.

Other professors at the same school invent simplified languages, write books by machinery, educate their pupils by inscribing the lesson on a wafer and causing them to swallow it, or propose to abolish individuality altogether by cutting of part of the brain of one man and grafting it on to the head of another. There is something queerly familiar in the atmosphere of these chapters, because, mixed up with much fooling, there is a perception that one of the aims of totalitarianism is not merely to make sure that people will think the right thoughts, but actually to make them *less conscious*. Then, again, Swift's account of the Leader who is usually to be found ruling over a tribe of Yahoos, and of the 'favourite' who acts first as a dirty-worker and later as a scapegoat, fits remarkably well into the pattern of our own times. But are we to infer from all this that Swift was first and foremost an enemy of tyranny and a champion of the free intelligence? No: his own views, so far as one can discern them, are not markedly liberal. No doubt he hates lords, kings, bishops, generals, ladies of fashion, orders, titles and flummery

[1] Tower.

generally, but he does not seem to think better of the common people than of their rulers, or to be in favour of increased social equality, or to be enthusiastic about representative institutions. The Houyhnhnms are organized upon a sort of caste system which is racial in character, the horses which do the menial work being of different colours from their masters and not interbreeding with them. The educational system which Swift admires in the Lilliputians takes hereditary class distinctions for granted, and the children of the poorest classes do not go to school, because 'their Business being only to till and cultivate the Earth . . . therefore their Education is of little Consequence to the Public'. Nor does he seem to have been strongly in favour of freedom of speech and the Press, in spite of the toleration which his own writings enjoyed. The King of Brobding-nag is astonished at the multiplicity of religious and political sects in England, and considers that those who hold 'opinions prejudicial to the public' (in the context this seems to mean simply heretical opinions), though they need not be obliged to change them, ought to be obliged to conceal them: for 'as it was Tyranny in any Government to require the first, so it was weakness not to enforce the second'. There is a subtler indication of Swift's own attitude in the manner in which Gulliver leaves the land of the Houyhnhnms. Intermittently, at least, Swift was a kind of anarchist, and part iv of *Gulliver's Travels* is a picture of an anarchistic society, not governed by law in the ordinary sense, but by the dictates of 'reason', which are voluntarily accepted by everyone. The General Assembly of the Houyhnhnms 'exhorts' Gulliver's master to get rid of him, and his neighbours put pressure on him to make him comply. Two reasons are given. One is that the presence of this unusual Yahoo may un-settle the rest of the tribe, and the other is that a friendly relationship between a Houyhnhnm and a Yahoo is 'not agreeable to Reason or Nature, or a Thing ever heard of before among them'. Gulliver's master is somewhat unwilling to obey, but the 'exhortation' (a Houyhnhnm, we are told, is never *compelled* to do anything, he is merely 'exhorted' or 'advised') cannot be disregarded. This illus-trates very well the totalitarian tendency which is explicit in the anarchist or pacifist vision of society. In a society in which there is no law, and in theory no compulsion, the only arbiter of behaviour is public opinion. But public opinion, because of the tremendous urge to conformity in gregarious animals, is less tolerant than any system of law. When human beings are governed by 'thou shalt not', the individual can practise a certain amount of eccentricity: when they are supposedly governed by 'love' or 'reason', he is under continuous pressure to make him behave and think in exactly the same way as everyone else. The Houyhnhnms, we are told, were unanimous on almost all subjects. The only question they ever *discussed* was how to deal with the Yahoos. Otherwise there was no room for disagreement among them, because the truth is always either self-evident, or else it is undiscoverable and unimportant. They had apparently no word for 'opinion' in their language, and in their conversations there was no 'difference of sentiments'. They had reached, in fact, the highest stage of totalitarian organization, the stage when conformity has become so general that there is no need for a police force. Swift approves of this kind of thing because among his many gifts neither curiosity nor good nature was included. Disagreement would always seem to him sheer perversity. 'Reason', among the Houyhnhnms, he says, 'is not a Point Problematical, as with us, where men can argue with Plausibility on both Sides of a Question; but strikes you with immediate Conviction; as it must needs do, where it is not mingled, obscured, or discoloured by Passion and Interest.' In other words, we know everything already, so why should dissident opinions be tolerated? The totalitarian society of the Houyhnhnms, where there can be no freedom and no development, follows naturally from this.

We are right to think of Swift as a rebel and iconoclast, but except in certain secondary matters, such as his insistence that women should receive the same education as men, he cannot be labelled 'Left'. He is a Tory anarchist, despising authority while disbelieving in liberty, and preserving the aristocratic outlook while seeing clearly that the existing aristocracy is degenerate and contemptible. When Swift utters one of his characteristic diatribes against the rich and powerful, one must probably, as I said earlier, write off something for the fact that he himself belonged to the less successful party, and was personally disappointed. The 'outs', for obvious reasons, are always more radical than the 'ins'.[1] But the most essential thing in Swift is his inability to believe that life — ordinary life on the solid earth, and not some rationalized, deodorized version of it — could be made worth living. Of course, no honest person claims that happiness is *now* a normal condition among adult human beings; but perhaps it *could* be made normal, and it is upon this question that all serious political controversy really turns. Swift has much in common — more, I believe, than has been noticed — with Tolstoy, another disbeliever in the possibility of happiness. In both men you have the same anarchistic outlook covering an authoritarian cast of mind; in both a similar hostility to science, the same impatience with opponents, the same inability to see the importance of any question not interesting to themselves; and in both cases a sort of horror of the actual process of life, though in Tolstoy's case it was arrived at later and in a different way. The sexual unhappiness of the two men was not of the same kind, but there was this in common, that in both of them a sincere loathing was mixed up with a morbid fascination. Tolstoy was a reformed rake who ended by preaching complete celibacy, while continuing to practise the opposite into extreme old age. Swift was presumably impotent, and had an exaggerated horror of human dung: he also thought about it incessantly, as is evident throughout his works. Such people are not likely to enjoy even the small amount of happiness that falls to most human beings, and, from obvious motives, are not likely to admit that earthly life is capable of much improvement. Their incuriosity, and hence their intolerance, spring from the same root.

[1] At the end of the book, as typical specimens of human folly and viciousness, Swift names 'a Lawyer, a Pickpocket, a Colonel, a Fool, a Lord, a Gamester, a Politician. a Whore-master, a Physician, an Evidence, a Suborner, an Attorney, a Traitor, or the like'. One sees here the irresponsible violence of the powerless. The list lumps together those who break the conventional code and those who keep it. For instance, if you automatically condemn a colonel, as such, on what grounds do you condemn a traitor? Or again, if you want to suppress pickpockets, you must have laws, which means that you must have lawyers. But the whole closing passage, in which the hatred is so authentic, and the reason given for it so inadequate, is somehow unconvincing. One has the feeling that personal animosity is at work.

Swift's disgust, rancour and pessimism would make sense against the background of a 'next world' to which this one is the prelude. As he does not appear to believe seriously in any such thing, it becomes necessary to construct a paradise supposedly existing on the surface of the earth, but something quite different from anything we know, with all that he disapproves of — lies, folly, change, enthusiasm, pleasure, love and dirt — eliminated from it. As his ideal being he chooses the horse, an animal whose excrement is not offensive. The Houyhnhnms are dreary beasts — this is so generally admitted that the point is not worth labouring. Swift's genius can make them credible, but there can have been very few readers in whom they have excited any feeling beyond dislike. And this is not from wounded vanity at seeing animals preferred to men; for, of the two, the Houyhnhnms are much liker to human beings than are the Yahoos, and Gulliver's horror of the Yahoos, together with his recognition that they are the same kind of creature as himself, contains a logical absurdity. This horror comes upon him at his very first sight of them. 'I never beheld,' he says, 'in all my Travels, so disagreeable an Animal, nor one against which I naturally conceived so strong an Antipathy.' But in comparison with what are the Yahoos disgusting? Not with the Houyhnhnms, because at this time Gulliver has not seen a Houyhnhnm. It can only be in comparison with himself, i.e. with a human being. Later, however, we are to be told that the Yahoos *are* human beings, and human society becomes insupportable to Gulliver because all men are Yahoos. In that case why did he not conceive his disgust of humanity earlier? In effect we are told that the Yahoos are fantastically different from men, and yet are the same. Swift has over-reached himself in his fury, and is shouting at his fellow-creatures: 'You are filthier than you are!' However, it is impossible to feel much sympathy with the Yahoos, and it is not because they oppress the Yahoos that the Houyhnhnms are unattractive. They are unattractive because the 'reason' by which they are governed is really a desire for death. They are exempt from love, friendship, curiosity, fear, sorrow and — except in their feelings towards the Yahoos, who occupy rather the same place in their community as the Jews in Nazi Germany — anger and hatred. 'They have no Fondness for their Colts or Foles, but the Care they take, in educating them, proceeds entirely from the Dictates of *Reason*.' They lay store by 'Friendship' and 'Benevolence', but 'these are not confined to particular Objects, but universal to the whole Race'. They also value conversation, but in their conversations there are no differences of opinion, and 'nothing passed but what was useful, expressed in the fewest and most significant Words'. They practise strict birth-control, each couple producing two offspring and thereafter abstaining from sexual intercourse. Their marriages are arranged for them by their elders, on eugenic principles, and their language contains no word for 'love', in the sexual sense. When somebody dies they carry on exactly as before, without feeling any grief. It will be seen that their aim is to be as like a corpse as is possible while retaining physical life. One or two of their characteristics, it is true, do not seem to be strictly 'reasonable' in their own usage of the word. Thus, they place a great value not only on physical hardihood but on athleticism, and they are devoted to poetry. But these exceptions may be less arbitrary than they seem. Swift probably emphasizes the physical strength of the Houyhnhnms in order to make clear that they could never be conquered by the hated human race, while a taste for poetry may figure among their qualities because poetry appeared to Swift as the antithesis of science, from his point of view the most useless of all pursuits. In part III he names 'Imagination, Fancy, and Invention' as desirable faculties in which the Laputan mathematicians (in spite of their love of music) were wholly lacking. One must remember that although Swift was an admirable writer of comic verse, the kind of poetry he thought valuable would probably be didactic poetry. The poetry of the Houyhnhnms, he says

must be allowed to excel [that of] all other Mortals; wherein the Justness of their Similes, and the Minuteness, as well as exactness, of their Descriptions, are, indeed, inimitable. Their Verses abound very much in both of these; and usually contain either some exalted Notions of Friendship and Benevolence, or the Praises of those who were Victors in Races, and other bodily Exercises.

Alas, not even the genius of Swift was equal to producing a specimen by which we could judge the poetry of the Houyhnhnms. But it sounds as though it were chilly stuff (in heroic couplets, presumably), and not seriously in conflict with the principles of 'reason'.

Happiness is notoriously difficult to describe, and pictures of a just and well-ordered society are seldom either attractive or convincing. Most creators of 'favourable' Utopias, however, are concerned to show what life could be like if it were lived more fully. Swift advocates a simple refusal of life, justifying this by the claim that 'reason' consists in thwarting your instincts. The Houyhnhnms, creatures without a history, continue for generation after generation to live prudently, maintaining their population at exactly the same level, avoiding all passion, suffering from no diseases, meeting death indifferently, training up their young in the same principles — and all for what? In order that the same process may continue indefinitely. The notions that life here and now is worth living, or that it could be made worth living, or that it must be sacrificed for some future good, are all absent. The dreary world of the Houyhnhnms was about as good a Utopia as Swift could construct, granting that he neither believed in a next world nor could get any pleasure out of certain normal activities. But it is not really set up as something desirable in itself, but as the justification for another attack on humanity. The aim, as usual, is to humiliate Man by reminding him that he is weak and ridiculous; and above all that he stinks; and the ultimate motive, probably, is a kind of envy, the envy of the ghost for the living, of the man who knows he cannot be happy for the others who — so he fears — may be a little happier than himself. The political expression of such an outlook must be either reactionary or nihilistic, because the person who holds it will want to prevent Society from developing in some direction in which his pessimism may be cheated. One can do this either by blowing everything to pieces, or by averting social change. Swift ultimately blew everything to pieces in the only way that was feasible before the atomic bomb — that is, he went mad — but, as I have tried to show, his political aims were on the whole reactionary ones.

From what I have written it may have seemed that I am *against* Swift, and that my object is to refute him and even to belittle him. In a political and moral sense I am against him, so far as I understand him. Yet curiously enough he is one of the writers I admire with least reserve, and *Gulliver's Travels*, in particular, is a book which it seems impossible for me to grow tired of. I read it first when I was eight — one day short of eight, to be exact, for I stole and furtively read the copy which was to be given me next day on my eighth birthday — and I have certainly read it not less than half a dozen times since. Its fascination seems inexhaustible. If I had to make a list of six books which were to be preserved when all others were destroyed, I would certainly put *Gulliver's Travels* among them. This raises the question: what is the relationship between agreement with a writer's opinions, and enjoyment of his work?

If one is capable of intellectual detachment, one can *perceive* merit in a writer whom one deeply disagrees with, but *enjoyment* is a different matter. Supposing that there is such a thing as good or bad art, then the goodness or badness must reside in the work of art itself — not independently of the observer, indeed, but independently of the mood of the observer. In one sense, therefore, it cannot be true that a poem is good on Monday and bad on Tuesday. But if one judges the poem by the appreciation it arouses, then it can certainly be true, because appreciation, or enjoyment, is a subjective condition which cannot be commanded. For a great deal of his waking life, even the most cultivated person has no aesthetic feelings whatever, and the power to have aesthetic feelings is very easily destroyed. When you are frightened, or hungry, or are suffering from toothache or sea-sickness, *King Lear* is no better from your point of view than *Peter Pan*. You may know in an intellectual sense that it is better, but that is simply a fact which you remember: you will not *feel* the merit of *King Lear* until you are normal again. And aesthetic judgment can be upset just as disastrously — more disastrously, because the cause is less readily recognized — by political or moral disagreement. If a book angers, wounds or alarms you, then you will not enjoy it, whatever its merits may be. If it seems to you a really pernicious book, likely to influence other people in some undesirable way, then you will probably construct an aesthetic theory to show that it *has* no merits. Current literary criticism consists quite largely of this kind of dodging to and fro between two sets of standards. And yet the opposite process can

also happen: enjoyment can overwhelm disapproval, even though
one clearly recognizes that one is enjoying something inimical.
Swift, whose world-view is so peculiarly unacceptable, but who is,
nevertheless, an extremely popular writer, is a good instance of this.
Why is it that we don't mind being called Yahoos, although firmly
convinced that we are *not* Yahoos?

It is not enough to make the usual answer that of course Swift
was wrong, in fact he was insane, but he was 'a good writer'. It is
true that the literary quality of a book is to some small extent
separable from its subject-matter. Some people have a native gift for
using words, as some people have a naturally 'good eye' at games. It
is largely a question of timing and of instinctively knowing how
much emphasis to use. As an example near at hand, look back at the
passage I quoted earlier, starting 'In the Kingdom of Tribnia, by
the Natives called Langdon'. It derives much of its force from the
final sentence: 'And this is the anagrammatic Method.' Strictly
speaking this sentence is unnecessary, for we have already seen the
anagram deciphered, but the mock-solemn repetition, in which one
seems to hear Swift's own voice uttering the words, drives home the
idiocy of the activities described, like the final tap to a nail. But not
all the power and simplicity of Swift's prose, nor the imaginative
effort that has been able to make not one but a whole series of
impossible worlds more credible than the majority of history books
— none of this would enable us to enjoy Swift if his world-view
were truly wounding or shocking. Millions of people, in many
countries, must have enjoyed *Gulliver's Travels* while more or less
seeing its anti-human implications: and even the child who accepts
parts I and II as a simple story gets a sense of absurdity from
thinking of human beings six inches high. The explanation must be
that Swift's world-view is felt to be *not* altogether false — or it
would probably be more accurate to say, not false all the time. Swift
is a diseased writer. He remains permanently in a depressed mood
which in most people is only intermittent, rather as though someone
suffering from jaundice or the after-effects of influenza should have
the energy to write books. But we all know that mood, and something in us responds to the expression of it. Take, for instance, one
of his most characteristic works, 'The Lady's Dressing Room': one

might add the kindred poem, 'Upon a Beautiful Young Nymph Going to Bed'. Which is truer, the viewpoint expressed in these poems, or the viewpoint implied in Blake's phrase, 'The naked female human form divine'? No doubt Blake is nearer the truth, and yet who can fail to feel a sort of pleasure in seeing that fraud, feminine delicacy, exploded for once? Swift falsifies his picture of the world by refusing to see anything in human life except dirt, folly and wickedness, but the part which he abstracts from the whole does exist, and it is something which we all know about, while shrinking from mentioning it. Part of our minds — in any normal person it is the dominant part — believes that man is a noble animal and life is worth living: but there is also a sort of inner self which at least intermittently stands aghast at the horror of existence. In the queerest way, pleasure and disgust are linked together. The human body is beautiful: it is also repulsive and ridiculous, a fact which can be verified at any swimming-pool. The sexual organs are objects of desire and also of loathing, so much so that in many languages, if not in all languages, their names are used as words of abuse. Meat is delicious, but a butcher's shop makes one feel sick: and indeed all our food springs ultimately from dung and dead bodies, the two things which of all others seem to us the most horrible. A child, when it is past the infantile stage but still looking at the world with fresh eyes, is moved by horror almost as often as by wonder — horror of snot and spittle, of the dogs' excrement on the pavement, the dying toad full of maggots, the sweaty smell of grown-ups, the hideousness of old men, with their bald heads and bulbous noses. In his endless harping on disease, dirt and deformity, Swift is not actually inventing anything, he is merely leaving something out. Human behaviour, too, especially in politics, is as he describes it, although it contains other more important factors which he refuses to admit. So far as we can see, both horror and pain are necessary to the continuance of life on this planet, and it is therefore open to pessimists like Swift to say: 'If horror and pain must always be with us, how can life be significantly improved?' His attitude is in effect the Christian attitude, minus the bribe of a 'next world' — which, however, probably has less hold upon the minds of believers than the conviction that this world is a vale of tears and the grave is a place of rest. It is, I am certain, a wrong attitude, and one which could have harmful effects upon behaviour; but something in us responds to it, as it responds to the gloomy words of the burial service and the sweetish smell of corpses in a country church.

It is often argued, at least by people who admit the importance of subject-matter, that a book cannot be 'good' if it expresses a palpably false view of life. We are told that in our own age, for instance, any book that has genuine literary merit will also be more or less 'progressive' in tendency. This ignores the fact that throughout history a similar struggle between progress and reaction has been raging, and that the best books of any one age have always been written from several different viewpoints, some of them palpably more false than others. In so far as a writer is a propagandist, the most one can ask of him is that he shall genuinely believe in what he is saying, and that it shall not be something blazingly silly. Today, for example, one can imagine a good book being written by a Catholic, a Communist, a Fascist, a pacifist, an anarchist, perhaps by an old-style Liberal or an ordinary Conservative: one cannot imagine a good book being written by a spiritualist, a Buchmanite or a member of the Ku-Klux-Klan. The views that a writer holds must be compatible with sanity, in the medical sense, and with the power of continuous thought: beyond that what we ask of him is talent, which is probably another name for conviction. Swift did not possess ordinary wisdom, but he did possess a terrible intensity of vision, capable of picking out a single hidden truth and then magnifying it and distorting it. The durability of *Gulliver's Travels* goes to show that, if the force of belief is behind it, a world-view which only just passes the test of sanity is sufficient to produce a great work of art.

W. B. YEATS

The Words upon the Window-Pane

Swift haunts me; he is always just round the next corner. Sometimes it is a thought of my great-great-grandmother, a friend of that Archbishop King who sent him to England about the first-fruits, sometimes it is St. Patrick's, where I have gone to wander and meditate, that brings him to mind, sometimes I remember something hard or harsh in O'Leary or in Taylor, or in the public speech of our statesmen, that reminds me by its style of his verse or prose. Did he not speak, perhaps, with just such an intonation? This instinct for what is near and yet hidden is in reality a return to the sources of our power, and therefore a claim made upon the future. Thought seems more true, emotion more deep, spoken by someone who touches my pride, who seems to claim me of his kindred, who seems to make me a part of some national mythology, nor is mythology mere ostentation, mere vanity if it draws me onward to the unknown; another turn of the gyre and myth is wisdom, pride, discipline. I remember the shudder in my spine when Mrs. Patrick Campbell said, speaking words Hofmannsthal put into the mouth of Electra, 'I too am of that ancient race':

> Swift has sailed into his rest:
> Savage indignation there
> Cannot lacerate his breast.
> Imitate him if you dare,
> World-besotted traveller; he
> Served human liberty.

'In Swift's day men of intellect reached the height of their power, the greatest position they ever attained in society and the State. . . . His ideal order was the Roman Senate, his ideal men Brutus and Cato; such an order and such men had seemed possible once more.'

The Cambridge undergraduate [a character in Yeats's play *The Words upon the Window-Pane*] into whose mouth I have put these words may have read similar words in Oliver, 'the last brilliant addition to English historians', for young men such as he read the newest authorities; probably Oliver and he thought of the influence at Court and in public life of Swift and of Leibniz, of the spread of science and of scholarship over Europe, its examination of documents, its destruction of fables, a science and a scholarship modern for the first time, of certain great minds that were medieval in their scope but modern in their freedom. I must, however, add certain thoughts of my own that affected me as I wrote. I thought about a passage in the Grammont *Memoirs* where some great man is commended for his noble manner, as we commend a woman for her beauty or her charm; a famous passage in the *Appeal from the New to the Old Whigs* commending the old Whig aristocracy for their intellect and power and because their doors stood open to like-minded men; the palace of Blenheim, its pride of domination that expected a thousand years, something Asiatic in its carved intricacy of stone.

'Everything great in Ireland and in our character, in what remains of our architecture, comes from that day . . . we have kept its seal longer than England.' The overstatement of an enthusiastic Cambridge student, and yet with its measure of truth. The battle of the Boyne overwhelmed a civilisation full of religion and myth, and brought in its place intelligible laws planned out upon a great blackboard, a capacity for horizontal lines, for rigid shapes, for buildings, for attitudes of mind that could be multiplied like an expanding bookcase: the modern world, and something that appeared and perished in its dawn, an instinct for Roman rhetoric, Roman elegance. It established a Protestant aristocracy, some of whom neither called themselves English[1] nor looked with contempt or

---

[1] Nor were they English: the newest arrivals soon intermarried with an older stock, and that older stock had intermarried again and again with Gaelic Ireland. All my childhood the Coopers of Markree, County Sligo, represented such rank and fashion as the County knew, and I had it from my friend the late Bryan Cooper that his supposed Cromwellian ancestor, being childless, adopted an O'Brien; while local tradition thinks that an O'Brien, promised the return of her confiscated estate if

dread upon conquered Ireland. Indeed the battle was scarcely over when Molyneux, speaking in their name, affirmed the sovereignty of the Irish Parliament.[1] No one had the right to make our laws but the King, Lords and Commons of Ireland; the battle had been fought to change not an English but an Irish Crown; and our Parliament was almost as ancient as that of England. It was this doctrine[2] that Swift uttered in the fourth *Drapier's Letter* with such astringent eloquence that it passed from the talk of study and parlour to that of road and market, and created the political nationality of Ireland. Swift found his nationality through the *Drapier's Letters*, his convictions came from action and passion, but Berkeley, a much younger man, could find it through contemplation. He and his fellow-students but knew the war through the talk of the older men. As a boy of eighteen or nineteen he called the Irish people 'natives' as though he were in some foreign land, but two or three years later, perhaps while still an undergraduate, defined the English materialism of his day in three profound sentences, and wrote after each that 'we Irishmen' think otherwise — 'I publish . . . to know whether other men have the same ideas as we Irishmen' — and before he was twenty-five had fought the Salamis of the Irish intellect. The Irish landed aristocracy, who knew more of the siege of Derry and the battle of the Boyne

she married a Cromwellian soldier, married a Cooper and murdered him three days after. Not, however, before he had founded a family. The family of Yeats, never more than small gentry, arrived, if I can trust the only man among us who may have seen the family tree before it was burnt by Canadian Indians, 'about the time of Henry VII'. Ireland, divided in religion and politics, is as much one race as any modern country.

[1] 'Until 1691 Roman Catholics were admitted by law into both Houses of Legislature in Ireland' (J. G. S. MacNeill, *Constitutional and Parliamentary History of Ireland* (Dublin, 1917), p. 10).

[2] A few weeks ago the hierarchy of the Irish Church addressed, without any mandate from Protestant Ireland, not the Irish people as they had every right to, even in the defence of folly, but the Imperial Conference, and begged that the Irish courts might remain subservient to the Privy Council. Terrified into intrigue where none threatened, they turned from Swift and Molyneux. I remind them that when the barons of the Irish Court of Exchequer obeyed the English Privy Council in 1719 our ancestors clapped them into gaol. (1931.)

delineated on vast tapestries for their House of Lords by Dublin
Huguenots than of philosophy, found themselves masters of a
country demoralised by generations of war and famine and shared
in its demoralisation. In 1730 Swift said from the pulpit that their
houses were in ruins and no new building anywhere, that the houses
of their rack-ridden tenants were no better than English pigsties,
that the bulk of the people trod barefoot and in rags. He exaggerated,
for already the Speaker, Conolly, had built that great house at
Celbridge where slate, stone and furniture were Irish, even the silver
from Irish mines; the new Parliament House had perhaps been
planned; and there was a general stir of life. The old age of Berkeley
passed amid art and music, and men had begun to boast that in these
no country had made such progress; and some dozen years after
Berkeley's death Arthur Young found everywhere in stately
Georgian houses scientific agriculturists, benefactors of their
countryside, though for the half-educated, drunken, fire-eating,
impoverished lesser men he had nothing but detestation. Goldsmith
might have found likeable qualities, a capacity for mimicry[1] perhaps,
among these lesser men, and Sir Jonah Barrington made them his
theme, but, detestable or not, they were out of fashion. Miss Edgeworth described her *Castle Rackrent* upon the title-page of its first
edition as 'the habits of the Irish squirearchy before 1782'. A few
years more and the country people would have forgotten that the
Irish aristocracy was founded, like all aristocracies, upon conquest, or
rather, would have remembered, and boasted in the words of a medieval Gaelic poet, 'We are a sword people and we go with the sword.'
Unhappily the lesson first taught by Molyneux and Swift had been but
half learnt when the test came — country gentlemen are poor politicians — and Ireland's 'dark insipid period' began. During the entire
eighteenth century the greatest landowning family of the neighbourhood I best knew in childhood sent not a single man into the
English army and navy, but during the nineteenth century one or
more in every generation; a new absenteeism, foreseen by Miss
Edgeworth, began; those that lived upon their estates bought no

---

[1] He wrote that he had never laughed so much at Garrick's acting as at
somebody in an Irish tavern mimicking a Quaker sermon.

more fine editions of the classics; separated from public life and ambition they sank, as I have heard Lecky complain, 'into grass farmers'. Yet their genius did not die out; they sent everywhere administrators and military leaders, and now that their ruin has come — what resolute nation permits a strong alien class within its borders? — I would, remembering obscure ancestors that preached in their churches or fought beside their younger sons over half the world, and despite a famous passage of O'Grady's, gladly sing their song.

He foresaw the ruin to come, Democracy, Rousseau, the French Revolution; that is why he hated the common run of men, — 'I hate lawyers, I hate doctors,' he said, 'though I love Dr. So-and-so and Judge So-and-so,' — that is why he wrote *Gulliver*, that is why he wore out his brain, that is why he felt *saeva indignatio*, that is why he sleeps under the greatest epitaph in history.'

The *Discourse of the Contests and Dissensions between the Nobles and the Commons in Athens and Rome*, published in 1703 to warn the Tory Opposition of the day against the impeachment of ministers, is Swift's one philosophical work. All States depend for their health upon a right balance between the One, the Few, and the Many. The One is the executive, which may in fact be more than one — the Roman republic had two Consuls — but must for the sake of rapid decision be as few as possible; the Few are those who through the possession of hereditary wealth, or great personal gifts, have come to identify their lives with the life of the State, whereas the lives and ambitions of the Many are private. The Many do their day's work well, and so far from copying even the wisest of their neighbours affect 'a singularity' in action and in thought; but set them to the work of the State and every man Jack is 'listed in a party', becomes the fanatical follower of men of whose characters he knows next to nothing, and from that day on puts nothing into his mouth that some other man has not already chewed and digested. And furthermore, from the moment of enlistment thinks himself above other men and struggles for power until all is in confusion. I divine an Irish hatred of abstraction likewise expressed by that fable of Gulliver among the inventors and men of science, by Berkeley in his

Commonplace Book, by Goldsmith in the satire of *The Good-Natured Man*, in the picturesque, minute observation of 'The Deserted Village', and by Burke in his attack upon mathematical democracy. Swift enforced his moral by proving that Rome and Greece were destroyed by the war of the Many upon the Few; in Rome, where the Few had kept their class organisation, it was a war of classes, in Greece, where they had not, war upon character and genius. Miltiades, Aristides, Themistocles, Pericles, Alcibiades, Phocion, 'impeached for high crimes and misdemeanours . . . were honoured and lamented by their country as the preservers of it, and have had the veneration of all ages since paid justly to their memories'. In Rome parties so developed that men born and bred among the Few were compelled to join one party or the other and to flatter and bribe. All civilisations must end in some such way, for the Many obsessed by emotion create a multitude of religious sects but give themselves at last to some one master of bribes and flatteries and sink into the ignoble tranquillity of servitude. He defines a tyranny as the predominance of the One, the Few, or the Many, but thinks that of the Many the immediate threat. All states at their outset possess a ruling power seated in the whole body as that of the soul in the human body, a perfect balance of the three estates, the king some sort of chief magistrate, and then comes 'a tyranny: first either of the Few or the Many; but at last infallibly of a single person'. He thinks the English balance most perfect in the time of Queen Elizabeth, but that in the next age a tyranny of the Many produced that of Cromwell, and that, though recovery followed, 'all forms of government must be mortal like their authors', and he quotes from Polybius, 'those abuses and corruptions, which in time destroy a government, are sown along with the very seeds of it' and destroy it 'as rust eats away iron, and worms devour wood'. Whether the final tyranny is created by the Many — in his eyes all Caesars were tyrants — or imposed by foreign power, the result is the same. At the fall of liberty came 'a dark insipid period through all Greece' — had he Ireland in his mind also? — and the people became, in the words of Polybius, 'great reverences of crowned heads'.

Twenty-two years later Giambattista Vico published that *Scienza Nuova* which Mr. James Joyce is expounding or symbolising in the

strange fragments of his *Work in Progress*. He was the opposite of
Swift in everything, an humble, peaceful man, son of a Neapolitan
bookseller and without political opinions; he wrote panegyrics upon
men of rank, seemed to admire all that they did, took their gratuities
and yet kept his dignity. He thought civilisation passed through the
phases Swift has described, but that it was harsh and terrible until the
Many prevailed, and its joints cracked and loosened, happiest when
some one man, surrounded by able subordinates, dismissed the
Many to their private business, that its happiness lasted some
generations until, sense of the common welfare lost, it grew
malicious and treacherous, fell into 'the barbarism of reflection', and
after that into an honest, plain barbarism accepted with relief by all
and started upon its round again. Rome had conquered surrounding
nations because those nations were nearer than it to humanity and
happiness; was not Carthage already almost a democratic state when
destruction came? Swift seemed to shape his narrative upon some
clairvoyant vision of his own life, for he saw civilisation pass from
comparative happiness and youthful vigour to an old age of violence
and self-contempt, whereas Vico saw it begin in penury like himself
and end as he himself would end in a long inactive peace. But there
was a greater difference. Swift, a practical politician in everything he
wrote, ascribed its rise and fall to virtues and vices all could understand, whereas the philosophical Vico ascribed them to 'the rhythm
of the elemental forms of the mind', a new idea that would dominate
philosophy. Outside Anglo-Saxon nations where progress, impelled
by moral enthusiasm and the Patent Office, seems a perpetual
straight line, this 'circular movement', as Swift's master, Polybius,
called it, has long been the friend and enemy of public order. Both
Sorel and Marx, their eyes more Swift's than Vico's, have preached
a return to a primeval state, a beating of all down into a single class
that a new civilisation may arise with its Few, its Many and its One.
Students of contemporary Italy, where Vico's thought is current
through its influence upon Croce and Gentile, think it created, or in
part created, the present government of one man surrounded by just
such able assistants as Vico foresaw. Some philosopher has added
this further thought: the classes rise out of the matrix, create all
mental and bodily riches, sink back, as Vico saw civilisation rise and

sink, and government is there to keep the ring and see to it that combat never ends. These thoughts in the next few generations, as elaborated by Oswald Spengler, who has followed Vico without essential change, by Flinders Petrie, by the German traveller Frobenius, by Henry Adams, and perhaps by my friend Gerald Heard, may affect the masses. They have already deepened our sense of tragedy and somewhat checked the naïver among those creeds and parties who push their way to power by flattering our moral hopes. Pascal thought there was evidence for and against the existence of God, but that if a man kept his mind in suspense about it he could not live a rich and active life, and I suggest to the Cellars and Garrets that though history is too short to change either the idea of progress or the eternal circuit into scientific fact, the eternal circuit may best suit our preoccupation with the soul's salvation, our individualism, our solitude. Besides we love antiquity, and that other idea — progress — the sole religious myth of modern man, is only two hundred years old.

Swift's pamphlet had little effect in its day; it did not prevent the impeachment and banishment a few years later of his own friends; and although he was in all probability the first — if there was another 'my small reading cannot trace it' — to describe in terms of modern politics the discord of parties that compelled revolutionary France, as it has compelled half a dozen nations since the war, to accept the 'tyranny' of a 'single person', it was soon forgotten; but for the understanding of Swift it is essential. It shows that the defence of liberty boasted upon his tombstone did not come from political disappointment (when he wrote it he had suffered none); and what he meant by liberty. Gulliver, in those travels written twenty years later, calls up from the dead 'a sextumvirate to which all the ages of the world cannot add a seventh': Epaminondas and Socrates, who suffered at the hands of the Many; Brutus, Junius Brutus, Cato the Younger, Thomas More, who fought the tyranny of the One; Brutus with Caesar still his inseparable friend, for a man may be a tyrant without personal guilt.

Liberty depended upon a balance within the State, like that of the 'humours' in a human body, or like that 'unity of being' Dante compared to a perfectly proportioned human body, and for its sake

Swift was prepared to sacrifice what seems to the modern man liberty itself. The odds were a hundred to one, he wrote, that 'violent zeal for the truth' came out of 'petulancy, ambition, or pride'. He himself might prefer a republic to a monarchy, but did he open his mouth upon the subject would be deservedly hanged. Had he religious doubts he was not to blame so long as he kept them to himself, for God had given him reason. It was the attitude of many a modern Catholic who thinks, though upon different grounds, that our civilisation may sink into a decadence like that of Rome. But sometimes belief itself must be hidden. He was devout; had the Communion Service by heart; read the Fathers and prayed much, yet would not press the mysteries of his faith upon any unwilling man. Had not the early Christians kept silent about the divinity of Christ; should not the missionaries to China 'soften' it? He preached as law commanded; a man could save his soul doubtless in any religion which taught submission to the Will of God, but only one State could protect his body; and how could it protect his body if rent apart by those cranks and sectaries mocked in his *Tale of a Tub*? Had not French Huguenots and English Dissenters alike sinned against the State? Except at those moments of great public disturbance, when a man must choose his creed or his king, let him think his own thoughts in silence.

What was this liberty bought with so much silence, and served through all his life with so much eloquence? 'I should think,' he wrote in the *Discourse*, 'that the saying, *vox populi, vox dei* ought to be understood of the universal bent and current of a people, not of the bare majority of a few representatives, which is often procured by little arts, and great industry and application; wherein those who engage in the pursuits of malice and revenge are much more sedulous than such as would prevent them.' That *vox populi* or 'bent and current', or what we even more vaguely call national spirit, was the sole theme of his *Drapier's Letters*; its right to express itself as it would through such men as had won or inherited general consent. I doubt if a mind so contemptuous of average men thought, as Vico did, that it found expression also through all individual lives, or asked more for those lives than protection from the most obvious evils. I remember J. F. Taylor, a great student of Swift, saying 'individual liberty is of no importance, what matters is national liberty'.

The will of the State, whether it build a cage for a dead bird or remain in the bird itself, must always, whether interpreted by Burke or Marx, find expression through some governing class or company identified with that 'bent and current', with those 'elemental forms', whether by interest or training. The men of Swift's day would have added that class or company must be placed by wealth above fear and toil, though Swift thought every properly conducted State must limit the amount of wealth the individual could possess. But the old saying that there is no wisdom without leisure has somewhat lost its truth. When the physical world became rigid; when curiosity inherited from the Renaissance, and the soul's anxiety inherited from the Middle Ages, passed, man ceased to think; his work thought in him. Spinoza, Leibniz, Swift, Berkeley, Goethe, the last typical figure of the epoch, recognised no compulsion but the 'bent and current' of their lives; the Speaker, Conolly, could still call out a posse of gentlemen to design the façade of his house, and though Berkeley thought their number too great, that work is still admired; Swift called himself a poor scholar in comparison with Lord Treasurer Harley. Unity of being was still possible though somewhat over-rationalised and abstract, more diagram than body; whereas the best modern philosophers are professors, their pupils compile notebooks that they may be professors some day; politicians stick to their last or leave it to plague us with platitudes; we poets and artists may be called, so small our share in life, 'separated spirits', words applied by the old philosophers to the dead. When Swift sank into imbecility or madness his epoch had finished in the British Isles, those 'elemental forms' had passed beyond him; more than the 'great Ministers' had gone. I can see in a sort of nightmare vision the 'primary qualities' torn from the side of Locke, Johnson's ponderous body bent above the letter to Lord Chesterfield, some obscure person somewhere inventing the spinning-jenny, upon his face that look of benevolence kept by painters and engravers, from the middle of the eighteenth century to the time of the Prince Consort, for such as he, or, to simplify the tale —

> Locke sank into a swoon;
> The Garden died;
> God took the spinning-jenny
> Out of his side.

'That arrogant intellect free at last from superstition': the young man's overstatement full of the unexamined suppositions of common speech. I saw Asia in the carved stones of Blenheim, not in the pride of great abstract masses, but in that humility of flowerlike intricacy — the particular blades of the grass; nor can chance have thrown into contiguous generations Spinoza and Swift, an absorption of the whole intellect in God, a fakir-like contempt for all human desire; 'take from her', Swift prayed for Stella in sickness, 'all violent desire whether of life or death'; the elaboration and spread of Masonic symbolism, its God made in the image of a Christopher Wren; Berkeley's declaration, modified later, that physical pleasure is the *summum bonum*, heaven's sole reality, his counter-truth to that of Spinoza.

In judging any moment of past time we should leave out what has since happened; we should not call the Swift of the *Drapier's Letters* nearer truth because of their influence upon history than the Swift who attacked in *Gulliver* the inventors and logicians; we should see certain men and women as if at the edge of a cliff, time broken away from their feet. Spinoza and the Masons, Berkeley and Swift, speculative and practical intellect, stood there free at last from all prepossessions and touched the extremes of thought; the Gymnosophists of Strabo close at hand, could they but ignore what was harsh and logical in themselves, or the China of the Dutch cabinet-makers, of *The Citizen of the World*: the long-settled rule of powerful men, no great dogmatic structure, few great crowded streets, scattered unprogressive communities, much handiwork, wisdom wound into the roots of the grass.

'I have something in my blood that no child must inherit.' There have been several theories to account for Swift's celibacy. Sir Walter Scott suggested a 'physical defect', but that seems incredible. A man so outspoken would have told Vanessa the truth and stopped a tragic persecution, a man so charitable have given Stella the protection of his name. The refusal to see Stella when there was no third person present suggests a man that dreaded temptation; nor is it compatible with those stories still current among our country people of Swift sending his servant out to fetch a woman, and dismissing that servant when he woke to find a black woman at his side. Lecky suggested dread of madness — the theory of my play — of madness already present in constant eccentricity; though, with a vagueness born from distaste of the theme, he saw nothing incompatible between Scott's theory and his own. Had Swift dreaded transmitting madness he might well have been driven to consorting with the nameless barren women of the streets. Somebody else suggests syphilis contracted doubtless between 1799, when he was engaged to Varina, and some date soon after Stella's arrival in Ireland. Mr. Shane Leslie thinks that Swift's relation to Vanessa was not platonic,[1] and that whenever his letters speak of a cup of coffee they mean the sexual act; whether the letters seem to bear him out I do not know, for those letters bore me; but whether they seem to or not he must, if he is to get a hearing, account for Swift's relation to Stella. It seems certain that Swift loved her though he called it by some other name, and she him, and that it was platonic love.

> Thou, Stella, wert no longer young,
> When first for thee my harp was strung:
> Without one word of Cupid's darts,
> Of killing eyes or bleeding hearts;
> With friendship and esteem possest,
> I ne'er admitted Love a guest.
> In all the habitudes of life,
> The friend, the mistress, and the wife,
> Variety we still pursue,
> In pleasure seek for something new;
> Or else comparing with the rest,
> Take comfort that our own is best;
> (The best we value by the worst,
> As tradesmen show their trash at first:)
> But his pursuits are at an end,
> Whom Stella chooses for a friend.

If the relation between Swift and Vanessa was not platonic there

[1] Rossi and Hone take the same view, though uncertain about the coffee. When I wrote, their book had not appeared.

must have been some bar that affected Stella as well as Swift. Dr. Delany is said to have believed that Swift married Stella in 1716 and found in some exchange of confidences that they were brother and sister, but Sir William Temple was not in Ireland during the year that preceded Swift's birth, and so far as we know Swift's mother was not in England.

There is no satisfactory solution. Swift, though he lived in great publicity, and wrote and received many letters, hid two things which constituted perhaps all that he had of private life: his loves and his religious beliefs.

'Was Swift mad? Or was it the intellect itself that was mad?' The other day a scholar in whose imagination Swift has a pre-eminence scarcely possible outside Ireland said: 'I sometimes feel that there is a black cloud about to overwhelm me, and then comes a great jet of life; Swift had that black cloud and no jet. He was terrified.' I said, 'Terrified perhaps of everything but death', and reminded him of a story of Dr. Johnson's.[1] There was a reward of £500 for the identification of the author of the *Drapier's Letters*. Swift's butler, who had carried the manuscript to the printer, stayed away from work. When he returned, Swift said, 'I know that my life is in your hands, but I will not bear, out of fear, either your insolence or negligence.' He dismissed the butler, and when the danger had passed, he restored him to his post, rewarded him, and said to the other servants, 'No more Barclay, henceforth Mr. Barclay.' 'Yes,' said my friend, 'he was not afraid of death but of life, of what might happen next; that is what made him so defiant in public and in private and demand for the State the obedience a Connacht priest demands for the Church.' I have put a cognate thought into the mind of John Corbet. He imagines, though but for a moment, that the intellect of Swift's age, persuaded that the mechanicians mocked by Gulliver would prevail, that its moment of freedom could not last, so dreaded the historic process that it became in the half-mad mind of Swift a dread of parentage: 'Am I to add another to the healthy rascaldom and knavery of the world?' Did not Rousseau within five years of the death of Swift publish his *Discourse upon*

---

[1] Sheridan has a different version, but as I have used it merely to illustrate an argument I leave it as Dr. Johnson told it.

Arts and Sciences and discover instinctive harmony not in heroic effort, not in Cato and Brutus, not among impossible animals — I think of that noble horse Blake drew for Hayley — but among savages, and thereby beget the *sans-culottes* of Marat? After the arrogance of power the humility of a servant.

IRVIN EHRENPREIS

The Origins of Gulliver's Travels[1]

I

UNTIL the publication of *The Letters of Jonathan Swift to Charles Ford*, literary scholars thought that Swift wrote *Gulliver's Travels* between 1715 and 1720, a period when he published almost nothing. His starting point was, they believed, sketches made up by the Scriblerus group — Pope, Swift, and others — in 1713 and 1714, and finally produced by Pope in 1741. Then D. Nichol Smith, in his edition of the Ford letters, proved that Swift wrote part I of *Gulliver* in about 1721–2, part II around 1722–3, part IV in 1723, and part III (after part IV) in 1724–5.[2] Swift continued to revise it, probably until it was published in the autumn of 1726.

But if Smith's facts have long been accepted, very few implications have been drawn from them. It is still normal for critics discussing the composition of the book to begin with Scriblerus, as it is still normal for them to seek later sources in literature and in political or intellectual history.[3] If, however, the Scriblerus papers seemed a probable beginning for *Gulliver* precisely because Swift worked on them just before he composed 'A Voyage to Lilliput' in 1715, surely the discovery of a six-year gap makes it less necessary

[1] Read, in a shortened form, before the International Association of University Professors of English (Jesus College, Cambridge, 23 Aug. 1956). I am indebted to Mr. Jonathan Wordsworth of Brasenose College, Oxford, for greatly improving the style of this paper. I have profited from the more general criticisms of Professor George Sherburn, who disagrees, however, with several of my conclusions.

[2] Oxford, 1935, pp. xxxviii–xlii and *passim*. Charles Firth used some of Smith's evidence (not quite correctly) in 'The Political Significance of *Gulliver's Travels*', *Proceedings of the British Academy*, vol. IX (1920), pp. 237–59.

[3] For recent examples, see Ricardo Quintana, *Swift, An Introduction* (Oxford, 1955), pp. 145 ff., and Charles Kerby-Miller (ed.), *Memoirs of ... Martinus Scriblerus* (New Haven, 1950), pp. 315–20.

to consider them. It may have seemed likely that Swift, after leaving both England and his friends of the Scriblerus Club in 1714, should in 1715 have projected a satire based on Scriblerian essays. It is less plausible that he should have waited six or seven years before hauling out sketches theretofore unused, and employing them as the frame for his greatest book.

Nevertheless, the original argument is useful: Ought one not to look at what Swift was indeed busy with, just before the genuine date of his start on 'Lilliput'? For not only were the early biographers and critics mistaken as to that date, they were also wrong to suppose that, because Swift published nothing in the years preceding *Gulliver*, he wrote nothing. It was during this period that he put together a succession of essays concerning English politics mainly from 1708 to 1715. Furthermore, these essays form stages in a long series of works and fragments dealing with the same subject, but none of them innocent enough to be published at the time. Finally, one remembers that part 1 of *Gulliver* is largely an allegory of English political history from 1708 to 1715, and that in this allegory Gulliver stands largely for Bolingbroke, the secretary of state from 1710 to 1714.

It seems to me more than a coincidence that Swift wrote essay after unprintable essay on English politics of the early eighteenth century, and then plunged into such an allegory. To ignore Swift's *History of the Four Last Years*, his *Some Free Thoughts upon the Present State of Affairs*, his *Memoirs ... 1710*, his various fragments on the same topics, and then to search for *Gulliver's* antecedents in a vague ur-*Scriblerus* is to contradict all we have learned of his literary method. What one knows of the *Memoirs of Scriblerus* belongs almost entirely to its form in 1741, fifteen years after the printing of *Gulliver*, a form which Pope had deliberately edited so as to connect the book with Swift's masterpiece.[1] Is it credible that an author should compose hundreds of poems practically all traceable to specific circumstances, and scores of essays or pamphlets which can hardly be understood except by reference to their occasions, and yet should compose his finest work

---

[1] Kerby-Miller, *Memoirs*, pp. 61–65.

in a library, referring to old drafts of hypothetical hoaxes?

I shall not only suggest that Swift created much of *Gulliver* out of his own memories, experiences, and reflections from 1714 to 1725; but, moving from this position, I shall try to indicate some new meanings for certain parts of the book.[1]

II

Arthur E. Case, refining on Charles Firth, has already explained the political allusions in 'A Voyage to Lilliput', and there is not a great deal to alter in his foundations.[2] Both scholars went astray, however, in comparing Lilliput with the actual events of 1708–15 and not with Swift's versions of those events. If Case had looked into Swift instead of history, he would have found that the political allegory is both more detailed and less consistent than he believed; that references to Bolingbroke (rather than Oxford) control the fable; and that Swift tended to choose, for dramatization, those episodes in which he could identify his own feelings with those of the ministry. There are many examples of these principles, though I shall limit myself to three.

In chapter ii of 'Lilliput', although Gulliver is under a strong guard, he is unavoidably exposed to the 'impertinence' and 'malice' of the 'rabble', some of whom shoot arrows at him. But 'the Colonel' delivers six of the ringleaders into his hands. Gulliver frightens each one by pretending he will eat the man alive and then setting him free.[3] In *The Battle of the Books*, Swift calls journalists 'a disorderly rout' of coatless 'rogues and raggamuffins'.[4] In his letters to Ford he calls Oxford 'the Colonel' and Bolingbroke 'the Captain'. In the *Journal to Stella* he complains that Whig pamphleteers are busy against the government: 'I have begged [Bolingbroke] to make

[1] For convenience, I call Oxford and Bolingbroke by their titles even before they became peers. In using quotations, I ignore the original capitals and italics where they do not bear on the meaning; and I indicate omitted words only within a quotation, not before or after.

[2] *Four Essays on Gulliver's Travels* (Princeton, 1945), pp. 69–80.

[3] Herbert Davis (ed.), *The Prose Works of Jonathan Swift*, vol. XI (Oxford, 1941), p. 15. Page references to *Gulliver's Travels* in the text are to this edition.

[4] D. Nichol Smith (ed.), *A Tale of a Tub* (Oxford, 1920), p. 238.

examples of one or two of them; and he assures me he will. They are very bold and abusive' (21 September 1711). The following month, he says that one journalist — Boyer — 'has abused me in a pamphlet, and I have got him up in a messenger's hands: [Bolingbroke] promises me to swinge him. [Oxford] told me last night that he had the honour to be abused with me in a pamphlet. I must make that rogue an example for warning to others.' A week later (24 October), he reports that 'every day some ballad comes out reflecting on the ministry', and Bolingbroke 'has seized on a dozen booksellers and publishers'.[1]

It was under Bolingbroke, as secretary of state, that 'we first see' the government trying to stamp out journalistic opposition 'by means of frequent arrests' rather than by court action. 'Warrants were issued in large numbers. Arrests were made, and printers were required to furnish sureties for appearance.' But the government's powers did not often permit anything more serious than such harrying and frightening manœuvres: 'And yet of these thirteen [Swift's dozen] who were seized, Boyer, who would not be likely to ignore martyrs for the Whig cause, mentions not one as suffering punishment. And in 1712 Bolingbroke was compelled to order the Attorney-General to release a number of persons under prosecution for libel.'[2] Swift, libelled like the government, has thus created an allegorical detail from Bolingbroke's method of dealing with the dart-throwing hack writers of 1710–14.

In chapter v of 'Lilliput', there is the crisis about which Case and Firth disagreed, the fire in the palace, which Gulliver quenches with his urine. Firth supposed this to mean *A Tale of a Tub*; Case interpreted it as the Treaty of Utrecht, ending the War of the Spanish Succession. Case is undoubtedly correct. The meaning appears from a sentence in a pamphlet written in 1714 by an underling with Swift's assistance: 'But the quarrelling with the peace, because it is not

[1] Four months afterward, there was a rumour that Swift had been arrested. In an odd coincidence he mentions this and the pamphleteers together, thus joining the themes of the episode in *Gulliver's Travels*: 'I doubt you have been in pain about the report of my being arrested. The pamphleteers have let me alone this month' (17, 18 Feb. 1712).

[2] Laurence Hanson, *Government and the Press 1695–1763* (Oxford, 1936), p. 62.

P   J.F.L.

exactly to our mind, seems as if one that had put out a great fire should be sued by the neighbourhood for some lost goods, or damag'd houses; which happen'd (say they) by his making too much haste.'[1] The figure of extinguishing a spreading blaze for stopping a tremendous military threat by allied action is ancient, natural, and ubiquitous. A few scattered modern instances are the Emperor Maximilian's declaration against the Venetians, 1509;[2] Samuel Daniel's *Breviary of the History of England*, *c.* 1610;[3] the Italian satirist, Boccalini, writing about the Fronde;[4] and (most relevantly) the London *Flying-Post*, 25 October 1712, applying Boccalini to the War of the Spanish Succession: 'A dreadful fire broke out in the palace of the French monarchy. . . . It raged so furiously, that the neighbouring monarchs, afraid that their own estates would be consumed by it, immediately ran one and all to quench it. The English . . . diligently carried thither the waters of their Thames.'

Yet Case mistakes the implications when he relates them to Oxford's difficulties with Queen Anne (pp. 75–76). It was not the queen who felt ungrateful for the peace, but those who impeached the ministers. The treaty was Bolingbroke's peculiar responsibility; and Swift's emphasis on it — as well as his preoccupation, throughout the first voyage, with foreign rather than domestic affairs — betokens Bolingbroke's predominance in the Lilliputian allegory. After all, by 1721 it was not Oxford who wanted defending: he had been discharged from his impeachment in 1717, and he acted a free role in the House of Lords until his death in 1724 — well before the completion of *Gulliver's Travels*. Bolingbroke, meanwhile, having fled to France in 1715, remained attainted and in exile until 1723;

---

[1] Davis (ed.), *Prose Works*, vol. VIII (1953), pp. xvi–xvii, 194.

[2] Raynaldus, *Annales ecclesiastici*, vol. XX (Rome, 1663), annus 1509, par. 2.

[3] Par. 27. R. B. Gottfried shows that it was written by Daniel, not Ralegh; and he dates it between 1605 and 1612 (*SP*, vol. LIII (April, 1956), pp. 172–190). Daniel uses the figure elsewhere as well: e.g. A. B. Grosart (ed.), *Complete Works* (London, 1896), vol. IV, pp. 162–3.

[4] See ch. iii of the *Politick Touchstone* in the 1704 translation of Boccalini's *Advertisements from Parnassus . . . [and] The Politick Touchstone*, vol. III, pp. 7–11 (following p. 256 of the same vol.).

and he never regained his seat in the House of Lords.

The same inferences emerge again from my final illustration; and this will carry us to a point after which, Case himself says, Gulliver's story is based on Bolingbroke's adventures, with only minor references to Oxford (p. 77). In chapter v of part I, Swift mentions the displeasure of the Emperor of Lilliput when Gulliver made friends with the ambassadors from Blefuscu and agreed to visit their emperor, thus creating a suspicion of high treason. Certain ministers, says Gulliver, 'represented my intercourse with those ambassadors, as a mark of disaffection, from which I am sure *my heart was wholly free*' (p. 38 — my italics). Here, one already knows, Blefuscu stands for France. From evidence in Swift's letters and pamphlets, it seems that the proposed visit to the Emperor of Blefuscu stands for Bolingbroke's visit (while he was secretary of state) to the French Court; and the suspicion of his disaffection would be due to Bolingbroke's having seen the Pretender during that visit.

In the *Enquiry into the Behaviour of the Queen's Last Ministry*, Swift has a portrait of Bolingbroke. Here is a pamphlet defending Swift's ministerial acquaintances against the charge (among others) of planning to bring in the Pretender and so to commit high treason. Swift opens the portrait of Bolingbroke with a lament that three of his most exalted friends are either in exile or awaiting trial. Then he applies to himself the same expression that Gulliver was to use: '*As my own heart was free* from all treasonable thoughts, so I did little imagine my self to be perpetually in the company of traitors.'[1]

This passage, written in 1715, has a further parallel in Swift's letter on the subject. The Archbishop of Dublin had suggested that Bolingbroke might turn informer, come back from France, and tell some 'ill story' about Swift. In reply, the Archbishop received a furious defence of the exile:

He was three or four days at the court of France, while he was secretary, and it is barely possible, he might then have entered into some deep negotiation with the Pretender; although I would not believe him, if he should swear it, because he protested to me, that he never saw him but once, and that was at a great distance, in public, at an opera. . . . But I am surprised to think your grace could talk, or

---

[1] Davis (ed.), *Prose Works*, vol. VIII, p. 134 (my italics).

act, or correspond with me for some years past, while you must needs believe me a most false and vile man; declaring to you on all occasions my abhorrence of the Pretender, and yet privately engaged with a ministry to bring him in.[1]

Finally, returning to 'Lilliput', one finds in chapter vii the fourth article of the impeachment against Gulliver, that 'contrary to the duty of a faithful subject, [he] is now preparing to make a voyage to the court and empire of Blefuscu ... [and] doth falsely and traitorously intend to take the said voyage, and thereby to aid, comfort, and abet the Emperor of Blefuscu, so late an enemy, and in open war with his imperial majesty aforesaid' (p. 53). In other words, the treason charged against Gulliver corresponds to the charge against Bolingbroke, which touches Swift as well; and Gulliver's projected trip corresponds to Bolingbroke's actual trip.

These echoes and parallels hold a few of the many clues which bear out my principal argument. Swift did not wait six years after 1714 to prepare his reflections on the ministry of the Earl of Oxford and Viscount Bolingbroke. He went over the material in one form after another, from personal letters, through unpublishable essays, into the entertainment of an allegory. 'Lilliput' is the sublimation of a series of unprintable pamphlets and fragments. The *Memoirs of Scriblerus* were an element in the allegory, but only an indeterminate element.

III

If the pygmies of Lilliput are dominated by a figure descended from Bolingbroke, the giants of Brobdingnag are ruled by one exactly the opposite in origin. This is the person to whom Swift immediately contrasted Bolingbroke the first time that he met the secretary. On the evening of that day, Swift wrote to Stella, 'I am thinking what a veneration we used to have for Sir William Temple, because he might have been secretary of state at fifty; and here is a young fellow, hardly thirty, in that employment.' A year later, he drew precisely the same contrast again, obviously forgetting that he

---

[1] F. E. Ball (ed.), *The Correspondence of Jonathan Swift* (London, 1910–14), vol. II, pp. 348–9.

had already noticed it. In fact, out of a total of seven times that Swift mentions Temple in the *Journal to Stella*, five are to link or contrast him with Bolingbroke.[1]

Indeed, between those two great men the similarities of interest and achievement and the differences of character are so startling that the image of one would naturally call up an image of the other. Bolingbroke talked too much, drank too much, systematically betrayed his wife, and sacrificed his integrity to political ambition. Temple spoke with reserve and formality, he lived with calculated moderation, he adored his wife, the brilliant Dorothy Osborne, and he withdrew from high office rather than injure his honour. Both men had their greatest successes in diplomacy. Temple arranged the Triple Alliance of England, Holland, and Sweden; he was largely responsible for the marriage of William of Orange to Princess Mary. Bolingbroke's supreme achievement was the Treaty of Utrecht. At forty-six Temple had refused to be made secretary of state; Bolingbroke at thirty-two had forced his way into that office.

If Swift's memory of Temple provided the outline for the King of Brobdingnag, certain other aspects of the second voyage slip into place. I have argued elsewhere that the child Stella, or Esther Johnson, has a similar relationship with the girl giantess, Glumdalclitch;[2] and of course Swift knew Stella as a child while they were both living with Temple. Lady Temple, or Dorothy Osborne, is naturally associated with a queen since she was the intimate friend of Queen Mary, whose death narrowly preceded her own. There is a further hint here; for in Brobdingnag the queen plays a far more dignified role, and has far more to do, than in any of the other courts which Gulliver visited. Yet the king remains emphatically in control of the monarchy. The reign of William and Mary duplicates this relationship, as did that of no other royal couple in Swift's lifetime before 1726; and that reign roughly coincides with the extent of Swift's residences at Moor Park. One might add, among Temple's links with kingship, that he bore the same name as William III, was a most esteemed friend of that ruler, and introduced Swift to him — the only king Swift met before 1726.

[1] 11 Nov. 1710; 3, 4, 15 April and 3 Nov. 1711.
[2] *PMLA*, vol. LXX (Sept. 1955), p. 715.

Gulliver's portrait of the King of Brobdingnag agrees in many essentials with the character of Temple. The giant had married a wife who, like Dorothy Osborne, possessed an 'infinite deal of wit and humour' and, when Gulliver first met him, the king was 'retired to his cabinet' (p. 87). Gulliver almost never describes him in society, almost always converses with him alone, and remarks that the geography of his country made him live in it 'wholly secluded from the rest of the world' (p. 117). But he 'delighted in musick', was 'educated in the study of philosophy', was 'as learned as any person in his dominions', and had an 'excellent understanding' (pp. 110, 87, 111). In examining Gulliver's body, the king showed up the quackery of certain pedants who pretended to be wise men (pp. 87–88).

Temple's own sister says that immediately after his marriage he had for five years lived a domestic and retired life, spending much time 'in his closet', studying history and philosophy. She comments on his excellent knowledge of Spanish, French, and Latin, and his regret at the decline of his Greek; and she says he was 'a great lover of musick'.[1] In an *Ode to Sir William Temple*, Swift has a stanza contrasting the baronet's polished but solid learning with the 'ill-mannered pedantry' of professional scholars (st. 3). During the decade when Swift lived with Temple, the baronet's sister says her brother utterly withdrew from court and town life, living in rural seclusion with his family.[2] The King of Brobdingnag spoke at first in a cold manner and produced an impression 'of much gravity, and austere countenance' (p. 87). Temple's reserve and aloofness are perhaps the best-known traits of his character, and Swift mentions them in the *Journal to Stella* (e.g. 3–4 April 1711).

In politics, the King of Brobdingnag 'professed both to abominate and despise all *mystery, refinement,* and *intrigue,* either [of] prince or a minister' (p. 119). In his *Ode* Swift devotes a stanza to Temple's destructive exposure of the deceits and frauds of ministers (st. 7). Temple's actual conduct as a diplomat was distinguished above all for its directness and its lack of intrigue or ceremony. The

[1] G. C. Moore Smith (ed.), *The Early Essays and Romances of Sir William Temple* (Oxford, 1930), pp. 8, 5, 6, 11, 28.

[2] Ibid. pp. 25, 28.

giant king feels overwhelmed by horror at Gulliver's description of human warfare, and cannot understand why the British in particular have engaged in 'such chargeable and extensive wars' (pp. 117–19, 115). Swift in his 'Ode' has two stanzas on Temple's repugnance for war (sts. 5, 6). Summing up the king's nature, Gulliver granted him 'every quality which procures veneration, love and esteem' (p. 119). In his 'Ode' Swift says that Temple is learned, good, and great all at once, and uniquely joins in himself the whole empire of virtue (sts. 1, 4). When Temple died, Swift wrote: 'With him [died] all that was good and amiable among men.'[1]

The King of Brobdingnag talks about government and politics in chapter vi of the second voyage. After hearing Gulliver explain the constitution of England, he asks many questions. Though these are satiric, they involve certain arguments which continue into the next chapter; and at the end of the latter, Gulliver delivers a few sentences on the political history of Brobdingnag. Those closing sentences of Gulliver's sound very much like *A Discourse of the Contests and Dissensions*, a work which Swift published in 1701; and this relationship has a special meaning.

The link between Brobdingnagian political history and Swift's *Discourse* was noted by Case,[2] but another scholar, Robert J. Allen, had already shown what I consider to be the significance of this link. In a study of the *Discourse*, Allen demonstrated that Swift's book was founded upon certain works by Sir William Temple;[3] and it is in fact possible to trace themes back from 'Brobdingnag' to Temple's essays either directly or through the intermediate stage of the *Discourse*.[4] I shall give only two of the simplest illustrations.

[1] Henry Craik, *Life of Jonathan Swift*, 2nd ed. (London, 1894), vol. 1, p. 95.

[2] See his edition of *Gulliver's Travels* (New York, 1938), p. 142 n.

[3] 'Swift's Earliest Political Tract and Sir William Temple's Essays', *Harvard Stud. and Notes in Philol. and Lit.*, vol. xix (1937), pp. 3–12. Myrddin Jones, in an unpublished B.Litt. thesis, adds further evidence to that of Allen; see his MS., 'Swift's Views of History' (1953), in the Bodleian Library, Oxford.

[4] To appreciate the connection of all this material with *Gulliver* one should first read Temple's essays, 'On the Original and Nature of Government' and 'Of Popular Discontents', then chs. i and v of Swift's *Discourse*, and finally chs. vi and vii of the 'Voyage to Brobdingnag'.

There is a particularly neat triangular relationship among the following specimens: Gulliver gives the giant king a most flattering account of the House of Commons. The king asks:

How it came to pass, that people were so violently bent upon getting into this assembly . . . often to the ruin of their families, without any salary or pension: because this appeared such an exalted strain of virtue and publick spirit, that his majesty seemed to doubt it might possibly not be always sincere: And he desired to know, whether such zealous gentlemen could have any views of refunding themselves for the charges and trouble they were at, by sacrificing the publick good to the designs of . . . a corrupted ministry. [pp. 113–14]

Temple, writing on popular assemblies, had said:

The needy, the ambitious . . . the covetous, are ever restless to get into public employments. . . . I have found no talent of so much advantage among men, towards their growing great or rich, as a violent and restless passion and pursuit for one or the other. . . . Yet all these cover their ends with most worthy pretences, and those noble sayings, That men are not born for themselves, and must sacrifice their lives for the public, as well as their time and health.[1]

The passage here quoted from Temple is part of a longer section picked out by Allen (pp. 9–10) as having influenced Swift's *Discourse*.

The King of Brobdingnag also asked Gulliver about the English army. The innuendo of his question is that a paid army in peacetime is needed only to maintain the power of a tyrant:

Above all, he was amazed to hear me talk of a mercenary standing army in the midst of peace, and among a free people. He said, if we were governed by our own consent in the persons of our representatives, he could not imagine of whom we were afraid, or against whom we were to fight; and would hear my opinion, whether a private man's house might not better be defended by himself, his children, and family; than by half a dozen rascals picked up at a venture in the streets, for small wages. [p. 115]

---

[1] Sir William Temple, *Works* (London, 1770 ed.), vol. III, pp. 42–43.

Temple, in his essay on government, says that a king and his people are like a father and his family; so a just and careful parent is willingly followed and obeyed by all his children. But a tyrant thinks he cannot be safe among his children, except by putting arms into the hands of hired servants:

> For against a foreign enemy, and for defence of evident interest, all that can bear arms in a nation are soldiers ... and these kind of forces [i.e. mercenaries] come to be used by good princes, only upon necessity of providing for their defence against great and armed neighbours or enemies; but by ill ones as a support of decayed authority, or as they lose the force of that which is natural and paternal....
>
> Yet this seems a much weaker principle of government ... [for] common pay is a faint principle of courage and action, in comparison of religion, liberty, honour, revenge, or necessity ... so as if the people come to unite by any strong passion, or general interest ... they are masters of [mercenary] armies.[1]

Most of the giant king's discussion of politics has a similar parallel in Temple's essays on government.

Now there should really be nothing to surprise one in Swift's reviving for *Gulliver's Travels* the ideas of his earlier work. The situation of his three great friends — Bolingbroke, Oxford, and Ormonde — in 1715 seemed to repeat the circumstances which had provoked the *Discourse*. In 1701 four former ministers were most unfairly impeached by the House of Commons, but they were dismissed and acquitted by the Lords. Swift thought the impeachments outrageous, and wrote his *Discourse* to prove them so. In 1715 his own ministerial friends were impeached. Though he might write a book then, however, nobody would dare to print it, and even *his* head was not out of danger. When, in 1721–2, he sublimated all these memories in a satiric fantasy, the arguments remained the same, and their origin was still, ultimately, Sir William Temple.

---

[1] Temple, *Works*, vol. 1, p. 45, Professor H. W. Donner has kindly pointed out to me that this motif is one more sign of *Gulliver's* connection (often slighted) with More's *Utopia*. The explosive attack on mercenaries in bk. ii, ch. viii, of the *Utopia* re-enforced the attitude which Swift had learned from Temple.

IV

For Houyhnhnmland (the third part of *Gulliver* in order of composition) my reasoning depends on two related assumptions. The first is that although the Houyhnhnms embody traits which Swift admired, they do not represent his moral ideal for mankind. The other is that the Houyhnhnms represent in general (though not wholly) what he considered to be a deistic view of human nature — a view against which, as a devout Anglican, he fought. By 'deistic' I mean the vague tradition in which men like Swift tended to lump freethinkers, deists, Socinians, and some Latitudinarians.[1]

Even a hasty reader might notice signs which support these assumptions. A rather light hint is the Houyhnhnms' ignorance of bodily shame: Gulliver says he asked his Houyhnhnm master's forgiveness 'if I did not expose those parts that nature taught us to conceal. He said...he could not understand why nature should teach us to conceal what nature had given' (pp. 220–1). Here, Gulliver's error resides in his logic rather than his modesty. It was not nature that taught us to conceal our genitalia; it was a supernatural moral law.

A more serious clue is a saying of Gulliver's master that '*Reason* alone is sufficient to govern a *rational* creature' (p. 243). This maxim runs contrary to the spirit of Christianity: except by removing men from the category of 'rational creatures', no sincere Anglican could agree with the wise Houyhnhnm. Swift devotes two of his extant sermons to annihilating such doctrines, and these sermons are the best of all commentaries on Houyhnhnmland. He excludes the possibility of virtue without Christianity except through rare 'personal merit', as in Socrates and Cato, who happened to be blessed with a disposition (not reason) naturally good.[2] 'There is no

---

[1] The term 'deist' was seldom used with any precision in the eighteenth century. Bolingbroke would not have admitted to the title, although his works were normally received as subversive of Christianity; cf. Boswell's *Johnson* (ed. Hill-Powell: Oxford, 1934–50), vol. I, pp. 268–9. Avowed deists were extremely rare, but Swift threw the label about with great freedom; cf. Davis (ed.), *Prose Works*, vol. III (1940), pp. 71, 79, 92, 122. For Swift's considered view of the deists, see Louis Landa's 'Introduction to the Sermons' in Davis (ed.), *Prose Works*, vol. IX (1948), pp. 108–16.

[2] Sermon, 'Upon the Excellency of Christianity', Davis (ed.), *Prose Works*, vol. IX (1948), p. 249.

solid, firm foundation for virtue, but in a conscience directed by the principles of religion.'[1]

Deistic philosophers run in another direction. William Wollaston, whom Swift detested, writes: 'To act according to right reason, and to act according to truth are in effect the same thing. . . . To be governed by reason is the general law imposed by the author of nature upon them, whose uppermost faculty is reason.'[2] Similarly, the inexhaustible benevolence of the Houyhnhnms sounds, even prima facie, like a parody of such antecedents of deism as the Earl of Shaftesbury, who says, 'To deserve the name of good or virtuous, a creature must have all his inclinations and affections, his dispositions of mind and temper, suitable, and agreeing with the good of his kind . . . this affection of a creature toward the good of the species or common nature is . . . proper and natural to him.'[3] Shaftesbury is at pains to show that the Christian doctrine of rewards and punishments can be inconsistent with virtue. It is also suggestive that William Godwin, one of the fullest flowers of the deistic tradition, should have been infatuated with the Houyhnhnms, calling them a description of 'men in their highest improvement',[4] and finding in Swift's exposition of their government 'a more profound insight into the true principles of political justice, than [in] any preceding or contemporary author'.[5]

Swift, for more than fifty years, was a priest in the Church of England. There is no doubt that he took his responsibilities as a pastor more seriously than most of his clerical colleagues took theirs. He reformed the worship in his cathedral to make it more regular and fuller than it had been for many years. He prayed in secret, went to church early so as not to be seen, wrote for his dearest friend some prayers which are models of intense but traditional religious

[1] Sermon, 'On the Testimony of Conscience', Davis (ed.), *Prose Works*, vol. IX, p. 154.

[2] *The Religion of Nature Delineated* (London, 1722), p. 36.

[3] J. M. Robertson (ed.), *Characteristicks* (London, 1900), vol. I, p. 280. Of course, Shaftesbury, in spite of his influence, was a sound Christian.

[4] *The Inquirer* (London, 1797), p. 134.

[5] F. E. L. Priestley (ed.), *Political Justice* (Toronto, 1946), vol. II, p. 209 n. For detailed evidence, see James Preu, 'Swift's Influence on Godwin's Doctrine of Anarchism', *JHI*, vol. XV (June 1954), pp. 371–83.

expression. He gave a third of his income to charity and saved half the remainder to leave a fortune to charity. His sermons, the remarks of his intimates, his own private papers, all confirm Swift's devotion to his faith and his calling. Nevertheless, he had suffered so many accusations of impiety — from misinterpreters of *A Tale of a Tub* and other works — that he would not bring religion openly into a satire like *Gulliver*.

In providing the Houyhnhnms with good qualities, he was therefore duplicating the method of More's *Utopia*; and only to this extent is R. W. Chambers correct in writing, 'Just as More scored a point against the wickedness of Christian Europe, by making his philosophers heathen, so Jonathan Swift scored a point against the wickedness of mankind by representing *his* philosophers, the Houyhnhnms, as having the bodies of horses.'[1] So in his sermon 'Upon the Excellency of Christianity', Swift argues that although there were 'great examples of wisdom and virtue among the heathen wise men', nevertheless, 'Christian philosophy is in all things preferable to heathen wisdom' (p. 243). As admirable creatures, the Houyhnhnms represent what could be accomplished by beings (neither horses nor men) capable of pursuing the natural virtues summed up in reason and given us by nature at one remove from God; in their way — which is not the human way — they are perfect, and do not want religion. As absurd creatures, they represent the deistic presumption that mankind has no need of the specifically Christian virtues. Gulliver is misled as, in *Joseph Andrews*, Mr. Wilson is ruined by a club of 'philosophers' who 'governed themselves only by the infallible guide of human reason', but who reveal their immorality when one of them withdraws, 'taking with him the wife of one of his most intimate friends', and another refuses to pay back a loan which Mr. Wilson had made to him. While under the spell, the victim says, 'I began now to esteem myself a being of a higher order than I had ever before conceived; and was the more charmed with this rule of right, as I really found in my own nature nothing repugnant to it. I held in utter contempt all persons who wanted any other inducement to virtue besides her intrinsic beauty

---

[1] *Sir Thomas More* (London, 1935), p. 128.

and excellence.'[1] Gulliver is not defrauded by the Houyhnhnms, for they are not human (or equine); but the rule of nothing-but-reason leads him to repudiate all human obligations and to detest his wife. Swift wished men to be as rational as possible; he believed that religion helps them to become so, and that reason leads them toward revelation. But the deistic effort to build a rational system of morals outside revelation he regarded as evil and absurd.

v

In the fourth voyage, Swift was aiming at a particular exponent of deistic thought, a correspondent with whom he was in argument about such doctrines while he was writing *Gulliver's Travels*. To identify the person, I shall limit myself at first to the most striking attributes of the Houyhnhnms: their emotionless serenity, their benevolence, and their reliance on reason.

Of the Houyhnhnms' indifference to such feelings as fear of death or filial love, one needs no reminding; this superiority to human passions appears throughout the fourth voyage. In chapter viii Gulliver surveys some of their other felicities. '*Friendship* and *benevolence*', he says, 'are the two principal virtues among the Houyhnhnms; and these not confined to particular objects, but universal to the whole race. For, a stranger from the remotest part, is equally treated with the nearest neighbour, and where-ever he goes, looks upon himself as at home. . . . They will have it that *nature* teaches them to love the whole species, and it is *reason* only that makes a distinction of persons, where there is a superior degree of virtue' (p. 252). In 1719 Swift reopened a correspondence with Bolingbroke which had been suspended for more than two years. In his answer Bolingbroke has a long passage on friendship, to which Swift replied in detail. After another exchange, the correspondence once more lapsed. When Swift wrote again, Bolingbroke sent him a very long letter which included further and extended reflections on friendship, such as, 'Believe me, there is more pleasure, and more merit too, in cultivating friendship, than in taking care of the state. . .

---

[1] Fielding's *Works*, ed. W. E. Henley (London, 1903), vol. 1, pp. 240–1 (bk. III, ch. iii).

none but men of sense and virtue are capable of [it].[1] It was Bolingbroke who wrote a whole treatise to prove that compassion, or
kindness to strangers, depends on reason and nothing else; and in it
he made such remarks as, 'An habit of making good use of our
reason, and such an education as trains up the mind in true morality,
will never fail to inspire us with sentiments of benevolence for all
mankind.' In another essay he has declarations like, 'Sociability is
the great instinct, and benevolence the great law, of human nature.'[2]

In Bolingbroke's next letter, he placed Swift on the opposite side
of a quarrel about the Christian religion and ancient morality. He
harps on the theme that 'a man of sense and virtue may be unfortunate, but can never be unhappy'. Almost two years later
(August 1723), Swift received a double letter from Pope and
Bolingbroke, both dilating on friendship; Pope's has so many
maxims relating to this subject that it is more an essay than a letter.
The two men emphasize their contentment, their indifference to
ordinary vicissitudes, their philosophical serenity. They preach a
cool moderation remote from the ordeals of Swift's preceding year.
'Reflection and habit', wrote Bolingbroke, 'have rendered the world
so indifferent to me, that I am neither afflicted nor rejoiced, angry
nor pleased, at what happens in it.... Perfect tranquillity is the
general tenor of my life.' While Swift may have envied such complacency, he could not imitate it. He sent a sarcastic riposte ridiculing
their pretensions to detached and philosophic calm. 'Your notions
of friendship are new to me,' Swift says; 'I believe every man is born
with his *quantum*, and he cannot give to one without robbing another.' As for their nonchalance, he told Pope, 'I who am sunk under
the prejudices of another education ... can never arrive at the
serenity of mind you possess.' It was their sort of vapidity that
Swift meant to deride, two years later, when he jeered at how
Bolingbroke in 1723 had been 'full of philosophy and talked *de
contemptu mundi*'.[3]

The next development of the correspondence is related to

[1] Ball (ed.), *Correspondence*, vol. III, pp. 24–28, 25, 30, 89.

[2] *Reflections concerning Innate Moral Principles* (London, 1752), p. 55;
Philosophical Works (London, 1754), vol. IV, p. 256.

[3] Ball (ed.), *Correspondence*, vol. III, pp. 111, 172, 175, 291.

Gulliver's most often quoted comment on the Houyhnhnms, his praise of their devotion to reason (i.e. to reason alone):

As these noble Houyhnhnms are endowed by nature with a general disposition to all virtues, and have no conceptions . . . of what is evil in a rational creature; so their grand maxim is, to cultivate *reason*, and to be wholly governed by it. Neither is *reason* among them a point problematical as with us, where men can argue with plausibility on both sides of a question; but strikes you with immediate conviction; as it must needs do where it is not mingled, obscured, or discoloured by passion and interest. [p. 251]

In the autumn of 1724 the undercurrent of Swift's quarrel with his friend becomes traceable; and it flows about this very problem of what reason unaided can do. Bolingbroke sent a long defence of deistic thought and an attack on Christianity (by implication), to rebut a letter that is now lost, from Swift. The dean had directly accused him of being an *esprit fort*, or freethinker.[1] In a tremendous harangue, Bolingbroke first takes the word to mean atheist, and repudiates that title; then he says:

If indeed by *esprit fort*, or free-thinker, you only mean a man who makes a free use of his reason, who searches after truth without passion or prejudice, and adheres inviolably to it, you mean a wise and honest man, and such a one as I labour to be. The faculty of distinguishing between right and wrong, true and false, which we call reason or common sense, which is given to every man by our bountiful creator, and which most men lose by neglect, is the light of the mind, and ought to guide all the operations of it. To abandon this rule, and to guide our thoughts by any other [Bolingbroke means Christian revelation], is full as absurd as it would be, if you should put out your eyes, and borrow even the best staff . . . when you set out upon one of your dirty journeys. . . . The peace and happiness of mankind is the great aim of these free-thinkers.[2]

In Bolingbroke's philosophical works there are many other similarities to the teachings of the Houyhnhnms. In fact, Gulliver's

[1] Nichol Smith (ed.), *Letters to Ford*, pp. 100–1.
[2] Ball (ed.), *Correspondence*, vol. III, pp. 208–9. That Bolingbroke means Christian revelation is clear from his parallel with Locke's *Essay concerning Human Understanding*, bk. IV, ch. xix, pars. 4, 8.

list of the subjects which generally come up in their conversation could serve almost as well for those works: friendship and benevolence, order and 'oeconomy', the visible operations of nature, ancient traditions, the bounds and limits of virtue, the unerring rules of reason, and so on (p. 261). Of course, however, Swift omits the purpose of Bolingbroke's philosophizing, which (according to his eighteenth-century critics) was the destruction of Christianity. Swift believed that a good Christian is a rational person, that reason leads one to Christian faith, that these two gifts are in harmony, and that man must strive to enlarge them both.

One final touch is that Bolingbroke's editor calls his philosophical writings for the most part 'nothing more than repetitions of conversations often interrupted, [and] often renewed'.[1] For I have assumed that the letters from Bolingbroke had the effect of reminding Swift of topics more freely canvassed when the two men had talked together.[2]

Although my observations pause here, there is a humorous postscript to the Houyhnhnms. Viscount Bolingbroke was no horse, and it would have been convenient to discover one which was not only a deistic thinker, but also a master of human beings. By a helpful chance, it happens that Swift once described such an animal in a letter. The episode may be no more than an odd coincidence, but it seems worth reporting. For on this occasion Swift's horse behaved more rationally than his servant, and the master treated the man like an animal.

At Christmas time 1714 the dean rode out of Dublin, planning to collect his groom and his valet on the way. When he met them, they were drunkenly incapable; and he found that the groom could not travel. Swift nevertheless rode on, but noticed that Tom, the valet, who usually rode behind him, failed to keep up. He waited, and Tom galloped up to him. Swift scolded him, and Tom answered foolishly. 'He was as drunk as a dog,' Swift wrote, 'tottered on his

[1] *Philosophical Works*, vol. III, p. 334.
[2] D. G. James saw the connection between the Houyhnhnms and Bolingbroke, but he quite misunderstood it; see his *Life of Reason* (London, 1949), pp. 256–61. Miss Kathleen Williams has reached conclusions similar to my own.

horse, could not keep the way, sometimes into the sea, then back to me; swore he was not drunk. I bid him keep on, lashed him as well as I could; then he vowed he was drunk, fell a crying, came back every moment to me. I bid him keep on.' At last, from the galloping and turning backwards and forwards, Tom's horse 'grew mad' and threw the valet down. Then Swift came up and called a boy and man to get the horse from him; but 'he resisted us all three, was stark mad with drink. At last we got the bridle from him, the boy mounted and away we rode, Tom following after us. What became of him I know not.'[1]

The episode has a peculiar interest, not only because the horse was English and the servants Irish, but because the name of the horse which 'grew mad' and threw Tom down was Bolingbroke. The editor of Swift's correspondence says that the horse Bolingbroke was a gift and that Swift named him; but we do not know who the donor was. In June 1713 Vanessa asked Swift, 'How does Bolingbroke perform?' Swift, *en route* to Ireland, said the horse fell under him; and in the end it was shipped over to its new country. Swift mentions Bolingbroke several times again, but after three years he exchanged him with a friend for another horse.[2] We never hear of him again, unless perhaps in *Gulliver's Travels*.

VI

Swift began to write the third voyage (last in order of composition) around January 1724, and he returned to Dublin, that month, from a visit which he had made to Quilca, the country home of his young and very dear friend, the Rev. Thomas Sheridan. Swift may have visited Quilca again the following April.[3] Meanwhile, the *Drapier's Letters* interrupted the writing of *Gulliver*, and Swift only finished the third voyage some time in 1725. At Quilca again the whole book was perfected and rewritten when Swift stayed there from April to the end of September 1725.[4]

[1] Ball (ed.), *Correspondence*, vol. II, p. 263.
[2] Ball (ed.), *Correspondence*, vol. II, pp. 44 and n., 242, 280–1, 305–6.
[3] Nichol Smith (ed.), *Letters to Ford*, p. 101; Harold Williams (ed.), *The Poems of Jonathan Swift*, 1st ed. (Oxford, 1937), vol. III, p. 1034.
[4] Ball (ed.), *Correspondence*, vol. III, pp. 235, 276; Nichol Smith (ed.), *Letters to Ford*, p. 122.

Sheridan provided Swift with more than a holiday. He gave him a model for the king and people of the flying island. Swift had met him in 1718, and their twenty-year friendship was perhaps never stronger than during the period when *Gulliver* was being written and they were meeting constantly in Dublin. Yet Swift found fault with his friend almost from the start. In letters, poems, and other papers, Swift continually bewailed Sheridan's absent-mindedness, his inability to listen carefully during conversations, his irresponsibility and forgetfulness, his neglect of the essential business of life in favour of peripheral occupations.

'Too much advertency is not your talent,' Swift told Sheridan. And, 'I believe you value your temporal interest as much as anybody, but you have not the arts of pursuing it.' And again, 'The two devils of inadvertency and forgetfulness have got fast hold on you.' Describing him at the same time to another acquaintance, Swift wrote, 'He hath not overmuch advertency. His books, his mathematics, the pressures of his fortune, his laborious calling, and some natural disposition or indisposition, give him an *egarement d'esprit*, as you cannot but observe.'[1]

In brief, Sheridan possessed to an extreme degree the characteristic on which Gulliver builds his portrait of the Laputans — that their minds are 'so taken up with intense speculations, that they neither can speak, [nor] attend to the discourses of others, without being rouzed' (p. 143).

Instead of caring for their common affairs, the Laputans and their king occupy themselves with three obsessions: music, mathematics, and abstract speculation. Swift described Sheridan as 'a man of intent and abstracted thinking, enslaved by mathematics'.[2] Sheridan's own son Thomas writes, 'As he was an adept in music both in the scientific and practical part, he had frequent private concerts at his house at no small cost.'[3] The King of Laputa was 'distinguished above all his predecessors for his hospitality to strangers' (pp. 144–5). Sheridan's son says his father was recklessly hospitable and generous: '[He] set no bounds to his prodigality.... [He had a]

---

[1] Ball (ed.), *Correspondence*, vol. III, pp. 267, 268, 275, 271.
[2] Ball (ed.), *Correspondence*, vol. III, p. 268.
[3] *Life of Jonathan Swift* (London, 1784), pp. 384–5.

large income . . . but not equal to the profuseness of his spirit. He was . . . the greatest dupe in the world and a constant prey to all the indigent of his acquaintance, as well as those who were recommended to him by others' (p. 384). Swift used to berate Sheridan for wasting money on the entertainment of false friends and random acquaintances.[1]

Sheridan also shared the Laputans' fecklessness in the management of his property. 'It is [his] great happiness,' Swift once observed of him, 'that, when he acts in the common concerns of life against common sense and reason, he values himself thereupon, as if it were the mark of great genius, above little regards or arts, and that his thoughts are too exalted to descend into the knowledge of vulgar management; and you cannot make him a greater compliment than by telling instances to the company, before his face, how careless he was in any affair that related to his interest and fortune.'[2] Gulliver blames the same defects in the Laputans: 'Although they are dextrous enough upon a piece of paper . . . yet in the common actions and behaviour of life, I have not seen a more clumsy, awkward, and unhandy people, nor so slow and perplexed in their conceptions upon all other subjects, except those of mathematics and music' (p. 147). In the same portrait in which he analysed Sheridan's pride at being incompetent, Swift also described him as proud, captious, quarrelsome, and argumentative.[3] After remarking that the Laputans are hopeless fumblers in practical affairs, Gulliver says, 'They are very bad reasoners, and vehemently given to opposition, unless when they happen to be of the right opinion' (p. 147).

Finally, there is the famous description by Gulliver of the desolation on the mainland subject to the King of Laputa: 'I never knew a soil so unhappily cultivated, houses so ill contrived and so ruinous', and so on (p. 159). While Swift was writing *Gulliver's Travels*, he also composed verses ridiculing the miserable condition of agriculture and buildings at Quilca:

[1] Ball (ed.), *Correspondence*, vol. III, pp. 246, 248.
[2] Temple Scott (ed.), *Prose Works* (London, 1897–1908), vol. XI, p. 156.
[3] T. Scott (ed.), *Prose Works*, vol. XI, pp. 156–8.

> A rotten cabbin, dropping rain . . .
> Stools, tables, chairs, and bed-steds broke
> Here elements have lost their uses,
> Air ripens not, nor earth produces.

Or, in another poem of the same time on the same subject:

> A church without pews.
> Our horses astray,
> No straw, oats, or hay;
> December in May.[1]

There is as well a prose diatribe dated April 1724, *The Blunders, Deficiencies, Distresses, and Misfortunes of Quilca*. Here Swift denounces the crazy state of the house and all its furniture, the lack of food, heat, and comfort, the savage behaviour of the servants, the barbaric manners of the natives: 'The new house all going to ruin before it is finished. . . . The kitchen perpetually crowded with savages. . . . Not a bit of mutton to be had in the country. . . . An egregious want of all the most common necessary utensils. . . . [The servants] growing fast into the manners and thieveries of the natives'.[2] In Balnibarbi, 'the whole country lies miserably waste, the houses in ruins, and the people without food or cloaths' (p. 161).[3]

There are many additional hints and clues to demonstrate the conclusion. Swift was not thinking *only* of Sheridan when he described the Laputans, but he was thinking more deeply of him than of anyone else.

VII

I am far from supposing that persons in *Gulliver's Travels* are portraits of men whom Swift knew. The King of Brobdingnag is not Sir William Temple; nor is Thomas Sheridan the King of

---

[1] Williams (ed.), *Poems*, vol. III, pp. 1035, 1036.

[2] T. Scott (ed.), *Prose Works*, vol. VII, pp. 75–77.

[3] Thomas Sheridan himself was no kinder when he put Quilca into verse, and he also wrote mercilessly concerning his house in Dublin; see Williams (ed.), *Poems*, vol. III, pp. 1043–7.

Laputa. In all the characters there are elements inconsistent with the originals that I have put forward. I suggest merely that the framework of the Houyhnhnms' character, for instance, goes back to Bolingbroke; that the giant king is derived from Swift's recollections of Temple, though with many additions and alterations; and so forth.

The most important question is how these observations alter one's reading of *Gulliver's Travels*. But to this the answers are so ramified that I shall no more than list a few implications. My analysis of the second voyage may go far to account for its *relative* placidity and its success, in comparison with the contemptuous tone of the first, the disjointedness of the third, and the harshness of the fourth; Swift had returned to the mood of his satisfying and fruitful years with Temple at Moor Park. The third voyage is one which has often been related to Scriblerian sketches ; and an explanation for its inadequacy has been that here Swift was stitching up ill-connected fragments.[1] My association of the Laputan king with Thomas Sheridan weakens that theory. Other scholars have shown that the political references and much of the satire on experimental science belong to the latter part of the reign of George I;[2] so does the connection with Sheridan. My commentary on the fourth voyage helps to destroy the misconceptions of innumerable scholars and critics who identify the author, through Gulliver, with the values of the Houyhnhnms. Swift was himself saying, in the fourth voyage, that anyone who believes in the adequacy of reason without Christianity must see himself as a Houyhnhnm and the rest of mankind as Yahoos. By innuendo, he argues that the deists cannot, with any consistency, believe their own doctrines.[3]

Finally, I suggest that the common approaches to Swift's satire, with an emphasis on manipulation of ideas, or else in terms of the

[1] e.g. Kerby-Miller, pp. 319–20.

[2] e.g. Case, *Four Essays, passim*; also Marjorie Nicolson and N. M. Mohler, 'The Scientific Background of Swift's 'Voyage to Laputa', in *Annals of Science*, vol. II (1937), pp. 299–334, and in this volume, pp. 226–69.

[3] I am indebted to Dr. Theodore Redpath for a discussion clarifying this statement.

technique of fiction, usually mislead one. Swift's imagination worked in terms of people. He did not invent a set of values to defend, or objects to attack; he started from human embodiments of those values or vices, and he addressed himself to people whom he wished to encourage, refute, or annihilate.

To consider *Gulliver's Travels* as a novel, to present it in language evolved for the criticism of prose fiction, and to study Swift's personae as people, is to misunderstand this book. *Gulliver* is admittedly an ancestor of stories like *Erewhon* and *Brave New World*. Swift, however, was writing a prose satire according to another pattern, curiously static and didactic, but not narrative as an epic or novel is. Its structure and its repetitive pattern help to explain both why it succeeds as a children's book and why it cannot be made into a satisfactory film or drama. Very little of the life in *Gulliver* belongs to its large 'story' or 'plot' line, or to the evolution of character. The life comes from the detached characterizations of individuals who otherwise exist as flat masks or as spokesmen and mouthpieces; from separate episodes loosely strung together; and, most of all, from the operations of Swift's irony. If Swift had unconscious models for his apparently narrative plan, they were books like the *Pilgrim's Progress* and not a foetal *Erewhon* or *Brave New World*.

Gulliver's characterizations are like the portraits in Swift's *History of the Four Last Years*, where he analyses statesmen in order to account for actions which the reader has already learned about outside the book: the motives, one might say, are revealed after the action is over and not through it — to explain and not to initiate it. So in *Gulliver* most episodes move independently of the characterizations and of one another. What if the King of Brobdingnag did dislike armies and had no use for them? He nevertheless possessed a militia of two hundred thousand men; and all of Gulliver's apologizing does not convince me that Swift put that army in for any other reason than to enhance the giant king's awfulness at the expense of his coherence. One finds consistency in neither the chronology, the geography, the persons, nor the points of view of this fable, although, like La Fontaine's poems, it has the coherence of the author's morality. If *Gulliver* were a novel, the scores of such contradictions would ruin it. Yet if Swift had been consistent in his technique, and built his characters *a posteriori* around the ideas they stood for, the book would have lost much of its life. But he portrayed them after sketches drawn from living creatures, and they possess a vividness and strength which have made them immortal.

MARJORIE NICOLSON
AND NORA M. MOHLER

The Scientific Background of Swift's
'Voyage to Laputa'

A MONG the travels of Gulliver, the 'Voyage to Laputa' has been
most criticized and least understood. There is general agreement that in interest and literary merit it falls short of the first two
voyages. It is marked by multiplicity of themes; it is episodic in
character. In its reflections upon life and humanity, it lacks the
philosophic intuition of the voyages to Lilliput and Brobdingnag
and the power of the violent and savage attacks upon mankind in
the 'Voyage to the Houyhnhnms'. Any reader sensitive to literary
values must so far agree with the critics who disparage the tale. But
another criticism as constantly brought against the 'Voyage to
Laputa' cannot be so readily dismissed. Professor W. A. Eddy, one
of the chief authorities upon the sources of *Gulliver's Travels*, has
implied the usual point of view when he writes:

> There seems to be no motive for the story beyond a pointless and
> not too artfully contrived satire on mathematicians. . . . For this
> attack on theoretical science I can find no literary source or analogue,
> and conclude that it must have been inspired by one of Swift's
> literary ideocyncracies [*sic*]. Attempts have been made to detect
> allusions to the work of Newton and other contemporary scientists,
> but these, however successful, cannot greatly increase for us the
> slight importance of the satire on Laputa.[1]

Three themes in the 'Voyage to Laputa' have been particularly
censured by modern critics. Some are repelled by the Laputans with

[1] W. A. Eddy, *Gulliver's Travels: A Critical Study* (Princeton and
London, 1923), p. 158; hereafter cited as Eddy, *Critical Study*.

their curious combination of mathematics and music and their dread of a comet and the sun[1]. Others are disturbed by the apparent lack of both unity and significance in the Balnibarians, particularly in the Grand Academy of Lagado (ch. 5). Most of all, the Flying Island has puzzled commentators who dismiss it as a 'piece of magical apparatus', a 'gratuitous violation of natural laws'[2] which offends the reader's sense of probability.

Yet is it conceivable that Swift, elsewhere so conscious of the unwritten law of probability, should have carelessly violated it in the 'Voyage to Laputa' alone? Professor Eddy in a later work has justly said:

> The compound of magic and mathematics, of fantasy and logic, of ribaldry and gravity, is a peculiar product of the disciplined yet imaginative mind of Swift. There are two distinct kinds of imagination: one is creative and mystical, the other is constructive and rational. Swift had no command over the faerie architects who decree pleasure domes in Xanadu without regard to the laws of physics. His imagination, like that of Lewis Carroll, had a method in its apparent madness. . . . What seems so lawless is the product of the most rigid law.[3]

Swift's imagination, we have long recognised, was eclectic; the mark of his genius lay less in original creation than in paradoxical and brilliant new combinations of familiar materials. Indeed, one of the sources of his humour to every generation of readers has been the recognition of old and familiar themes treated in novel fashion. Pygmies and giants, animals with the power of speech, have been the perennial stuff of fairytale and legend. The novelty in *Gulliver's Travels* lies less in the material than in new combinations and the mood of treatment. The study of the sources of Swift has been particularly rewarding in showing what the 'constructive and rational' imagination may do to time-honoured themes. The very

[1] 'Voyage to Laputa', in *Gulliver's Travels*, ed. W. A. Eddy (Oxford, 1933), ch. ii. References to the 'Voyage to Laputa' in the text are always to this edition.
[2] Eddy, *Critical Study*, p. 158.
[3] Introduction to *Gulliver's Travels*, ed. W. A. Eddy, p. xviii.

fact that the literary[1] and political[2] background of *Gulliver's Travels* has been established so completely leads the inquisitive reader to inquire whether the unrecognized sources of the 'Voyage to Laputa' may not be equally capable of verification. If the most assiduous searchers into sources can find 'no literary source or analogue' for the peculiar themes in this voyage alone, must not those sources be sought elsewhere than in the literary traditions which Swift inherited?

There were other important materials accessible to writers of romance and fantasy in Swift's generation, of which many availed themselves. The attempt of this study will be to show that Swift borrowed for the 'Voyage to Laputa' even more than for the other tales, but that the sources of his borrowings were different. The mathematicians who feared the sun and comet, the projectors of the Grand Academy, the Flying Island — these came to Swift almost entirely from contemporary science.[3] The sources for nearly all the theories of the Laputans and the Balnibarians are to be found in the work of Swift's contemporary scientists and particularly in the *Philosophical Transactions of the Royal Society*.

I

Only during the last few years have students of literature become aware of the part played by the 'new science' in the stimulation of literary imagination in the seventeenth and eighteenth centuries. Among the various themes which have been studied, the relation of

[1] The most important study of literary sources is Eddy's *Critical Study*, which incorporates the earlier work of Borkowsky, Conant, Hönncher, Poll and others.

[2] The political satire of *Gulliver's Travels* has been definitively treated by Sir Charles Firth, 'The Political Significance of Gulliver's Travels', in *Proceedings of the British Academy*, vol. IX (1919), pp. 1–23.

[3] An occasional commentator has recognised the scientific background of one or another of the details. M. Émile Pons, in *Gulliver's Travels* [*Extraits*] ... *avec une introduction et des notes* (Paris, 1927), p. 204 n., remarks: 'It must be acknowledged, also, that in several of the numerous scientific hints and suggestions contained in these chapters, Swift reveals to us a remarkable and quite unexpected power of divination which is a cause of wonderment for many a scientist of our day.'

men of letters to the Royal Society has proved a rewarding field. Shadwell's *Virtuoso*, for example, takes on entirely new meaning when read in connection with experiments reported by Wilkins, Hooke, Boyle and many others,[1] and the interest of Restoration audiences in such drama becomes clear when we realise the number of men in the audience who had attended meetings of the Royal Society and had heard first-hand reports of the experiments which Shadwell satirizes through 'Sir Nicholas Gimcrack'. Wilkins, Waller, Dryden, Comenius and Evelyn in England, John Winthrop and Cotton Mather in America, are among those who have been shown to have reflected in their works the discoveries of the Society. Pepys's interest may be traced through the frequent references in his diary and letters. Addison and Steele in their periodicals played to a gallery not only of gentlemen but also of ladies interested in science. No reader of *Hudibras* and of the minor poems can fail to be aware of the extent to which Butler, too, found the *virtuosi* an amusing and profitable theme. Foreign visitors to England paid particular attention to 'Gresham Colledge', sending home observations, both serious and satiric, upon collections and experiments. It has indeed been suggested that the 'early development of Anglomania' during the last years of the seventeenth century and the first quarter of the eighteenth century in France was largely the result of French interest in the Royal Society, particularly in the reports published in the *Philosophical Transactions*.[2]

The widespread interest in scientific discovery among English men of letters was in large part a natural result of the rapid strides made by science during the seventeenth and eighteenth centuries. More specifically, it was the result of the attendance at meetings of the Royal Society by men of letters, many of whom claimed the title of *virtuosi*, and of the publication of the *Philosophical Transactions*, which were widely read. In addition to the complete *Transactions*, various abridged editions were published in the early eighteenth century. In 1705 many of the papers were made still more accessible

[1] See Claude Lloyd, 'Shadwell and the Virtuosi', in *PMLA*, vol. XLIV (1929), pp. 472–94.
[2] Minnie M. Miller, 'Science and Philosophy as Precursors of the English Influence in France', in *PMLA*, vol. XLV (1930), pp. 856–96.

in an edition in three volumes under the title *Miscellanea Curiosa*.[1]
Reports of discoveries, inventions and experiments were therefore
available in various ways to Jonathan Swift in Ireland, and even
more after his return to England where he 'corrected, amended, and
augmented' his voyages.[2] The influence of the *Philosophical
Transactions* upon Swift appears in two ways. Both in the complete
and in the abridged editions, these volumes were storehouses of
such accounts of travel as those imitated by Swift in *Gulliver's
Travels*. In addition they offered him specific sources for his
scientific details in the 'Voyage to Laputa'.

[1] *Miscellanea Curiosa. Containing a Collection of Some of the Principal
Phenomena in Nature, Accounted for by the Greatest Philosophers of this
Age; Being the Most Valuable Discourses, Read and Delivered to the Royal
Society, for the Advancement of Physical and Mathematical Knowledge. As
also a Collection of Curious Travels, Voyages, Antiquities, and Natural
Histories of Countries; Presented to the same Society.* The first volumes
appeared at London 1705–7; a second edition, revised and corrected by
W. Derham, was published in 1723–7. According to the catalogue of the
Library of Congress, the first edition appeared under the auspices of
Edmond Halley, the second under the auspices of William Derham.

[2] It is clear, from references in his letters, that Swift was engaged upon
Gulliver's Travels from at least 1720 until their publication in 1726. He
himself points out that he completed, corrected and augmented the travels
in 1726, before their publication. Critics disagree about the order of
composition, the majority holding that the 'Voyage to Laputa' was the
earliest and that its imperfections are to be accounted for by the fact that it
was written before Swift conceived the work as a whole. One or two critics
however have considered the work as the latest of the voyages. The
evidence given in this paper tends to bear out the idea that a large part of
the 'Voyage to Laputa' was a late composition. Several of the experiments
which Swift followed most closely were performed as late as 1724. Robert
Boyle's complete scientific works appeared in 1725, and though individual
papers were available earlier, Swift's close following of Boyle and his
many references to him seem to indicate that the complete scientific works
were used. The actual dating which Swift himself gives, in the case of the
comet — discussed later — and the beginning of the trouble in Balnibari,
about forty years earlier, both point to 1726 as the most probable date of
the composition of the scientific portions of the 'Voyage to Laputa'. It
would seem that, while Swift was undoubtedly working upon some sections of this voyage in 1724, as references in his letters show, he put aside
the more technical portions until his return to England; and that the
scientific sections of the 'Voyage to Laputa' were among the latest of
Gulliver's Travels.

The various sources of the general idea of such 'voyages' as those of Gulliver have been traced so often and are so obviously part of the great interest in travel that had persisted in England since the time of the earliest voyagers that it seems almost a work of super-erogation to suggest the *Philosophical Transactions* as still another source for the main idea of *Gulliver's Travels*. Yet it is at least interesting to see the space devoted in the *Transactions* — particularly between 1700 and 1720[1] — to accounts of travel. From them Swift may well have gleaned many a suggestion not only for the proper style of Captain Lemuel Gulliver, but also for the pattern of such tales of travel and observation, for such a pattern there was in the actual accounts.[2] The newly discovered islands of the Philippines, reported in the *Transactions*, must greatly have appealed to the creator of Gulliver, who discovered so many islands, some inhabited, some desolate;[3] the Hottentots, as they appear in the accounts sent to the Royal Society, are as curious a people as any discovered by Gulliver.

More specifically, Swift may well have picked up from these actual voyages a hint for his 'men who never die', the Struldbrugs. The authors who reported this particular group of travels to the Royal Society showed an almost morbid interest in 'antient' men who live too long. Mr. G. Plaxton, a clergyman, who seemed to have an uncanny affinity for livings in remote districts, reported from the parsonage of Kinnardsey: 'I took the Number of the Inhabitants, and found that every sixth Soul was sixty Years of Age, and upwards; some were 85, and some 90'.[4] His next incumbency

---

[1] The abridged edition of the *Transactions* from 1700 to 1720 devotes a long section (vol. v, ch. iii) to 'Travels and Voyages'. The third volume of the *Miscellanea Curiosa* is entirely devoted to 'Curious Travels, Voyages . . . and Natural Histories'.

[2] Swift's borrowing from contemporary travel tales has been pointed out particularly by W. H. Bonner, *Captain William Dampier* (Stanford, 1934), ch. ix; and by R. W. Frantz, 'Swift's Yahoos and the Voyagers', in *Modern Philology*, vol. XXIX (1931), pp. 49–57.

[3] *Phil. Trans.* vol. XXVI (1708), p. 189: 'An Extract of Two Letters from the Missionary Jesuits, concerning the Discovery of the New Phillippine-Islands, with a Map of the Same.'

[4] 'Some Natural Observations in Natural History in Shropshire', in *Phil. Trans.* vol. XXV (1707), p. 2418; abridged ed. vol. v, ii, pp.

proved even more remarkable; the number of the aged was much greater and the parishioners lived so long that the Reverend Mr. Plaxton seldom had the pleasure of burying a member of his flock.[1] Cotton Mather sent back from New England 'an Account of some Long-Lived Persons there', many of whom were more than a century old.[2] Closer parallels are found in 'An Account of the Bramines in the Indies': 'It is reported, that upon the Hills by Casmere there are Men that live some hundreds of Years . . . .'[3] Like the Struldbrugs, they have passed beyond curiosity, and beyond interest in life. With Tithonus they seem to have found immortal life but not immortal youth. Gulliver saw the Struldbrugs as 'the most mortifying sight I ever beheld. . . . Besides the usual deformities in extreme old age, they acquired an additional ghastliness in proportion to their number of years, which is not to be described' (p. 254). The voyager to the 'Bramines' saw his old men in much the same way: 'The Penances and Austerities that they undergo are almost incredible; Most of them, through their continual Fastings, and lying upon the parching hot Sand in the Heat of the Sun, are so lean, dry'd and wither'd, that they look like Skeletons or Shadows, and one can scarce perceive them to breathe, or feel their Pulse beat'.[4]

Whether such voyages as those in the *Philosophical Transactions* combined in Swift's mind with literary sources already well established to lead him to the general idea of the travels of Gulliver, we may conjecture, though not prove. That the *Philosophical Transactions*, together with the more complete works of the *virtuosi*, were the specific source of Swift's Laputans, his projectors of the Grand

---

112–15. (In general, in reference to the *Transactions*, the authors have endeavoured to give references to both the complete and the abridged editions. The first number refers to the complete edition, the second to the abridged, which is more accessible to general readers. We have used the 1749 edition of vols. II, III, IV and V, the 1734 edition of vols. VI and VII.)

[1] *Phil. Trans.* vol. XXV (1707), p. 2421; vol. V, ii, p. 114.

[2] 'An Extract of several Letters from Cotton Mather, D.D.', in *Phil. Trans.* vol. XXIX (1714), p. 62; vol. V, ii, pp. 159–65.

[3] J. Marshal, 'An Account of the Bramines in the Indies', in *Phil. Trans.* vol. XX (1700–1), p. 729; vol. V, ii, pp. 165–71.

[4] 'Account of the Bramines', vol. V, ii, p. 169.

Academy of Lagado, and his Flying Island, can be proved beyond the possibility of doubt.

II

The section of the 'Voyage to Laputa' which deals with the mathematical peculiarities of the Laputans has been generally recognized to be of a piece with others of Swift's pronouncements upon mathematicians.[1] Although several of the critics incline to think that such satire is peculiar to Swift, there is little in the main idea of this section that is unique. Behind the Laputans lay the rapidly growing interest of the seventeenth century in mathematics, embodied in the work of Kepler, Descartes, Leibnitz and many others, and a persistent attitude of the seventeenth-century layman toward the 'uselessness' of physical and mathematical learning.[2] Bacon's discrimination between 'Experiments of Light' and 'Experiments of Fruit' had only put into pictorial language a persistent conflict between 'pure' and 'applied' science. To the layman, and particularly to the satirist of the last quarter of the seventeenth century, when the Royal Society was attracting its greatest attention, the apparent 'uselessness' of the new science was a common point of attack. Samuel Butler in *Hudibras* and in minor poems, Shadwell in the *Virtuoso*, Ned Ward in the *London Spy*, William King in the *Dialogues of the Dead* — these and a host of minor writers laughed at the impractical *virtuosi*. A close parallel for Swift's point of view in *Gulliver's Travels* may be found in the *Spectator* papers, those mirrors of the age. In spite of Addison's profound response to many of the new concepts of the day — his interest in Cartesianism, in Newtonianism, his fascination with the vastly expanded universe of astronomy and biology — he lost no chance for laughter at impractical experimenters and at absent-minded

[1] Cf. *Memoirs of Martin Scriblerus*, in *Satires and Personal Writings*, by Jonathan Swift (ed. W. A. Eddy: New York, 1933), p. 133: 'In his third Voyage he discover'd a whole kingdom of Philosophers, who govern by the Mathematicks.'

[2] Passages which illustrate this point of view will be found in M. H. Nicolson, 'The Microscope and English Imagination', in *Smith College Studies in Modern Languages*, vol. XVI (1935), pp. 22–37.

mathematicians who in their preoccupation with one subject forgot the world about them.

Swift's Laputans excel in theoretical learning; the abstractions of 'higher mathematics' are their meat and drink. They can solve equations — but they cannot build houses, because of the 'contempt they bear to practical geometry, which they despise as vulgar and mechanic' (p. 191). Unfortunately their theoretical learning is too abstruse and 'too refined for the intellectuals of their workmen'. One may well wonder whether the passage in which Swift discusses their sharp divergence between theory and practice reflects a point of view suggested by many of the theorists of the day, and expressed by Robert Boyle in these words:

> Let us now consider how far the knowledge of particular qualities, or the physical uses of things, will enable men to perform, philosophically, what is commonly done by manual operation. And here, methinks, 'tis a notable proof of human industry, as well as a great incitement thereto, that philosophy can supply the want to strength, or art, and the head prevent the drudgery of the hand.[1]

If a specific source must be found for Swift's laughter at the uselessness of mathematical learning, it may be discovered in Fontenelle's 'Defence' of mathematical and natural philosophy and in his insistence that such publications as those of the Royal Society and the Paris Academy justified themselves. Swift's attitude toward Fontenelle is shown clearly in his earlier work *The Battle of the Books*, which was largely a reply to Fontenelle's defence of the 'moderns'. Another paper by Fontenelle so clearly suggests the position that Swift attacks in the 'Voyage to Laputa' that it seems impossible it should not have been in Swift's mind when he wrote. In 1699 Fontenelle, as part of his defence of the 'moderns', had upheld mathematical learning in a preface to the *Memoirs of the Royal Academy at Paris*, which was republished as a preface to the *Miscellanea Curiosa* in 1707.[2] The general points attacked by Swift are to be found in this preface. Fontenelle begins his defence:

[1] Peter Shaw, *The Philosophical Works of the Honourable Robert Boyle, Abridged, methodized and disposed* (London, 1725), vol. 1, p. 131. (The pagination in this volume is duplicated in pp. 129–36.)

[2] 'A Translation of Part of Monsieur Fontenelle's Preface to the

But to what purpose should People become fond of the Mathematical and Natural Philosophy? Of what use are the Transactions of the Academy? These are common Questions, which most do not barely propose as Questions, and it will not be improper to clear them. People very readily call useless, what they do not understand. It is a sort of Revenge; and as the Mathematicks and Natural Philosophy are known but by few, they are generally look'd upon as useless.

Fontenelle proceeds with a defence of such 'useless' knowledge, pointing out on the one hand that supposedly theoretical learning has resulted in practical discoveries, but, on the other hand, defending the intellectual curiosity of mathematicians and natural philosophers as an end in itself. 'Altho' the Usefulness of Mathematicks and Natural Philosophy is obscure,' he declares, 'yet it is real.'[1]

The 'contempt they bear to practical geometry' is sufficient to explain the miscalculation of the Laputan tailors in making Gulliver's clothes (p. 190). The mistaking of 'a figure in the calculations' may be intended as a satire upon Newton, as has been suggested.[2] But like the corresponding passage in the 'Voyage to Lilliput', in which tailors make clothes for the 'man mountain', the passage in the 'Voyage to Laputa' in which the tailor 'first took my altitude by a quadrant' is chiefly a satire upon the current interest in surveying and particularly upon attempts to determine the altitude of the sun, moon, stars and mountains, both lunar and terrestrial, by quadrants and other instruments.[3] Many such papers are included in the Memoirs of the Royal Academy at Paris, in the Year 1699, treating of the Usefulness of Mathematical Learning', in *Miscellanea Curiosa*, 2nd ed. (London, 1708), vol. I, Preface. There are striking similarities between the aspects of science defended by Fontenelle and attacked by Swift.

[1] Swift possessed in his own library a copy of Fontenelle's *Histoire du renouvellement de l'Académie Royale* (Amsterdam, 1709). See *A Catalogue of Books: The Library of the late Rev. Dr. Swift* (Dublin, 1745), no. 137, p. 4. This has been republished in *Dean Swift's Library*, by Harold Williams (Cambridge, 1932).

[2] G. R. Dennis, *Gulliver's Travels*, p. 167, n. 1, has suggested 'an error made by Newton's printer in adding a cipher to the distance of the earth from the sun, which drew down some ridicule upon the astronomer'.

[3] R. T. Gunther, *Early Science in Oxford* (London, 1923), vol. I, pp. 345 ff., lists a long series of books and articles on surveying, and discusses, with illustrations, surveying instruments invented in the period, some of

Philosophical Transactions; the original paper is frequently followed by a rejoinder on the part of another mathematician, pointing out errors in either method or calculation.

But the mathematical interests of the Laputans are not, as a rule, satirized alone; they are included with their interest in music, for in Laputan minds, mathematics and music are one, as they suggest in their clothing, their food and their customs. Here again Swift follows an attitude common enough in the seventeenth century, reflecting Kepler, Descartes, Newton, Leibnitz; more specifically, his ideas go back to Dr. John Wallis, who contributed many papers to the Royal Society on the general subject of the analogies between music and mathematics,[1] prefacing his 'discoveries' by the suggestions that they 'may not be unacceptable to those of the Royal Society, who are Musical and Mathematical'.[2] In music and mathematics, many writers of the seventeenth century found the two eternal and immutable verities. Indeed, the mathematician and astronomer, Christian Huygens, went so far as to declare that, no matter how inhabitants of other planets might differ from man in other ways, they must agree in music and geometry, since these are 'everywhere immutably the same, and always will be so'.[3] The interest of the Laputans in music is not, as has frequently been

them as curious as those found in Laputa. The reader may well be reminded of the political significance of such toys implied in the *Spectator*, no. 262: 'The air-pump, the barometer, the quadrant, and the like inventions, were thrown out to those busy spirits [the *virtuosi*], as tubs and barrels are to a whale, that he may let the ship sail on without disturbance, while he diverts himself with those innocent amusements.'

[1] See particularly Wallis, 'Imperfections in an Organ', in *Phil. Trans.* vol. xx (1698), p. 249; vol. I, pp. 612–17. Here Wallis gives an account of the work of his predecessors, and a discussion of 'the Degree of Gravity', or Acuteness of the one Sound to that of the other' and of the 'Proportions' in music expressed in mathematical formulae. See also 'Of the Trembling of Consonant Strings', in *Phil. Trans.*, abridged, vol. I, pp. 606 ff.

[2] 'Dr. Wallis's letter to the Publisher, concerning a new Musical Discovery', in *Phil. Trans.* vol. xii (1677), p. 839.

[3] *C. Hugenii, ΚΟΣΜΟΘΕΩΡΟΣ, sive de Terris cœlestibus, earumque ornatu, conjecturæ*, 1698; editio altera, 1699. The work was translated as *The Celestial Worlds Discover'd: or Conjectures Concerning the Inhabitants, Plants, and Productions of the Worlds in the Planets* (London, 1698). The above reference is to this English translation, p. 86.

suggested, a satire upon the interest shown in London in Swift's day in opera; the Laputan interest is diametrically opposed and shows the Laputans on the side of those who were resisting the idea that music was a handmaiden to language. Swift's main point is that the Laputans are concerned with the theory, not with the application, of both mathematics and music. Like many of Swift's contemporaries, they expressed their theory of music in mathematical formulae.[1] The Laputans, we are told, express their ideas 'perpetually in lines and figures'. Such lines and figures — almost equally divided between mathematical and musical symbols — Gulliver saw displayed upon their garments and in the king's kitchen, where 'all kinds of mathematical and musical instruments' were used to cut the food into 'rhomboides' and 'cycloids', flutes, fiddles and hautboys. It was entirely natural that, with ideas of beauty founded upon the 'Proportions' of music and mathematics, the Laputans should have transferred their figures of speech from one realm to another:

If they would, for example, praise the beauty of a woman, or any other animal, they describe it by rhombs, circles, parallelograms, ellipses, and other geometrical terms, or by words of art drawn from music. (p. 191)[2]

[1] For such mathematical interpretations of music, see 'The Defects of a Trumpet, and Trumpet Marine' (*Phil. Trans.* vol. XVII (1692), p. 559; vol. I, pp. 660 ff.), in which the author writes of the general agreement of 'all Writers on the Mathematical Part of Music'. Wallis (ibid. vol. XX (1698), pp. 80, 297; vol. I, pp. 610, 618) discusses the mathematical divisions of the monochord in terms of 'Proportions of Gravity' and offers other mathematical analogies. S. Salvetti, in 'The Strange Effects reported of Musick in Former Times, examined', points out (vol. I, p. 618) the decadence of contemporary music, in that it was tending away from emphasis on mathematical principles and was coming to be applied merely to 'particular Designs of exciting this or that particular Affection, Passion, or Temper of the Mind' — a matter, he feels, to be regretted by true musicians.

[2] Cf. Fontenelle, 'Of the Usefulness of Mathematical Learning', ed. cit.: 'A Geometrical Genius is not so confin'd to Geometry but that it may be capable of learning other Sciences. A Tract of Morality, Politicks, or Criticism and even a Piece of Oratory, supposing the Author qualify'd otherwise for those Performances, shall be the better for being composed by a Geometrician. That Order, Perspicuity, Precision and Exactness, which some time since are found in good Books, may originally proceed from that Geometrical Genius, which is now more common than ever.'

No specific source is needed for such an idea; and in view of the long succession of the predecessors of the Laputans who had found evidence of eternal and perfect beauty in mathematics and music, no specific source can really be posited. Yet the musico-mathematical notions of the Laputans may be conveniently found in a paper by the Rev. T. Salmon on 'The Theory of Musick reduced to Arithmetical and Geometrical Progressions'.[1] The paper followed an earlier one in which Salmon had reported a 'Musical Experiment before the Society', the propositions of which were: 'That Music consisted in Proportions, and the more exact the Proportions, the better the Music.' In his second paper, Salmon discussed 'the Theory of Music, which is but little known in this Age, and the Practice of it which is arriv'd to a very great Excellency', both of which, he suggested, 'May be fixed upon the sure Foundations of Mathematical Certainty'. He offered in conclusion two tables 'wherein Music is set forth, first Arithmetically, and then Geometrically'. It required only one more step for the Laputans to apply the certain 'Proportions' of music and mathematics to the praise of feminine beauty.

III

More specific satire with more immediate source is found in the sections in which Swift discusses the two predominant prepossessions of the Laputans — their fear of the sun and of a comet (pp. 192–3). In spite of Swift's suggestions that the Laputans still share astrological fears, he has made them a people whose dread is founded less upon tradition than upon celestial observation. They possess 'glasses far excelling ours in goodness', by means of which they have extended 'their discoveries much further than our astronomers in Europe' (p. 200).[2] They have made important discoveries with their

---

[1] *Phil. Trans.* vol. XXIV (1705), p. 2072; vol. IV, i, pp. 469–74.

[2] Gulliver adds: 'Although their largest telescopes do not exceed three feet, they magnify much more than those of an hundred yards among us, and at the same time show the stars with greater clearness.' This passage does not appear in the 1726 edition, but was added in 1727. The addition of the sentence may indicate the current interest in such small instruments. Cf. 'An Account of a Catadioptrick Telescope, made by Mr. J. Hadley': *Phil. Trans.* vol. XXXII (1723), p. 303; vol. VI, i, p. 133. The telescope described was six feet long and magnified some 220 times.

telescopes, none more remarkable than that of the two satellites of Mars — which actually remained hidden from all eyes but those of the Laputans until 1877![1] They are careful observers, among whom one would expect to find science rather than superstition. Yet their dread of the sun and of a comet is greater than had been their ancestors', for their fear is more profoundly rooted in contemporary science.

Three ideas of the sun particularly disturbed the Laputans:

that the earth, by the continual approaches of the sun towards it, must in course of time be absorbed or swallowed up. That the face of the sun will by degrees be encrusted with its own effluvia, and

---

[1] M. Pons (*Gulliver's Travels*, p. 234 n.) pays particular attention to this apparently remarkable discovery of Swift's, and points out the similarity not only in the number of satellites but in their periods to the actual discovery made in the nineteenth century. The Laputans found two satellites, 'whereof the innermost is distant from the centre of the primary planet exactly three of the diameters, and the outermost five; the former revolves in the space of ten hours, and the latter in twenty one and a half; so that the squares of their periodical times are very near in the same proportion with the cubes of their distance from the centre of Mars, which evidently shows them to be governed by the same law of gravitation, that influences the other heavenly bodies' ('Voyage to Laputa', pp. 200–1). In spite of a natural desire to agree with M. Pons and Camille Flammarion that this discovery of the satellites of Mars was 'second sight' on Swift's part, we are forced to the conclusion that it was only a happy guess. It was inevitable that many writers, scientists and laymen, should have raised the question of the satellites of Mars. (See, for example, Fontenelle, *Plurality of Worlds*, trans. Glanvill, London, 1702, pp. 120 ff.) Our own planet was known to have one satellite; Galileo had discovered four about Jupiter; in Swift's time, Cassini had published his conclusions in regard to the five satellites of Saturn. (See *Phil. Trans.* abridged, vol. I, pp. 368, 370 and 377; vol. IV, p. 323.) Swift, using no telescope but his imagination, chose two satellites for Mars, the smallest number by which he could easily indicate their obedience to Kepler's laws, a necessity clearly shown him by Cassini; this number fits neatly between the one satellite of the earth and the four of Jupiter. To indicate the Keplerian ratio, he has made one of the simplest of assumptions concerning distances and period, that of $3 : 5$ for the distances, and 10 for the period of the inner satellite. It was not a difficult computation, even for a Swift who was no mathematician, to work out the necessary period of the outer satellite ($3^3 : 5^3 = 10^2 : x$). His trick proved approximately correct — though it might easily have been incorrect.

give no more light to the world. . . . That the sun daily spending its rays without any nutriment to supply them, will at last be wholly consumed and annihilated; which must be attended with the destruction of this earth, and of all the planets that receive their light from it. (p. 193)[1]

Such fears were in no way original with the Laputans; many a thoughtful man of the day found himself pondering the same possibilities. Behind the fear that their planet might fall into the sun lay the potent influence of Newton, 'Britain's justest pride, The boast of human race'.[2] Newton's analysis of planetary motion showed that there must exist a nice balance between the velocity with which the earth is falling toward the sun and its tangential velocity at right angles to that fall. Any disturbance of this 'due proportion of velocity' would be disastrous. The most obvious possibility of disturbance is the gradual decrease of our tangential velocity, for then the earth's orbit would no longer repeat itself year after year, but would approach the sun with ever-increasing speed, eventually to fall into it. This possibility is recognised in the *Principia* by general calculations of the time required for such falls,[3] and by an estimate of the density of the material in space through which the earth spins and the retarding effect to be expected from it.[4] While Newton's conclusion was, on the whole, an optimistic one that the loss of velocity would be quite inappreciable even for 'an immense tract of time',[5] other conclusions were drawn from the

[1] Cf. *Memoirs of Scriblerus*, p. 136: 'A Computation of the Duration of the Sun, and how long it will last before it be burn'd out.'

[2] David Mallet, 'The Excursion', in *Poems*, ed. A. Chalmers (London, 1810), vol. xiv, p. 22.

[3] *Philosophiæ Naturalis Principia Mathematica* (1687). Translated into English by Andrew Motte (1729). References are to the recent revision, *The Mathematical Principles*, ed. Florian Cajori (Stanford, 1934). Cf. particularly book i, sections vii and viii.

[4] Ibid. book iii, proposition x, theorem x: 'That the motions of the planets in the heavens may subsist an exceedingly long time.'

[5] Newton goes on to prove that the life of a comet may be more rudely concluded if its approach to the sun is so near that it is slowed down by friction in the atmosphere of the sun (ibid. book iii, proposition xlii, problem xxii). See below, p. 247, n. 1.

same premises. The Laputans might well have found reason for their doubt in Robert Hooke, who, opposing his wave-theory to Newton's theory of light, recognised clearly that there is difficulty in describing the medium which carried these waves and that any imaginable medium would have a retarding effect upon the earth's motion.[1]

Die we must, it would seem, if we are fearful eighteenth-century Laputans. Even if we follow the conclusion of Newton in regard to our earth's falling into the sun, there still remains the warning of the sun-spots and of the consumption of the sun's energy. From the time of Galileo's first observation of sun-spots, astronomers had been concerned to explain these phenomena, and the explanations had led in many different directions. During the early years of the eighteenth century the *Philosophical Transactions* devoted much attention to the problem of these phenomena. A letter of 'Mr. Crabtrie', written in 1640, was revived and republished, and his theory debated, that the spots were 'fading Bodies. . . . no Stars, but unconstant (in regard of their Generation) and irregular Excrescences arising out of, or proceeding from the Sun's body'.[2] At the least, these spots indicated 'a Smoak arising out of the Body of the Sun'.[3] At the worst, the 'Smoak' suggested volcanic action. This point of view was developed in detail by William Derham:

From these preceding Particulars, and their Congruity to what we perceive in our own Globe, I cannot forbear to gather, That the Spots on the Sun are caused by the Eruption of some new Vulcano therein; which at first, pouring out a prodigious Quantity of Smoak, and other opacous Matter, causeth the Spots: And as that fuliginious Matter decayeth and appendeth itself, and the Vulcano at last becomes more torrid and flaming, so the Spots decay and grow to Umbræ, and at last to Faculæ; which Faculæ I take to be no other

---

[1] Cf. 'A Discourse of Earthquakes', in *The Posthumous Works of Robert Hooke* (1705), p. 322.

[2] Crabtree's opinion, in a letter to Mr. Gascoigne, is included in the *Phil. Trans.* vol. XXVII (1711), p. 270; vol. IV, pp. 241 ff.

[3] Ibid. vol. XXVII (1711), p. 278. A series of articles on the subject will be found in the *Phil. Trans.*, abridged, vol. IV, pp. 229–47.

than more flaming brighter Parts than any other Parts of the sun.[1]

The Laputans, it would seem, were incorrigible pessimists. Granted we escape, through Newton's optimism, falling into the sun, and granted too — though it seems highly improbable — that the sun-spots indicate only 'Smoak', not 'Vulcano', our fate, though different, will be as surely sealed, if the sun cools or dwindles to a vanishing point. The natural explanation of the heat of the sun, that it is a tremendous burning mass, had been made even more plausible by the discovery of those spots on the sun, which look suspiciously like smoke. Here Hooke was the chief source for concern. 'I question not', he wrote, 'but that there may be very cogent Arguments drawn to prove, that the Light of this Body of the Sun may be caused by an actual Fire, or Dissolution of the superficial Parts thereof ... which being proved, or supposed so, all the Appearances that have been hitherto taken notice of concerning Clouds, Spots and Blazes, will be very naturally and clearly solved. . . . But some may object and say, that if this were so, certainly the Body of the Sun in so many Thousand Years would have been all consumed, at least it would have grown sensibly less. Suppose this were granted and said, that it has grown some Minutes less since it first began to give Light, none could contradict it by any Observations we have upon record.'[2]

Fear of the sun was not all; even greater than dread of such changes was the Laputan dread of comets and of one comet in particular. 'The earth very narrowly escaped a brush from the tail of the late comet, which would infallibly have reduced it to ashes', Gulliver learned in Laputa (p. 193). It is however not the 'last comet' that terrifies the Laputans so much as one that is to come 'which will probably destroy us'. Is this mere pointless satire, or is there method in this apparent madness? Swift's imagination here, as so often, is making of the real something apparently unreal. His reference — as every reader of his day must have realised — was not merely to a comet, but to 'Halley's comet' — the first comet whose period of return was definitely predicted, with resultant great

---

[1] 'Spots on the Sun from 1703 to 1708', by Mr. W. Derham. Ibid. vol. IV, p. 235.

[2] 'Lectures of Light', in *Posthumous Works of Robert Hooke*, p. 94.

excitement both to literary and to scientific imagination.[1] Thomson, writing only a year later than Swift, shows the same response to a scientific idea, when he turns it into poetry in 'Summer':

> Lo! from the dread immensity of space
> Returning with accelerated course,
> The rushing comet to the sun descends:
> And as he sinks below the shading earth,
> With awful train projected o'er the heavens,
> The guilty nations tremble . . .
> While, from his far excursion through the wilds
> Of barren ether, faithful to his time,
> They see the blazing wonder rise anew.[2]

In this passage Swift has told us the date of composition of at least part of the 'Voyage to Laputa'. The Laputans calculated the return of their comet in 'one and thirty years'; and one and thirty years after 1726 — the date of the first publication of *Gulliver's Travels* — English laymen expected the return of Halley's comet. True, Halley himself had predicted that the comet of 1682 would return not in 1757 — as Swift's passage implies — but in 1758; but Halley's prophecy left some reason for doubt. Laymen, then as now, grasped the main point, but neglected the careful mathematics in which Halley corrected a generalization.[3] Seventy-five years had

[1] Swift had already satirized the popular excitement occasioned by the prediction of a comet's return in 'A True and Faithful Narrative of What Passed in London' (*Satires and Personal Writings*, p. 90): 'But on Wednesday morning (I believe to the exact Calculation of Mr. Whiston) the Comet appear'd: For at three Minutes after five, by my own Watch, I saw it. He, indeed, foretold that it would be seen at five Minutes after Five, but as the best Watches may be a Minute or too [*sic*] slow, I am apt to think his Calculation Just to a Minute.'

[2] Chalmers (ed.), *Poems*, vol. XII, pp. 434–5.

[3] Halley's earliest complete publication on the periods of comets appeared as the 'Astronomiæ Cometicæ Synopsis', published in the *Phil. Trans.* for 1705. An English translation, published at Oxford, appeared in the same year. The latter paper may be found appended to *The Elements of Astronomy, Physical and Geometrical*, by David Gregory (London, 1715), vol. II, pp. 881–905. The inclusion of this paper in Gregory's volume seems to have escaped the notice of Halley's bibliographers. It is not mentioned in the 'Halleiana' in *Correspondence and Papers of Edmond Halley*, ed. E. F. MacPike (Oxford, 1932), pp. 272–8, although the later Latin edition of 1726 in Gregory's volume is noted, p. 278.

elapsed between the appearance of the comet in 1607 and its reappearance in 1682; years, not days, are important to the layman. The 'Mean period' Halley himself calculated at '75 Years and a half'.[1] The general public was not at all concerned with the careful table of Halley's 'inequalities', nor with his masterful application to his theory of comets of the explanation which he had earlier proposed for the deviation from equality in the case of Jupiter and Saturn. As he had suggested that that inequality was the result of the attraction of these planets for each other, in addition to the attraction of the sun for both, so he concluded that the inequalities in the comet's return might arise from a similar cause. The layman understood only that the comet would appear in approximately seventy-five years; and he vaguely recognized that, if it did, it would put beyond question Newton's theory of gravitation.[2]

In the period of the Renaissance, 'Comets importing change of time and states' had brandished their bloody tresses, and predicted 'disasters in the sun'. But during the seventeenth century, under the impact of the new astronomy, the attitude toward comets began gradually to change, as men questioned whether these strange phenomena, too, might not prove to have a natural place in the great cosmic scheme. There are indications in almanacs and other popular literature of the day that this was one result of Newton's discoveries. Nevertheless, old beliefs still largely dominated popular imagination.[3] As Swift himself wrote: 'Old men and comets have been reverenced for the same reasons; their long beards, and pretenses to foretell events.'[4]

[1] In the later edition of the *Synopsis*, Halley wrote: 'Now it is manifest that two periods of this Comet are finished in 150 Years nearly, and that each alternately, the greater and the less, are compleated in about 76 and 75 Years; wherefore, taking the mean period, to be 75 Years and a half...'

[2] Halley himself was incorrect in his computations, as events proved, since the theory of perturbations was not sufficiently advanced for him to make exact prophecy; in addition, Uranus and Neptune were unknown to his generation. The comet passed perihelion on 13 March 1759, though it was observed on Christmas night, 1758.

[3] For the popular attitude towards comets in this period see C. P. Olivier, *Comets* (Baltimore, 1930), ch. i.

[4] T. Scott (ed.), *Prose Works*, vol. i, p. 281.

The dread of the Laputans rested however less upon such superstition than upon scientific discovery. With their telescopes they had 'observed ninety-three different comets, and settled their periods with great exactness' (p. 201).[1] If therefore they feared that a comet 'one and thirty years hence' would destroy them, they must have had scientific grounds for their belief. The basis for their fear was implied even in Halley's earlier *Synopsis*, in connection with his discussion of the approach of various comets to the earth. His paper concluded with the statement: 'But what might be the Consequences of so near an appulse; or of a contact, or, lastly, of a shock of the Celestial Bodies,(which is by no means impossible to come to pass,) I leave to be discussed by the Studious of Physical matters'.[2] In his later amplification of the *Synopsis*,[3] Halley went further and expanded this section in connection with the comet of 1680:

Now this Comet, in that part of its Orbit in which it descended towards the Sun, came so near the paths of all the Planets, that if by chance it had happened to meet any one of the Planets passing by,

[1] This is characteristic Laputan exaggeration. No such number of comets had been observed; and the periods of only three had been fully calculated by Halley. Gulliver adds characteristically: 'It is much to be wished that the observations were made public, whereby the theory of comets, which at present is very lame and defective, might be brought to the same perfection with other parts of astronomy.' Among the advantages which Gulliver at first thought might come from the immortality of the Struldbrugs, he suggested (p. 250): 'What wonderful discoveries should we make in astronomy, by outliving and confirming our own predictions, by observing the progress and return of comets, with the changes of motion in the sun, moon, and stars.'

[2] *The Elements of Astronomy*, vol. II, p. 905. Cf. *Memoirs of Scriblerus*, p. 136. One of the 'Philosophical and Mathematical Works' of Martin Scriblerus was 'Tide-Tables for a Comet, that is to approximate towards the Earth'.

[3] There is no mention in the 'Halleiana' referred to above of the fact that Halley published a later edition of the *Synopsis*, with several corrections and additions. Such a paper appeared however in *Astronomical Tables with Præcepts Both in English and Latin, For Computing the Places of the Sun, Moon, Planets, and Comets*, by Edmond Halley (London, 1752). The volume is not paginated. The editor states that the tables were 'sent to the press in 1717 and printed off in 1719'. The chief changes are in the tables; the rest follows the original until the conclusion, to which we refer, which is expanded.

it must have produced very sensible effects, and the motion of the Comet would have suffered the greatest disturbance. In such case the plane and species of its Ellipsis and its periodic Time would have been very much changed, especially from meeting with Jupiter. In the late descent, the true path of this Comet left the Orbits of Saturn and Jupiter below itself a little towards the South: It approached much nearer to the paths of Venus and Mercury, and much nearer still to that of Mars. But as it was passing thro' the plane of the Ecliptic, viz., to the southern Node, it came so near the path of the Earth, that had it come towards the Sun thirty one days later than it did, it had scarce left our Globe one semidiameter of the Sun towards the North: And without doubt by its centripetal force (which with the great Newton I suppose proportional to the bulk or quantity of matter in the Comet), it would have produced some change in the situation and species of the Earth's Orbit, and in the length of the year. But may the good GOD avert such a shock or contact of such great Bodies moving with such forces (which however is manifestly by no means impossible), lest this most beautiful order of things be intirely destroyed and reduced into its antient chaos.

Although this suggestion alone would have been sufficient to explain the Laputans' dread of the return of the comet, there is little doubt that popular imagination was even more deeply stirred by another paper which Halley presented to the Royal Society — on the subject of Noah and the Flood! This was one of many papers published in the period by important men of science in which an attempt was made to explain difficult passages in Scripture in such a way as to keep the reverence for the Bible, yet make it consistent with modern scientific thought. Straining at the gnat, Halley and others swallowed the Deluge.[1] In an earlier version of the paper, read before the Royal Society in 1694,[2] Halley had suggested 'the

[1] Cf. *Memoirs of Scriblerus*, p. 135: 'To him we owe all the observations of the Parallax of the Pole-Star, and all the new Theories of the Deluge.'

[2] 'Some Considerations about the Cause of the Universal Deluge', *Phil. Trans.* abridged, vol. VI, ii, pp. 1–5. The original paper, which differed in several important respects, was read before the Society on 12 Dec. 1694. The later paper was read in 1724. To some extent the ideas suggested in the earlier paper were intended as a confutation of Thomas Burnet's *Sacred Theory of the Earth* (London, 1681–2), 2 vols., a copy of which, containing annotations in his own hand, was in Swift's library. See *A Catalogue of Books*, no. 375.

casual Choc of a Comet, or other transient Body' as 'an Expedient change instantly the Poles and Diurnal Rotation of the Globe'. But in the later paper he went further: 'At that Time', he says, 'I did not consider the great Agitation such a Choc must necessarily occasion in the Sea.' Halley's description of the probable consequences of such a 'Choc' was sufficient to strike terror into braver hearts than those of the Laputans. He visualizes the Deluge:

raising up Mountains where none were before, mixing the Elements into such a Heap as the Poets describe the Old Chaos; for such a Choc impelling the solid Parts would occasion the Waters, and all fluid Substances that were unconfined, as the Sea is, with one Impetus to run violently towards that Part of the Globe were [*sic*] the Blow was received; and that with Force sufficient to rake with it the whole Bottom of the Ocean, and to carry it upon the Land; heaping up into Mountains those earth Parts it had born away with it, in those Places where the opposite Waves balance each other, *miscens ima summis*.

Thus Halley, discovering that the comets, like the stars in their courses, obey the universal law of gravitation, established in 1705 the point of view that was to free men from their long dread of 'those stars with trains of fire and dews of blood'; but through a few sentences in a paper in which he announced the law of comets, and, most of all, through republishing in 1724 a paper largely written thirty years before on the subject of that Deluge weathered only by an ark, put into the minds of the Laputans — and many others of Swift's contemporaries — a greater dread, of the complete annihilation of this globe which we inherit.[1] Small wonder that in the morning

[1] The Laputans may also have found reason for their fear of a collision in Newton's passage (referred to above p.240, n. 5) in the *Principia*, book III, proposition XLII, problem XXII: 'The comet which appeared in the year 1680 was in its perihelion less distant from the sun than by a sixth part of the sun's diameter; and because of its extreme velocity in that proximity to the sun, and some density of the sun's atmosphere, it must have suffered some resistance and retardation; and therefore, being attracted something nearer to the sun in every revolution, will at last fall down upon the body of the sun.' After a discussion of the appearance and disappearance of *novæ*, Newton concludes: 'The vapours which arise from the sun, the fixed stars, and the tails of the comets, may meet at last with, and fall into, the atmospheres of the planets by their gravity . . .'

the Laputans exchanged no trivial greetings. 'The first question is about the sun's health, how he looked at his setting and rising, and what hopes they have to avoid the stroke of the approaching comet' (p. 193). Like small boys who have listened to tales of hobgoblins, the Laputans 'dared not go to bed for fear'.

IV

After his visit to the Laputans, Gulliver descended to the main-land, Balnibari, and proceeded at once to the capital Lagado, whose Grand Academy was to prove one of the chief interests of his voyage. He was impressed, both in town and country, by many 'odd appearances'. The houses were 'very strangely built and most of them out of repair'. Though the fields were filled with labourers and the soil appeared excellent, he saw neither corn nor grass. As he journeyed with the 'great lord Munodi' to his country estate, he observed 'the several methods used by farmers in managing their lands, which to me were wholly unaccountable' (p. 208). Only in the privacy of the country-house did Munodi venture to explain to Gulliver the source of the evident difference between his own well-ordered estate and the 'ill contrived' buildings and 'unhappily cultivated' fields of the rest of Balnibari. In so far as this section of the 'Voyage to Laputa' has been studied, critics have taken for granted that the source of its satire was in contemporary politics. Balnibari is England, or more often Ireland, with its houses out of repair, its fields badly cultivated, its people in misery and want. Yet, though Swift undoubtedly intended some such double meaning, there is another sort of satire here also, which leads backward to Swift's part in that particular chapter of the long warfare of 'ancient' and 'modern', which Swift himself called *The Battle of the Books*.

The aspect of the old quarrel reflected in the 'Voyage to Laputa' is not the controversy between 'ancient' and 'modern' literature, but the broader implications of the quarrel which in England had be-come largely a scientific controversy. Munodi, with whom alone the conservative Gulliver found real sympathy, is clearly an 'ancient' and for that reason ridiculed by his 'modern' neighbours. His sympathy with the party of the 'ancients' is shown most im-mediately in his surroundings. His house is 'a noble structure, built according to the best rules of ancient architecture' (p. 209) and therefore, Swift slyly suggests, still standing! 'The fountains, gardens, walks, avenues, and groves were all disposed with exact judgment and taste' (p. 209). 'Everything about him was magnificent, regular, and polite' (p. 208). 'He was content to go on in the old forms, to live in the houses his ancestors had built, and act as they did in every part of life without innovation' (p. 210). Yet in the eyes of his countrymen he was not only a failure, but also an enemy to progress, an 'ill commonwealth's man'. His example would have been considered dangerous, had it not been that that example was followed only by 'such as were old, and wilful, and weak like himself' (p. 208). So strong was the pressure of public opinion that Munodi sadly faced the necessity of tearing down his noble structure to rebuild in the present ill mode.

The trouble had begun, he tells Gulliver, 'about forty years before', when certain Balnibarians had visited progressive Laputa and, falling under the spell of Laputan philosophy, 'came back with a very small smattering in mathematics, but full of volatile spirits acquired in that airy region' (p. 209). Here, as so often, Swift's figures are significant. 'About forty years before' the composition of the 'Voyage to Laputa' — thirty-nine years, if we are to continue accepting 1726 as the year of composition of these sections — the first gun in the *Battle of the Books* had been fired by Charles Perrault's *Siècle de Louis le Grand*, followed the next year by Fontenelle's *Digression sur les anciens et les modernes* and the first volume of Perrault's *Parallèle des anciens et des modernes*, as a result of which Sir William Temple wrote his essay 'On Ancient and Modern Learning' and ultimately drew Swift into the combat. From the time of their visit to Laputa, the Balnibarians 'fell into schemes of putting all arts, sciences, languages, and mechanics upon a new foot' (p. 209). Most of all, they had established an 'Academy of Projectors' which had come to dominate the nation — as the Royal Society dominated England. Its 'professors contrive new rules and methods of agriculture and building, and new instruments and tools for all trades and manufactures'.[1] They promised a new Utopia if

[1] The terminology here recalls that of the Royal Society. Cf. *The History of the Royal Society of London, For the Improving of Natural*

their methods were followed. True, their magnificent projects had been brought to no perfection at the time of Gulliver's visit; but with Baconian optimism, they persisted in their prosecution of schemes to reform the kingdom by science, centred in a later 'Salomon's House'.

v

It has been generally recognized that in the Grand Academy of Lagado, Swift was to some extent following a fashion, common enough in literature of the seventeenth and eighteenth centuries, of satirizing academicians in general and the Royal Society in particular; but the full extent of that satire has not been appreciated. Long before the incorporation of the Royal Society, Rabelais had introduced a somewhat similar passage in his Court of Queen Whim; Joseph Hall in 1610 described another such Academy in his *Mundus Alter et Idem*.[1] Bacon's enthusiastic proposals for his scientific Academy in the *New Atlantis* offered new fuel. The establishment of the Royal Society tended to make specific the former general satire. From the time of Samuel Sorbière's visit to London in 1663,[2] journeys, whether 'real' or 'philosophical', tended to include accounts of academies which are usually only thinly veiled pictures of the Royal Society. Ned Ward's tour of London, described in the *London Spy* in 1698,[3] led him to Gresham College as well as to the 'Colledge of Physicians'; in both institutions he examined the supposed 'rarities' and 'Philosophical Toys'. From both he went away

Knowledge, by Tho. Sprat, 3rd ed. (London, 1722), p. 190: 'They have propounded the composing a Catalogue of all Trades, Works, and Manufactures, wherein Men are employ'd . . . by taking notice of all the physical Receipts or Secrets, the Instruments, Tools, and Engines . . . and whatever else belongs to the Operations of all Trades.' The interest of the Society in 'instruments and tools . . . trades and manufactures' is clear throughout.

[1] On similarities between Swift and Rabelais and Hall, see Eddy, *Critical Study*, pp. 57 ff.

[2] Cf. Vincent Guilloton, 'Autour de la Relation de Samuel Sorbière en Angleterre', in *Smith College Studies in Modern Languages*, vol. XI (1930), no. 4, pp. 1–29.

[3] *The London Spy. Compleat in Eighteen Parts*, by Ned Ward, with an Introduction by Ralph Straus (London, 1924), pp. 50 ff. and 125 ff.

with a poor opinion of scientists, who seemed to him only less mad than the inmates of the lunatic asylum which he also visited. Dr. Martin Lister, in the account of his journey to Paris,[1] paid high tribute to both French and English scientists. The subsequent parody by William King in his *Journey to London*[2] in the same year introduces satirically the theme of visits to the *virtuosi*. King carries his attack further in the Ninth Dialogue of the *Dialogues of the Dead*[3] and in the *Transactioneer*.[4] Even closer similarities to Swift's Academy may be found in Tom Brown's 'Philosophical or Virtuosi Country' in *Amusements Serious and Comical*, and in Ludwig Holberg's *Journey to a World Underground*.[5] If we are to trust the evidence of literature, Swift hardly exaggerated when he said through the lips of Munodi: 'There is not a town of any consequence . . . without such an academy' (p. 209). While there is no doubt that some of the details in the 'Voyage to Laputa' reflect such earlier works as that of Rabelais, nevertheless Swift's Grand Academy of Lagado was drawn rather from life than from literature.

On 13 December 1710 Swift himself had paid a visit to Gresham College. With many other visitors, his itinerary included other institutions often grouped together in the memory of travellers to London: 'then to Bedlam; then dined at the Chophouse behind the Exchange; then to Gresham College (but the keeper was not at home), and concluded the night at the puppet-show . . .'[6] Puppet-

---

[1] *A Journey to Paris in the Year 1698* (London, 1698), pp. 78 ff. and *passim*.

[2] *A Journey to London. In the Year 1698. After the Ingenious Method of that made by Dr. Martin L. . . . to Paris, in the same year* in *Miscellanies in Prose and Verse*, by William King (London, 1705), pp. 224 ff. and *passim*. A modern edition may be found in *A Miscellany of the Wits: Select Pieces by William King, D.C.L., John Arbuthnot, M.D., and other Hands*, with an Introduction by K. N. Colville (London, 1920), pp. 15 ff. and *passim*.

[3] In *Miscellanies in Prose and Verse*, pp. 324–38; *A Miscellany of the Wits*, pp. 69–80.

[4] William King, *The Transactioneer, with some of his Philosophical Fancies, in Two Dialogues* (London, 1700).

[5] The similarities between Swift, Brown and Holberg have been pointed out by Eddy, *Critical Study*, pp. 160–3.

[6] *Journal to Stella*, in *Prose Works* (ed. T. Scott), vol. II, p. 72.

shows, lunatic asylums, colleges for the advancement of research —
they were all one to the satirists of that generation. If, in spite of the
absence of the keeper, Swift saw any of the collections of the Royal
Society, we may perhaps detect reminiscences of his visit in his later
references to the loadstone of the Flying Island and in his brief
suggestion of projectors who were 'petrifying the hoofs of a living
horse to preserve them from foundering' (p. 216). The collection of
petrified objects belonging to the Royal Society was shown with
pride to all visitors and was known throughout Europe. One section
of their earliest catalogue was devoted to 'Animal Bodies Petrified',
another to 'Vegetable Bodies Petrified'.[1] Yet on the whole Swift's
Academy reflects less Swift's own visit than accounts in the
Philosophical Transactions.

In his account of the Grand Academy, Swift first describes the
institution briefly: 'This Academy is not an entire single building,
but a continuation of several houses on both sides of a street, which
growing waste was purchased and applied to that use' (p. 212).
Gulliver later estimates that there were at least five hundred rooms
in the institution. This is certainly not the Royal Society as it
appeared in the years when Swift was at work on *Gulliver's Travels*.
Yet it is possible that this is one of Swift's sly digs at the Society's
ambition for greatly expanded quarters, which threatened to divide
the Council into two factions.[2] There were those among the

---

[1] Nehemiah Grew, *Musæum Regalis Societatis. Or a Catalogue and
Description of the Natural and Artificial Rarities Belonging to the Royal
Society and preserved at Gresham Colledge* (London, 1681), pp. 253 and
265.

[2] From the time that the president, Newton, had declared it necessary
that they 'have a being of their own' (C. R. Weld, *History of the Royal
Society* (London, 1848), vol. 1, p. 387), one of the most persistent problems reflected in the records is that of moving to larger quarters. When in
1705 the Council received word from the Mercers' Company that the
latter had decided 'not to grant the Society any room at all' (ibid.),
purchase of property became imperative. In 1710 two houses in Crane
Court in Fleet Street were bought, though the Council was far from
unanimous in its decision as a pamphlet of the day indicates (*An Account
of the late Proceedings in the Council of the Royal Society, in order to remove
from Gresham College into Crane Court in Fleet Street*, London, 1710).
During the next few years the Society came to pride itself upon its

members who continued to entertain the noble ambition, proposed by Bacon in his description of 'Salomon's House', not only of 'great and spacious houses', but of 'deep caves ... high towers', great lakes and artificial wells, orchards, gardens, parks and enclosures.

The members of the Academy whom Gulliver encountered were of various groups — experimental scientists, 'projectors in speculative learning', professors in the 'school of languages' and politicians. Since our concern for the moment is with the scientific background of the voyage and particularly its relation to the *Philosophical Transactions*, we may limit ourselves to the first group of experimentalists.[1] Since Swift's own larger outline cannot be followed, we may watch his subdivisions of the experiments of his projectors according to a scheme suggested by Fontenelle: 'Physick ... is divided in the Academy into three Branches, which make three different sorts of Members of the Society, Anatomy, Chymistry, and Botanicks.'[2] The experiments of these projectors have impressed literary historians chiefly by their apparent exaggeration and have been dismissed as so obviously impossible that they become grotesque rather than humorous. Swift, the critics say, 'simply tortured his memory and his fancy to invent or recall grotesque

increasing importance. On 15 Dec. 1710, the Society was appointed Visitors and Directors of the Royal Observatory at Greenwich (Weld, op. cit. vol. I, pp. 400 ff.). Its property, received by deed and bequest, was so extensive that a petition to the King in 1724 mentions 'two messuages in Crane Court; certain lands and hereditaments in Mablethorpe, Lincolnshire; two houses in Coleman Street ... and a fee-farm in Sussex' (ibid. vol. I, p. 431 n.).

[1] Each of these other groups has, however, its relation to the Royal Society. I have treated elsewhere the 'projectors in speculative learning' and the 'school of languages', since, in spite of their scientific heritage, each of these groups has its part in the literary controversies of the day. I may, however, mention at this point that, although Professor Eddy feels that the division into 'experimental' and 'speculative' scientists follows a similar division in Tom Brown's *Amusements* (Eddy, *Critical Study*, p. 162), my own impression is that both Brown and Swift were reflecting a common enough division in the minds of men — that between the 'Baconians' and the 'Cartesians' of the Royal Society. It is hardly possible here to go into the evidence for this belief. M. H. N.

[2] 'Of the Usefulness of Mathematical Learning' (unpaged).

illustrations of scientific pedantry'.[1] Yet there was humour in these passages when they were written, and humour of a sort particularly popular today. Swift's is the *reductio ad absurdum* frequently employed by modern satirists who reduce to nonsense scientific papers and doctoral dissertations, not by inventing unreal subjects of research, but — more devastatingly — by quoting actual titles of papers and theses. What, asks a modern reader, could be more absurd than 'A Study of the Bacteria Found in a Dirty Shirt'? Removed from its context, read by laymen instead of scientists, the real serves often as a more powerful weapon against scientific research than can anything invented by fancy. Such is Swift's technique. For the most part he simply set down before his readers experiments actually performed by members of the Royal Society, more preposterous to the layman than anything imagination could invent and more devastating in their satire because of their essential truth to source. The 'invention' in Swift's passages usually consists in one of two things: sometimes he neatly combines two real experiments on different subjects — as in the case of the spiders who not only spun silk stockings, but also went one better than the scientists by colouring them naturally; at other times Swift carries a real experiment only one step further — and the added step carries us over the precipice of nonsense.

Two of the 'projects' alone seem to have had a literary source. The purposely disgusting experiment of the 'most ancient student of the Academy', who attempted to 'reduce human excrement to its original food', was based upon Rabelais' 'Archasdarpenin'.[2] The 'Ingenious architect' who built his house, like the bee and spider, by beginning at the roof and working downwards, had also a literary source, though one may suspect that Swift found at least partial authority for the idea in contemporary accounts of architectural experiments.[3] With these two possible exceptions, all of Swift's

[1] Eddy, *Critical Study*, p. 163.

[2] Cf. Eddy, *Critical Study*, p. 162. Swift himself would seem to indicate this source in his phrase, 'the most ancient student of the Academy'. It is possible that there may also be a reflection here of Leeuwenhoek's microscopical observations upon human excrement.

[3] Eddy points out (op. cit. p. 163) the similarity between this passage

major experiments may be found in the *Philosophical Transactions* or in more complete works of members of the Royal Society.

The 'astronomer who had undertaken to place a sun-dial upon the great weather-cock on the town-house, by adjusting the annual and diurnal motions of the earth and sun, so as to answer and coincide with all accidental turnings by the wind' (p. 214) was proposing nothing impossible. Such sun-clocks had been invented both in France and in England. Sir Christopher Wren in 1663 had contrived an automatic wind-recorder, by annexing a clock to a weather-cock, and, by an ingenious combination of a pencil attached to the clock and a paper on a rundle moved by the weather-cock, procured automatic records of the wind.[1] An English correspondent of the Royal Society in 1719, taking exception to the assertion of a Frenchman that 'clocks to agree with the Sun's apparent Motion' had been invented first in France, wrote:

[He] supposed that it was a Thing never thought of by any before himself: I shall therefore give this short Account of what I have performed in that Matter myself.... [The account follows].... But these Clocks that I then made to agree with the Sun's apparent Time, were done according to the Equation Tables, which I found not to agree very exactly with the Sun's apparent Motion.... I made

and one in Tom Brown's *Amusements*. There were however certain architectural experiments not entirely dissimilar, which might well have attracted Swift's attention. Wallis had proposed in 1644 'A Geometrick Flat Floor', working on the problem of how to support a floor over an area wider than the length of the timbers available for joists (cf. R. T. Gunther, *Early Science in Oxford*, vol. i, p. 211). Of a similar nature was the roof of the Sheldonian Theatre, designed by Wren. Cf. also 'A Bridge without any Pillar under it', 'Journal of the Philosophical Society of Oxford', in *Phil. Trans.* vol. xiv (1684), p. 714; vol. i, p. 594. In an earlier passage on the architecture of Balnibari ('Voyage to Laputa', p. 210), Gulliver finds that a palace may be built in a week 'of materials so durable as to last for ever without repairing'. Swift at this point may well have remembered a man who discovered, after the event, that he had built his house not of stone but of asbestos (*Phil. Trans.*, abridged, vol. iv, ii, p. 285).

[1] R. T. Gunther, *Early Science in Oxford*, vol. i, pp. 317–19.

a Table myself by Observation. . . . Since then I have made many of these Clocks.[1]

Others of Swift's experiments follow actual accounts as closely. Among the many remarkable professors of Lagado was 'a man born blind, who had several apprentices in his own condition; their employment was to mix colours for painters, which their master taught them to distinguish by feeling and smelling' (p. 213).[2] One might suspect that here Swift was having his fun — as so often — with Newton, and particularly with the corpuscular theory of light, which had been reported in the *Philosophical Transactions*.[3] But the source was much more direct; not Newton, but Boyle, was the villain of this piece. Material made to his hand Swift found either in Boyle's 'Experiments and Observations upon Colours' or more probably — since Boyle's earlier reports had been made in 1663 and 1664 — in the ponderous *Philosophical Works of Robert Boyle*, which had been 'abridged, methodized, and disposed under various heads' by Peter Shaw in 1725. The blind professor whom Gulliver saw had in the preceding century been a real blind man, whose case was reported to Boyle by 'Dr. Finch, anatomist extraordinary to the great duke of Tuscany'.[4] Finch had told Boyle of 'a blind man at Maestricht, in the Low Countries, who at certain times could

[1] 'The Invention of making Clocks to keep Time with the Sun's apparent Motion, asserted by Mr. J. Williamson' (*Phil. Trans.* vol. xxx (1719), p. 1080; vol. iv, i, p. 394).

[2] Much the same idea — without the mention of a blind man — is used in *Memoirs of Scriblerus,* p. 135: 'He it was that first found out the Palpability of Colours; and by the delicacy of his Touch, could distinguish the different Vibrations of the heterogeneous Rays of Light.' The fact that Swift does not in this earlier work attribute the technique to a blind man may indicate that in the earlier period he was satirizing Newton, while in 1725, in the collected works of Boyle, he found the perfect story for his purposes.

[3] Cf. Sir Isaac Newton, *Opticks: or, A Treatise of the Reflections, Refractions, Inflections, and Colours of Light* (1704; 2nd ed. 1717), book ii, query 29.

[4] 'Dr. Finch' was evidently Sir John Finch, whose career is described by Archibald Malloch, *Finch and Baines: A Seventeenth Century Friendship* (Cambridge, 1917), and in the *Conway Letters*, ed. M. H. Nicolson (New Haven, 1930). Boyle's original paper was written in 1663 and published in 1664. At that time Boyle was prescribing for Lady Anne

distinguish colours by the touch with his fingers'. After several scruples on Boyle's part, he was forced to believe in the account, which he relates in these words:

The name of the man was John Vermaasen, at that time about thirty-three years of age, who, when he was two years old, had the small pox, which render'd him absolutely blind, tho' he is at present an organist in a public choir. The doctor discoursing with him over night, the blind man affirmed, that he could distinguish colours by feeling, but not unless he were fasting; for that any quantity of drink deprived him of that exquisite touch which is requisite to so nice a sensation. Upon this, the doctor provided against the next morning seven pieces of ribbon of these seven colours, black, white, red, blue, green, yellow, and grey; but as for mixed colours, this Vermaasen would not undertake to discern them; tho', if offer'd, he could tell that they were mixed. To discern the colour of the ribbon, he places it betwixt his thumb and his fore-finger, but his most exquisite perception is in his thumb, and much better in the right than in the left. After the man had four or five times told the doctor the several colours, whilst a napkin was tied over his eyes, the doctor observed he twice mistook, for he called the white black, and the red blue; but still before his error, he would lay them by in pairs, saying, that tho' he could easily distinguish them from all others, yet those two pair were not easily distinguishable from one another. Then the doctor desired to know what kind of difference he found in colours by his touch. To which the blind man reply'd, that all the difference he observed, was a greater or less degree of asperity; for, says he, black feels like the points of needles, or some harsh sand, whilst red feels very smooth ... [1]

Boyle goes on to point out that before he saw the notes from which the account was taken he had believed that the blind man might have distinguished the colours not by feeling, but by smelling — another point which Swift was quick to catch. Boyle's account continues:

for some of the ingredients employ'd by dyers, have different and strong scents, which a very nice nose might distinguish; and this I

Conway, sister of Sir John Finch, who received his medical degree at Padua, spent much of his life in Italy and was in close contact with the Grand Duke of Tuscany.

[1] *Philosophical Works*, vol. II, pp. 10–12.

the rather suspected, because he required that the ribbons he was to judge of, should be offer'd him in the morning fasting; for I have observ'd in setting-dogs, that the feeding of them greatly impairs their scent.

In others of his experiments, Swift has cleverly welded together two or more accounts and has made a new combination. The cure 'of a small fit of the colic' (pp. 214–15) is of this sort. Here Swift applies to Gulliver a series of experiments which Shadwell had already made famous in the *Virtuoso*[1] and implies, in addition, various later experiments performed by members of the Royal Society on the general subject of respiration and artificial respiration. The work of Swammerdam, Hooke, Boyle and others on these subjects had long been familiar; but in addition to this general satire — in which otherwise he might be said to follow Shadwell — Swift has suggested something more specific. It is not enough that 'a large pair of bellows' should convey air into the intestines or that, when the dog dies from the treatment, artificial respiration should be used to revive it. Swift needed another element, which he found in an account of 'An extraordinary Effect of the Cholick', in which Mr. St. Andre had already suggested Swift's principle of 'curing that disease by contrary operations':

The Peristaltick Motion of the Intestines is by all Anatomists supposed to be the proper Motion of those Cylindrical Tubes. The use of this Motion is to propel the Chyle into the *Vasa lactea*, and to accelerate the grosser parts of the Aliment downwards, in order to expel them, when all their nutritive Contents are extracted. This Motion, thus established, it naturally seems to follow, that an Inversion of it (call'd for that Reason an Antiperistaltick Motion) should force the Aliments, Bile, Pancreatic Juice, and lastly the Fæces, to ascend towards the Mouth.[2]

The same trick of combining two sources is found in the remarkable experiment of the projector who was able to make silk stockings and gloves from spiders' webs. Swift's projector was found

[1] The experiment, satirized by Shadwell, was reported in Sprat's *History of the Royal Society*, p. 232: 'By means of a Pair of Bellows, and a certain Pipe thrust into the Wind-pipe of the Creature', artificial respiration was established and its effects observed.

[2] *Phil. Trans.* vol. XXX (1717), p. 580; vol. v, i, pp. 270–2.

in a room 'where the walls and ceiling were all hung round with cobwebs' (p. 214). He lamented 'the fatal mistake the world had been so long in of using silk-worms, while we had such plenty of domestic insects, who infinitely excelled the former, because they knew how to weave as well as spin'. One critic has suggested that this idea went back to the proposal of a Frenchman;[1] but it has not been noticed that that Frenchman's proposal appeared in the *Philosophical Transactions*, whence it came to Swift's attention. In a paper on 'The Silk of Spiders', M. Bon in 1710 first gave an account of various sorts of spiders, which reminds the English reader of the satirical interest in these insects in Shadwell's earlier parody. Shadwell's Sir Nicholas Gimcrack had become intimately acquainted with many kinds of spiders; but M. Bon was concerned only with two: '*viz.* such as have long legs, and such as have short Ones: The latter of which furnishes the Silk I am going to speak of.' M. Bon, however, was aware, as was Sir Nicholas Gimcrack, that spiders 'are distinguished by their Colour, some being Black, others Brown, Yellow, Green, White, and others of all these Colours mixed together'. Unlike Sir Nicholas Gimcrack, M. Bon was less concerned with species of spiders than with their utilitarian value. He wrote:

The first Thread that they wind is weak, and serves them for no other Use than to make that Sort of Web, in which they catch Flies: The second is much stronger than the first; in this they wrap up their Eggs, and by this means preserve them from the Cold, and secure them from such Insects as would destroy them. These last Threads are wrapt very loosely about their Eggs, and resemble in Form the Bags of Silk-Worms, that have been prepared and loosened between the Fingers, in order to be put upon the Distaff. These Spiders Bags (if I may so call them) are of a grey Colour when they are new, but turn blackish when they have been long exposed to the Air. It is true, one may find several other Spiders Bags of different Colours, and that afford a better Silk, especially those of the Tarantula; but the Scarcity of them would render it very difficult to make Experiments upon them; so that we must confine ourselves to the Bags of such Spiders as are most common, which are the short-legg'd Ones. . . . And by getting together a great many of

---

[1] Emile Pons, *Gulliver's Travels*, p. 254 n.

these Bags, it was that I made this new Silk, which is no-way inferior in Beauty to common Silk. It easily takes all sorts of Colours; and one may as well make large Pieces of it, as the Stockings and Gloves which I have made . . .[1]

Only one significant difference appears in Swift's account. M. Bon still found it necessary to dye his stockings and gloves in the usual way. But the projector of Lagado had had access to another paper in the *Philosophical Transactions* and was able to produce colours without added expense by a natural method:

He proposed farther that by employing spiders the charge of dyeing silks should be wholly saved, whereof I was fully convinced when he showed me a vast number of flies most beautifully coloured, wherewith he fed his spiders, assuring us that the webs would take a tincture from them; and as he had them of all hues, he hoped to fit everybody's fancy, as soon as he could find proper food for the flies, of certain gums, oils, and other glutinous matter to give a strength and consistence to the threads. (p. 214)

This trick Swift learned from another paper in the *Transactions*, of the very sort that must have delighted his ironic mind. Here Dr. Wall, beginning with a discourse on amber and diamonds, concluded with gum-lac, pismires and artificial and natural dyes, and unconsciously gave rise to experimentation in Lagado:

I don't know in the Animal Kingdom any Thing but Pismires, that affords a Volatile Acid, and in the East-Indies there's a large kind of them that live on the Sap of certain Plants, affording both a Gum and a Colour, which Sap passing through the Body of those Insects and Animals, is by their Acid Spirit converted into an Animal Nature; which is the Reason, that with the Colour extracted from Gum-Lac (which Gum-Lac is nothing else but the Excrements of these Insects or Animals) almost as good, and full as lasting, Colours are made as from Cochineal: I am the more confirmed herein, because I know of an Artificial Way of converting Vegetable Colours into an Animal Nature very much like this, by which the Colours are made much more pleasant and permanent. After the same Manner the remaining Gum, which is an Oleosum, being digested and passing through the Bodies of those Insects or Animals,

---

[1] *Phil. Trans.* vol. XXVII (1710), p. 10; vol. V, ii. pp. 21–24.

is by their Volatile Acid converted into a Vegetable Animal Phosphorus or Noctiluca.[1]

The projector whom Gulliver saw 'at work to calcine ice into gunpowder' (p. 213) may have been moved by nothing more esoteric than the report of 'Haile of so great a Bigness' which 'fell at Lisle in Flanders': 'One among the rest was observed to contain a dark brown Matter, in the Middle thereof; and being thrown into the Fire, it gave a very great Report'.[2] But since Swift's projector had already written a treatise on the 'malleability of fire', and since a group of his fellow-projectors, by 'condensing the air into a dry intangible substance, by extracting the nitre, and letting the aqueous fluid particles percolate' (p. 215), showed close familiarity with the work of Boyle and his followers, it is more probable that the gun-powder-projector had been studying Boyle's 'Experiments and Observations upon Cold',[3] and had been impressed not only by the similarities between heat and cold, but also and more particularly by the long series of experiments on 'the expansive forces of congela-tion'[4] with their recurrent motif of explosion and violence. In all these experiments water is introduced into tubes of various types and allowed to freeze. In all, the tubes break 'with a considerable noise and violence' or 'the ball of the glass was burst to pieces with a loud report'.[5] Occasionally, 'the compress'd air flew out with a great noise, and part of the pipe . . . . appear'd filled with smoke'.[6] Such reports would have been enough for Swift's imagination, even if he had not also read Boyle's paper on 'The Mechanical Origins of Heat and Cold'[7] with its discussion of the apparent extravagances of 'heating cold liquors with ice'. Boyle's persistent interest in both ice and gunpowder is clear enough to the layman, so that Swift need not

---

[1] *Phil. Trans.* vol. XXVI (1708), p. 69; vol. IV, ii, pp. 275–8.
[2] *Phil. Trans.* vol. XXVII (1693), p. 858; vol. II, p. 145. There are several accounts in the *Transactions* of hail and ice, emphasizing the explosive noise of their bursting.
[3] *Philosophical Works*, vol. I, pp. 573–730.
[4] Ibid. section XV, pp. 626–9.
[5] Ibid. p. 627.
[6] Ibid. vol. I, p. 568.
[7] Ibid. pp. 550–72.

have entered — though he may — upon the problem of the 'effluvia' of both, which Boyle raises in this work.

Of all the experiments of Swift's projectors, none has excited more contemptuous laughter than that of the man who 'had been eight years upon a project for extracting sun-beams out of cucumbers, which were to be put into vials hermetically sealed, and let out to warm the air in raw inclement summers' (p. 212). Preposterous as this may seem, it is no more incredible than the other experiments which prove to have scientific sources — and it leads the reader into the last of the groups suggested by Fontenelle — 'Botanicks'. The basis of the project is obvious. Swift merely combined a group of experiments, adding to them little — except the cucumbers! The 'cucumber projector' may have been an assiduous student of Grew, Boyle, Hooke and Newton; he may have read a paper by Halley on 'The Circulation of Watery Vapours[1], in which many of his ideas were suggested. But it is more likely that he was a follower of Hales, who, working upon principles laid down for him by these predecessors, made the final experiments which were imitated in the Grand Academy of Lagado. Over a period of years Hales had reported to the Royal Society experiments on the respiration of plants and animals, which he welded into a whole in 1727 in his two volumes of *Statical Essays*.[2]

Hales's work also presupposed certain conclusions made by Boyle and Newton on the nature of the 'particles of the air',[3] which gave rise to long discussion among men of science. Hales had been

---

[1] *Phil. Trans.* vol. XVII (1693), p. 468; vol. II, pp. 126–9.

[2] *Statical Essays: Containing Vegetable Staticks: Or, An Account of some Statical Experiments On the Sap in Vegetables*, 1st ed. 1727, 2nd ed. 1731. The book is, of course, too late to have served as Swift's source; but, as the title-page indicates, the two volumes 'incorporate a great Variety of Chymico-Statical Experiments, which were read at several Meetings before the Royal Society'. These experiments concerned 'the quantities imbibed and perspired by Plants and Trees', in which Hales followed and improved upon Boyle and Hooke. Hales had followed Boyle's experiments, performed with his air-pump and exhausted and unexhausted receivers, upon 'Grapes, Plums, Gooseberries, Cherries, Pease' and several other sorts of fruits and grains.

[3] *Optics*, queries 30 and 31.

particularly impressed by the great quantities of air generated from certain fruits and vegetables, most of all, apples.[1] Swift's projector was familiar not only with the general principles involved in such experiments on plant respiration, but also with a series of experiments reported by Hales upon the effect of sunbeams upon the earth and with the principles by which these sunbeams were alleged to enter into plants:

The impulse of the Sun-beams giving the moisture of the earth a brisk undulating motive, which watery particles, when separated or rarefied by heat, do descend in the form of vapour: And the vigour of warm and confined vapour . . . must be very considerable, so as to penetrate the roots with some vigour . . . 'Tis therefore probable that the roots of trees and plants are thus, by means of the Sun's warmth, constantly irrigated with fresh supplies and moisture . . . whence, by the same genial heat, in conjunction with the attraction of the capillary sap vessels, it is carried up thro' the bodies and branches of vegetables, and thence passing into the leaves, it is there most vigorously acted upon, in those thin plates, and put into an undulating motion, by the Sun's warmth, whereby it is most plentifully thrown off, and perspired thro' their surface; whence, as soon as it is disentangled, it mounts with great rapidity in the free air.[2]

Such sunbeams, sinking into the ground, as Hales reported, 'for a distance of two feet' and then rising through root and branch of the plant to be 'perspired' or 'respired', Swift's projector, like Hales, caught in his 'hermetically sealed vials'. The second step in his experiment needed only the authority of Shadwell's Sir Nicholas Gimcrack, who motivated by Boyle and Hooke collected air from all parts of the country so that his guests might choose 'Newmarket, Banstead-down, Wiltshire, Bury Air; Norwich Air; what you will';[3]

[1] *Vegetable Staticks*, experiment LXXXVII.
[2] Ibid. pp. 63–66. This was a controversial question in Swift's time, involving as it did questions of the nature of air and of heat. Three years later all these theories of Boyle, Newton and Hales and also that of the Dutch scientist Nieuwentyt were brought together and discussed in a paper in the *Phil. Trans.* by J. T. Desaguliers ('An Attempt to Solve the Phenomenon of the Rise of Vapours', vol. XXXVI (1729), p. 6; vol. VI, ii, p. 61).
[3] *The Virtuoso*, in *Dramatic Works of Thomas Shadwell*, 4 vols. (London, 1720), vol. I, p. 387. The many parallels between Shadwell's

when Sir Nicholas grew weary of the closeness of London and had
'a Mind to take Country Air', he sent for 'may be, forty Gallons of
Bury Air, shut all my Windows and Doors close, and let it fly into
my Chamber'. So Swift's projector, having collected the sunbeams,
let them out 'to warm the air in raw inclement summers'.

Practical as was the application of a theory in the case of this
botanist, Swift's projectors concerned with 'new methods of agriculture' were more practical still. To be sure, they had already, as
Gulliver had seen, reduced the fields of Balnibari to desolation and
were responsible for those 'wholly unaccountable' methods of
managing lands which Gulliver had observed. Because of his interest in Ireland, Swift may have noticed particularly a paper 'On
the Manuring of Lands by Sea-shells in Ireland, by the Archbishop
of Dublin',[1] with its suggestions of the great improvements to be
wrought in agriculture by this method. Swift may also have noticed
the many reports on agriculture in distant countries — particularly
Ceylon and China — and the proposals in the *Philosophical
Transactions* for carrying over to English soil methods applicable to
agriculture in very different climates. Certainly there seem to be
reminiscences of such papers in the experiments of the agricultural
projectors of Lagado. The professor, for example, who proposed to
plough the land by driving six hundred hogs into a field, that they
might 'root up the whole ground . . . at the same time manuring it
with their dung' suggests that he had studied a paper on the 'Culture
of Tobacco in Zeylan'.[2] The custom in Ceylon was this:

They clear a little piece of Ground, in which they sow the Seed
of Tobacco, as the Gardeners here sow Parsley and Coleworts;
against the Time that this is ready for transplanting, they choose a
piece of Ground, which they hedge about; when the Buffalo's begin
to chew the Cud, they are put within this Hedge-Ground and let

work and Swift's would suggest that the *Virtuoso* was one of the important literary sources of the 'Voyage to Laputa'. In each instance, however,
Swift has brought Shadwell up to date by material drawn from contemporary science.

[1] *Phil. Trans.* vol. XXVI (1708), p. 59; vol. IV, pp. 298–301.

[2] Ibid. vol. XXIII (1702), p. 1164; vol. IV, pp. 312–14. (For other possible sources of this passage cf. Pons, *Gulliver's Travels*, p. 254 n.)

stand until they have done, and this they continue Day and Night, until the Ground be sufficiently dunged.

The 'universal artist' who devoted himself to agriculture among his various pursuits, proposed to 'sow the land with chaff, wherein he affirmed the true seminal virtue to be contained'. The 'seminal virtue' of plants had engrossed English botanists since the discovery of Nehemiah Grew that plants possessed sex. Swift needed no source for this interest in Lagado; he could have found it in Grew himself, or in such suggestions as that 'Of Manuring of Land by Sea-Sand',[1] in which the author suggests the mixing 'of these Male and Female Salts; for the Sea Salt is too lusty and active of itself'. The 'Propagation of Vegetables' from this point of view was discussed at length in another paper which, following Grew's discovery 'that the Farina . . . doth some way perform the Office of Male Sperm', went on to prove 'that this Farina is a Congeries of Seminal Plants, one of which must be convey'd into every Ovum before it can become prolifick'.[2]

The most specific proposal of the agriculturists of Lagado Gulliver had observed even before his visit to the Academy. On Munodi's property stood a mill, turned by the current of a river, which had for years proved satisfactory. However, some seven years before, the projectors had come to Munodi

with proposals to destroy this mill, and build another on the side of that mountain, on the long ridge whereof a long canal must be cut for a repository of water, to be conveyed up by pipes and engines to supply the mill; because the wind and air upon a height agitated the water, and thereby made it fitter for motion; and because the water descending down a declivity would turn the mill with half the current of a river whose course is more upon a level. (pp. 210–11)

Behind this sage conclusion of the theorists of the Academy lay a long series of experiments reported to the Royal Society first by Francis Hawksbee, later by James Jurin, who from 1720 until 1727 was the editor of the *Philosophical Transactions*. Beginning with a discussion of the cause of ascent of water in capillary tubes,

[1] Ibid. vol. XXVI (1708), p. 142; vol. IV, p. 301.
[2] Ibid. vol. XXIII (1703), p. 1474; vol. IV, pp. 305–8.

Jurin continued with a study of the effect on the flow of water at various heights, and finally with two papers, one in English, the other in Latin, 'Of the Motion of Running Water'.[1] Here Swift seems to have found, couched in the terms of mathematical proof which never failed to amuse and irritate him, a study of the force of running water at various heights, the effect of gravity, the mathematical ratio between 'the Altitude of the Water' and the 'Motion of the Cataract'. Here he may even have found his 'Canal'; for Jurin's experiment is in large part a study of the relation between the 'Length of the Canal', the 'Motion of the Water' and the 'Velocity of the Water'. To Jurin, to be sure, 'Canals' were only a part of laboratory equipment; but by the projectors — and by Swift — the small laboratory model was readily expanded in size and easily translated to the side of a mountain in Balnibari, where water flowed (or did not flow, as Munodi learned to his cost) with the same 'Force' and 'Velocity' as in Jurin's tubes.

Of all the experimenters in the Grand Academy of Lagado, there remains only that 'universal artist' who, like Bacon, believed that the end of science was the 'benefit and use of man' and who 'had been thirty years employing his thoughts for the improvement of human life' (pp. 215–16). So common were 'universal artists' in Swift's day that it is perhaps idle to seek to identify the original of a passage which is clearly intended as a satire upon the tendency of many scientists of the time to take all knowledge to be their province. Such a universal artist was the earlier Martin Scriblerus, 'this Prodigy of our Age; who may well be called The Philosopher of Ultimate Causes, since by a Sagacity peculiar to himself, he hath discover'd Effects in their very Cause; and without the trivial helps of Experiments, or Observations, hath been the Inventor of most

---

[1] *Phil. Trans.* vol. xxx (1718), p. 748; vol. iv, pp. 435–41; vol. xxxii (1722), p. 179; vol. vi, i, pp. 341–7. In the second, presented to the Society in 1726, Jurin reviews the history of the subject. In the same year J. T. Desaguliers presented (vol. xxxiv (1726), p. 77; vol. vi, i, pp. 347–50) 'An Account of several Experiments concerning the Running of Water in Pipes, as it is retarded by Friction and intermixed Air.... With a Description of a new Machine, whereby Pipes may be clear'd of Air, as the Water runs along, without Stand-Pipes, or the Help of any Hand.'

of the modern Systems and Hypotheses'.[1] The 'universal artist' of the 'Voyage to Laputa' was, however, an experimenter; and his experiments covered many fields. He was at once a specialist on the nature of the air, on petrification, on marble, on agriculture and on the breeding of sheep. Allowing for the obvious exaggeration of the passage, we may suspect that, if Swift intended his thrust at any one man, it was at Robert Boyle, who spoke with authority on all these subjects and who, more perhaps than any other man of his age, had been a pioneer in all fields of investigation. Swift's many other references to Boyle, and his obvious familiarity with the three large volumes in which Dr. Peter Shaw had treasured up his master to a life beyond life, bear out this theory. But theory it must remain; for Boyle was not alone in his encyclopaedic knowledge and in his tendency to express himself on any and every subject. If vice it was, it was, as Bacon would have said and as Swift seems to imply in his passage, less a vice of the individual than of the age.

VI

'It is highly probable', Swift wrote ironically in the 'Voyage to the Houyhnhnms', 'that such travellers who shall hereafter visit the countries described in this work of mine, may, by detecting my errors (if there be any), and adding many new discoveries of their own, justle me out of vogue, and stand in my place, making the world forget that I was ever an author.'[2] Swift himself would have been the last to object to the attempts of 'later travellers' to recognize the specific sources of his satire. He, who delighted in the setting of riddles, wrote with some regret: 'Though the present age may understand well enough the little hints we give, the parallels we draw, and the characters we describe, yet this will all be lost the next.' Yet he added more hopefully: 'However, if these papers should happen to live till our grandchildren are men, I hope they may have curiosity enough to consult annals and compare dates, in order to find out.'[3] Letters exchanged between Swift and his contemporaries offer

---

[1] *Memoirs of Scriblerus*, p. 135.
[2] *Gulliver's Travels*, p. 349.
[3] Temple Scott (ed.), *Prose Works*, vol. ix, p. 110. Sir Charles Firth, one of the most acute of the commentators on *Gulliver's Travels*, said

evidence that Swift's own age was quick to catch the implications in the scientific portion of the voyage. Ten days after the publication of *Gulliver's Travels*, Gay and Pope wrote to Swift a joint letter, in which they said that there was general agreement by the politicians that the work was 'free from particular reflections, but that the satire on general societies of men is too severe'.[1] They added: 'Not but that we now and then meet with people of greater perspicuity, who are in search for particular applications in every leaf, and it is highly probable we shall have keys published to give light into Gulliver's design.'[2] Erasmus Lewis complained that he wanted such a key.[3] Dr. Arbuthnot, recognizing the satire upon his colleagues in the Royal Society, wrote critically to Swift: 'I tell you freely, the part of the projectors is the least brilliant';[4] Gay and Pope reported to Swift that Arbuthnot had said 'it is ten thousand pities he had not known it, he could have added such abundance of things upon every subject'.[5] To the joint letter Swift replied, still pretending to preserve his anonymity, reporting other criticisms which had come to him. He added a sentence which may well be significant in connection with the 'Voyage to Laputa': 'I read the book over, and in the second volume observe several passages, which appear to be patched and altered, and the style of a different sort, unless I am much mistaken'.[6] Various explanations may be suggested for that self-criticism. In the light of the evidence which has been offered here, is it not possible that Swift intended an apology for the haste with which the scientific portions of the 'Voyage to Laputa' were

(*The Political Significance of Gulliver's Travels*, p. 1): 'A critic who seeks to explain the political significance of *Gulliver's Travels* may be guilty of too much ingenuity, but he cannot fairly be charged with exaggerated curiosity. He is searching for a secret which Swift tells us is hidden there, and endeavouring to solve riddles which were intended to exercise his wits.'

[1] *Works of Alexander Pope . . . with Introduction and Notes*, by Rev. Whitwell Elwin (London, 1871), vol. VIII, p. 88.

[2] Ibid. vol. VIII, p. 88.

[3] F. E. Ball (ed.), *The Correspondence of Jonathan Swift* (London, 1910–14), vol. III, p. 357.

[4] Scott, *Prose Works*, vol. VIII, p. xvi.

[5] *Works of Pope*, vol. VII, p. 89.

[6] Ibid. vol. VII, pp. 91–92.

completed, after his return from Ireland?[1]

Whatever the artistic inferiorities of the 'Voyage to Laputa', Swift has left to posterity in these chapters a record of the greatness and the limitations of his time. No age will be a 'Century of Genius' that does not also appear to its coevals a century of absurdities. Perhaps the final word on this adventure of Gulliver may best be said, not by posterity, but by one of Swift's contemporaries, John, Earl of Cork and Orrery, who wrote to his son:

'However wild the descriptions of ... the manners, and various projects of the philosophers of Lagado may appear, yet it is a real picture embellished with much latent wit and humour. It is a satir upon those astronomers and mathematicians, who have so entirely dedicated their time to the planets, that they have been careless of their family and country, and have been chiefly anxious, about the oeconomy and welfare of the upper worlds. But if we consider Swift's romance in a serious light, we shall find him of opinion, that those determinations in philosophy, which at present seem to the most knowing men to be perfectly well founded and understood, are in reality unsettled, or uncertain, and may perhaps some ages hence be as much decried, as the axioms of Aristotle are at this day. Sir Isaac Newton and his notions may hereafter be out of fashion. There is a kind of mode in philosophy, as well as in other things ...[2]

[1] Cf. *Remarks on the Life and Writings of Dr. Jonathan Swift ... In a Series of Letters from John Earl of Orrery To his Son* (London, 1752), p. 99: 'He seems to have finished his voyage to Laputa in a careless hurrying manner, which makes me almost think that sometimes he was tired of his work, and attempted to run through it as fast as he could.'

[2] Ibid. p. 97.

MARJORIE W. BUCKLEY

Key to the Language of the Houyhnhnms
in Gulliver's Travels

FOR more than two centuries scholars have pondered the question of significant satire in the names *Houyhnhnm* and *Yahoo* in Swift's 'A Voyage to the Houyhnhnms'. At last it seems possible that the question may be answered. The key appears to be phonetic and it may be applied to all the Houyhnhnm words in the fourth book of *Gulliver*. The first section of the paper will set forth a brief explanation of the key's basic form. The second will offer supporting evidence proving that the key is valid, and finally the study will demonstrate the detailed working of the key in the text of 'A Voyage to the Houyhnhnms'.

The word *Yahoo* spoken phonetically in the eighteenth century would be pronounced 'Yay who', which, correctly spelt, would be 'Ye who'. *Houyhnhnm* pronounced phonetically with the final *mn* transposed becomes 'Who inhuman'. Transposition is found elsewhere in Swift, notably in the title of his poem 'Cadenus and Vanessa', 'Cadenus' being taken from the Latin, *decanus*, 'a dean'. *Yahoo* is used as 'Ye who' in the sense of an indictment: 'Ye who behave thus.' *Houyhnhnm* is used as an indictment, also, in the sense of 'You who, inhuman, behave thus.' The word 'inhuman' has a vastly different connotation from 'un-human' previously applied to the satiric significance of Swift's horses. It will be seen, therefore, that in the phonetic interpretation of the words *Yahoo* and *Houyhnhnm* lies the secret of a deeper level of satire than hitherto realised.

Swift provides many clues in his text in support of the view that he intended to demonstrate the Houyhnhnms' behaviour as inhuman. Many pertinent passages occur in chapter iii. In Ricardo Quintana's edition, pp. 190–1, we read of the Houyhnhnms: 'To help my Memory, I formed all I learned into the *English* Alphabet, and writ the Words down with the Translations. This last, after some time, I ventured to do in my Master's Presence. It cost me much Trouble to explain to him what I was doing; for the Inhabitants have not the least Idea of Books or Literature.'[1] It seems clear that Swift is telling us that the Houyhnhnms are without the gift of creativity. They have no means of communicating by the written word therefore no means of preserving ideas in a lasting and communicable form. An idea communicated only by speech could not retain its original form beyond a very short time. Swift is recording, therefore, that the Houyhnhnms lack the human quality of wishing to record their history and ideas, a quality common to all communities where human intelligence exists. We must be careful to recognise that Swift does not deny his horses' intelligence, it is the human quality that is missing.

On p. 191 we read: 'The Word *Houyhnhnm*, in their Tongue, signifies a *Horse*; and in its Etymology, *the Perfection of Nature*.' But, as we know, the perfection of nature has nothing to do with humanity. And on p. 193 Gulliver describes the ship which brought him to the land of the Houyhnhnms. His Honour was mystified that a ship could be made and managed by Yahoos, and had never before heard of a ship although he lived on an island. Thus again Swift demonstrates the lack of creativity in his horses. The same deficiency is clear again on pp. 196–7 in the passage: 'He said, I differed indeed from other Yahoos . . . but in point of real Advantage, he thought I differed for the worse. That my Nails were of no Use either to my fore or hinder Feet: As to my fore Feet, he could not properly call them by that Name, for he never observed me to walk upon them; that they were too soft to bear the Ground; that I generally went with them uncovered, neither was the Covering I sometimes wore on them, of the same Shape, or so strong as that on my Feet behind.' His Honour was unable to realise the need for creative manual work.

The chief Houyhnhnm expressed great indignation on hearing that in Gulliver's country horses were used as beasts of burden. Gulliver says: 'I described as well as I could, our Way of Riding; the Shape and use of a Bridle, a Saddle, a Spur, and a Whip . . .'

[1] *Gulliver's Travels and other writings* (New York, 1958). Reference throughout the study will be to Quintana's edition.

His Honour replied that he 'wondered how we dared to venture upon a Houyhnhnm's Back ... that the meanest Servant in his House would be able to shake off the strongest *Yahoo*; or by lying down, and rouling upon his Back, squeeze the Brute to Death'. Yet on p. 196 comes the antithetical statement that 'if it were possible there could be any Country where *Yahoos* alone were endowed with Reason, they certainly must be the governing Animal, because Reason will in Time always prevail against Brutal Strength. But, considering the Frame of our Bodies, and especially of mine, he thought no Creature of equal Bulk was so ill-contrived, for employing that Reason in the common Offices of Life ...' Thus Swift shows us that whilst paying lip-service to reason His Honour is expressing the negation of reason. Therefore if reason is a human quality then it is not conspicuous in the Houyhnhnms. It seems incredible that they have been credited with a high standard of reasoning power for over two hundred years.

Evidence of inhuman characteristics in lack of emotion occur throughout the text. On page 219 we read: 'They have no Fondness for their Colts or Foles; but the care they take in educating them proceedeth entirely from the Dictates of *Reason*. ... In their Marriages they are exactly careful to chuse such Colours as will not make any disagreeable Mixture in the Breed.' Another example of extreme placidity appears on p. 224: 'I remember, my Master having once made an Appointment with a Friend and his Family to come to his House upon some Affair of Importance; on the Day fixed, the Mistress and her two Children came very late ... Her excuse for not coming sooner, was, that her Husband dying late in the Morning, she was a good while consulting her Servants about a convenient Place where his Body should be laid.' There are other examples of absence of emotion in the Houyhnhnms, but it is unnecessary to cite them for the purposes of our study. We have established that Swift appears to have provided his horses deliberately with a lack of human qualities, often disguised as an advantageous lack. It seems to be clear from the text therefore, irrespective of the phonetic qualities of the word *Houyhnhnm*, that the correct interpretation is 'Who inhuman'.

We must consider now the term *Yahoo* — the ostensible object of scorn in the book. It seems plain that Swift had no intention of offering praise of the Yahoos, but our study sets out to prove that he is bent on holding them up for inspection, that their true condition may be known, pitied, and possibly improved. In order to carry out such a project Swift must therefore have given us evidence that the Yahoos exhibited an essential humanity beyond the inhuman Houyhnhnms' comprehension.

Let us examine three quotations from Swift's text where evidences exist in the Yahoos of the three human characteristics we studied in the passages on the Houyhnhnms. The qualities are creativity, reason, and emotion. Swift cloaks the human qualities in a disguise of filth and depravity for the purposes of his satire. Under the disguises we find vestiges of creativity on p. 212, where we read of the neighbourhood battles of the Yahoos: 'Those of the District watching all Opportunities to surprise the next before they are prepared.' And on p. 215 Swift gives us a description of emotion in a Yahoo, accompanied, incidentally, by a description of His Honour's inability to understand the condition. The passage reads: 'My Master likewise mentioned another Quality, which his Servants had discovered in several *Yahoos*, to retire into a Corner, to lie down and howl, and groan, and spurn away all that came near him, although he were young and fat, and wanted neither Food nor Water; nor did the Servants imagine what could possibly ail him. And the only Remedy they found was to set him to hard Work, after which he would infallibly come to himself.'

In spite of constant avowals from the Houyhnhnms that the Yahoos are completely devoid of reason,[1] we read on p. 212: 'That, if a Cow died of Age or Accident, before a *Houyhnhnm* could secure it for his own *Yahoos*, those in the Neighbourhood would come in Herds to seize it.' Again, we read on p. 217: 'the *Yahoos* appear to be the most unteachable of all Animals, their Capacities never reaching higher than to draw or carry Burthens. Yet I am of Opinion this Defect ariseth chiefly from a perverse, restive Disposition. For they are cunning, malicious, treacherous and revengeful.' Both the passages quoted above display understandable

[1] Quintana, pp. 190, 191, 196, 211.

emotional reactions and reasoning power in the Yahoos under the treatment accorded them by the Houyhnhnms.

Having established for the purpose of our study that Swift uses the behaviour of both Houyhnhnms and Yahoos as material for indictment, our phonetic interpretations of both names as phrases of indictment 'Who inhuman' and 'Ye who' apply perfectly as the key phrases in the meaning of the satire.

Applying the phonetic key, the reader may unlock Swift's meaning with relative ease. The method is simple. Between the letters of each Houyhnhnm word, unwritten vowel sounds occur in speech. Many of the speech-inserted diphthongs are varied by Swift between similar letters in the text according to the sound he wishes to produce. The sounds implied coincide with the meaning of the word or phrase, thus giving added fascination to Swift's puzzles. He uses also the usual alternative sounds for letters in the text of the Houyhnhnm words, i.e. *Y* is used as in 'sky' or as in 'you' exactly as in ordinary writing. Unlike some previously suggested interpretations of Swift's invented language,[1] there are no anagrams in the language of the Houyhnhnms. Nor are there any transpositions apart from the final *nm* in *Houyhnhnm*. The phonetic spelling is accurate in the text and the interpretation of the spelling is straightforward, requiring no rearrangement.

Evidence of an exactly similar technique used by Swift occurs in his letters to Sheridan where he writes 'IstmuaDt' for 'I esteem you a Deity'.[2] Further support for the phonetic interpretation comes from the *Journal to Stella* (7 March 1710–11), where he says, 'When I am writing in our language, I make up my mouth just as if I was speaking it.'[3]

In order to facilitate phonetic interpretation a list of similar letters with different pronunciations must be applied to the study of the Houyhnhnm words. The key to the different sounds of similar letters is:

[1] H. D. Kelling, 'Some Significant Names in Gulliver's Travels', in *SP*, vol. XLVIII, no. 4 (Oct. 1951).
[2] F. E. Ball (ed.), *The Correspondence of Jonathan Swift, D.D.* (London, 1910–14), vol. V, p. 436.
[3] Kelling, p. 766.

A   Pronounced as in *lay*.

A   Pronounced as in *hernia*.

A   Pronounced as in *hand*.

H   May be silent as in *doh*.

HN   May develop an intervening vowel *er* as in h*er*nia.

HN   May develop an intervening vowel as in h*oof*.

HN   A diphthong forms when N is pronounced as *en*, the sound becoming *hoo-en*, which becomes 'when'.

HN   May develop an intervening vowel sound of *er*, *oo*, or 'when' as described above. The N may be followed by the vowel sound *o* as in *no*; thereby producing a phrase (when the intervening vowel is *oo*) *hoo-no*, which becomes 'who know'. The other combinations are obvious.

L   May be pronounced unvoiced as an initial letter, thus becoming 'ill'.

L   May be pronounced *ell*.

U   May be pronounced as in *nun*.

U   May be pronounced as in *you*.

Y   May be pronounced as in *you*.

Y   May be pronounced as in *shy*.

Y   May be unvoiced as in *layn* 'lane'.

Y   May be pronounced as in *tin*.

Let us examine a Houyhnhnm word after applying our key. On pp. 213–14 we read: 'Neither has their language any more than a general Appellation for those Maladies; which is borrowed from the Name of the Beast, and called *Hnea Yahoo*, or the *Yahoo's-Evil*.' Applying our key we find that *HN* produces an intervening vowel sound *er* and the disease is shown in the word 'hernia'. As the general name for disease in the Yahoos, hernia is an excellent choice. It comes from strain in bearing burdens heavier than the body should bear. As the Houyhnhnms found it expedient to employ the Yahoos mainly as beasts of burden the disease is appropriate, particularly as in man's environment horses, as beasts of burden, often contract hernia.

Another simple example of the efficacy of this phonetic key occurs in the word *Hnhloayn*, which appears on p. 229 in the following context: 'I should here observe to the Reader, that a Decree of the general Assembly in this Country, is expressed by the Word *Hnhloayn*, which signifies an *Exhortation.*'

We discover that between *H* and *n* the spoken vowel is *oo*. Therefore the first syllable becomes 'Who'. Between *n* and *h* the voiced vowel is *o* and the sound becomes *noh* producing 'know'. Between *h* and *l* the interposed vowel is *a*. The last five letters *loayn* are spoken as 'lone'. Adding together the four syllables we find the 'Decree' to be 'Who-know-alone'. It is decreed among the Houyhnhnms that the members of the Assembly are those 'Who-know-alone'. It is a type of decree which has been popular among many legislative assemblies.

On p. 225 we find an interesting list of Houyhnhnm words. Studying them in context we read: 'I know not whether it may be worth observing, that the *Houyhnhnms* have no Word in their Language to express any thing that is *evil*, except what they borrow from the Deformities or ill Qualities of the *Yahoos*. Thus they denote the Folly of a Servant, an Omission of a Child, a Stone that cuts their Feet, a Continuance of foul or unseasonable Weather, and the like, by adding to each the Epithet of *Yahoo*. For Instance, *Hhnm Yahoo*, *Whnholm Yahoo*, *Ynlhmnawihlma Yahoo*, and an ill-contrived House, *Ynholmhnmrohlnw Yahoo.*'

Possibly as an added hurdle Swift has given us four clues and only three Houyhnhnm phrases, for the last item on the list carries its own free interpretation. Bearing in mind the information in the text and regarding Yahoo as a derogatory adjective, we shall decipher each phrase in turn. It would seem that we must discard 'a Stone that cuts their Feet' as the extra phrase.

The first item, *Hhnm Yahoo*, meaning 'the Folly of a Servant', is simply *Houyhnhnm Yahoo*, the spelling *Hhnm* being an alternative form of *Houyhnhnm*. The twist must have appealed to its wry author!

The second phrase, *Whnaholm Yahoo*, meaning 'an Omission of a Child', develops the vowel sound *ee* between *W* and *h* thus producing the syllable *Wee*. The other letters in the word, *hnaholm*, form yet another spelling of *Houyhnhnm*. Thus *Whnaholm* becomes *Wee Houyhnhnm*. After adding our derogatory adjective *Yahoo* we find that the erring child has been described adequately as 'Wee Houyhnhnm Yahoo'. The variation in spelling must have been devised to make the puzzle doubly baffling, for the list is a direct invitation to interpreters.

The third phrase, *Ynlhmnawihlma Yahoo*, meaning a 'Continuance of foul or unseasonable Weather', uses *Y* as in *you* developing the vowel sound *oo* between *Y* and *n*. Thus the first syllable becomes You'. Between *n* and *l* the voiced vowel is *o* as in *no*. The vowel *o* shades into the unvoiced consonant *w* before *l* producing the sound *no-well* which becomes 'know well'. Between *h* and *m* the sound developed is *i* producing the syllable *in*. The remainder of the word *awihlma* reads quite simply as 'a while may'. Therefore when we assemble our syllables we produce the result 'You-know-well-home-in-a-while-may'. The following adjective *Yahoo* gives the 'evil' connotation to the phrase. Swift says in the passage quoted above: 'The Houyhnhnms have no Word in their Language to express any thing that is *evil*.' Therefore the foul weather over a long period must be described by its effect. And its effect is to keep the Houyhnhnms at home.

The last phrase, *Ynholmhnmrohlnw Yahoo*, meaning an 'ill-contrived House', uses the initial letter *Y* with *n* as *in*. *Holm* becomes 'home'. *Hnm* is another spelling of *Houyhnhnm*. *Rohl* is 'roll'. Between *n* and *w* the vowel sound *ow* occurs, thus the final syllable becomes 'now'. Therefore, assembling our syllables once more, we find that the phrase becomes 'In-home-Houyhnhnm-roll-now Yahoo'. Analysing the description we find that the Houyhnhnms, being horses, roll in their homes. The phrase indicates one particular home as Swift uses the singular of *Houyhnhnm*. Therefore with the added stigma of *Yahoo* the home becomes 'an ill-contrived House'.

One more example will serve to demonstrate our key. On p. 221 we read: 'That those Creatures [Yahoos] could not be *Ylnhniamshy* (or *Aborigines* of the Land) because of the violent Hatred the *Houyhnhnms* as well as all other Animals, bore them: which although their evil Disposition sufficiently deserved, could never have arrived at so high a Degree, if they had been *Aborigines*, or else they would have long since been rooted out.' Reading the word *Ylnhniamshy* in Swift's phonetic key we find that between *Y* and *l* is developed the vowel sound *oo* merging into 'well' before *l*, thus forming the two words 'You well'. Between *n* and *h* the vowel sound *o* occurs, producing the syllable *noh*, which becomes 'know'. Between *h* and *n* the sound 'when' develops, and the end of the word *iamshy* reads just as it is written: 'I am shy.' Adding together our syllables we find the phrase is 'You-well-know-when-I-am-shy', which fits into the context admirably in describing an aborigine.

It is superfluous to offer other examples of elucidation. Once the key is grasped the rest is easy. Swift's brilliance in adapting so closely his invented language to the natural sounds made by the horses, has helped materially in obscuring the key for so long. We must credit him with having invented a device which has occupied scholars with his text almost from the date when it was published. Thus his work, designed 'to vex the world rather than to divert it', has had more close attention than even Swift could have hoped for.

VIVIAN MERCIER

Swift and the Gaelic Tradition

IT would be a noble achievement to abolish the Irish language in this kingdom. . . .'[1] Bearing in mind this statement and others similar to it in the writings of Jonathan Swift, the reader will doubtless think it paradoxical for me to discuss the great Dean's relationship to the Gaelic tradition, as I am proposing to do in this article. Yet I believe I can show that Swift fits into that tradition in three distinct ways.

First of all, his conception of the power and prestige of the satirist agrees closely with that held by the Gaelic poets from time immemorial. Indeed, his reputation for wit and wilful eccentricity, so similar to that of many Gaelic poets, has won him a permanent place beside them in Gaelic folklore and its Anglo-Irish continuation.

In the second place, an apparent direct impact of the Gaelic tradition upon Swift can be traced at several points in his works. I do not say that he had any true awareness of the characteristics of Gaelic satire or even of its bulk; nevertheless, certain hints from a Gaelic source seem to have found their way into *Gulliver's Travels*.

Finally, and this is both the strangest and, to my mind, the least disputable aspect of Swift's relations with the Gaelic tradition, at least two later Gaelic poets show indebtedness to his example in their satirical poetry.

II

Admittedly, one could argue that Swift's apparent faith in the power of satire to terrify and injure its victims was a mere literary convention, inherited from Greek and Roman times and adhered to

[1] 'An Answer to Several Letters Sent Me from Unknown Hands', in Temple Scott (ed.), *The Prose Works of Jonathan Swift, D.D.*, VII (1905), p. 133.

by all the English Augustans. When Swift describes himself in 'Cadenus and Vanessa' as 'Of half mankind the dread and hate', the reader can easily recall parallel passages from Pope — 'Let Sporus tremble . . .', for instance. Swift's conviction of his own rightness may be similarly conventional, even when he denounces a victim who had the temerity to answer an attack,

> . . . as if the whole Satire had been
> The oppression of Virtue, not wages of Sin.[1]

Pope says similar things; for instance, he cites as the only provocation necessary for his satire 'The strong antipathy of good to bad'. Nevertheless, such attitudes are endemic in Gaelic satire too, along with an intemperateness, a propensity for what I may call 'total ridicule', which is alien to Pope but not to Swift — at any rate not to the later Swift who conceived the Yahoos. Let the Irish bishops disagree with Swift, and at once he is ready to compare them to Judas or Satan himself.[2] Let the Irish Parliament disregard Swift's notion of what is due to the clergy by opposing the tithe of agistment, and he immediately reacts by characterising the entire parliament as a madhouse, 'The Legion Club', while singling out thirteen members for specially obscene and sadistic ridicule like the following:

> *Dick Fitz-Baker*, *Dick* the Player,
> Old Acquaintance, are you there?
> Dear Companions hug and kiss,
> Toast *old Glorious* in your Piss.
> Tye them Keeper in a Tether,
> Let them stare and stink together;
> Both are apt to be unruly,
> Lash them daily, lash them duly,
> Though 'tis hopeless to reclaim them,
> Scorpion Rods perhaps may tame them.[3]

To find parallels for Swift's uncontrolled rage we must seek out David O'Bruadair's denunciation of the woman who refused him

---

[1] 'The Yahoo's Overthrow', in Harold Williams (ed.), *The Poems of Jonathan Swift*, 2nd ed., 3 vols. (Oxford, 1958), III, 814–17.

[2] Williams (ed.), *Poems*, vol. III, pp. 801–6.

[3] Williams (ed.), *Poems*, vol. III, pp. 835–6.

a glass of ale,[1] or Owen Roe O'Sullivan's curse on the woman who kept his socks as a pledge for fourpence.[2]

I don't wish to labour the resemblances between Swift and the Gaelic satirists, because many of them are due to the world-wide tradition of satire so vividly illustrated in Fred Norris Robinson's 'Satirists and Enchanters in Early Irish Literature'[3] and in Robert C. Elliott's recent book, *The Power of Satire*.[4] I do, however, want to suggest that these resemblances enabled Swift to slip very easily into Gaelic folklore. Several traditional anecdotes, for example, connect him with Turlough Carolan, alleging that Swift prompted and admired certain Gaelic epigrams by the harper-composer-poet; the Dean is even reputed to have translated one of them, on a cantankerous doorkeeper named Dermot O'Flynn:

> 'Tis a pity Hell's gates are not kept by O'Flynn:
> So surly a dog would let nobody in.[5]

There is also a large body of Anglo-Irish folklore about Swift, much of it doubtless carried over from the Irish. Some of the most entertaining and significant anecdotes may be found in Patrick Kennedy's *The Banks of the Boro*. One of these goes so far in appropriating Swift for the native Irish as to give a circumstantial account of how he outwitted a fellow-clergyman of the Church of Ireland and became a Roman Catholic on his deathbed.[6]

---

[1] John C. Mac Erlean (ed.), *Duanaire Dháibhidh Ul Bhruadair: The Poems of David Ó Bruadair*, vol. II, Irish Texts Society XIII (1913), pp. 220–1. See also James Stephens, *Collected Poems*, 2nd ed. (London, 1954), p. 185.

[2] Patrick S. Dinneen (ed.), *Amhráin Eoghain Ruaidh Ul Shúilleabháin*, 2nd ed. (Dublin, 1902), pp. 73–75, 125–6.

[3] David Gordon Lyon and George Foot Moore (ed.), *Studies in the History of Religions Presented to Crawford Howell Toy* (New York, 1912), pp. 95–130.

[4] Princeton, 1960.

[5] Standish Hayes O'Grady, *Catalogue of Irish Manuscripts in the British Museum*, vol. I (London, 1926), p. 577. See also Donal O'Sullivan, *Carolan*, 2 vols. (London, 1958), vol. I, pp. 85–86.

[6] Patrick Kennedy, *The Banks of the Boro* (London and Dublin, 1867), pp. 211–14.

III

It would be very strange if Gaelic culture had had no direct impact upon Swift's work, since a knowledge of Irish was far more widespread among the Protestant Anglo-Irish than most Swift scholars seem to realise. For instance, during Swift's time at Trinity College both the successive Provosts of the College encouraged the study of Irish as a means of reaching the Roman Catholic population with a view to their conversion. Provost Narcissus Marsh, who resigned in 1683, knew Irish himself and employed a converted Roman Catholic priest, Paul Higgins, as lecturer in the Irish language. Some eighty students and Fellows attended the lectures. Marsh's successor, Robert Huntington, at least shared his predecessor's interest in having the Old Testament translated into Irish. Even after the Williamite war had made all things Irish suspect, we find Provost Benjamin Pratt (1710–17) employing a lecturer in the Irish language.[1]

Furthermore, Donal O'Sullivan suggests in his study of Carolan that the harper's patrons among the country gentry of English stock 'must have been thoroughly familiar with Irish, for we can hardly suppose that songs would have been sung in their praise in a language that was unintelligible to them'.[2] Swift's close friend Dr. Patrick Delany was one of these patrons, whether he knew Irish or not. Carolan composed a tune in Delany's honour, and after the harper's death Delany aided the publication of a volume of his music.[3]

We cannot be sure that Carolan and Swift ever met, but they are intimately associated in one respect: Carolan composed the music for Hugh MacGauran's humorous poem, 'Pléaráca na Ruarcach', the only Gaelic work known for certain to have been 'translated' by Swift. 'The Description of an Irish Feast. Translated Almost Literally out of the Original Irish' was, of course, merely versified by Swift, from a literal translation by somebody else — possibly MacGauran himself.[4]

If we are to believe a long footnote in Warburton, Whitelaw and

---

[1] Constantia Maxwell, *A History of Trinity College, Dublin, 1591–1892* (Dublin, 1946), pp. 73, 76 n., 89.

[2] O'Sullivan, *Carolan*, vol. I, p. 45.   [3] O'Sullivan, *Carolan*, vol. I, p. 84.

[4] Williams (ed.), *Poems*, vol. I, p. 244.

Walsh's *History of the City of Dublin*, cited by Mr. O'Sullivan,
Carolan helped Swift with the translation. The footnote's only
authority for a series of 'traditional anecdotes' about Carolan and
Swift is an anonymous 'old gentleman'. The following story, of
which I do not believe a word, is too good to omit:

The Dean admired Carolan's genius, had him frequently at the
Deanery House in Dublin, and used to hear him play and sing the
pléaráca. He was particularly struck with the happy and singular
onomatopoeia in several passages of the original, particularly that
which represented the sound of the wet in the dancers' shoes,
'*glug-glug i n-a mbróg*'. This was thought to be inimitable by
English words, till Carolan bade him send his servant to walk over
shoes in a pool of water and then dance before him. This coincided
with the Dean's own whimsical fancy. The experiment was made,
and the Dean caught the sound and expressed it by
Splish, splash in their pumps . . .[1]

MacGauran's rollicking poem, very much after the 'stage Irishman' pattern, would naturally attract Swift, especially as it is partly
satirical: a jolly celebration turns into a free-for-all. More interesting,
however, is the possibility that whoever translated 'Pléaráca na
Ruarcach' for Swift may also have translated or summarised for him
a prose tale which several Gaelic scholars regard as an important
source for *Gulliver's Travels*. I am referring to 'Imtheachta Tuaithe
Luchra agus Aidheadh Fhearghusa' ('The Proceedings of the People
of Luchra and the Death of Fergus'), of which a text is given, with
expurgated translation, as no. XIV in Standish Hayes O'Grady's
Silva Gadelica.[2] O'Grady's sixteenth-century text, from British
Museum MS. Egerton 1782, shows some very close parallels with
Gulliver's Travels. The king of the leprechauns displays the same
overweening pride and sense of his own omnipotence as the King of
the Lilliputians. Aedh, the King of Ulster's dwarf, who visits the
leprechaun kingdom, resembles Gulliver in his admiration for the
flawless complexions of the little people. The leprechauns' size is
similar to that of the Lilliputians: Aedh describes how seventeen

[1] O'Sullivan, *Carolan*, vol. I, pp. 84–85.
[2] Standish Hayes O'Grady (ed.), *Silva Gadelica*, 2 vols. (1892), vol.
I, pp. 238–52 (Irish texts), and vol. II, pp. 269–85 (English trans.).

pretty girls could lie in his bosom and a man could hide in his beard without his being aware of it.

Conversely, the leprechauns' adventures in Ulster remind us of Gulliver's in Brobdingnag. Eisirt, the leprechaun poet, is nearly drowned in a tankard of ale, just as Gulliver was in a bowl of cream. The leprechauns object to the 'infected breaths' of the Ulstermen, as Gulliver objected to the body odour of the Brobdingnagians and the Lilliputians to his.

The most curious parallel arises from the love affair between King Fergus of Ulster and the queen of the leprechauns. In spite of their totally disproportionate sizes, they succeed in consummating the relationship. The Gaelic text records some obscenely explicit dialogue between the pair and between Fergus and the cuckolded king of the leprechauns — which O'Grady forbears to translate.[1] Is it far-fetched to regard this as the source of the passage where Gulliver feels 'obliged to vindicate the Reputation of an excellent Lady' among the Lilliputians?

The Treasurer took a Fancy to be jealous of his Wife, from the Malice of some evil Tongues, who informed him that her Grace had taken a violent Affection for my Person; and the Court-Scandal ran for some Time that she once came privately to my Lodging. This I solemnly declare to be a most infamous Falshood....[2]

Note that instead of ridiculing the notion of any guilty connections being possible between them, Gulliver simply denies that they ever had the opportunity to become intimate.

Any one of these parallels, taken alone, might be a coincidence, but the whole series of resemblances suggests a direct influence. It is known that many Gaelic scholars, familiar with the literature as well as with folklore and colloquial speech, were resident in Dublin during Swift's lifetime. T. F. O'Rahilly edited a poem composed by Tadhg Ó Neachtain in 1728 which lists twenty-six such learned Dubliners.[3] Most of these men would have belonged to 'the hidden

---

[1] O'Grady (ed.), *Silva Gadelica*, vol. 1, p. 244.

[2] *Gulliver's Travels*, with an Introduction by Harold Williams (Oxford, 1941), p. 49.

[3] Thomas F. O'Rahilly, 'Irish Scholars in Dublin in the Early Eighteenth Century', *Gadelica*, vol. 1 (1912–13), pp. 156–62. Hugh MacGauran figures as 'Aodh Mac Gabhráin' on p. 159.

Ireland' as far as Swift was concerned, including those who were members of the Roman Catholic clergy, but a practising physician, Dr. John Fergus, figures among them, as does Hugh MacGauran, who seems to have been accorded the status of a country squire by his Protestant contemporaries. Any of the twenty-six might be expected to know the 'Aidheadh Fhearghusa', but since Charles Wilson's *Swiftiana* claims that MacGauran met Swift and translated the 'Pléaráca' for him, there is no great harm in imagining that MacGauran supplied the link in the other case too.[1]

For the sake of completeness, I shall mention the reference to 'Tom Mac Lobe' in one of the epigrams against Charles Carthy's translation of Horace. Under the title 'Irish Epigram English'd', one of Swift's circle, but probably not Swift himself, wrote the following:

> While with the Fustian of thy Book
> The witty Ancient you enrobe,
> You make the graceful *Horace* look
> As pitiful as *Tom Mac Lobe*.[2]

The original note describes Tom as 'a notorious Irish poetaster', but the name suggests rather Tomás Mac Lóbuis, supposed ancestor of Clan Thomas, a contemptuous name for the Irish peasantry. A whole cycle of Gaelic social satire grew from the original seventeenth-century work, 'Pairlement Chloinne Tomáis' ('The Parliament of Clan Thomas'), which popularised the nickname.[3] MacGauran's description of lower-class behaviour in the 'Pléaráca' is conceived in the spirit of the 'Parliament'.

IV

On the basis of the evidence already given, it is clear that Swift's contact with Gaelic satire, or indeed with Gaelic literature of any kind, was extremely limited. On the other hand, I have suggested that his satirical method, together with his unique personality, made

[1] Quoted in Williams (ed.), *Poems*, vol. I, p. 244.
[2] Williams (ed.), *Poems*, vol. II, p. 670.
[3] *Pairlement Chloinne Tomáis*, ed. Osborn J. Bergin, *Gadelica*, vol. I (1912–13), pp. 35–50, 127–31, 137–50, 220–36. Excerpts from an excellent translation by Francis MacManus appeared in vols. VI and VII of the *Bell* (Sept.–Dec. 1943).

him a figure highly congenial to the Gaelic poets and their audience. *The Drapier's Letters* and other pro-Irish pamphlets made him even more acceptable in the guise of an Irish patriot. Consequently those later Gaelic poets who were familiar enough with the English language would read Swift eagerly and imitate him if they could (*imitare, si poteris*).

Brian Merriman, author of 'Cúirt an Mheadhón Oidhche' ('The Midnight Court'),[1] was the greatest of these imitators. At the prompting of that fine Celtic scholar Robin Flower, W. B. Yeats argued that the 'Court of love' framework in 'The Midnight Court' was derived from Swift's 'Cadenus and Vanessa'.[2] True, the court of Venus appears only at the beginning and end of Swift's poem, whereas the entire action of Merriman's takes place at the midnight court presided over by Aoibheal, the fairy queen; nevertheless, it is hard to see where else Merriman could have encountered the idea of a court of law in which each sex blames the other for the decay of love. The only medieval literature Merriman is likely to have known is that in Irish — remember that he lived in the second half of the eighteenth century, when England's medieval heritage was still known mainly to scholars — and the 'court of love' motif seems not to occur earlier in Gaelic literature.

I have seen it suggested that Merriman's peculiar verse form, which had never before been employed in Gaelic poetry, was devised in conscious imitation of the English heroic couplet. Now, there is no denying the couplet pattern, but since the Gaelic lines contain only four stresses each throughout the poem, it would be far more accurate to describe the metre as an imitation of the tetrameter couplet so dear to Swift. Given the wide fame of Swift in Ireland and Merriman's apparent familiarity with 'Cadenus and Vanessa', one need not assume that the Gaelic poet was merely following Swift's own model, *Hudibras* Butler.

[1] Newly edited by Risteárd Ó Foghludha, Dublin, 1949. Translations abound, of which the best is Frank O'Connor's in *Kings, Lords, & Commons* (New York, 1959; London, 1962), pp. 136–66.

[2] In his introduction to *The Midnight Court and The Adventures of a Luckless Fellow*, translated by Percy Arland Ussher (London, 1926), pp. 5–6. Yeats provides an amusing bit of Swift folklore in the footnote to p. 6.

In support of the view that Merriman was imitating the tetrameter couplet, I can cite the first translator of the 'Court', Dennis Woulfe, who was not far removed from Merriman in either time or place, having flourished during the 1820's in Merriman's native County Clare. Woulfe used the tetrameter couplet; moreover, the brief excerpts from his manuscript translation that have been printed often yield a Swiftian ring; for example:

> Your cabin sluiced from soot and rain,
> And springing fluids that oozed amain;
> Its weed-grown roof so rudely shaped
> By hens at roost all scooped and scraped.[1]

Or better still:

> Favour not for rank or riches
> Lazy men or Moll in breeches.[2]

It is quite possible that Woulfe knew Merriman personally and had direct knowledge of his intention to imitate Swift's metre.

According to T. F. O'Rahilly, Merriman's unique metre is the key to his originality:

In so far as Merriman employs 'the spoken speech' it is to a considerable extent due to the metre in which he wrote; when he writes the lyric 'Mac Alla' he is much like any other contemporary.[3]

Merriman's colloquialism, singled out for special mention by Piaras Béaslaí as well as by O'Rahilly, again reminds us of Swift; indeed, Béaslaí himself draws the parallel.[4] All in all, if Swift had never lived, Merriman might never have written his great satire.

Sustained irony, such as we find throughout *A Modest Proposal* and in so many passages of *Gulliver's Travels*, seems alien to the Gaelic tradition. The typical Gaelic satirist employs irony only in brief sallies, amid quantities of direct vituperation. Therefore, when

[1] Bryan Merryman, *Cúirt an Mheadhón Oidhche*, ed. Riseárd [*sic*] Ó Foghludha (Dublin, 1912), p. 122.
[2] Ibid. p. 129.
[3] T. F. O'Rahilly, reviewing Ó Foghludha's first edition, *Gadelica*, vol. 1 (1912–13).
[4] In his introduction to Ó Foghludha's 1912 edition, p. 5.

we find a Gaelic poem, however brief, which is completely ironical, and when we know that the author greatly admired Swift, I think we are entitled to say that it was written under Swift's influence. The ironic elegy 'Eoghan Cóir', by the County Mayo poet Richard Barret (1748–1819), is such a poem.[1] The 'honest Owen' of the title was, says James Hardiman, 'one of the most rapacious "land-agents" of his time', but at his death, according to Barret, 'The like of the bawling and keening was never heard in the land before'. The poet does not wonder at this, in view of Owen's generosity and lovable character. Two men, doubtless bitter enemies of the dead man, are singled out as inconsolable. The two editions of the poem I have seen, Hardiman's and Donal O'Sullivan's, both contain a rather pointless final stanza; the true ending, to my mind, is that of the second-last stanza, with its ironical sting: 'According as he was to others, may Christ be the same to him.'

As we would naturally expect, Swift's irony found more would-be imitators among Anglo-Irish writers than among the Gaels, but none of them was able to sustain it at any great length. Maria Edgeworth made the most successful attempt — so much so that some readers miss the irony of *Castle Rackrent* entirely. Thomas Moore's *Memoirs of Captain Rock* and John Mitchel's *Apology for the British Government in Ireland* are two quite self-conscious imitations of Swift, both of which fall pathetically short of his standard.[2] Mitchel was far happier when imitating Carlyle. Still, anyone might be excused for lacking the emotional control which irony demands, in face of the appalling series of disasters attending the Great Irish Famine.

In the twentieth century James Joyce's two verse satires, 'Gas from a Burner' and 'The Holy Office', are pastiches of Swift — metre, scatology and all.[3] This kind of influence was doubtless

[1] See Roderic O'Flaherty, *A Chorographical Description of West or H-Iar Connaught*, ed. James Hardiman (Dublin, 1846), pp. 292–3. Also Donal O'Sullivan, *Songs of the Irish* (New York, 1960), pp. 155–6.

[2] *Memoirs of Captain Rock, the Celebrated Irish Chieftain, with Some Account of His Ancestors. Written by Himself* (London, 1824). John Mitchel, *An Apology for the British Government in Ireland* (Dublin, 1905).

[3] Ellsworth Mason and Richard Ellmann (eds.), *The Critical Writings of James Joyce* (New York, 1959), pp. 149–52, 242–5.

predictable, given the status of Swift in English literature. It is his impact upon Gaelic literature that I find amazing, yet at the same time entirely understandable. A traveller in the wilds of Mayo who met Richard Barret records the significant fact that the poet 'did not seem to admire Burns, but he talked of Swift with rapture'.[1] However much Swift may have prided himself on being an Englishman, the Irish have never been deceived, but have accepted him, 'with rapture' even, as one of themselves.

[1] Patrick Knight, *Erris in the 'Irish Highlands' and the 'Atlantic Railway'* (Dublin, 1836), pp. 120–2, quoted in Thomas F. O'Rahilly, 'A Song by Richard Barret', *Gadelica*, i (1912–13), p. 115.

GEORGE P. MAYHEW

Jonathan Swift's Hoax of 1722 upon Ebenezor Elliston

WHILE examining some Dublin newspapers from the period
1719–22 I lately came upon additional information which
may be useful to readers of Dr. Daniel L. McCue's recent scholarly
account of 'A Newly Discovered Broadsheet of Swift's *Last Speech
and Dying Words of Ebenezor Elliston*'.[1] In addition to Swift's
parody, the three other sources of information about Ebenezor
Elliston, the victim of Swift's hoax of 1722, have hitherto been: 'The
Last Farewell of Ebenezer Elliston To This Transitory World', an
autobiographical Dublin broadsheet of 1722 preserved now in
Archbishop Marsh's Library, Dublin, and printed by Professor
Herbert Davis as an appendix (pp. 363–7) to volume IX of his
edition of Swift's *Prose Works*;[2] George Faulkner's headnote to
Swift's broadsheet as published in the 1735 Dublin edition of Swift's
Works;[3] and a note appended to the same piece by Thomas Sheridan,
the younger, in his 1784 edition of Swift's *Works*.[4] These last two
pieces of information were accepted without question and have been
merely paraphrased or summarized by such later editors of Swift's
works as John Nichols, who mistakenly attributed Sheridan's
note to Faulkner, by Sir Walter Scott, and by Temple Scott.[5]

The two following accounts from *Whalley's [Dublin] Newsletter*,

[1] *Harvard Library Bulletin*, vol. XIII (Autumn 1959), pp. 362–8. Hereafter referred to within the text by page number alone.

[2] 14 vols. (Oxford, 1939–   ). Hereafter referred to within the text by
volume and page number alone and in the footnotes as Davis (ed.), *Prose
Works*. Swift's broadsheet as printed by Faulkner is contained in vol. IX,
pp. 35–41.

[3] vol. IV, p. 375.

[4] vol. IX, p. 300.

[5] See vol. XII, p. 55 of Nichols's ed. of 1801; vol. VI, p. 296 of Scott's
2nd ed. of 1824 (reprinted 1883–4), hereafter referred to as W. Scott (ed.),

a report of the action of the Dublin burgesses upon a petition by Elliston, and an advertisement from *Harding's Impartial* [*Dublin*] *News-letter*, published by John Harding, the printer of both Swift's broadsheet and of Elliston's 'Last Farewell', furnish additional information about Elliston's life of crime and the perpetration of Swift's hoax upon him. In fact, the advertisement seems to me to refer to the forthcoming publication of the very broadsheet discovered at Harvard by Dr. McCue.

These newspaper accounts show that the method of Jonathan Swift's macabre joke upon Ebenezer Elliston follows the pattern earlier established by Swift in such other hoaxes as, for instance, the famous one on Partridge in 1708.[1] The date and wording of Harding's advertisement show that Swift's realistic parody of a criminal's 'dying' speech was set up some time in advance of the actual, and in this case, the literal, springing of the trap on 2 May 1722, the day of Elliston's execution. The additional information from Dublin records and newspapers permits us also to trace more clearly Swift's motives in singling out Elliston as his victim, to evaluate with some precision the efficacy of Swift's method of satiric verisimilitude, and, finally, to establish the significance of his hoax on Elliston within the wider scope and aims of Swift's satire between 1720 and 1727, during which time *The Drapier's Letters* and *Gulliver's Travels* were being written and eventually published.

At almost the very moment in 1720 when the miserable condition of the weavers of Dublin compelled Swift to break his six years of silence and once more to take up his pen in aid of his oppressed country, the first notice of Ebenezor Elliston, a 'much reduced'

Swift's *Works*; vol. VII, p. 55 of Temple Scott's ed. of 1897–1908, hereafter referred to as T. Scott (ed.), *Prose Works*.

[1] See also Irvin Ehrenpreis, 'Swift's April Fool for a Bibliophile', *Book-Collector*, vol. II (1953), pp. 205–8. There (p. 208) Professor Ehrenpreis remarks that 'Swift's notions for hoaxes were not often original. He generally picked them up from other sources and bettered the instruction.' It might be added that Swift's hoaxes (as with the ones on Partridge and Elliston) were often macabre, employing the grim humour of reporting upon the death of someone, and that they also show evidence of having been planned well in advance, as here. See also 'Swift's Bickerstaff Hoax as an April Fool's Joke', in *Modern Philology*, vol. LXI (May 1964), pp. 270–80.

weaver of silk stockings, appeared as a news report in *Whalley's News-Letter* for Saturday, 5 March 1719/20:

> *Dublin*, Mar. 5. At the Quarter-Sessions of this City Yesterday [Friday, 4 March 1720] *Derby MacCormuck* a famous Robber, who for some time past, has pestered this City and the Roads, leading to it, *Jam. McManus* and *James Keating*, a Boy about 16 or 17 Years of Age, all of the Gang of *Mc.Cormuck* were convicted, and receiv'd Sentance to die this Day Se'ennight upon the Evidence of *John Seymour*, an Apothecary, who[s]e Mother formerly was known to belong to, and to give out Tokens at the Tholsel, and *Ebeneʒir Elison*, a Stocking-Weaver Try'd at the King's-Bench last Michaelmas Term for Burglary but acquitted; but now Confesses Fact, and with *Seymour* owns he was with Mc.Cormuck Mc.Manus & Keating at breaking open and Robbing Hous[e]s of *Mr. Ongs Mr. Bodin* and *Mr. Brelord* and who I am told says he was in above 24 Robber[ie]s, in which he will discover 4 Gangs and some of'em Sons of Men of Note in this City, but The Particular keepes Secret as yet. . . .

The Derby MacCormack mentioned (his first and last names, like those of Elliston, are variously spelt) was the leader of the gang to which Ebenezor Elliston belonged. As 'The Last Farewell' (IX. 365) explains, MacCormack 'Justly deserved' to be executed, together with the other members of his gang, at St. Stephen's Green on 12 March 1720 for his own crimes as well as for those which he committed but for which such an innocent man as '*John Lynham*' suffered (IX. 366). According to *Whalley's News-Letter* for Saturday, 20 June 1719 '*Derby Cormuck*', along with many others who were 'out on their Keeping', was ordered to be proscribed by the Lord-Lieutenant and Privy Council, all of them outlawed as '*Tories, Robers and Raparees*'. Although he was described in the proclamation as being formerly a yeoman, 'late of *Grallagh*', Co. Dublin, after 1 August 1719 MacCormack was a hunted and probably a desperate man on the run. It was undoubtedly about this time in 1719 that the 'much reduced' Elliston fell in with Mac-Cormack and became involved in the burglary for which he was tried but acquitted at Michaelmas term, 1719. James McManus, also executed at St. Stephen's Green on the same day as his leader, was probably the 'Other person' who was said by Elliston in 'The Last

Farewell (IX. 366) to have been with MacCormack at the time of the robbery for which Lynham was later prosecuted. '*James Keating*, a Boy about 16 or 17', was evidently Elliston's own apprentice in the trade of stocking-weaving. He is mentioned in the account below of his master's, Elliston's, own later conviction.

In March 1720 it was Elliston's informing upon them that helped to hang Keating, McManus, and MacCormack. By serving as an evidence Elliston also procured a pardon for his own part in their crimes, and in a short time he was publicly rewarded and even seems to have become, temporarily, something of a local hero. The following account is taken from the records of the City of Dublin for July 1720, four months after Elliston turned informer:[1]

[July 22, 1720]

Ebenezir Elliston, setting forth that he hath been serviceable to the public in detecting several robberies and prosecuting the offenders, and being much reduced prays consideration for the same: ordered that the treasurer do pay, on the Lord Mayors warrant, to the petitioner the sum of ten pounds, sterling, as a reward for discovering several notorious offenders who were convicted and executed for the same.

Since it has direct bearing upon Swift's satiric thesis in his hoaxing broadsheet that real criminals are never truly sorry or repentant for their crimes, it is worth noticing here that, although Elliston had been tried and acquitted 'at the King's-Bench last Michaelmas Term for Burgalary', by his own admission in 'The Last Farewell' (IX. 366) he instantly thereafter commenced his own major career in crime which lasted, he said, 'from October 1719 to January 1720' and which consisted, for the most part, of robberies and house-breakings in and about the city of Dublin in the company of his old friend MacCormack and his gang. Finally, it should also be re-marked that Elliston, having chosen to save his own neck and eventually to be rewarded for it, in March 1720 anticipated Swift and was himself then willing to implicate others even more highly placed than MacCormack. Whether as a deterrent, for the public good, or as a kind of blackmail, against would-be avengers from

[1] Sir John T. Gilbert, *Calendar of Ancient Records of Dublin*, 7 vols. (Dublin, 1889–98), vol. VII, p. 130.

other gangs, Elliston, in 1720, like Swift in 1722, threatened to reveal the names of members of other Dublin gangs 'some of 'em Sons of Men of Note in this City', 'but The Particulars keepes Secret as yet'. Elliston's well-publicized threat would be of special interest to Swift. It probably caught his eye, reminded him of his own earlier thoughts on the subject, and implanted the idea for his own future hoax and broadsheet. For Swift (if he is the author) as early as *Tatler*, no. 68, for 1709 (II. 242) had once himself entertained a similar notion of publishing a list of the names of those men of better quality and education who aided gangs of London thieves, pick-pockets, and card-sharps to fleece the innocent, unless such men were deterred by this threat and speedily reformed their ways. As in some of his other hoaxes, and notably the one on Partridge, Swift seems once more to have had in mind for some time the basic notion of how to expose his victim.

The second newspaper account, from *Whalley's News-Letter* for Monday, 30 April 1722 reports the trial of Ebenezor Elliston on Wednesday, 25 April 1722, exactly a week before the day of his execution. The news of the trial and sentencing of Elliston probably provoked Swift into composing his *Last Speech and Dying Words of Ebenezor Elliston* on the day of the trial, or between that date and Saturday, 28 April 1722 when John Harding announced its forthcoming publication. In what follows the nature of the crime for which Elliston was condemned and executed should be especially noted:

On Wednesday [25 April 1722], were Try'd at the King's-Bench for Stealing a Mare from Councillor Sweeney Rich. Otway a Boy and Ebenezer Alison who about two Years since was Pardon'd upon becoming an Evidence against Macmanaus and his own Apprentice, who thereupon were Executed at Stephens-green, for several Robberies Committed by Alison, and them in Company.

'Otway', the name of Elliston's boy accomplice, as it is here spelt, is more likely to be correct than the 'Oroway' of 'The Last Farewell' (IX. 366), since the first is a common Dublin name, as with that of the Restoration dramatist, while the last was probably a printer's error, indicating the carelessness of Harding's printers in setting up Elliston's broadsheet. However innocent he may have been of the burglary for which he was tried and acquitted in late September or October 1719, however guilty he may have been of the robberies and housebreakings which he admitted, but for which, as Swift recalled in his broadsheet, he was pardoned in March 1720, Ebenezor Elliston, in April 1722, was tried and finally executed for horse-stealing, and not for burglary, housebreaking, or robbery. As Elliston himself so deferentially and impenitently put it, in his 'Last Farewell' (IX. 366), 'Unfortunately I was concerned with another Person in taking Counsellor Sweeny's Mare'. And getting caught at it, he might have added.

The point here is that Swift, in his *Last Speech and Dying Words of Ebenezor Elliston*, has his mouthpiece, the 'I' who is 'Ebenezor Elliston', make no mention of horse-stealing. Yet, if Swift's broadsheet, as seems likely, was actually hawked about the gallows, interested Dublin citizens would well know that the real Elliston was then being executed for stealing Sweeney's mare. And yet, the remarks made by the fictitious 'Ebenezor Elliston' of Swift's broadsheet all seem to assume that the real Elliston was at that moment being hung for the robberies and housebreakings for which, as even Swift's own account acknowledges, he had long since been pardoned. It is possible, of course, but I think unlikely, that Swift really did not know the crime for which Elliston was executed. In any case, the question thus arises whether the circumstantial authenticity and convincing verisimilitude which has sometimes been claimed for Swift's parody and hoax, and upon which it depended to become effective, was, in fact, operative at the moment the hoax was perpetrated. For the moment the question need only be raised and not answered.

As though deliberately to confuse in advance and further to bewilder his prospective audience Swift appears to have inspired John Harding to place the following announcement in *Harding's Impartial News-Letter* for Saturday, 28 April 1722, a date midway in the week between Elliston's trial and his execution:

Dublin, April 28 [1722]. The last and true Speech of Ebenezar Ellison will be printed by the Printer hereof (containing several Things for the Common Good) and by no other in this city.

N.B. This Publick Notice is given that the Town may not be impos'd on by any sham one Printed by one Fitzgerald in Montrath-Street, who makes it his constant Practice to Impose on the Publick.

'The last and true Speech', an approximate rendition of Swift's eventual title, the phrase 'containing several Things for the Common Good', which echoes Swift's sub-title, make it certain that Harding's advertisement refers to Swift's broadsheet discovered by Dr. McCue, and not to Elliston's own 'Last Farewell', the printing of which was also entrusted to Harding. Unless it be taken as a deliberate and daring attempt to alert and confuse the public in advance, Harding's warning to prospective buyers to beware of a sham 'last speech' is peculiarly without point, since it would otherwise give away the hoax which he had meanwhile so well in hand. For by Saturday, 28 April, with Sunday, not a work-day, intervening, and the execution set for the early morning hours of Wednesday, 2 May, Harding's printers would have required Swift's copy as well as Elliston's to hand. It seems to me possible that Swift may even have had a chance to read over Elliston's effort before he put the finishing touches to his own composition. In the opening paragraph of his own broadsheet Swift's analysis of the triple heads of discourse usual in such compositions, 'such Nonsense and false English', corresponds quite well with the three-part division of Elliston's rival broadsheet.

Elliston's 'Last Farewell', 'Delivered in the Presence of *George Derry*, Clerk', although it was somewhat carelessly set by the printer (as with the mis-spelling of 'Oroway'), is not bad reading in its lengthy second paragraph, a torrential non-stop sentence of more than thirty lines of print (IX. 365–6). The opening and closing paragraphs, however, in another vein, are written in the usual pious and canting manner to which Swift referred so contemptuously in his own broadsheet. They express the Christian sentiments of forgiveness and forbearance, of repentance and hope of salvation, and they suggest that the hand of the prison chaplain was at work there. The style and content of the opening and closing paragraphs are in striking contrast to the realistically detailed expression, the almost breathless, certainly bitter and betrayed, 'confessional' tone of the middle section, where Elliston himself was probably writing. They also contrast very strikingly with the circumstantially detailed, the slangily realistic manner, the bold and unrepentant tone, of Swift's own broadsheet, which sufficiently resembles the middle portion of Elliston's 'Last Farewell' to be an almost perfect parody. Sir Walter Scott has most appropriately remarked that the execution of Elliston 'gave Swift an opportunity of exercising that remarkable versatility of composition, by which he could assume any character which he chose to personate'.[1] That the task of parodying Ebenezor Elliston was not a difficult one for Swift in April 1722 may be shown by the fact that Swift's talent, at this same time, was also busy creating and sustaining the 'plain simple Style' of Captain Lemuel Gulliver.

If, as Professor Davis surmises (IX. 371), Elliston's own account was 'cried about in his own hearing, as he was carried to execution', it seems to me just as likely that Swift's broadsheet was also hawked about the place of execution, or along the route leading to it. And if John Harding had enough confused the minds of the Dublin citizens about which was the authentic and which the sham 'dying' speech, Swift's broadsheet, despite its uncertainty about the crime for which Elliston was being executed, must have been received with a credulity at least equal to that given Elliston's own account, which was all the advantage Swift's art required. As the printer and joint distributor of Elliston's broadsheet, as well as the printer and sole distributor of Swift's, John Harding was in a position to manipulate the sale of both, to his own advantage. After the event, at least one of the rival authors would not be present to chide him for the calculated confusion.

As in some of his earlier hoaxes Swift was also absent at the moment when his joke reached its climax, at the execution of Ebenezor Elliston. Sometime during the last week of April 1722, and probably between 25 April and 28 April, as he later wrote to Vanessa, Swift left Dublin for five weeks of solitary riding through isolated parts of the north of Ireland, a jaunt which eventually took him to call upon several of his country friends and which kept him

---

[1] W. Scott (ed.), Swift's *Works*, vol. I, p. 263.

away from Dublin for five months.[1] When Swift returned to the city in early October 1722, William Wood in England had possessed his patent to coin Irish half-pence for several months. The economic, political, and moral forces which were to engage Swift in controversy for the next several years and were to hinder the completion of his half-finished *Gulliver's Travels* were already at work once more.

II

Insignificant and parochial as it may seem by comparison, I believe that Jonathan Swift's interest from 1720 to 1722 in the increasing corruption and reversal of values of a world turned upside down by such seemingly successful criminals as Ebenezor Elliston led him logically and inevitably to engage in the manner he did in the Drapier controversy of 1724, and that the widening circles of his thoughts about the psychology of the criminal mind eventually informed even the satiric art of *Gulliver's Travels*, parts of which Swift was composing at the time that Elliston lived out his brief life of crime. Beginning with the specific case of a contemporary local 'great' man Swift's study of the nature of criminal psychology seems to me to have led him, by 1726 or 1727, to conclude generally that corruption was widespread and universal and was practised by 'great' men of the past as well as the present. When Swift, in his third *Drapier's Letter* of September 1724, wished to suggest the criminal nature of William Wood, he had only to associate Wood's name with the name of '*Elliston*' and, to a Dublin audience at least, no further explanation was necessary.[2] Since such a 'greatness' had no concern with 'goodness', Swift found in it little or no incentive to that vanishing 'virtue', which he defined, in 1724, as 'This love of the public, or of the commonwealth, or love of our country [which] was in ancient times properly known by the name of *Virtue*, because it was the greatest of all virtues, and was supposed to contain all virtues, in it' (IX. 233).[3]

[1] F. Elrington Ball (ed.), *The Correspondence of Jonathan Swift, D.D.*, 6 vols. (London, 1910–14), vol. III, p. 131.

[2] Herbert Davis (ed.), *The Drapier's Letters* (Oxford, 1935), pp. 37, 229.

[3] 'Doing Good: A Sermon.' Cf. Davis (ed.), *Prose Works*, vol. x, p. 90 (fifth Drapier's Letter).

In 1720, however, and to start with, it was the economic rather
than the political or spiritual condition of Ireland, 'the growing
poverty of the nation', as Swift later said (XII. 131), and especially
the wretched condition of such unemployed weavers of Dublin as
Elliston, at that time a master-weaver of thirty years old with a
family and at least one apprentice dependent upon him, that
prompted Swift to engage once more in pamphleteering. Swift
proposed a boycott of English cloth and wearables and the support
of Irish trade and home industries. Almost at once, however, in
May 1720, Edward Waters, the printer of Swift's *Proposal for the
Universal Use of Irish Manufacture*, was prosecuted, its author
presented by a Dublin Grand Jury, as persons politically 'dis-
affected' to the Government, 'the said pamphlet to be False, Scandalous and Seditious'.[1]

And yet surely Swift's chief aims were economic and sociological
rather than political, to encourage desperately needed home manufacture and trade and to reduce unemployment and to discourage
crime. Swift later estimated that in mid-1720 'about 1500 weavers
were forced to beg their bread, and had a general contribution made
for their relief, which just served to make them drunk for a week:
and then they were forced to turn rogues, or strolling beggars, or to
leave the Kingdom' (XII. 121). Less than a year later Archbishop
King of Dublin estimated that there were 'near 1700 weavers'
families starving . . . the persons near 6000'.[2] Both Swift and Archbishop King were quick to realize that unless something were done
about it, out of such widespread unemployment would come
inevitably a rise in Dublin's crime rate. Such, in fact, became the
case from 1719 to 1722.

Despite the partisan and political charges of the Dublin Grand
Jury, which put Swift and his printer in the same class as other
felons, the Dean continued to work toward alleviating the extreme
poverty that led to crime among the unemployed weavers of Dublin. By such positive practical measures as collecting money at St.

[1] *Dublin Gazette*, no. 1626 for Tuesday, 31 May to Saturday, 4 June
1720.
[2] Ball (ed.), *Correspondence*, vol. III, p. 75, n. 2.

Patrick's for the general contribution towards their relief,[1] by composing an epilogue for a performance of *Hamlet* benefiting the weavers held on 1 April 1721,[2] by proposing the formation of charity Church schools (IX. 202), and by inaugurating what Swift called 'industrious money',[3] an interest-free personal loan made by him to the penniless weavers and artisans of his Liberty of St. Patrick's, Swift worked hard to improve or to alleviate the circumstances which made criminals out of good citizens.

Negatively, but just as practically and vigorously, from the winter of 1719–20 onward, Swift also set about combating, in what might be called a one-man war on crime, the rising rate of crime in and about Dublin. For instance, Swift admonished those drapers and weavers who still maintained some semblance of trade about their short-sighted policy of skimping and cheating such custom as remained (IX. 17; XII. 69). Later, he proposed that beggars of each parish be badged to weed out the cheats (XIII. 127). It is against such a background as this one-man war on crime, especially after it became clear that some officials in Dublin were either politically corrupt, or preferred to buy off criminals rather than punish them, that Swift's hoax upon Elliston should probably be judged.

In the winter of 1719–20, when the growing audacity of organized gangs like MacCormack's made the streets and roads about Dublin unsafe after darkness, when the gangs included unrepentant and vicious men like Elliston, who was, according to the younger Thomas Sheridan, brought up in a rigid Dissenting family, or the sons of men of note in the city, or renegades frightened out of England by the enforcement of harsher penal laws there, and when their attacks affected his own friends, then Swift began to concern himself as much with the nature of local crimes and criminal psychology and its operations as with the economic and political oppression which bred the conditions encouraging such crimes.

---

[1] Ball (ed.), *Correspondence*, vol. II, p. 75, n.2.

[2] Sir Harold Williams (ed.), *The Poems of Jonathan Swift*, 3 vols. (Oxford 1937), vol. I, p. 273.

[3] Ball (ed.), *Correspondence*, vol. III, p. 99, n. 1, and William Monck Mason, *The History and Antiquities of the Collegiate and Cathedral Church of St. Patrick* (Dublin, 1820), pp. 416–17, nn. *l* and *m*.

Whalley's News-Letter of 16 February 1719/20 gives a good account of the situation in and around Dublin at that time. It reports as news the robbery, within gun-shot of St. Stephen's Green, of two unescorted women in broad daylight. Among the advertisements are rewards offered for information concerning the recent house-breakings and robberies at Joseph Bernard's of Ballyhide, Queens Co., and at Lady Mountcashel's estate of St. Catherine's, Leixlip, just outside Dublin. Lady Mountcashel had recently became acquainted with Swift through Dr. Thomas Sheridan, a frequent guest at her house, and master of the Dublin school attended by her brilliant son and heir.[1] Among the advertisements are also some for stolen horses. Sheridan and possibly Swift may have themselves been victims of horse-thieves about this time.[2] The crime situation, in and around Dublin, was therefore brought home to Swift in a meaning-ful, and even a personal, way.

The same issue of *Whalley's News-Letter* also contains the following report which suggests that the rise in crime in Ireland was in part caused by the enforcement of new and harsher penal laws in England:

Dublin, Feb. 13 [1719/20]. The late Act of Parliament in England has already so prevailed, that several Robbers have been frightened thence, are returned hither, and a gange or two of them, having lately committed several Roberies on the Road leading to and near this City, and kill'd 2 Men therefore [it is?] advisable for all honest Men to provide against those Vermine.

The language here is not far removed from the words of Swift's mouthpiece, 'Ebenezor Elliston', who, in the broadsheet of 1722, is made to refer to himself and to other criminals as 'common Enemies of Mankind; whose Interest it is to Root us out like Wolves, and other mischievous Vermin' (IX. 41). Behind both expressions looms the King of Brobdingnag's contemptuous dismissal of all of puny mankind as 'the most pernicious Race of little odious Vermin that Nature ever suffered to crawl upon the Surface of the Earth'.

The 'late Act of Parliament' mentioned in the news-sheet may

---

[1] Williams (ed.), *Poems*, vol. III, pp. 1013, 1017.
[2] Ball (ed.), *Correspondence*, vol. III, p. 83.

refer to an Act of March 1718,[1] which increased the severity of the laws having to do with transportation to the colonies of criminals, especially highwaymen and robbers. In his *Last Speech and Dying Words* Swift has Elliston scoff at the ineffectiveness of such punishment (IX. 38). As he wrote, Swift had before him an actual case of a vessel that was taken over by mutinous felons being transported from Dublin to the colonies, the ship deliberately run aground on the coast of northern Ireland, and the criminals once more dispersed over the countryside.[2] As Swift's mouthpiece said in his broadsheet, when criminals were successfully transported to the colonies they sooner or later managed to drift back to England or Ireland and were then worse offenders than ever (IX. 38). A further Royal Proclamation of January 1719/20, which offered £100 per head for the apprehension and conviction of highwaymen and street-robbers in England, may also have speeded up the exodus of criminals from England to Ireland.[3] Here was another English export the Irish could well do without.

Swift's stern and ruthless attitude towards confirmed criminals, and especially towards those who attacked women, had probably been earlier shaped by the attack of robbers upon Stella's isolated Dublin dwelling in 1705 or 1706. In his essay *On the Death of Mrs. Johnson* (1728) Swift recalled her vigorous methods of self-defence and her unusual degree of personal courage upon that occasion.[4] Stella's conduct contrasted most tellingly with the cowardly behaviour or timidity of some of the gentlemen of Dublin in 1719–22. Although armed, when confronted by highwaymen or robbers they weakly and tamely allowed themselves to be robbed, and for their cowardice Swift threatened, in his broadsheet (IX. 39), to expose their initials to the world, just as he threatened to expose by name future criminals and their associates.

There are therefore many reasons, some of them personal, why

---

[1] *Pue's Occurrences*, vol. xv, no. 11, for 8–11 Feb. 1717/18, and vol. xv, no. 19, for 18 22 March 1717/18.

[2] *Whalley's News-Letter* for Saturday, 20 May 1721.

[3] Abel Boyer, *The Political State of Great Britain*, vol. xix (for January 1720), pp. 108–9.

[4] T. Scott (ed.), *Prose Works*, vol. xi, p. 130.

Swift should have singled out Ebenezor Elliston to become the victim of his hoax in 1722. As a master-weaver and as a relatively well-to-do and well brought up young man Elliston may have seemed to Swift to be a person who was only too easily pardoned, although unrepentant, for crimes for which he had less excuse than thousands of other less fortunate Dublin artisans. Elliston, by being rewarded for his part in the crimes about which he informed upon such other gang members as his own young apprentice, towards whom he had special responsibilities, seems to have become, for a brief moment in 1720, to his less fortunate fellow-weavers and to his fellow-citizens, a kind of 'great' man who made crime pay. To Swift he probably represented the creeping corruption of the enforcement of law and order in Dublin about this time. As a member of a gang which had committed, as he boasted, 'above 24 Robberies' in and about Dublin in 1719–20, as a member of the tribe of informers, who were, as Swift wrote to Pope on 10 January 1720/21, 'the most accursed and prostitute and abandoned race that God ever permitted to plague mankind',[1] Elliston was doubly Swift's, or any honest man's, natural enemy. But it was probably Elliston's own blackmailing or deterrent threat in March 1720 to produce a list of fellow-criminals, a notion which Swift had earlier considered and to which he returned with a vengeance in May 1722, that focused Swift's attention upon Ebenezer Elliston in 1720 and inevitably marked him out as a proper victim for the eventual hoax. We may surmise that in the meanwhile, between 1720 and 1722, Swift, as he conducted his examination into the psychology of the true criminal type, kept a close eye upon Elliston as a fine local example of the species.

Swift's method, in his superb parody that sprang the joke, is, despite the exception noted above, a wonderfully detailed and most realistically convincing 'confession' and unrepentant 'last speech'. In his account Swift also demonstrated a surprisingly intimate and detailed knowledge of the practices current in the Dublin underworld of his time. We may a little doubt Faulkner's pious and

[1] George Sherburn (ed.), *The Correspondence of Alexander Pope*, 5 vols. (Oxford, 1956), vol. II, p. 71.

sweeping claim, made thirteen years after the event, that '*this Speech had so good an Effect that there have been very few Robberies of that kind committed since*'.[1] As late as 1724 or 1725 Swift himself continued to complain that 'our Streets [are] so dangerous to those who are forced to walk in the Night' (IX. 208). But despite its seeming ignorance of the crime for which Elliston actually was being executed, and especially because of the authenticity and well-informed air with which Swift employed details of criminal life in Dublin's underworld, *The Last Speech and Dying Words of Ebeneʒor Elliston* may well have had a temporary deterrent effect upon local robbers and highwaymen who read the broadsheet.

For, as Swift seems shrewdly to have calculated, most decent people and even some fellow-criminals, remembering in 1722 the earlier escapades of Elliston in 1719–20, must have felt as Swift did, that Elliston, no matter what the present crime, had certainly deserved to be hung for his earlier robberies and betrayals, instead of being pardoned for them and even rewarded. To be hung for horse-stealing is a mean and ignominious — even ludicrous — fate. It was Swift's moral and satiric purpose in 1722 to recall as subtly as he could to his readers' minds Elliston's more heinous earlier crimes and the collusion of those in authority at the time, to buttress these recollections with a wealth of other authentic detail, so that the broadsheet might then convince the criminals in his audience that Elliston was truly speaking, and the decent people that some such determined 'good man' as Swift himself was the person with whom the list of names was to be left.

Sir Walter Scott believed that Swift composed his parody speech 'as an experiment in aid of the police',[2] a most unlikely supposition when one examines the corruption of some of those who served as officers of the law in the Dublin of the 1720s. With an irony that only Swift could have fully relished, Elliston, in his own 'Last Farewell' (IX. 366), claimed most bitterly and probably correctly that he, in his turn, had been informed upon by one Elizabeth Gorden and falsely accused by her to the Lord Mayor for com-

---

[1] *Works* (1735), vol. IV, p. 375.
[2] W. Scott (ed.), Swift's *Works*, vol. VI, p. 296.

mitting robbery upon a captain in Gravel Walk about mid-December 1721. Elliston said darkly that he had been framed 'by the persuasions of a Man in power'. A few lines farther along in his 'Last Farewell' the identity of that person was hinted at as directly as Elliston, or the printer, dared say: 'Mr. H——s made it his Business [after the false charges were made] to Haunt Night and Day for me, and also informed several Persons, that there was Twenty Pounds Reward for anyone who would apprehend me.' For a Judas the amount of the reward seems right, and again it cannot have escaped Swift's sense of the irony of life as it did not Archbishop King's, that the amount offered for the apprehension of a notorious criminal in 1722 was fifteen times less than that offered in 1724 for information concerning the author of *The Drapier's Letters*.[1]

But more than anything Swift, if he knew Elliston's own 'Last Farewell', would have relished best the final irony of one rogue accusing another of framing him before the law. For the 'Mr. H——s' referred to by Elliston is surely none other than John Hawkins, the predecessor and prototype of his opposite number in England, the Jonathan Wild of Dublin in the 1720s. Formerly the Keeper of Dublin's Bridewell, and, since April 1721, the notorious Gaoler of Newgate, Hawkins had paid the Lord Mayor and Sheriffs of Dublin £100 'gratuity' for his powerful and lucrative position as thief-catcher of Dublin.[2] As later investigation showed, Hawkins, with the aid of his wife, an underkeeper, a turnkey, and other unsavoury associates, managed to squeeze out, by means of receiving stolen goods, protecting criminals, selling perquisites, and by direct extortion, a yearly income of more than £1100 on an annual salary of £10.[3] In November 1729 the Irish House of Commons finally dismissed Hawkins from his office, because of his corruption and perversion of the law, but it hardly was 'in aid of the police' and such men as Hawkins that Swift composed his broadsheet. Rather,

---

[1] Mason, *History of St. Patrick*, p. 344, n. *n*, reports that at that time Archbishop King said in a letter that the reward was five times greater than had ever been offered for discovery of the most atrocious felony.

[2] Sir John T. Gilbert, *A History of the City of Dublin*, 3 vols. (Dublin, 1861), vol. 1, p. 265.

[3] Gilbert, *History of Dublin*, vol. 1, p. 268.

it seems to me that Swift recognized the corruptions which had already undermined the forces of law and order in Dublin and that in his broadsheet he attempted to circumvent them with a shrewd psychological trick by instilling, at least momentarily, a very real fear of betrayal into the hearts of the criminals in his audience.

To achieve his aim Swift had to be thoroughly convincing in his hoax and parody. Dr. McCue has noticed (pp. 366–7) that 'the four convicts mentioned at the end of the Harvard broadsheet were presumably real persons', and that the two final paragraphs not found in Faulkner's version of the broadsheet 'add a further note of verisimilitude and authenticity to the *Last Speech*'. So too with Swift's knowing reference to the ways by which £1000 worth of stolen goods would hardly bring in £50, after the profits had been taken and cuts received by various tapsters, whores, inn-keepers, and fences, and considering 'the Bribes we must give for Concealment', probably a glance on Swift's part at the practice of Hawkins and his associates (IX. 40). Stylistically, too, a liberal sprinkling of such current and slangy underworld jargon and thieves' argot as the expressions 'Setters', 'to go Snacks with', 'to get a Booty' also lend an air of convincing verbal authenticity to the broadsheet. And with a psychological insight worthy of Milton's Satan 'Ebenezor Elliston' is made to observe acutely and poignantly of the criminal's state of mind that 'something heavy always hangs about us, I know not what it is' (IX. 40). That observation illustrates how remarkably well, by 1722, Swift was able to penetrate psychologically and to express convincingly the vague and uneasy sense of guilt permeating the unrepentant criminal's subconscious mind.

But perhaps the most remarkable instance of Swift's detailed knowledge of the practices of the Dublin underworld in the 1720s as exemplified in *The Last Speech and Dying Words of Ebenezor Elliston* is the passage in the second paragraph where Swift makes his mouthpiece speak as follows:

I can say further from my own knowledge, that two of my Fraternity after they had been Hanged and wonderfully came to life, and made their Escapes, as it sometimes happens, proved afterwards the wickedest Rogues I ever knew, and so continued untill they were Hanged again for good and all. . . .

According to Sir John T. Gilbert's *History of the City of Dublin*[1] such famous ballads from Dublin's Newgate as 'The Night before Larry was Stretch'd' and its sequel, 'Larry's stiff', record an actual contemporary practice, current in the 1720s, which Swift seems to have known about, by which the friends of the deceased cut down the executed criminal as quickly as possible, rushed him to the nearest tavern and, sometimes successfully, 'made an incision in his juglar vein, in the hope . . . of "cheating Jack the breath-stopper" '. In Dublin thieves' argot the process was called 'tipping a snig in de juglar'.[2] It is to this sometimes successful contemporary method of reviving an executed 'great' man that Swift, in his broadsheet, refers with an air of authenticity and as something personally witnessed to show decent people how unrepentant most hardened criminals were, and to convince the criminals in his audience that it was someone like Ebenezor Elliston writing the broadsheet.

For, as Swift seems early to have realized, to have consistently thereafter pursued, even after Elliston's execution, and finally to have formulated in some of his greatest satires, the chief difference between the psychology of the petty criminal and the 'great' but unscrupulous man of political affairs was merely one of scope of operation and degree of daring. The equation of a 'greatness' with the opposite of goodness or of true 'virtue', as Swift defined it, was developed throughout the Drapier controversy of 1724-5,[3] was

[1] Vol. i, pp. 271-3.
[2] Gilbert, *History of Dublin*, vol. i, p. 273.
[3] Page references in what follows are from Davis (ed.), *Prose Works*, vol. x. As well as being a draper, Swift's mouthpiece, 'M. B. *Drapier*', was also a weaver, as was Elliston (p. xiii; cf. pp. 82-83). Through his mouthpiece one of Swift's purposes in *The Drapier's Letters* was to blacken William Wood's reputation and to reduce him to the level of a common criminal, some 'great' man like Ebenezor Elliston. Thus Swift calls Wood 'a *Sharper*' (p. 57), someone not 'fit to be trusted in any *honest* Man's shop' (p. 48), a criminal with a previous record (p. 29), the unscrupulous leader of a gang, 'Wood and his Associates' (p. 17; cf. pp. 15, 63, 122), among whom was an '*Elliston*' (p. 29) and other criminal types (p. 28). By direct comparison, or by shrewd use of suggestive metaphor and simile, what Swift called 'putting Cases', 'Wood and his Accomplices' (p. 46) were frequently compared to highwaymen, housebreakers, and robbers (pp. 19-20, 22, 23, 46, 48, 84, 105, 137). Just as Swift had earlier composed a

pursued in such poems as 'The Ballad upon Blueskin' (?1725) and
'Clever *Tom Clinch*' (?1726),[1] found expression in some parts of
Gulliver's Travels[2] and was most succinctly stated by Swift in his

hoaxing account of Elliston's end, so he now wrote a punning *Full and
True* Account *of the solemn Procession to the* Gallows, *at the Execution of*
William Wood, *Esquire, and Hard-ware-man* (pp. 145–9), an account of
the mock-hanging and attempted burning of Wood in effigy by the
Dublin mob on 7 Sept. 1724. See Richard Dickson's *Dublin Intelligencer*,
no. 3219, for Tuesday, 8 September 1724 and Mason, *History of St.
Patrick*, p. 332, n. *w.*

Another of Swift's purposes in *The Drapier's Letters* was to suggest, as
openly as was possible without bringing the law down upon him, the
vicious collusion that existed between such 'great' persons as Sir Robert
Walpole and the Duchess of Kendal in England and others in Ireland and
so mean a 'great' man as William Wood. The first *Drapier's Letter* said
bluntly (p. 5) that Wood 'had GREAT FRIENDS' at court who were bribed
to help him get his Patent. In his fourth letter (p. 67) the Drapier complained that Wood was openly boasting about what 'the same great man',
Sir Robert Walpole, would do to punish the Irish. He therefore concluded
(p. 67) that 'If Mr. *Wood* hath no better a Manner of representing his
Patrons; when I come to be a *Great Man*, he [Wood] shall never attend
at my *Levee*'. In the fifth letter (p. 121) the Drapier said that now even
'*great Folks*' in Ireland were abandoning their country's cause and were
become 'Grand Compounders'. By December 1724 the Drapier, in his
fifth letter, was thoroughly convinced of the almost universal vice and
corruption of 'great' men in both the highest and lowest estates and that
Virtue, here (p. 91) briefly defined as 'publick Spirit', resided only among
the middle ranks of society (p. 90): 'That, as Philosophers say, *Vertue is
seated in the Middle*; so in another Sense, the little *Virtue* left in the World
is chiefly to be found among the *middle* Rank of Mankind; who are neither
allured out of her Paths by *Ambition*, nor *driven* by *Poverty*.'

[1] Williams (ed.), *Poems*, vol. II, p. 399; vol. III, p. 1111.

[2] Page references in what follows are from Davis (ed.), *Prose Works*,
vol. XI. In *Gulliver's Travels* perhaps the most striking example of Swift's
reduction of 'greatness' to its extremes occurs at the end of chap. vii,
Voyage III (p. 196). As one climax to the varied series of physical and
spiritual confrontations which run throughout *Gulliver* the Roman
Senate is made to appear for comparison and contrast with a contemporary English or Irish Parliament assembled. It is worth remarking that
this particular invidious comparison is a double one: between the godlike
Roman Senate and its modern but corrupted and degenerate counterpart,
and between the assemblages of modern 'great' men and their counterparts
in the underworlds of London or Dublin: 'I desired that the Senate of
Rome might appear before me in one large Chamber, and a modern
Representative, in Counterview, in another. The first seemed to be an

'Character of Sir Robert Walpole' (1731)[1] and in his little known *Proposals for Virtue* (1727),[2] from the conclusion of which the following quotation is taken:

A contemptuous character of court-art, how different from true politicks; for, comparing the [. . .] talents of two professions that are thought very different. I cannot but think that in the present sense of the word Politician a common Sharper or pick pocket has every quality that can be required in the other, and accordingly I have personally known more than half a dozen who in their time esteemed equally to excell in both.

In such a view the only difference to Swift between a Sir Robert Walpole of the year 1726 or 1727 and an Ebenezor Elliston of the year 1720 or 1722 was that the former turned the world and its values upside down on a grander scale and got away with it more successfully. Nor was Swift the only person to entertain such a notion. The idea was developed by John Gay in his *Beggar's Opera*

Assembly of Heroes and Demy-Gods; the other a Knot of Pedlars, Pick-pockets, Highwaymen and Bullies.'

Within moments, however, another confrontation was arranged between a true hero and demi-god of antiquity, the tyrant Julius Caesar, and his virtuous assassin, the patriot Brutus. Caesar was made to confess his inferiority to Brutus, who was grouped with five other patriotic men of history as the only truly virtuous and 'great' men the world has produced, or is likely to produce.

Other examples that might be cited from *Gulliver's Travels* are Gulliver's remarks, in Voyage I, chap. vi (pp. 58–60), upon the treatment given informers, of 'Fraud as a greater Crime than Theft', of the original system of rewards and punishments in Lilliputia before the morals of that country had degenerated through vice and corruptions. Or Gulliver's brief remarks, in the following chapter (p. 67), upon the malignity of 'great Princes and Ministers'. In the second Voyage the condemnation by the King of Brobdingnag of all kinds of 'great' men in Europe as 'little odious Vermin' has been noticed above. When, in the tenth chapter of Voyage IV (pp. 276–7), Gulliver came to sum up the kinds of evils he was free of in Houyhnhnmland he indiscriminately lumped together in an abusive catalogue of invidious comparisons 'Pick-pockets, Highwaymen, Housebreakers' and 'Gamesters, Politicians, Wits', or 'Ravishers, Murderers, Robbers', and 'Leaders or Followers of Party and Faction'.

[1] Williams (ed.), *Poems*, vol. II, pp. 539–40.

[2] I take my next text from Huntington MS. HM 14346, p. 2. Cf. T. Scott (ed.), *Prose Works*, vol. VII, p. 376.

(1728), traditionally thought to have been suggested to Gay by Swift, and most memorably and sustainedly by Henry Fielding in his *History of Jonathan Wild, the Great* (1743). First in the brief career of Ebenezor Elliston and then perhaps more typically in the career of Elliston's nemesis, John Hawkins, the Dublin prototype of the notorious Jonathan Wild, Swift found in real life examples of the 'great' men who posed as upholders of law and order, but who actually, under cover of their positions and by turning the normal world and its values upside down, robbed and plundered, blackmailed and coerced quite safely and for their own selfish ends. Eventually Swift extended his knowledge of criminal psychology so far as to condemn and satirize conquering monarchs of the past and domineering kings or prime ministers of the present. But at the start, in the Dublin of the early 1720s, and with his study of the career of his victim, the petty criminal and informer, Ebenezor Elliston, Swift, it seems to me, first began to perceive how the circles of crime and vice widened out until they included, in his mind, other 'great' men of his own time and of the past. In his eventual satiric equation Swift compared even heroes, demi-gods, and 'great' personages of antiquity on the same moral level with the petty thieves, pickpockets, and highwaymen of his own time and place, some of whom, like Ebenezor Elliston, he had studied at first hand.[1]

[1] For a cogent development and exposition of Swift's ability to reverse the values and to turn upside down the ideals of Augustan society see J. C. Maxwell, 'Demigods and Pickpockets: The Augustan Myth in Swift and Rousseau', in *Scrutiny*, vol. XI (1942), pp. 34–39.

MACKIE L. JARRELL

'Jack and the Dane': Swift traditions in Ireland

D. J. O'DONOGHUE'S 'Swift as an Irishman' is one of the warmest tributes which Swift has received from an Irishman in the twentieth century.[1] O'Donoghue strongly affirms Swift's right to the name of Irish patriot and adds playfully that the name 'Sinn Feiner and Cattle Driver' would not be inaccurate. Yet he recognizes that Swift's right to the name of either Irish patriot or Irishman will not go uncontested.

The question is, to put it most simply, whether Swift spoke for the Irish people or only for the English settlers in Ireland, and few of his biographers or critics have written in firm accord with O'Donoghue. (Swift's early biographers were, of course, Anglo-Irish, entirely committed to the English rule, and his later ones have been largely English, with little interest in Ireland, or even, like Craik, anti-Irish.)[2] A recent study, Oliver Ferguson's *Jonathan Swift in Ireland*, emphasizes 'the significance of his part in Ireland's slow progress toward legislative independence' but concludes that ' "Ireland's rights" meant for Swift (as it did for Molyneux) the rights of the Anglo-Irish'.[3]

The Irish attitude toward Swift has been understandably mixed, and often gingerly. He has had some notable defenders among Irish

[1] *Irish Review*, June–Aug. 1912, pp. 209–14, 256–63, 305–11.

[2] See, for example, such remarks as 'I would trust no Irishman upon such a point' [authenticity of Swift's autobiographical fragment, preserved in Trinity College] and 'Was there ever an Irish man of genius who did not get himself turned into an Englishman as fast as he could, except Curran?' (Letters from Henry Craik to John Forster, Forster Collection, MS. 48.E.25).

[3] Oliver Ferguson, *Jonathan Swift in Ireland* (Urbana, Ill., 1962), p. 186.

nationalists, Catholic and Protestant,[1] and some vigorous detractors (like John Mitchel, whose dislike of Swift was unrelenting)[2] who could find in him no love for Ireland and who dismissed his Irish pieces as 'cheap and noisy patriotism'.[3] Although the two camps persist in Ireland today, the English have more and more claimed him for their own, and the Irish have become more reluctant to do so.

The dual attitude in Ireland is, of course, quite understandable historically, and in view of the contradictions which Swift himself displayed and expressed. He said, in his *Thoughts on Religion*, that he looked upon himself as 'one appointed by Providence for defending a post assigned' him.[4] The post, which he certainly knew, as his will and his letters show, to be a desperate one, was that of a clergyman of the Church of Ireland — the name itself now reads like a piece of Swiftian irony. He attacked the Protestant dissenters with considerably more violence than he did the Catholics; but, as he said several times, the Catholics had been reduced to helplessness.[5] He was undoubtedly deeply moved, to wretchedness

[1] Among the best-known tributes to Swift are Grattan's 'Curse of Swift' speech, in *The Speeches of the Right Honourable Henry Grattan* (London, 1882), vol. II, p. 355; John W. Croker's *A Sketch of the State of Ireland Past and Present* (London, 1808); and E. Berwick's *A Defence of Dr. Jonathan Swift* (London, 1819). Less well-known are James Hardiman's statements that Swift was 'the best and purest Patriot that Ireland ever produced' and that 'the Dean may be considered the Father' of the Volunteer Movement (For. MS. 48.E.25, No. 1538). W. B. Yeats in several works echoes Croker in the statement that Swift 'created the political nationality of Ireland' (Introduction to *The Words upon the Window-Pane*, in *Wheels and Butterflies* (New York, 1935), vol. II, and in this volume).

[2] Mitchel's judgements of Swift are consistently severe. His animus sometimes leads him into curious positions, as in his notes on Whitshed: 'Swift persecuted the Chief Justice with his bitter wit, until he stung him to death'; 'he died of grief, and of the Dean's wicked verses'. See *Irish Political Economy* (Dublin, 1847), pp. 12, 24.

[3] 'For all his cheap and noisy patriotism Swift did not love Ireland nor its people' (Dublin *Daily Express*, 11 March 1899, p. 3).

[4] Herbert Davis (ed.), *The Prose Works of Jonathan Swift*, vol. IX (Oxford, 1948), p. 262.

[5] See, for example, Davis (ed.), *Prose Works*, vol. II (1939), p. 120; vol. XII (1955), p. 273. It is difficult to be certain of the extent of Swift's

and despair as well as to courageous action, by the poverty and misery of Ireland; but in spite of his almost lifelong residence there his library contained 'hardly ten books of Irish interest', and he evidently knew only a few words of Irish.[1] His charities were many, becoming in the end his chief concern; but there is little evidence that — like the Rev. Philip Skelton, whose failure to rise in the Church exceeded even Swift's[2] — he distributed them to Catholic and Protestant alike. He maintained in his apologia as in his epitaph that 'Fair Liberty was all his Cry', he stubbornly refused to accept the concept, or fact, of a 'dependent' Ireland, and he himself declared that '*Government* without the Consent of the *Governed, is* the *very Definition of Slavery*';[3] yet he found himself engaged in forcing on a dispossessed people a religion which they wanted no more than they wanted Poyning's Law or Wood's fireballs. He correctly diagnosed Carteret's position —

> And what Condition can be worse?
> He comes to *drain a Beggar's Purse*:
> He comes to tye our Chains on faster,
> And shew us, *E*[ngland] is our Master[4]

— and possibly he saw that his own was hardly more enviable. He was, in spite of his post, driven beyond dissatisfaction to sedition and open defiance of the authority of church and state, although the

disingenuousness in many of his political pieces, where he is master of the expedient argument and the effective pose, as in his praise of George I and of Walpole in *The Drapier's Letters*. His descriptions of Ireland as 'a Kingdom distinguished for its Loyalty, perhaps above all others upon Earth' and of the Irish Catholics as 'altogether as inconsiderable as the Women and Children' (vol. II, p. 120; vol. X (1941), p. 35) are fair samples of remarks which may be interpreted as evidence that he spoke only for the English in Ireland, or as O'Donoghue suggested, that he posed as a settler in order to work effectively for Ireland.

[1] 'Nescio' comments on his library in the *Irish Book Lover*, vol. XXI (1933), p. 64; for his knowledge of Irish, see, for example, Davis (ed.), *Prose Works*, vol. IV (1957), p. 279.

[2] See Samuel Burdy's life of Skelton in *The Complete Works of Philip Skelton* (London, 1824), vol. I, pp. lxxxiii ff.

[3] Davis (ed.), *Prose Works*, vol. X, p. 63.

[4] 'A Libel on Dr. Delany', in *The Poems of Jonathan Swift*, ed. Harold Williams, 2nd ed. (Oxford, 1958), vol. II, p. 484.

defiance, obscured by more than two centuries, may be too easily dismissed today as trivial or wrong-headed.

The Irish attitude toward Swift in his own day deserves more investigation than it has received, even though the evidence for assessing it is scanty — and scantier because of the great destruction of records in the struggles of those centuries. Ferguson, among others, says that after 1720 'Swift had the trust and affection of the common people' (p. 58), but it has never been demonstrated that the acclaim and adulation Swift received as patriot during his lifetime came from the common people, except from Kevan Bail and the Coombe weavers, or sifted down below the Protestant ascendancy. Certainly he came to pride himself on his mob following, and certainly he was idolized by an extremely articulate group who called him 'Father Swift' and 'Pater Patriae' and who predicted that the

> *Drapier, Dublin, Wood,* in Times to come,
> Shall sound like *Tully, Catiline,* and *Rome.*[1]

There is ample evidence of the many Drapier's Head signs, showing him in canonicals, throughout Dublin; of ships named the *Drapier*; and of the bonfires built to celebrate his birthday.[2] O'Keeffe's *Recollections* and numerous other accounts tell how he was venerated and blessed, and how the children ran to hold his cassock as he walked through the Dublin streets.[3]

Yet these accounts are largely Anglo-Irish; and, remembering the nature of the Pale, one can hardly help wondering whether Swift's fame extended beyond Dublin or what was the impact of the Drapier's fourth letter on 'the whole people of Ireland', to whom it was addressed. One would suppose that the language barrier and the

---

[1] 'A Dish of Chocolate [i.e. satire] for the Times. Address'd to the Reverend Edward Young' (Dublin, 1754), lines 259–60. Swift is addressed as both 'Father Swift' and 'Pater Patriae' in *A New Collection of Poems on Several Occasions* (Dublin, 1741), and many tributes are even more enthusiastic.

[2] 'Scarce a street in town [is] without a representation of him for a sign', *Mist's Weekly Journal,* 23 Sept. 1726. For ships, see, e.g., *Dublin Evening Post,* 6–10 Aug. 1734; *Reilly's Dublin News-Letter,* 17–20 Jan. 1740–1.

[3] *Recollections of the Life of John O'Keeffe, Written by Himself* (London, 1826), vol. I, p. 18.

Penal Laws, which produced illiteracy as well as penury, would narrowly limit his range; but the supposition needs testing. One of the few ways of testing it today is to see what Swift traditions are still preserved in Ireland, and fortunately the collections made by the Irish Folklore Commission offer an approach.[1]

The manuscript records of the Irish Folklore Commission contain collections of Swiftiana made from oral sources by fieldworkers and by schoolchildren, as a school assignment. The total collection is heterogeneous but is largely anecdotal in character, and a very large proportion of it consists of anecdotes about 'Jack and the Dane', that is, the witty Dean and his wittier servant Jack or Seán (occasionally Larry, Roger, or Paddy). (Swift's contemporaries were fond of pointing out that he early became '*the* Dean' and that no other identification was necessary.[2] His exclusive right to the title has never been questioned; it appears in the collection much more frequently than his surname.) One may still hear 'Jack and the Dane' stories in Dublin; but they are fast disappearing, and are likely to be mentioned now as stories which the speaker's aunt or father might remember, but which he himself has forgotten.

Analysis of the material recorded from oral tradition by the Irish Folklore Commission shows that it is largely literary in origin, deriving in the main from jestbooks. Many of the anecdotes can be found in seventeenth- and eighteenth-century collections, and also in such late popular collections as Patrick Kennedy's *The Banks of the Boro* (1867) and *The Book of Modern Irish Anecdotes* (1872). The motifs are familiar to all students of folklore. A surprising proportion of the stories concern the hiring of a servant, but the

---

[1] I should like to express my gratitude to the Irish Folklore Commission for their extraordinary kindness and helpfulness: to Professor J. H. Delargy, who made the collections available to me; to Dr. Kevin Danaher, who translated the Irish; to Dr. Thomas Wall, Librarian, who located materials; and to Mr. Seán O'Sullivan, Archivist, who furnished other information. Swift was fond of saying that a few men of genius could change the world. A few groups like the Irish Folklore Commission could transform scholarship.

[2] See, e.g., the broadside 'A Letter to The Dean, on the late Edition of Don Quixote' (Dublin, 1734): 'no Body can be meant by THE Dean, but Dean *Swift*'.

most common pattern is how the servant gets the better of his master, in repartee or in action.

The material is grouped here into four main categories, although the divisions sometimes overlap: (1) anecdotes showing Jack triumphing over the Dean, (2) anecdotes telling how he came to be employed, most often as coachman, (3) traditions concerning places connected with Swift, and (4) recollections of his works. The first category contains the stories encountered most frequently; the second includes some miscellaneous tales.

The story recorded most often is that of 'the leg of the goose' (K402.1).[1] The servant eats one leg of the roast goose before it is served for dinner; and when the Dean inquires about the missing leg, he is told that geese have only one leg. Later, when the Dean and Jack are out riding, Jack points out the geese standing by the pond on one leg. The Dean claps his hands (or cracks his whip, or says 'Cush' or 'Whoosh'), and the geese put down their other legs. Jack says, 'You should have clapped your hands at dinner.' This familiar story was sent to John Forster in 1856 by William John Fitzpatrick as one of the many 'humorous and traditional stories of Swift' which 'are constantly in the mouths of the lower orders in Ireland, but especially those of Dublin', although in Fitzpatrick's version Swift himself makes the witty reply to his host.[2] One IFC version (MS. 1112) records the tradition that Swift mistreated his servant and that the boy ate the goose because he was actually hungry.

[1] The parenthetical numbers in the text refer to Stith Thompson's *Motif-Index of Folk-Literature*, rev. ed. (Bloomington, n.d.). MS numbers in text or notes refer to the IFC collected volumes; and *S* added before the number indicates that the material was collected by schools. No attempt has been made to trace the jestbook history of the anecdotes; ordinarily a jestbook reference is given only when the anecdote has been found in jestbooks printed before Swift's death, or when it is earlier than the sources cited in standard editions. The goose anecdote appears in MSS. 8, p. 329; 86, pp. 355–9; 166, pp. 542–3; 259, pp. 305–6; 362, p. 143; 480, pp. 87–88; S531, pp. 87–88; 600, pp. 393–4; 779, pp. 430–31; S969, p. 163; 1112, p. 217. It is also found in *England's Jests Refin'd and Improved*, 3rd ed. (London, 1693), as quoted by John Ashton in *Humour, Wit, & Satire of the Seventeenth Century* (New York, 1884), p. 291.

[2] For. MS. 48.E.25, no. 1555. Fitzpatrick published several works which are largely anecdotal.

A comparable story about roast ducks is also found in early jest-books (K2137).[1] The Dean, fond of bringing home eccentric characters, invited 'a queer-looking old tract-dropper' to dinner. Jack was tempted to eat one of the two ducks roasted for dinner, and 'he never cried whack until he had it finished'. Naturally he then ate the second. To save himself, he told the visitor that he was 'a terrible foolish man to come home with the mad Dane. . . . He'll castrate you. He'll cut the testicles out of you. He has a room above full of them.' The visitor didn't believe him until the Dean came into the room sharpening his carving-knife. When the man fled from the house, Jack told the Dean that the tract-dropper had stolen the two ducks. ' "Give me one of them," roared the Dean, starting after him with the knife in his hand. "Oh no, oh no," cried the poor fellow, "I want the two of them myself." '

Like other folk heroes, Jack is generally able to get out of what-ever pickle he falls into or, if he gets his come-uppance, as he does in the 'dirty boots' story, he may still manage to give back as good as he gets. When he is reproved for neglecting to clean Swift's boots, he says, 'It's no use cleaning them; they'll only be dirty tomorrow. Next morning, when it is past breakfast-time and Jack announces that he is hungry, the Dean says, 'It's no use eating breakfast; you'll only be hungry tomorrow.'[2] This anecdote is often combined with another, told as its sequel. The Dean and his servant continue their journey, Swift reading his prayer-book, until they meet a man who asks them where they are going. 'To heaven,' says Jack; 'he's praying and I'm fasting.'[3] (In one version, MS. 98, Swift is so em-barrassed by Jack's reply that he says, 'Whist! or ye'll make a show

---

[1] MS. 482, pp. 291–3. This anecdote appeared as 'The Parson and the Fowls: Or, The Maid too Cunning for her Master' in *Laugh and be Fat: Or, An Antidote against Melancholy*, 11th ed. (London, 1733), pp. 1–7.

[2] MSS. 98, pp. 344–6; 715, p. 405; 966, p. 27; S1003, p. 13. The volume numbers are given throughout in mathematical sequence; or, if there is a significant difference in versions, the example used in the text is placed first in the note. Liberties have been taken with the language only for brevity's sake. The phrasing of the original has in general been retained; quotation marks are used only when it has been transcribed exactly.

[3] MSS. 98; 166, pp. 541–2; 715; S982, pp. 56–57. Fitzpatrick reports, separately, both parts of the anecdote.

of me. I'll get your breakfast the first town we'll go into.')

This anecdote is not listed in the folklore indexes, nor have I encountered it in any early jestbook. It is, however, one of the Swift anecdotes told by Monck Berkeley in his *Literary Relics*.[1] In Berkeley's version two servants who had disputed over which one of them should clean the Dean's boots were made to go without their breakfasts. Swift overheard the response of one, 'the butler', to the stranger's question and was so delighted by it that he 'presented the fellow with a guinea'. The wild tale which Berkeley tells (on the authority of Richard Brennan, the servant in whose arms Swift is said to have died) of the child of Swift's and Stella's who sometimes dined at the Deanery does not inspire confidence in the *Literary Relics*,[2] but the 'dirty boots' anecdote may have some basis in fact. It recalls, at any rate, Sheridan's account of how Swift reacted to a dispute between the two servants who always attended him[3] as

to which of their offices it belonged to carry the spatterdashes [large over-boots] and spurs. Swift soon settled the matter, by making each of them carry one of each, and in that manner walk behind him through the streets. The blackguards of Dublin, who are remarkable for low humour, soon smoked the design, and ridiculed the fellows as they passed along in such a way as to make them quite ashamed of themselves, and willing to come to a compromise. But Swift, to punish them, made them continue their progress in the same way, enjoying the low jokes of the mob as they passed; till at their earnest entreaty afterwards they were allowed to take it turn about.[4]

[1] London, 1789, pp. liv–lv.

[2] It is sad to see this tale turn up again in Sybil Le Brocquy's *Cadenus* (Dublin, 1962), where the child is Vanessa's rather than Stella's.

[3] The two servants are substantiated by several contemporary poems, e.g.:

No more shall we view our darling Dean
Between his servants, ride along the Plain

in *A New Collection of Poems on Several Occasions*, p. 7.

[4] *The Life of the Reverend Dr. Jonathan Swift* (London, 1784), p. 441. The spatterdashes or gambadoes which Swift wore to enable him to ride when he was lame are often mentioned in his 1732 letters. See F. E. Ball (ed.), *The Correspondence of Jonathan Swift* (London, 1910–14), vol. IV, pp. 313, 315, 336, 340.

Jack is left master of the field in two other frequently told tales, both versions of 'the biter bit'. On their travels Swift and his servant sleep in the same bed, the boy at the Dean's feet. In the morning, when Swift wakes, he says with humorous superiority, 'Well, how are you at my feet?' 'Oh, I am well, and how are you at my feet?' In one account Swift is so pleased by the wit and independence of the answer that he tells the boy to come up to him. Jack does so and 'lies beside him just as if he had been his own son'.[1]

In another inn the Dean has his dinner upstairs and, when he has finished, takes down the plate of bones to his servant Paddy. Seeing the disgusted look on Paddy's face, he says, 'The nearer the bone, the sweeter the meat.' Paddy then catches the Dean's horses and ties them with their noses to a rock. The Dean is enraged when he sees them, but Paddy assures him that 'The nearer the rock, the sweeter the grass.'[2]

The servant instructs again in an anecdote which Kennedy prints as 'A Lesson in Manners and Generosity'.[3] A messenger boy sent by his master with a present of fish for the Dean walks into the house, places the parcel on the table, and is about to leave when the Dean says, 'You are very rude; sit there until I show you how you should have behaved.' Swift leaves the room, knocks loudly, enters when he is bid, and presents the fish to the boy with a polite speech. The boy makes an equally pretty reply and concludes it, to the Dean's discomfiture, with 'And here's a half crown for you.' In a variant (MS. 600), the Dean does not receive the lesson but instead instructs Jack before sending him on an errand to a stingy man who never gives anything to messenger boys. Instructed and instructing, Jack comes away with five shillings.

[1] MSS. 963, p. 81; S167, p. 402; S642, p. 234; 779, p. 431; 966, p. 26.

[2] MSS. 166, pp. 543–4; S167, pp. 402–3; 275, pp. 677–9; 820, pp. 446–7.

[3] MSS. S1004, pp. 25–26; 600, pp. 388–9; and *The Banks of the Boro*, p. 12. Cf. the anecdote of how a poor poet instructed Augustus in generosity and obtained money from him by a similar method, in G. M.'s *Delight and Pastime: Or, Pleasant Diversion for both Sexes* (London, 1697), pp. 74–75.

A story which Yeats cited and apparently accepted as genuine[1] tells of Swift's custom, when he is away from home — the setting is usually London, once Tralee — of sending his servant out to find him a woman for the night. The servant brings him, for economy's or the joke's sake, an old and ugly woman. Sometimes she is black; in one version (MS. 166) she has a wooden leg. When Swift wakes up, or sobers up, in the morning and discovers her defects (as an Irish version has it, sees the 'article' in his bed), he fires the boy in a fury. When Jack is asked why he has been fired, his answer is that the Dean sent him out to get a chicken and he brought him an old hen. It is often the Dean's wife who questions him. He says, 'Well, I'll tell you; the other evening the Dean sent me out to get a pullet for him, and 'twas an ould hen I brought him and the next morning he gave me the sack.' When Swift comes home, she pleads for Jack, protesting that he couldn't be expected to know anything about fowl. The Dean is so delighted when he learns what Jack has told her that he not only takes him on again but rewards him and tells him that he can be his coachman for life. He 'wouldn't part with Jack for anything after that'.

The story of the lamenting woman, related to 'the Ephesian Matron' of the jestbooks (K2213.1),[2] portrays Swift as the defender of womanly virtue and fidelity — until his boy proves him wrong. In one highly embroidered account the Dean and, here, Seán argue at length about the nature of women. Swift says that if it weren't for the women, the men would go completely mad, that they would

---

[1] 'The refusal to see Stella when there was no third person present suggests a man that dreaded temptation; nor is it [the theory that Swift has a 'physical defect'] compatible with those stories still current among our country people of Swift sending his servant out to fetch a woman, and dismissing that servant when he woke to find a black woman at his side.' (*Wheels and Butterflies*, p. 24). MSS. 600, pp. 395–7; S.167, pp. 403–4; 98, p. 348; 166, pp. 549–51; 306, pp. 70–72; 480, p. 406; 820, pp. 445–6; 963, pp. 82–90. A crude version of this anecdote appeared in *Teagueland Jests, Or, Bogg-Witticisms* (London, 1690), 97–98.

[2] MSS. 11, p. 252; 8, pp. 330–1; 98, pp. 346–8; S329, pp. 63–64; 480, p. 408; 966, p. 26. William Dunkin, Swift's young protégé, wrote a lengthy version in verse, 'The Ephesian Matron, From Petronius Arbiter'. He says that Swift read his poem 'with some glee'. *The Poetical Works of the Late William Dunkin* (London, 1774), vol. II, p. 412.

have no pity and no conscience, that they would not even wear clothes and would rush about like wild beasts, but that, because of the company and counsel of women, they remain in a reasonable state. Seán, on the other hand, blames Eve for all human ills, says that all women are like her, and that men would never fight if it weren't for women. As they talk they see a woman in mourning in a churchyard, weeping at the grave of her husband. They see her there, always lamenting, for three days in succession; and the Dean now glares at Seán when he doubts woman's virtue. When Seán says that she would marry again tomorrow if she could find a man, they make a bet. Seán goes to her — he may dishevel his hair and lament for his dead wife a while first, ending by comparing their situations, or he may merely ask her directly, saying that there is a priest on the road who will marry them. The Dean is sadly shocked and horrified when she accepts him; sometimes he is in such a rage that he seizes his coachwhip to beat them. But Seán always collects his bet — and leaves the lady.

In a simple tale of successful laziness the boy, sent to cut bracken, fools his master by carrying the same bundle of bracken back and forth without troubling to cut more (cf. W11).[1] An even simpler bit of repartee has no doubt gratified many a schoolboy's need for profanity: 'Dane Swift and the boy, they were going on a journey one time, and before they left home the boy wrote DDDD on the door, four D's. "What's the meaning of those four D's?" "Don't you know it?" "I'm sure I do not." "The Devil Double Damn Dane Swift." '[2]

It is well to stop here briefly, since these stories are among those found most frequently in the total collection and are also of a distinct folk type. They are all 'success' stories, with the servant victorious over the master through mother-wit. With the possible exception of the 'dirty boots' story, they have no actual biographical basis, but have merely become attached to a name associated with wit, the point being that a clever master has a servant even cleverer than himself. The Dean is little more than straight man, except for the important role of opening his purse. His rewarding of wit with

<hr>

[1] MS. 715, p. 407.   [2] MS. 820, p. 447.

cash is of course essential to the story pattern; and it is interesting in view of the conflicting tradition of Swift's avarice that this pattern was established as early as 1752, in the anecdotes attached to the *Memoirs of the Life and Writings of Jonathan Swift*.[1]

Of other particulars included in these anecdotes, only two have any known factual basis: the tradition that Swift was unkind to his servants, and his remarks that the company of woman is civilising.[2] His behaviour to his servants was argued by the early biographers. Orrery reported that 'To his domestics he was passionate and churlish', and Delany replied that he was 'churlish only in appearance' and 'in truth, one of the best masters in the world'.[3] The many evidences of Swift's kindness do not need re-collecting; but in spite of authenticated reports of his politeness, his manner to his intimates, especially in his old age, was sometimes rough, and there is sufficient reason for suspecting that he was a difficult master. Acheson's son, Lord Gosford, told a story which is at least chilling: Swift, who had brought a lobster to his hostess, was so infuriated when he learned at dinner that a servant had cracked the lobster's claws between the hinges of a door that he 'flew into a violent Passion and snatcht up a Whip, with which he gave the younker some Stripes. And he was so much displeased that he did not recover his temper the whole Evening.'[4]

[1] London, 1752, pp. 116–19. It has never been noticed that these *Memoirs* are a reworked piracy of Orrery's *Remarks*. The anecdotes, however, are additional and of unusual interest. The *Memoirs* are, I believe, for reasons unnecessary to summarize here, the product of Henry Jones, 'the Bricklayer' (1721–70). The 'author' is clearly an Irishman, with some direct knowledge of Swift. Three of the anecdotes mention the Dean's habit of rewarding wit: e.g. 'he rewarded the fellow's humour with a shilling'.

[2] Swift speaks in several places of the need for women in society and of their civilizing influence. See, for example, Davis (ed.), *Prose Works*, vol. IV, p. 95.

[3] Orrery's *Remarks*, 3rd ed. (London, 1752), p. 146; Delany's *Observations upon Lord Orrery's Remarks* (London, 1754), p. 185. Berwick also replied (p. 25) to the charge in the *Edinburgh Review*, vol. XXVII (1816), pp. 1–58, that Swift 'in hiring servants always chose to insult them, by inquiring into their qualifications for some filthy and degrading office'.

[4] 'Anecdotes of Dean Swift told by Lord Gosford, 1790' (B.M. Egerton MS. 201, fo. 91); printed in Ball (ed.), *Correspondence*, vol. V, p. 454.

It is noteworthy that of all the early stories about Swift's servants which have been repeated in biography after biography — such as his instructing 'Sweetheart' to take the joint back and 'do it less', his promotion of his butler Robert Blakeley to verger, and his epitaph for the beloved Saunders — not one is encountered in oral tradition. Jack is, of course, to be taken as a 'real' name no more than Paddy; but perhaps it is worth recalling that the authenticated names of Swift's servants were John, Patrick, Hugh, Ned, William, Tom, Robert, Archy, and Saunders (Alexander McGee), as well as Richard Brennan, Henry Land (his butler), and Mrs. ('Walpole') Brent, his housekeeper.[1]

Although a wife (and child) are conferred on Swift in some anecdotes, no hint of familiarity with the problem which has plagued his biographers — whether he was actually married to Stella — appears in any one. Yeats's apparent acceptance of the story of promiscuity is hardly more astonishing than the other sexual charges, ranging through incest, homosexuality, impotence, and venereal disease, brought against Swift. His friends and his enemies have fathered on him several children. Monck Berkeley's account of the child 'commonly reported to be the Dean's son by Mrs. Johnson' (p. xxxvi) has already been mentioned. O'Donoghue was, I believe, the first to record the tradition that the Rev. William Pilkington was Swift's son by Mrs. Pilkington, and that he looked remarkably like the Dean and had his satirical gifts.[2] The belief is maintained among the Homrighs living in the United States that they are the descendants of a child of Swift's by Vanessa.[3] A child by Rebecca Dingley is still to be produced.

Another group of stories falls into the classification of hiring a

[1] See For. MS. 44.D.5, which contains Forster's summary of Swift's account books; Ball (ed.), *Correspondence*, vol. III, p. 146; and Hugh Jackson Lawlor, *The Fasti of St. Patrick's* (Dundalk, 1930). Perhaps it is worth noting in connection with the well-known Robert Blakeley story that Blakeley was made verger on 16 Dec. 1725, although no mention is made of his being Swift's butler. Henry Land, however, sexton for thirty-eight years, is so described (Lawlor, pp. 259–61). The Robert in Swift's service in 1722 was, according to Ball, his valet.

[2] *The Poets of Ireland* (Dublin, 1912).

[3] Private letter in my possession.

servant, generally a coachman; and here the 'Male Cinderella' motif emerges more clearly, or, to put it another way, Swift unerringly chooses the leaden casket rather than the silver or gold.

These anecdotes often set out to tell how the Dean first came to employ Jack. In one account of their first meeting Jack was fishing in the river when the Dean came by and asked what he was fishing for. 'The devil,' said Jack. 'What bait do you use?' At the reply 'A minister' (jestbooks are likely to say 'an exciseman'), the Dean asked the boy to work for him and came to prefer his company to that of others.[1]

Having advertised for a man servant, Swift asked the three who answered to repeat after him, 'Lamb of God, who takest away the sins of the world, have mercy on us', and promised to keep whoever 'would have that off in a year's time'. When the time came, two repeated it exactly, but the third, Roger, said ' " Sheep of God. . . ." "Moonshine," said the Dean, "that's not what I told you"; "but," said Roger, "what was a lamb a year ago, is a sheep now." ' And the Dean kept Roger for his wit.[2]

The name Roger may possibly be a reminiscence of Roger Cox, Swift's clerk at Laracor. Although the 'dearly beloved Roger' story, first told by Orrery, does not appear in the IFC collection, one manuscript contains a jest which appeared in *Swiftiana* (1804) and in earlier collections: Roger has been told by Swift to bid a certain sum for a pen of poultry but is outbid by a man named Hatch. Roger tells the Dean, 'They're useless, they're all going to Hatch.'[3]

In another tale of applications for employment, Swift questions twenty boys about their abilities, sowing, reaping, etc. All say that they can do great things. When it is Jack's turn, he, 'the small chap', says, 'Oh, sir, it is not necessary for me to do anything. These men have done everything already.'[4]

In other stories the point is giving the prudent rather than the witty answer. The applicants who answer Swift's advertisement for

[1] MSS. 966, p. 26; 480, p. 404. Abel Boyer's *The Wise and Ingenious Companion* (London, 1700), p. 191, contains this jest, with an exciseman used as bait.

[2] MSS. 1272, pp. 103–5; 600, p. 398.

[3] MS. 1272, p. 105; *Swiftiana* (London, 1804), vol. I, pp. 8–9.

[4] MSS. 715, pp. 405–7; 166, pp. 536–7.

a coachman vie with each other in boasting of their driving skill. One says, 'I could gallop a coach and six through a wood'; another, 'I could drive a coach and six within an inch of the edge of a cliff.' Jack says that he would prefer to drive slowly through the wood and to stay farther away from the cliff. He is of course hired.[1] The boasts may concern how close the driver can come to another coach (MS. S167); and truth rather than prudence is the issue in a naïver version: Swift, wanting a safe coachman for his family, hires an applicant and sends him out driving with his wife and child. He then dresses up in a white sheet and gets in front of the horses. The carriage is wrecked; and when the coachman reports that a big black monster came up out of the river and would have killed the woman and child except for him, he is fired for telling lies (MS. 600).

Sometimes the boy is hired out of pleasure in his laziness as well as his wit. In a story placed near Portrane Castle, Donabate, where 'Swift used to visit his wife Stella', he is walking through the fields when he sees a boy lying lazily along a fence, and stops to ask him the way to a certain place. The boy stretches out his leg and points to the direction with the toe of his boot (W111.53). The Dean smiles and says that he will give him a shilling if he can do anything lazier than that. The boy says, 'Put the shilling in my pocket,' and the Dean laughs with pleasure. When he asks which way the wind is blowing and is told 'Sou' southwest', he says he will give the boy another shilling if he can add anything to that; and the boy promptly says, 'Sou' southwest, sir.' The Dean again laughs heartily and takes the boy into his household.[2]

The perennial jokebook favourite about repairing the roof (J2171.2.1) appears once. The boy about to be hired says that he cannot go to be the Dean's servant until he repairs his mother's roof. 'Why don't you repair it now?' says the Dean. 'It's a fine day.' 'But,' says the boy, 'it doesn't need to be repaired on a fine day.'[3]

In a few tales the boy is the foolish ne'er-do-well, familiar in *Märchen*, epic, and romance. The son of a poor widow, Jack is thought to be a kind of idiot. When he tells his mother that he is

---

[1] MSS. S.329, p. 63; II, p. 250; S167, p. 402; 600, pp. 384–5.
[2] MS. S789, pp. 303–4.   [3] MS. 480, p. 412.

going to apply for the job of coachman, she says that he knows nothing about driving. Undaunted, he applies anyhow and makes foolish answers to Swift's questions. ' "What can you do?" says the Dane. "I can do nothing." "Begor, you're a quare fellow." ' After more talk the Dean instructs him to come to him tomorrow, but he must be 'neither dressed nor undressed, nor riding, nor walking' (H1053.1; H1054.1).[1] Jack says all right and goes home to his mother. They have a big pocán (buck goat) at home, and the next day Jack puts a halter on the pocán and a bag on his back. 'Then he got a big fishing net; and he stripped off mother-naked, and he put the net around him. He'd get upon the pocán; and the pocán would carry him a bit. Then he'd get down and walk for a while, till the pocán would get his wind and be able to carry him a bit.' The Dean is delighted by Jack's solution and hires him.

Another tale of the paradoxical or impossible demand is told by the same teller. Locking the boy in a kitchen with no meat in it, the Dean tells him that he must get meat somewhere and prepare it for breakfast. The boy cuts off the tops of the Dean's boots, boils them, and prepares them as if they were tripe. Swift is, as always, delighted; but when he learns that Jack has boiled his boot-tops, he says that he must be punished and is to get no breakfast until they meet water running against the hill. When the horses stop to drink from a running stream, Jack says that here is water running against the hill. The Dean agrees that he has won his breakfast and gives him five shillings (391–3).

Two other variants of the King and the Peasant's Son motif add a touch of the mysterious and of the riddle to the comic. In these the boy is the son of Swift's tenant. The tenant, who is a bit short of the total sum, comes to pay his rent. When the Dean won't accept it, he goes and starts drinking up what he has. Regretting his decision, the Dean goes to the tenant's house and finds the son there. To his three questions (What is your father doing? Your mother? Your sister?), the boy gives three mysterious answers: the father is adding to the

---

[1] MS. 600, pp. 386–8. These motifs appear in early Irish literature. See Tom Peete Cross, *Motif-Index of Early Irish Literature* (Bloomington, n.d.).

evil, the mother is sieving the meal they ate last year, and the sister is lamenting last year's laughter (H583.2.1; H583.4.2; H583.5). That is, the father is drinking; the mother is sifting borrowed meal, since their own supply is exhausted; and the sister is crying in childbirth. The Dean is so taken with the boy that he offers him five pounds then and five pounds when they next meet. The boy promptly runs out the back door and meets him at the corner. The Dean obtains permission from the father to take the boy on as his servant.[1]

Another teller makes Jack's method of getting the money in hand even more direct. When the Dean, impressed by his wit, says, 'I'll give you money the next time I see you,' he says, 'Why not give it to me now?' and so gets the money and a job.[2]

The Dean receives another riddling reply when the boy tells him that his brother is fowling and everything he catches he throws away and what he does not catch he keeps (H583.3).[3] The answer to the riddle is that he is catching lice.

Two other tales told by the teller of the pocán and the boot-tops stories show Jack saving Swift from the humiliation of losing his rash bets. Both stories present Swift as a great drinker. He could outdrink his friends because he 'would swallow about a quarter pound of butter before he'd start drinking. All the drink used to float on top of that, and it wouldn't go to his head at all.' Swift bets that he can drink the Liffey dry but becomes desperate when the testing day approaches. Jack tells him to say that if they'll 'stop the ocean from coming in you'll do it' (H704; cf. H951).[4]

He makes another rash bet with a minister — Swift is not identified as one himself — who 'bet him an awful amount of money that he'd ask him three questions, and that he wouldn't [be able to] answer them'. When Swift again gets worried, the boy says he'll take his place. The questions are: (1) What is the centre of Europe? (2) [The teller forgets the second.] (3) What am I worth? Jack makes a mark on the ground and says, 'Well, if yous are not able to

[1] MSS. 1112, p. 269; 166, p. 536.
[2] MS. 98, p. 344.
[3] MS. 166, p. 536. Also found in early Irish literature; see Cross.
[4] MS. 600, pp. 399–400. For analogues see F. J. Child, *English and Scottish Popular Ballads* (Boston, 1882), vol. 1, pp. 10 ff.

tell me, that must be it' (H681.3.1). To the third he says, 'Our
Saviour was sold for thirty pieces of silver, and you're surely not
near as good a man as Him' (H711.1).[1]

At times Jack is all fool, at others all rogue. In a tale which re-
joices in nonsense names (X951),[2] he is completely unteachable,
unable to remember anything at all. The Dean, presumably in
despair, has told him to call the cat Whitehead, the fire Hot
Gogglyorum, the fence Highmount, water Salvation, and the Dean's
slippers Farting Clappers. One morning Jack runs to the Dean's
chamber and, in words at least as startling as Macaulay's first ones,
shouts, 'Arise, Master. Put on your Farting Clappers. Whiteface
[*sic*] leaped into Gogglyorum, and he went from that to Highmount,
and only for Salvation all would be lost.'

A story which has little point beyond its pleasure in outraged
propriety (cf. K1252)[3] is set in the Dean's garden. The Dean has a
party, and Jack is showing the guests the flowers. He has earlier,
however, 'made a s - - -' in the garden and put his hat over it for
fear he would forget it. Two grand ladies come up to him asking
questions. He tells them there is a strange flower in the garden, takes
them to see it, and raises the hat. ' "This," he says, "is the strangest
flower in the garden." So, begor, they told him to go away.'

The Dean has no active role in two other rogue tales. In one he
has left Jack to pay the bill at an inn, but without money to pay it.
Declaring he can prove that there are three different kinds of drink
in a barrel of porter, Jack makes the innkeeper helpless by getting
him to use two fingers and his tongue to stop the holes. Swift has
only to extricate the innkeeper from his predicament.[4]

---

[1] MS. 600, pp. 398–9. Jack the Fool and a bishop fill Jack and the Dean's
roles in a version of 'The Three Questions' reported by Delargy; for this
and other versions see *Béaloideas, The Journal of the Folklore of Ireland
Society*, vol. II (1929–30), pp. 382, 197. Cf. the Cobbler and the Chaplain
in *England's Jests Refin'd and Improved*, quoted by Ashton, p. 173: and
Vernam Hull and Archer Taylor, *A Collection of Irish Riddles* (Berkeley,
1955), p. 75.

[2] MS. 600, p. 395.

[3] MS. 98, pp. 348–50.

[4] MS. 715, p. 408.

In another Jack defends his master's or perhaps his horses' honour by a scurvy trick (J1169.5). The Dean always lets his horses' manes and tails grow long, but at a big party other coachmen cut off their manes and tails (or ears). Jack then cuts the sides (or mouths) of the other horses, and announces that the Dean's horses have eaten one another's manes and tails and that the other horses have split their sides laughing at them.[1] In one version (MS. 166) Jack succeeds in being well paid for his trick. One of the gentlemen says that he will give fifty pounds to whoever can inform him how it all happened. Jack agrees to tell if the man will give him the money first. He gets the money and gives the familiar explanation.

Jack's customary role is taken over by an outsider in a splendid encounter with regional pride. Swift was making a circuit of Munster to learn what kind of people the Munster people were. The Kerry people knew that he was coming and sent a very intelligent man, Aodagán O'Rahille, out to meet him (cf. J31.1).[2] 'Aodagán was dressed in the garb of a cowboy with two dogs with him. "You have a lot of bullocks," says the Dane to Aodagán. "Who made them?" "Oh," says Aodagán, " 'twas God made um but my father made bullocks of um." '

Aodagán then turned toward the cows, spoke Latin to some, Greek to others, and

some very high terms of Old Irish to some more of them. When the Dane heard that, he turned to his boy and he says: ' 'Tis no use for us to go any further. The cowboys here can speak different languages.' 'My good man,' says he to Aodagán, 'do you drink?' 'Ah,' says Aodagán, 'I drink from a gentleman.' So on they went and went to the ale house anyway, and the Dane called for one pint of porter and he left it on the counter and the Dane turned to Aodagán and says, 'What does that look like?' says he. 'Oh dear,' says Aodagán, 'it looks black and muddy like the Reformation.'

' 'Tis no use for us,' says the Dane, 'trying to compete with them,' turning on his heel and going away.

[1] MSS. 600, pp. 390–1; 166, p. 536; S451, p. 410; S460, pp. 104–5; 1112, pp. 273–4.
[2] MS. 820, pp. 444–5. Swift did travel in Munster in 1723, at the time of Vanessa's death. R. Wyse Jackson gives some account in 'Swift's Munster Tour', *Swift and His Circle* (Dublin, 1945), pp. 60–71.

Rostrevor, County Down, is complimented in a remark usually
ascribed to Lady Carteret in the jestbooks, but here to the Dean's
sister, who is visiting him. When she remarks that the Rostrevor air
is very bracing, ' "Oh, for heaven's sake," says he to her, "don't
say that when you get back to England, or they'll tax it." '[1]

Swift also usurps Jack's role in another anecdote of religious
conflict. Underneath a notice that 'No Catholic Need Apply' (or
'No Papishes Wanted') Swift writes:

> Whoever wrote this wrote it well,
> For the same is wrote on the Gates of Hell.

In the accepted version, however, it is the servant, not the Dean,
who writes the couplet.[2]

A final anecdote, which omits Jack entirely, is a fitting end for
the collection; it shows Swift becoming a Catholic on his deathbed.
When he becomes ill, he sends for a minister and says, 'I owe a debt
to a man in the town.' 'I shall bring him to you. Who is he?' 'He is
the priest of the parish.' The minister returns with the priest and
offers to witness that the debt is paid. 'You were not here when I
contracted the debts and you shall not be here when they are paid.
So please go away.' The minister listens at the door, however, and
discovers that the priest is baptizing the Dean. Very angry, he
forces his way into the room and says, 'If you recover, you will pay
for this.' 'If I recover you are finished as a minister because it was you
who brought the priest to me.'[3]

Swift was frequently charged with Catholicism, as with Jacobitism, by his political enemies; and although Swift scholarship has
rarely taken them seriously, the charges may have obtained some
credence during his lifetime, in years when his old enemy Dick
Tighe began every speech in the Irish House with, 'Mr. Speaker, A
Papist I hate, A Papist I detest.'[4] Mrs. Pilkington's recollection

---

[1] MS. 976, p. 359. Sherlock said that Voltaire told him of Swift's *bon
mot* (*Anecdotes, Bons-Mots, and Characteristic Traits, collected by the
Rev. John Adams* (Dublin, 1789), p. 15).

[2] MSS. 1112, p. 217; 976, pp. 358–9.

[3] MSS. 480, pp. 413–14; 8, p. 331. *The Banks of the Boro*, p. 214.

[4] Berwick, p. 35.

that Swift's bows to the Holy Table in church service brought forth accusations of Popery; Wilson's account of his refusal, after direct orders, to remove Ormonde's escutcheon from St. Patrick's; and the criticism of the St. Cecilia's Day concerts held in the Cathedral[1] — these show, at any rate, that the charges, for whatever motives, received considerable attention: and an unnoticed essay by Thomas Barry, 'Ragionamento Istorico sopra Il Dottore Swift, da T. B., Irlandese' (1768), considers the case with some care.[2] Barry states that many Catholics, in and outside of Ireland, are convinced that Swift was a good Catholic at heart and that he lived in seclusion in his last years so that he might die in the communion of the Church. Barry summarizes, at some length, the reasons for believing Swift a Catholic, mentioning, for example, his celibacy ('Che non mai violare voleste il suo Celibato con Stella') and his attempts to preserve and restore the ancient relics and monuments of Catholicism, such as Archbishop Tregury's gravestone ('piena di Croci sull' effigie in basso rilievo') which he restored in St. Patrick's in spite of severe criticism. Barry concludes, nevertheless, that since there is no certain evidence that Swift was a Catholic, he should probably be numbered among those who were Protestants 'per disgrazie, più che per malizia' and whom political rather than religious reasons kept

[1] *Memoirs of Mrs. Letitia Pilkington, 1712–1750, Written by Herself,* with an Introduction by Iris Barry (New York, 1928), p. 50; 'Collections Made for a History of St. Patrick's Cathedral by Wilson' (B.M. Add. MS. 43,687, fo. 62); and *A Letter To the Revd. Dr. Thomas Sheridan. Occasion'd by a Sermon Preach'd at St. Patrick's Church on St. Cæcilia's Day* (Dublin, 1731).

[2] Barry's 'Ragionamento' was written to accompany Francesco Vanneschi's translation of Hawkesworth's life of Swift, *Vita del Dottore Gionata Swift, Irlandese,* printed in Lucca, 1768. The particulars of Barry's identity are unknown. The genealogy furnished by Vanneschi relates him to the Barrys of Cork and of Santry, but stops short of his parentage. He is, in 1786, a 'Molto Reverendo Signore' of Florence; he is also the Barry mentioned in *Brookiana* as 'a clergyman then resident in Rome', whose translations Henry Brooke gave to Swift (London, 1804), vol. II, p. 46. Barry says that he knew Swift through having lived in the same parish with him for many years (p. 77). A Thomas Barry was a 'guardian [i.e. churchwarden] of Santry' in 1713 (B. W. Adams, *History and Description of Santry* (London, 1883), p. 77).

from returning to Catholicism.[1]

The jokebook anecdote of Swift's deathbed acceptance of Catholicism is, of course, far removed from a genuine tradition; and no clear belief that he was in fact a Catholic is preserved in the IFC collection, although a record from Dundalk, County Down, mentions that he was 'intent on uplifting the Catholic population'.[2] There is little else in this second group of stories that can have much factual basis except for two details: he did journey through Munster, and, as two persons mention, he did have a lame leg.[3] Swift's legs troubled him on many occasions: he suffered from a 'pitifull broken shin' in 1719,[4] and in 1732 he was able to ride only by wearing spatterdashes. The fact that Jack is often a coachman is in itself an indication, although a superfluous one, that the anecdotes are apocryphal, since Swift did not keep a coach until his last few years. Bishop Rundle's account (1742) of Swift's vow to obtain a coach when Walpole was out of office and of his refusal to re-enter it when he learned that the report of Walpole's dismissal was premature is well known. The name of his coachman is apparently not recorded.[5]

The traditions related to places associated with Swift have, as one would expect, more factual basis. The recollections of Quilca are especially vivid, whether because of the Sheridans or of Swift. Charles Farrelly, who died about 1910 at the age of 90, recalled

[1] Barry, pp. 96–97, 100. The Dean and Chapter restored Tregury's monument in 1730 (see J. Warburton and J. Whitelaw, *History of the City of Dublin* (London, 1818), vol. I, p. 482). Barry mentions that Swift restored other ancient monuments as well. The local belief that he raised the fallen Market Cross at Kells was told to John O'Donovan during his Ordnance survey, as Helen M. Roe notes in *The High Crosses of Kells* (Longford, 1959), p. 26; the tradition is also mentioned in S. Lewis's *Topographical Dictionary of Ireland* (London, 1846). Kells was 'eight Irish miles' from Quilca, and the Sheridans purchased provisions there (*The Letters of Jonathan Swift to Charles Ford*, ed. D. Nichol Smith (Oxford, 1935), p. 123).

[2] MS. 1112, p. 216.

[3] MS. S329, p. 63 (Co. Cork) mentions that he had a lame leg and walked a great deal. MS. 11, p. 252 (Co. Kerry) also records the lame leg.

[4] Nichol Smith (ed.), *Letters to Ford*, p. 82; Walter Scott, *Memoirs of Jonathan Swift* (Edinburgh, 1814), p. 470.

[5] Scott, *Memoirs*, p. 430 n.; Ball (ed.), *Correspondence*, vol. VI, p. 179, n. 2.

details quite similar to those recorded in Sheridan's biography and in John Brooke's 'A Pilgrimage to Quilca in 1852'.[1] Farrelly said that Sheridan's Quilca house was 'about four miles to the west of Mullagh and midway in the parish', that Swift was said to have been a frequent visitor, and that a group of old hawthorn-trees, nearly obliterated, overlooking the little lake and 'about eighty yards to the northwest of Carrick-a-Craw' had been known as Stella's Bower. The Dean himself was supposed to have supervised the tree-planting carried out by Dr. Sheridan, and 'the Dark Walk, a fine beech-lined avenue', still remained when the record was made. In Swift's time an 'open-air theatre' was built on the crest of the mound of Carrick-a-Craw in a ring of lime-trees. The ring had a diameter of about thirty feet, and the trees had been cut off at a height of about twelve feet from the ground. Farrelly also located at Quilca, 'in the lawn shading a cool well spring', the tree under which Swift was supposed to have performed, in a thunderstorm, the famous marriage service:

> Beneath this tree, in stormy weather,
> I bind this man and maid together,
> And none but he who rules the thunder,
> Whom God has joined, can put asunder.[2]

The story first told by Sheridan about his father's workman Doughty, who was said to have given Swift the idea of the Brobdingnagians, was told by a Rantavan farmer, although the names are altered and Lilliput is heaped upon Brobdingnag:

Long ago when Dr. Sheridan lived in Quilca he employed as

---

[1] Sheridan, pp. 400–2; *Dublin University Magazine*, vol. XL (November, 1852), pp. 509–26. The article is signed only with the initial *B*, but a letter from J. S. LeFanu to Forster identifies the author as John Brooke (For. MS. 48.E.26).

[2] MSS. S1003, pp. 11–12; 820, p. 442; S1004, p. 18. The usual version appeared in *Swiftiana*, vol. II, p. 2, and is given in Williams (ed.), *Poems*, vol. III, p. 1146; the verse has been said to have been composed near Lichfield. The earliest jestbook version I have encountered is in *The Agreeable Companion; Or, An Universal Medley* (London, 1745), p. 227, where it is attributed to Swift.

workmen some members of a family named Sheridan [*sic*]. These men were of gigantic size and the Doctor was quite proud of their appearance and took pleasure in parading them occasionally before his visitors.

Now the Brookes family [the parents of Henry Brooke, a pupil of Sheridan's] employed on their farm some men named Bradley. These happened to be the smallest men in the whole district, being almost dwarfs. Their descendants who live in Rantavan still are of very small stature.

Dr. Sheridan and Mr. Brookes were close friends and assisted each other at many farming operations. On one occasion when Dean Swift was visiting in Rantavan Dr. Sheridan happened to send some of his huge Sheridan labourers to help at Mr. Brookes' hay-making, and the Dean was so amused at the contrast, and at seeing the giant Sheridans lift up the dwarf Bradleys in their hands and place them like dolls on the haycocks that he joked and laughed with Mr. Brookes at what he had seen that day in the hayfield.

The recorder adds that it is still firmly believed in the locality that Swift got his idea of Lilliput from this incident.[1]

Sheridan also mentioned that, when his father was called away, Swift sometimes kept his school for him. County Cavan reports the tradition that Swift taught — no mention is made of Dr. Sheridan — 'in the house facing Cornahill school' and gives a remarkable portrait:

Mr. Jonathan Swift sat before the huge fire of turf with a large bowl of punch at his elbow, imbibing to his heart's content. A reading lesson was supposed to be in progress, but in reality the boys took it in turn to keep up a mumbling noise which sounded to their teacher like reading while the remainder of the class were having the times of their lives as we say nowadays. Should the supposed reading discontinue, Mr. Swift belaboured all the boys with a stout stick and thereby restored order for the time being.[2]

The only other tradition reported from County Cavan is that Swift is said to have been a visitor, on more than one occasion, at

---

[1] MS. S1003, pp. 12–13; Sheridan, p. 407.
[2] MS. S1022, pp. 330–1; Sheridan, p. 374.

Swanlinbar, which was 'much frequented by the members of the Irish Parliament, who came . . . to drink the waters'.[1]

As early as 1859 Percy Fitzgerald wrote that the Celbridge traditions had 'quite died out among the people' and that 'Even the name "Marlay" is forgotten'.[2] Marlay Abbey has become Celbridge Abbey in the IFC collections, but a few memories of Swift and Vanessa endure. The Abbey is described as the oldest inhabited house in County Kildare, the home first of VanHomrigh, then of Vanessa, Swift's fiancée, and later of Henry Grattan. The name of 'Vanessa's Bower' is said to have been changed by Sir Gerald Dease and his lady to 'St. Anthony's Chair'. ('Vanessa's Bower' has apparently become confused with 'the Dean's Chair'; Fitzgerald reported that one spot was called both 'the Dean's Chair' and 'St. Anthony's Chair'.) The estate was bought by a Major Gough in the 1930s. Mention is made of two tunnels, one going to the estate of Oakley Park and the other to Castletown, Speaker Conolly's famous house. The people are 'afraid to enter [the tunnels] on account of the rats and otters which infest them, but it is said also that there are gold vessels and other valuables to be found there'.[3]

The only ghost story in the collection is reported of Celbridge Abbey. Vanessa's ghost (her name is 'Irished' as Vennessa Vonbhombret) is said to have appeared to Jack Macan as he was crossing the rock bridge [near the rustic seat formerly called 'the Dean's Chair']. She told him not to go home by that way any more. He persisted, after still another warning, and on the third night she threw him into the river. 'It is said that if a person walks at twelve o'clock at night by the gate on the Temple Mill road he will see this noted Lady with a dog and fire coming from its mouth.' (The same manuscript tells that Swift rode out to visit Vanessa every night and that one evening he sat down by the river and wrote *The Drapier's Letters*.)[4]

[1] MS. S969, p. 6. 'Swandlingbar' is etymologized in 'On Barbarous Denominations in Ireland', Davis (ed.), *Prose Works*, vol. IV, p. 282.

[2] 'Sketches by Percy Fitzgerald of Dublin and by Anthony Stannus of Bath of Places of Swiftian Interest' (For. MS. 48.E.25 — letter to Forster).

[3] MS. S772, pp. 58, 66–78.

[4] MS. S772, pp. 96–97.

A clergyman informed another schoolchild that Swift 'officiated [during his Laracor residence] in Rathbeggan Church, which is now in ruins, and while doing so lived at a place called the Woodlands opposite the Flathouse. This house had twisted chimneys and only a portion of it now stands.'[1]

From Donabate come two accounts of Swift's residence there. One, already mentioned, says that Swift used to visit his wife Stella, 'who spent her summer holidays in Portrane Castle, Donabate'. The second locates 'Dean Swift's Castle', again described as 'the summer residence of Swift and his wife Stella' in 'a field facing the back gates of the Mental Hospital. . . . Gold was supposed to be buried here. Once men came and dug and removed a pot of gold. No matter what they did they could not fill up the hole made. It is still shown, though the castle is in ruins.'[2]

The tradition of Stella's summer residence at Portrane is undoubtedly an accurate recollection of her visits in the home of Swift's cousin, Mrs. Swanton, the daughter of Willoughby Swift. Elrington Ball mentions a castle 'in which the Swantons are said to have resided' and a hospital built nearby in recent years.[3] Interest in Swift at Portrane and Donabate may have been greater because of Matthew Pilkington, who was vicar of Donabate from 1741 until his death in 1784, and because of Lady Acheson, the last occupant of the Castle.[4]

Recollections of Swift's works are scanty and are often doubtful attributions as well. Some of them, like the marriage service already mentioned, were frequently reprinted in the mid-eighteenth-century jestbooks, where they are described as the Dean's extemporaneous compositions. The epigrams which he and Carteret are supposed to have exchanged in Dublin Castle appear in one manuscript, without

[1] MS. S687, p. 327.

[2] MS. S789, pp. 303, 321.

[3] Ball (ed.), *Correspondence*, vol. IV, pp. 456–7.

[4] The date of Pilkington's collation has not been known, but the information is given in 'Extracts from the Register of the Diocese of Dublin' (in the hand of the Rev. John Lyon) found in manuscripts preserved in the safe at the Archbishop of Dublin's Registry and compiled by the Rev. Canon J. L. Robinson, 1945 — on loan to Trinity College. Lewis records Lady Acheson's residence in the castle.

Carteret's name, and with the explanation that they were written in chalk on the wall of a room of the Castle.[1]

Another couplet, which appears in various forms in four manuscripts, is based on the incident commemorated by Sheridan's *Intelligencer*, no. 11, and was first printed, I believe, by Scott, apparently from oral tradition. The 'Squire Wether' of the *Intelligencer* was Abel Ram, of Gorey, whose coachman forced Swift and Sheridan into a ditch. As he rose to his feet, Swift is supposed to have recited lines similar to these:

> England's pride [or dread] and Ireland's glory
> Was thrown in the ditch by the Ram of Gorey.[2]

The accompanying story varies considerably from Sheridan's indignant account and from one version to another. In one manuscript (MS. 1272) Ram is only a ram. Another (MS. S891) traces the genealogy of the Rams and says that the Dean, a friend of the family, was on his way to the spa at Tubberneering when the collision occurred. Ram invited him home to dinner and

with a view of having a good joke at the expense of the famous wit . . . gave orders that rabbit and rabbit alone should be served at the meal. The Dean made no comment on this during the meal nor gave the slightest sign that anything beyond the ordinary was occurring. However at the conclusion when asked to say grace he changed the usual form and substituted the following:

> We had rabbits young and rabbits old,
> We had rabbits hot and rabbits cold,
> We had rabbits tender and rabbits tough,
> We thank Thee, Lord, we had rabbits enough.

Here is a good example of the accretion around an actual incident. The couplet ascribed to Swift has no authority, and the extempore

---

[1] MS. 1272, pp. 104–5; Williams (ed.), *Poems*, vol. 11, p. 368. It has not been noted that the first attribution of these epigrams to Swift and Carteret was in the *Dublin Intelligencer*, 18 Feb. 1725. They were much reprinted.

[2] MSS. 820, 441; S823, p. 158; S891, pp. 6–7; 1272, p. 104. See also F. Geoghegan's letter in Ball (ed.), *Correspondence*, vol. IV, p. 63; and Scott, *Memoirs*, p. 368.

grace is a late attribution. The anecdote is told in an 1814 jestbook of a 'lord of a certain manor' and the curate of the parish.[1]

Two other extempore poems are claimed for Swift in the IFC collection. Meeting a lawyer's funeral, he said:

> One rogue over, and four under;
> The body's goin' to the grave, an' the soul's goin' a journey;
> The divil's in law an' wants an attorney.[2]

And when asked about the characteristics of the four provinces of Ireland, he wrote:

> Leinster for seeding,
> Ulster for breeding,
> Munster for reading,
> And Connaught for stealing.[3]

A couplet which did not appear in any edition of Swift's work until it was reported by W. C. Taylor in his introduction to *Gulliver's Travels* (London, 1840) concerns the 'base Apostate Vesey' of 'The Legion Club':

> Agmondesham Vesey, out of his bounty,
> Built a fine bridge, at the cost of the county.[4]

The bridge in question, according to the same manuscript, was said to be at Lucan (where the Vesey seat was located).

---

[1] *The Festival of Wit, or Cabinet of Humour* (London, 1814), p. 76.

[2] MS. 1112, p. 215. Cf. an anecdote, widely reprinted, about Swift's severity to lawyers in an assize sermon and, on his being asked whether a clergyman could be found to preach the devil's funeral sermon, his reply that he 'would gladly be the man, for I would then give the Devil his due, as I have this day his Children' (*The Tell-Tale: or, Anecdotes Expressive of the Characters of Persons . . .* (London, 1756), vol. I, p. 12).

[3] MS. 820, p. 441. Cf. Williams (ed.), *Poems*, vol. III, p. 1072 (17), patterned on
> Beckles for a puritan, Bungley for the poor,
> Halesworth for a drunkard, and Bliborough for a whore
in John Ray, *A Collection of English Proverbs* (1670), p. 253.

[4] MS. S794, pp. 64–65; Taylor (p. xlv) does not give Vesey's name. The couplet does not appear in Williams (ed.), *Poems*. The only other printing I recall is in Walter Cox's *A Short Sketch of the Present State of the Catholic Church in the City of New York* (New York, 1819), p. 6, where Swift is said to have immortalized the Squire.

Fourteen lines of the 'Elegy on Damer' were recalled with high accuracy in County Cork,[1] and some lines from 'To Quilca, A Country House' were mingled with the ending of another 'Grace after Dinner', also of doubtful authority, printed in *Swiftiana*.[2] The most remarkable attribution in the collection is thirty-two lines which the Dean is said to have penned after a trip to Sleabh-na-Caillighe (County Meath, near Kells), where he was persuaded to go by a Mr. Winslow (or Hounslow) of Fore. The poem mentions both Finn and Caoilte. The first stanza is as follows:

> Twelve giant elks trained to the car,
> Had brought the warlike dame from far. [*sic*]
> Bengore where reigned the dreadful war
> When morning dawned, the board was spread
> With cresses, nuts, and berries, red;
> And Garvogue left her heather bed
> Black Ramor, Creide [?] and glossy Sheel,
> Send up the bream, the break, the eel
> At midday for her ample meal.[3]

The single recollection of Swift's prose, besides the association of *Gulliver* with Quilca and of *The Drapier's Letters* with Celbridge, is of the line which Swift quoted as one he had heard from 'the late Archbishop of Tuam', John Vesey: 'The Dean you know was appointed to Christ Church in Dublin, an' he only had the one congregation. Oh, he was gettin' about four hundred a year for it. But he never had more nor the one congregation. The first Sunday he went into the pulpit, y'see, he told them to burn everythin' that come from England bar her coals.'[4]

It is clear that the Swift of Irish oral tradition is very different from the Swift of the biographers. Of all the familiar anecdotes

---

[1] MS. 820, p. 443; in Williams (ed.), *Poems*, vol. I, pp. 233–4; lines 1–4, 9–12, 23–28. In Ireland the name Damer early became synonymous with great wealth.

[2] MS. 820, pp. 443 ff. See Williams (ed.), *Poems*, vol. III, p. 1034, lines 1–4, 7–8; and p. 1146, line 6. Williams does not note that the 'Grace after Dinner', attributed to Swift in *Swiftiana* (1804), appeared in *The Festival of Wit*, 16th ed. (Dublin, 1791), with no mention of Swift.

[3] MS. S1004, pp. 164–5.

[4] MS. 976, p. 358. Davis (ed.), *Prose Works*, vol. IX, p. 17.

which pyramided from Mrs. Pilkington, Orrery, Delany, Deane Swift, and Sheridan to Scott, and which have always formed a sizeable portion of the biographies, not one is found in the IFC collection. Their place is taken by older stories common to many peoples. (The substitution might well have amused the creator of Glubbdubdrib, where Gulliver discovers 'the Roguery and Ignorance of those who pretend to write Anecdotes'.)

Little of the material identifies Swift so clearly with the interests of the Irish people as does the last recollection of *A Proposal for the Universal Use of Irish Manufacture*; but throughout the collection there is hardly a grain of enmity expressed and a great deal of sympathy ('Why, they even charged their own [Protestants] sixpence each to see him when he was lyin' for death, an' the poor man astray in the head').[1] Although most of the anecdotes, like the works attributed to him, are apocryphal, and although the material demonstrates little precise knowledge of him, the total collection does indicate that Swift's impact on Ireland was considerable. A twentieth-century schoolchild may call him 'Mr. Swift', an old man may say that he lived at 112 O'Connell Street, and another may attach him to Christ's Church rather than St. Patrick's;[2] but he is still *the* Dean, and his visits to certain localities are remembered with the same jealous regard with which Johnson's visits to parts of the Hebrides are still remembered in Scotland. Although 'poor Seán' (MS. 11), the eternal and ubiquitous Jack of many nations, triumphs over him, as Brer Rabbit and Coyote triumph over their betters in two well-known Trickster cycles, the legend which emerges from the collected material does, in a curious way, preserve some of his identity. His contempt for lawyers, his distrust of Connaught, his lame leg, his obsession with walking, his beliefs about the society of women, his trip through Munster, his hatred of Vesey, his relations with Sheridan — these are small but valid details which spring from actual knowledge. Much has undoubtedly been lost ('If only I could come at all the cracks about him. An' they used to have a lot of what they

[1] MS. 1112, p. 216. Scott, *Memoirs*, gives some evidence that the servants did accept money for showing Swift to 'curious strangers' (p. 459 n.).

[2] MSS. S1022, p. 330; 8, p. 329; 976, p. 358.

called Dane Swift's sayin's,' a woman from Dundalk said in 1945) and some has been preserved by chance encounter (' 'Twas from Donal O'Leary the old teacher I heard all that').[1] Yet it is worth noting that even the jestbook anecdotes which, early and late, became attached to his name can be attached only to a great name and one renowned for wit.

The warmest tribute to him in the collection was recorded in County Kerry in 1933: He was 'a headstrong man, rough in his mind, and very cunning. People say he was honest, and a good friend to this country while he lived. He was witty and well-spoken, and his intellect and his learning and his cunning were better than that of anybody before him or since.'[2] It is an epitaph which should content either saint or sage.

[1] MSS. 1112, p. 215; 820, p. 447.
[2] MS. 11, p. 249.

RICARDO QUINTANA

A Modest Appraisal: Swift scholarship and criticism, 1945-65

M ORE than two hundred years ago Swift sailed into his rest, but he has been exciting the scholars and the critics to activity ever since. At no time has this lack of repose been more apparent than in our own period, which in the present instance we may date from 1945. Since the close of the Second World War the sheer number of books, essays, and articles which have appeared devoted to various aspects of Swift and ranging in tone and manner from the popular to the austerely scholarly — not to mention the new, authoritative editions which Swift's modern editors have been giving us — is over-whelming. The truth seems to be that something approaching a Swift Industry has been establishing itself in our midst — a minor affair, undoubtedly, in comparison with the gigantic Shakespeare Industry, but awe-inspiring nevertheless.

It is not difficult to account for this acceleration of activity, to which several obvious factors have contributed. Swift's fascination does not diminish with the years. He is as provocative, as per-plexing, as hypnotic today as he has ever been, and the judgements arrived at in our own time are as challengingly diverse as those which have been delivered in the past. That there are more readers of Swift today and far more attending critics and scholars is a statistical fact bringing us face to face with certain sociological and economic aspects of contemporary society: there are paperbacks everywhere; the reading public is being constantly enlarged, less as a result of our new leisure than of the spectacular growth of our undergraduate population; and since our modern humanists are for the most part university inhabitants, they are engaging in criticism and scholarship with a zeal that perhaps is not wholly disinterested. Yet no one who has been following the modern work on Swift can help feeling, in the end, that socio-economic explanations are inadequate to explain what has been happening. The nature of our response to a great writer — to the man himself and to his art — has been undergoing a fundamental change. Polite impressionism, no matter how polished in voice, no longer satisfies us. In every way — historically, aesthetically — we seek more exact analysis, and this we pursue along the multiple lines of enquiry now established within the field of humanistic studies, doing so with a newly released energy and enthusiasm. Simplistic answers are no longer forthcoming, but we are succeeding, nevertheless, in getting closer to the writer's art. Most of us would agree that this is as it should be — that this is the right response and the best tribute.

The present survey of Swift scholarship and criticism during the 1945–65 period is divided into two parts. The first takes in the new editions of Swift which have appeared, bibliographical items, and the principal books of scholarship and criticism. The listing given in this part is fairly comprehensive. It is intended primarily as a bibliographical record, and therefore carries with it a minimum of evaluative commentary.

The second part is concerned with the more specialised essays and articles — though the books previously mentioned are not wholly excluded — directed at particular aspects of Swift and of his work. The number of such items is so large that anything approaching a complete listing is here quite out of the question, and would moreover only interfere with the kind of discussion aimed at in this second part — a discussion of selective items, evaluating and summarizing.

Editions

Our period has been a distinguished one in respect of Swiftiana if only by reason of the new and authoritative editions of Swift which have been forthcoming. Herbert Davis's indispensable edition of *The Prose Works* (Oxford), of which four volumes were in print before 1945, is now complete save for the final, fourteenth volume, to consist of the Index. Sir Harold Williams's equally important edition of *The Poems* (Oxford, 1937) has made its appearance in a second edition (Oxford, 1958), and to this has now been added his definitive edition of the *Journal to Stella* (Oxford, 1948) and most recently his edition of *The Correspondence* (5 vols.: Oxford, 1963–1965), described as 'to some extent a reissue' of the Ball edition, but including all the items in A. Martin Freeman's *Vanessa and her Correspondence with Jonathan Swift* (London, 1921) and David Nichol Smith's *Letters of Jonathan Swift to Charles Ford* (Oxford, 1935) and based on all the available autographs and preserving the original spelling and punctuation. And happily we have been given a second edition of the authoritative Guthkelch and Smith 1920 edition of *A Tale of a Tub* (Oxford, 1958).

A few textual problems may be noted. In his *Text of 'Gulliver's Travels'* (Cambridge, 1952) Sir Harold Williams defended compellingly the authority of the 1735 Faulkner edition, and his view has been widely accepted. Whether the Faulkner version — in which Swift himself no doubt had a hand — should be used as copy text for our present-day editions is, however, another and perhaps still open question. Another problem pertains to the *Letter of Advice to a Young Poet*, which Davis (see *Prose Works*, vol. IX) has hesitated to accept as Swift's. In his as-yet unpublished doctoral dissertation, *A Quantitative Approach to the Style of Jonathan Swift* (1963), Louis T. Milic sets forth his reasons for believing that tests involving the use of an electronic computer show the *Letter* to be the definite work of Swift, with the possible exception of the first two pages, which may have been tampered with by someone else.

Of special editions there have been several: *The Art of Sinking in Poetry*, edited by Edna L. Steeves (New York, 1952), pretty certainly Pope's, but bearing closely on Swift; *An Enquiry into the Behaviour of the Queen's Last Ministry*, edited by Irvin Ehrenpreis (Bloomington, Indiana, 1956); *Polite Conversation*, with extensive — and admirable — commentary by Eric Partridge (London and New York, 1963); and *Directions to Servants*, with the amusing drawings by Joseph Low (London and New York, 1964).

For the general reader and the student there are now available numerous selections from the prose and verse, one of the most interesting being the volume prepared by the late Emile Pons — with the collaboration of Jacques and Marius Pons and Benedicte

Lilamand — with French translations of all the chosen pieces together with provocative commentary (*NRF*, 1965).

Bibliographies

The most important addition to Swift bibliography has been the revised and corrected edition, edited by Arthur H. Scouten (Philadelphia, 1963), of the 1937 Teerink *Bibliography of the Writings of Jonathan Swift*.

In addition to the standard bibliographical listings of items of Swift scholarship in the *Cambridge Bibliography of English Literature* — volume v goes through 1954 — and in the annual *PMLA* 'International Bibliographies' (available for 1956–65) as well as the annual '18th-Century Bibliographies' in *PQ*, there is Milton Voigt's *Swift and the Twentieth Century* (Detroit, 1964), a valuable and interesting critical review of Swift criticism.

Biographical Items, etc.

Many minor items of a biographical nature have appeared in the journals, but the most comprehensive new biography will, when finished, be Irvin Ehrenpreis's *Swift: The Man, his Work, and the Age*, of which only the first volume, *Mr. Swift and his Contemporaries* (London and Cambridge, Mass., 1962), has appeared to date. Embodying such facts as have thus far been established, it is a work notable for its clear, straightforward manner and its complete avoidance of sensationalism. When completed, it may well find a place beside the great nineteenth-century *Life* by Henry Craik, hitherto unchallenged as straight biography. It is a pity that there have not been more studies like R. Wyse Jackson's delightfully informal *Swift and His Circle* (Dublin, 1945).

Have any new facts of importance been uncovered? Denis Johnston's *In Search of Swift* (Dublin, London, and New York, 1959) makes highly exciting reading, but it can only be said that the startling theories it advances concerning Swift's parentage and his relationship to Stella have won no support from the leading Swift authorities of our time. Nor has Mrs. Sybil Le Brocquy's *Cadenus: A Reassessment in the Light of New Evidence of the Relationships between Swift, Stella and Vanessa* (Dublin and London, 1962) found acceptance on the part of most competent Swiftians. New facts concerning Swift's parentage and his relations with Stella and Vanessa — concerning, that is, what is still popularly referred to as 'the mystery of his life and loves' — may of course turn up, but conjectures are not to be confused with facts established through indisputable evidence.

The medical aspects have recently been discussed by two highly qualified experts, Lord Brain and T. G. Wilson, the former in an essay on 'The Illness of Dean Swift' (1952), reprinted in his *Some Reflections on Genius and Other Essays* (London, 1960), the latter in 'The Mental and Physical Health of Dean Swift' (*Medical History*, 1958) and 'Swift's Personality and Death-Masks' (*REL*, 1962). Swift suffered from Ménière's disease; he was never — not even in the terrible final years — 'insane'; and he was not a homosexual — this is the burden of the testimony. But as everyone is aware, Swift — or something called 'Swift' — is well-known to the Freudian psychoanalysts of our time. Evelyn Hardy's *The Conjured Spirit* (London, 1949) reflects this fact and has been called a Freudian biography, but it is in this respect a tame affair in comparison with Phyllis Greenacre's *Swift and Carroll: A Psychoanalytic Study of Two Lives* (New York, 1955). A most amusing summary of the things solemnly attributed to Swift by the Freudians will be found in Milton Voigt's *Swift and the Twentieth Century*. But the Freudian approach has recently been remapped by Norman O. Brown, who in his influential essay on 'The Excremental Vision', included in his *Life against Death: The Psychoanalytical Meaning of History* (London, 1959), finds the thing that has aroused most suspicion, Swift's scatology, the sign of a kind of psychic sanity which we must all attain if we hope to salvage civilization. Thus the whirligig of time.

Books of Scholarship and Criticism

(A) At least eight or nine books have appeared which treat Swift in more or less general terms: R. C. Churchill's *He Served Human Liberty* (London, 1946); Bernard Ackworth's *Swift* (London, 1947); W. van Ravesteyn's *Satyre als medicijn*; *Jonathan Swift* (Arnhem, 1951); a reprint with revisions (1953) of Ricardo Quintana's *Mind and Art of Jonathan Swift* (London and New York, 1936); Quintana's *Swift: An Introduction* (London, 1955); J. Middleton Murry's *Jonathan Swift* (London, 1954); Murry's *Swift* ('Writers and Their Work': London, 1955); Kathleen Williams's *Jonathan Swift and the Age of Compromise* (Kansas, 1958); and Nigel Dennis's *Jonathan Swift: A Short Character* (New York, 1964). Murry's full-length study of 1954 has the kind of resonance which we associate with traditional criticism of the more impressionistic order. Quintana's *Swift: An Introduction* is essentially a summary of facts. Kathleen Williams's *Age of Compromise* has had a strong influence, particularly on those younger critics who are preoccupied with Gulliver's fourth voyage. Its effective style contributes greatly to its persuasiveness, but whether its central theory, conferring on Swift the sense of compromise said to be characteristic of his time, will continue to satisfy Professor Williams herself remains to be seen. Though a practising satirist in his own right, and a very clever one, Nigel Dennis has less to say in his *Short Character* about Swift's satiric achievement than about Swift's struggles and disappointments in the world, his desire for power, and the nature of his personality, the latter established by inference from the fact that people like him are priests, teachers, celibates, and homosexuals. If Swift has been explained, surely his satiric career has not been.

(B) A more concentrated kind of criticism marks another group of books concerned, each in its own fashion, with the nature of Swift's satire. The earliest of these studies is Herbert Davis's *The Satire of Jonathan Swift* (New York, 1947), the most recent *Swift and the Satirist's Art* (Chicago, 1963), by Edward W. Rosenheim, jr., with three appearing during the 1950s: Martin Price's *Swift's Rhetorical Art: A Study in Structure and Meaning* (New Haven, Conn., 1953), John M. Bullitt's *Jonathan Swift and the Anatomy of Satire* (Cambridge, Mass., 1953), and *The Masks of Jonathan Swift* (Oxford and Cambridge, Mass., 1954), by William B. Ewald, jr.

Perhaps nothing would throw more light upon the entire subject of Swift criticism today than a detailed comparison of the above five studies with respect to their different methods and their different yields. Davis has chosen a fairly broad approach, having in mind the general reader; his observations are anything but superficial, but they do not derive from any unusual or special point of view or special analytical techniques. But by the end of the 1940s the so-called rhetorical nature of satire had begun to be emphasised, and it is Swift's rhetoric that is being examined by Price, Bullitt, and Ewald. This 'rhetoric' means different things: Price thinks of it in terms of Swift's prose style; to Bullitt it is such things as invective, diminution, the exemplum, and the satiric enthymeme; Ewald concentrates on Swift's masks or personae. In the meantime the new interest in satire — an interest which has been growing steadily in our century — has placed the satiric in a much expanded context, which takes in many elements besides the stylistic or rhetorical ones. In his interesting approach to satiric statement as such and to Swift's art Rosenheim has this wider context constantly in mind.

(C) Closely associated with the studies mentioned immediately above are several which confine themselves to a certain side of Swift, to some particular work of his, or to some special aspect of his writings. Outstanding are Miriam K. Starkman's *Swift's Satiric Learning in 'A Tale of a Tub'* (Princeton, 1950) and Philip Harth's *Swift and Anglican Rationalism: The Religious Background of 'A Tale of a Tub'* (Chicago, 1961), both of which, through perceptive scholarship, add significantly to our knowledge of the background of Swift's first major satire. The only lengthy critical work of our period devoted wholly to Swift's poetry is *The Sin of Wit: Jonathan Swift as a Poet* (New York, 1950), by Maurice Johnson, which lays to rest some of the old misapprehensions concerning Swift's verse, at the same time establishing one of the lines along which modern criticism can profitably move. The most arresting of these more specialized studies is unquestionably Ronald Paulson's *Theme and Structure in Swift's 'Tale of a Tub'* (New Haven, Conn., 1960), where modern literary analysis is exhibiting itself in its most complex state. It would, however, be unfair to suggest that Paulson has prepared an elaborate hoax, for he has succeeded — be it said most emphatically — in bringing forth the seventeenth-century vituperative tradition in which much of the *Tale* stands. Charles A. Beaumont has contributed two useful monographs: *Swift's Classical Rhetoric* (Athens, Georgia, 1961), and *Swift's Use of the Bible: A Documentation and a Study in Allusion* (Athens, Georgia, 1965).

(D) Certain of the more specialized books of recent years have been more historical than critical in emphasis. The most important of these is Louis A. Landa's *Swift and the Church of Ireland* (Oxford, 1954), which establishes once and for all the factual details of Swift's career as a churchman. Similarly, his career as an Irish patriot and statesman is the subject of *Jonathan Swift and Ireland* (Urbana, Ill., 1962), by Oliver W. Ferguson. Swift's journalistic activities during the 1710–14 period have been the subject of two studies somewhat different in manner. Michael Foot, in *The Pen and the Sword* (London, 1957), has added fresh drama to the exciting events of these years by centring his account on what he regards as a personal contest between Swift and Marlborough. Bertrand A. Goldgar, on the other hand, in *The Curse of Party: Swift's Relations with Addison and Steele* (Lincoln, Neb., 1961), is more interested in Swift's relation with his two fellow-writers. The latter study is more cautious and the better documented of the two, but *The Pen and the Sword* makes livelier reading.

(E) It remains to take note of three books containing, in each case, the essays of a single writer. In *Four Essays on 'Gulliver's Travels'* (Princeton, 1945) Arthur E. Case argued against the 1735 Faulkner edition, added something to our knowledge of the political allegories woven into *Gulliver's Travels*, and maintained, rather too dogmatically, that the chief significance of the work lies in its politico-sociological nature. Something of what Irvin Ehrenpreis has to say in *The Personality of Swift* (London and Cambridge, Mass., 1958) has been incorporated into the opening volume of his comprehensive biography, while the interpretation of the fourth voyage of *Gulliver's Travels* set forth in this earlier book of essays has been superseded by his own more recent and drastically different reading. In *Jonathan Swift: Essays on His Satire and Other Studies* (London and New York, 1964) Herbert Davis has brought together his *Stella* (New York, 1942), *The Satire of Jonathan Swift* (New York, 1947), and seven essays, all well known, of which five made their first appearance within our period.

Modern Trends in Swift Criticism

In the present section it is proposed to consider recent Swift criticism by observing the areas of its greatest concentration and by noting, within each area, the discernible trends or, in some cases, the points at issue. The books already mentioned will not be entirely excluded from the ensuing discussion, but the criticism here under review — treated of necessity in a highly selective manner — is to be found for the most part in essays and articles.

(A) Helpful bibliographical guides through these disconcertingly extensive regions of Swift criticism are the following: Donald M. Berwick's *The Reputation of Jonathan Swift: 1781–1882* (Philadelphia, 1941); *Jonathan Swift: A List of Critical Studies Published from 1895 to 1945* (New York, 1945), by Louis A. Landa and James E. Tobin, a revised, up-to-date edition of which is badly needed; the Swift items listed, as mentioned in the previous section, in the *Cambridge Bibliography of English Literature*, the *PMLA* 'International Bibliographies', and the eighteenth-century bibliographies in *PQ*; and, in expressly limited terms, Ricardo Quintana's 'Emile Pons and the Modern Study of Swift's *Tale of a Tub*' (*EA*, 1962).

The availability of this critical material sometimes presents problems. For those who do not have easy access to the complete files of the magazines and journals in which so many of these Swift items have appeared, there are several collections of recent critical essays: '*Jonathan Swift: 'Gulliver's Travels'. An Annotated Text with Critical Essays* (New York, 1961), edited by Robert A. Greenberg; *A Casebook on Gulliver Among The Houyhnhnms* (New York, 1961), edited by Milton P. Foster; *Discussions of Jonathan Swift* (Boston, 1962), edited by John Traugott; and *Swift: A Collection of Critical Essays* (New Jersey, 1964), edited by Ernest Tuveson. Also to be noted is the July 1962 issue of *REL*, largely devoted to Swift and containing five essays on him. Histories of eighteenth-century literature as a matter of course contain commentary on Swift: e.g. D. W. Jefferson's 'An Approach to Swift' in *From Dryden to Johnson* (vol. IV of *The Pelican Guide to English Literature*: London, 1957), and Bonamy Dobrée's discussion in his *English Literature in the Early Eighteenth Century: 1700–1740* (vol. VII of *The Oxford History of English Literature*: Oxford, 1959). Separate essays or chapters on Swift have found their way into many books the titles of which give no clue to this fact, examples being George Orwell's essay 'Politics *vs.* Literature: an examination of *Gulliver's Travels*', in his *Shooting an Elephant and Other Essays* (London, 1950) and in this volume, and Vivian Mercier's 'Swift and Irish Satire in the English Language', in his *Irish Comic Tradition* (Oxford, 1962). And many important essays have been contributed to the *Festschrifts* honouring such eighteenth-century scholars as David Nichol Smith (1945), George Sherburn (1949), R. F. Jones (1951), Arthur Case (1952), Alan McKillop (1963), and Leo Strauss (1964).

(B) The first area of discussion is readily distinguishable though hard to describe briefly. Here the questions that arise concern, broadly speaking, Swift's *Weltanschauung*: his views of human nature, of reason, of religion, of society. Naturally we find a wide spectrum of stated opinions as to the kind of man Swift was in these and similar respects. Are we talking about Swift the everyday person, whom we do or do not find an agreeable acquaintance, or about the ideas he entertained? When we find — if we do — that he believed in reason and order, do we interpret this against the cultural background of his period, or do we reject him on the grounds that the sooner his kind of reason and order give way to our modern imagination and change the better off our unstructured world will be? On the one hand we find George Orwell, for instance, in the essay referred to above, concluding that Swift's world view is one 'which only just passes the test of sanity'; and in his recent book on Swift Nigel Dennis tells us that the opinions he expressed on major matters 'were always ineffectual and almost un-influential'. On the other hand, more than one scholar has under-taken to show that Swift's controlling ideas belonged to a particular age and ought, in fairness, to be first considered in their context: such is the burden of J. J. Hogan's penetrating essay, 'Bicentenary of Jonathan Swift, 1667–1745' (*Studies*, 1945) and of Ricardo Quintana's book, *Swift: An Introduction*, and most recently of Kathleen Williams's 'Restoration Themes in the Major Satires of Swift' (*RES*, 1965). Many essays fall somewhere between these two poles: Arland Ussher's 'Swift and Mankind' (*Dublin Magazine*, 1947); James Gray's 'The Modernism of Jonathan Swift' (*QQ*, 1960); John A. Yunck's 'The Sceptical Faith of Jonathan Swift

(*Personalist*, 1961); and Paul West's 'Swift and Dry Religion' (*QQ*, 1963).

Scholars have likewise shown interest in other reaches of Swift's thought. Ernest Tuveson in 'Swift and the World-Makers' (*JHI*, 1950) has studied Swift's repudiation of the theories being advanced by certain of the physico-theologians of his age. Increasingly the sincerity of Swift's religion has been emphasized. Louis A. Landa, in 'Jonathan Swift and Charity' (*JEGP*, 1945), helped clear the air, and he has been followed here by Ernest Tuveson in 'Swift: The Dean as Satirist' (*UTQ*, 1953), and by James Brown in 'Swift as Moralist' (*PQ*, 1954). Swift's churchmanship is the subject of J. C. Beckett's 'Swift as an Ecclesiastical Statesman', in *Essays . . . in Honour of James Eadie Todd* (London, 1949) and in this volume. 'Swift's Historical Outlook' (*JBS*, 1965) by James W. Johnson, is an illuminating treatment of still another aspect of Swift's intellectual position.

(C) But it is to *Gulliver's Travels* that the critics of our time, old and new alike, have most frequently directed their attention, the articles devoted solely to this one work accounting for a very considerable part of all recent Swiftiana. Unfortunately, little of genuine significance seems to have emerged. Too frequently the operative assumption has been that a work of literary art stands by itself, free of its background: it is an autonomous object, and only when approached as such can it reveal its true nature. *Gulliver's Travels* has too often been discussed as though it had no background at all — none in the period, none in the rest of Swiftian satire. Quite as unfortunate has been the tendency to forget the first three voyages and to concentrate almost exclusively on the final one.

It is round the last voyage that there has raged what can be called 'the Battle of the Fourth Book'. Swift's Ancients and Moderns, his Big-Endians and Small-Endians, have in this case been replaced by the Hard and the Soft Expositors. How, briefly, are we to interpret the Houyhnhnms and their effect on Gulliver? Happily, all the important episodes in this battle, together with the names of the chief combatants and the nature of their individual exploits, have been set forth in summary more than once — the criticism of criticism coming, as it were, to the aid of the Goddess herself. One of the earlier of these summaries is to be found in 'The Fifth Voyage of Lemuel Gulliver: A Footnote' (*MP*, 1962), by Edward Rosenheim, jr. And there are several later ones: viz. 'Gulliver, Yahoos, and Critics' (*CE*, 1965–6), by Curt A. Zimansky; 'The Houyhnhnms as Menippean Horses' (*CE*, 1965–6), by W. E. Yeomans; 'The Role of the Horse in "A Voyage to the Houyhnhnms" ' (*UTQ*, 1965), by Conrad Suits; and 'Houyhnhnms Est Animal Rationale' (*JHI*, 1965), by William H. Halewood and Marvin Levich. The 'soft' interpretation seems to be peculiar to our own time. According to this view, Swift meant the Houyhnhnms to be a *reductio ad absurdum* and Gulliver to be a figure of folly for allowing himself to be brain-washed by them, the corollary being that Swift himself was essentially a non-rationalist. For a time the 'soft' line was being exploited with great enthusiasm by the younger critics. Recently, it is the 'hard' line which seems to be prevailing: Swift's adherence to rationalism, at least of the ethical variety, has been vigorously reasserted, and Gulliver's eventual plight has been seen as pointing in its own comic fashion at the human condition.

(D) The *Bickerstaff Papers*, the *Argument against Abolishing Christianity*, and *The Drapier's Letters* have all received some attention, but it is the tripartite *Tale of a Tub* which, after *Gulliver's Travels*, has called forth the greatest amount of comment. The books by Philip Harth, Miriam K. Starkman, and Ronald Paulson (see comment on p. 348) all have to do with the *Tale*, and in addition there have been a number of interesting articles. It can be said that the recent criticism of the *Tale* has proceeded along a great many more lines of enquiry — some historical, others thematic, formal, or stylistic — than has the critique of *Gulliver's Travels*. The article by Ricardo Quintana mentioned on p. 350 gives a brief survey of the work done on the *Tale* during the past forty years. Clearly, the *Tale* has now come into its own as satiric art.

It is, however, in regard to Swift's poetry that the most marked shift in opinion has occurred. Far less has been done on the verse than on *Gulliver's Travels* and *A Tale of a Tub*, but the criticism which has appeared has been generally of a high order. Maurice Johnson's *The Sin of Wit* is the only book-length study. Herbert Davis's 'Alecto's Whip' (*REL*, 1962; rptd. in his *Jonathan Swift:*

Essays on His Satire, 1964) is general in its consideration and defence, but the other articles have usually taken up single poems: ' "Rage or Raillery"; Swift's "Epistle to a Lady" and "On Poetry: A Rhapsody" ' (*HLQ*, 1960), by George P. Mayhew; 'Meaning in Swift's "Description of a City Shower" ' (*ELH*, 1960), by Brendan O Hehir; Charles Peake's 'Swift's "Satirical Elegy on a Late Famous General" ' (*REL*, 1962); Barry Slepian's 'The Ironic Intention of Swift's Verses on his Own Death' (*RES*, 1963); Peter Ohlin's 'Cadenus and Vanessa' (*SEL*, 1964); and Marshall Waingrow's 'Verses on the Death of Dr. Swift' (*SEL*, 1965).

(E) Swift's artistry in the broad sense and, more narrowly, his stylistic characteristics raise a group of related questions — questions which modern criticism has attempted to answer in a number of different ways. In his 'Irony and Conciseness in Berkeley and Swift' (*Dublin University Magazine*, 1952) Donald Davie has viewed the style and the satiric vision as co-ordinates. Louis T. Milic, in his doctoral dissertation referred to on p. 344, has subjected the style, without direct reference to the meanings it carries, to what he calls a quantitative analysis, thus revealing the structural variety and complexity and in other respects the copiousness of Swift's prose. Others have seen the persona as used by Swift to be a factor of first importance, and have shown the extent to which it controls the satiric idioms present in the particular piece. Ricardo Quintana's 'Situational Satire: A Commentary on the Method of Swift' (*UTQ*, 1948) proceeds in this direction; Ian Watt in 'The Ironic Tradition in Augustan Prose from Swift to Johnson' (in *Restoration and Augustan Prose*; Los Angeles: Clark Memorial Library, 1956) speaks of the complex problems arising 'when you have several *personae* engaged in ironic counterpoint'; and Paul Fussell, jr., in 'Speaker and Style in *A Letter of Advice To A Young Poet*' (*RES*, 1959), cautions against easy generalizations about Swift's 'own style' in view of the ventriloquial masks through which he is so often addressing us.

A slightly different angle of approach brings into prominence the rhetorical aspects of Swift's writings — in certain cases their conformity to the principles of traditional rhetoric, in others merely their measured effect upon a public audience. In his book on *Swift's*

Classical Rhetoric, Charles A. Beaumont shows how closely an ironic argument like the *Modest Proposal* follows the prescribed form of the oration. Richard I. Cook has discussed Swift's 'Tory rhetoric' in a number of articles, the most recent being 'The Audience of Swift's Tory Tracts, 1710–14' (*MLQ*, 1963).

Swift's copiousness — or copy, to use the older form — stands in amusing contrast to his repeated demands for an English style marked by 'simplicity'. He was, as Emile Pons has rightly said, a 'créateur linguistic'. His conjured spirit was for ever doing mischief with words, playing with them, inventing new ones, piling them up in overwhelming inventories. The wonderful colloquialism of his verse has finally been recognized, and in the commentary included in his edition of *Polite Conversation* Eric Partridge has called attention to the fact that this brilliant linguistic *tour de force* is, among other things, a 'superb record of literate English at the colloquial level'. Thanks largely to Swift, *simplex munditiis* did not always mean to the Augustans stylistic stiffness and unbending formality.

Swift's art is multiphasic, and not all the elements are of the stylistic order. Several writers, taking their lead from F. R. Leavis's well-known essay on 'The Irony of Swift', in *Determinations* (London, 1934) and in this volume, have sought to interpret the Swiftian vision through the Swiftian irony: so A. E. Dyson in 'Swift: The Metamorphosis of Irony' (*E&S*, 1958, rptd. in his *The Crazy Fabric*, 1965). Still another aspect has been the concern of Vivian Mercier in 'Swift and the Gaelic Tradition' (*REL*, 1962 and in this volume). But it is perhaps significant that the critical studies which seem to bring us closest to the sources of Swift's satiric energy are ones having much to say about the compositional forms through which his imagination found vent. In his essay on 'The Ironic Tradition in Augustan Prose', referred to above, Ian Watt points out the ironigenic character of understatement and abstraction as used by Swift, while John Holloway in his 'Analysis of Swift's Satire' (in his *The Charted Mirror: Literary and Critical Essays*: London, 1960) unravels a little of Swift's complexity, as he puts it, by examining Swift's figurative language, particularly his use of metaphor and complex analogy.

CLAIRE LAMONT

A Checklist of Critical and Biographical Writings on Jonathan Swift, 1945-65

The entries are arranged alphabetically, under authors, for each year. A list of the abbreviations used is given on p. xxi. I wish to acknowledge the invaluable assistance of Peter J. Schakel of Wisconsin in the compilation of this checklist.   C.L.

For Biography and Criticism before 1945 see:

Teerink, H. *A Bibliography of the Writings of Jonathan Swift.* 2nd ed. revised and corrected by Dr. H. Teerink; ed. Arthur H. Scouten. University of Pennsylvania Press, Philadelphia, 1963. Section VII: Biography and Criticism, 1709–1895, pp. 405–31.

Landa, Louis A., and Tobin, James Edward. *Jonathan Swift: a list of critical studies published from 1895 to 1945, to which is added 'Remarks on some Swift manuscripts in the United States', by Herbert Davis.* Cosmopolitan Science and Art Service Co., New York, 1945, pp. 17–62.

1945

Babcock, R. W. 'A Pilgrimage to Moor Park.' *Dalhousie Review,* XXV (1945), pp. 39–45.

Bergh, Gerhard van den. *Der Pessimismus bei Thomas Hardy, George Crabbe und Jonathan Swift.* Baumann, Menziken, 1945, pp. 247.

Case, Arthur E. *Four Essays on 'Gulliver's Travels'.* Princeton University Press, 1945, pp. ix + 133.

—— 'Swift and Sir William Temple — a Conjecture.' *MLN,* LX (1945), pp. 259–65.

Clewes, Winston. *The Violent Friends.* Appleton-Century, New

York, 1945, pp. 225. A novel based on the life of Swift.

Connolly, Cyril. 'Sterne and Swift.' *Atlantic Monthly*, CLXXV (1945), pp. 94–96.

Davies, Godfrey. 'A New Edition of Swift's *The Story of an Injured Lady*.' *HLQ*, VIII (1945), pp. 388–92.

Davis, Herbert. 'The Conciseness of Swift.' *Essays on the Eighteenth Century presented to David Nichol Smith*. Clarendon Press, Oxford, 1945, pp. 15–32.

Davis, Kathryn. 'A Note on the *Spectator 459*.' *MLN*, LX (1945), p. 274.

Friends of the Library of Trinity College, Dublin. Catalogue of the Exhibition held in the Library from October 19 to November 23, 1945, to Commemorate the Bicentenary of the Death of Jonathan Swift. Dublin University Press, 1945, pp. 16.

Gould, S. H. 'Gulliver and the Moons of Mars.' *JHI*, VI (1945), pp. 91–101.

Grennan, Margaret R. 'Lilliput and Leprecan: Gulliver and the Irish Tradition.' *ELH*, XII (1945), pp. 188–202.

[Hayward, John.] *A Catalogue of Printed Books and Manuscripts, by Jonathan Swift, D.D., Exhibited in the Old Schools in the University of Cambridge. To Commemorate the 200th Anniversary of his Death, October 19, 1745*. Cambridge University Press, 1945, pp. 45.

Hogan, J. J. 'Bicentenary of Jonathan Swift, 1667–1745.' *Studies*, XXXIV (1945), pp. 501–10.

Jackson, R. Wyse. 'Stella's Signatures.' *TLS*, 29 Dec. 1945, p. 624.

—— *Swift and his Circle: a book of essays*. Talbot Press, Dublin, 1945, pp. xii + 112.

Jonathan Swift, 1667–1745: An Exhibition of Printed Books at the University of Texas, October 19–December 31, 1945, described by Autrey Nell Wiley. University of Texas Press, Austin, 1945, pp. 48.

Kliger, Samuel. 'The Unity of *Gulliver's Travels*.' *MLQ*, VI (1945), pp. 401–15.

Landa, Louis A. 'Jonathan Swift and Charity.' *JEGP*, XLIV (1945), pp. 337–50.

—— 'Swift, the Mysteries, and Deism.' *Studies in English, 1944*. University of Texas Press, Austin, 1945, pp. 239–56.

—— and Tobin, James Edward. *Jonathan Swift: a list of critical studies published from 1895 to 1945, to which is added 'Remarks on some Swift manuscripts in the United States', by Herbert Davis.* Cosmopolitan Science and Art Service Co., New York, 1945, pp. 62.

O'Hegarty, P. S. 'Jonathan Swift: Irishman.' *Bell*, x (1945), pp. 478–83.

Scouten, A. H. 'Swift at the Moving Pictures.' *N&Q*, CLXXXVIII (1945), pp. 38–39.

'The Melancholy of Swift: Society and Solitude.' Leading article in *TLS*, 20 Oct. 1945, p. 498.

Williams, Harold. 'Deane Swift, Hawkesworth, and *The Journal to Stella.' Essays on the Eighteenth Century presented to David Nichol Smith.* Clarendon Press, Oxford, 1945, pp. 33–48.

—— 'Old Mr. Lewis.' *RES*, XXI (1945), pp. 56–57.

—— 'Swift Exhibition at Cambridge.' *TLS*, 20 Oct. 1945, p. 504.

1946

Briggs, H. E. 'Swift and Keats.' *PMLA*, LXI (1946), pp. 1101–8.

Churchill, R. C. *He Served Human Liberty: An Essay on the Genius of Jonathan Swift.* Allen and Unwin, London, 1946, pp. 56.

Jaggard, W. ' "The Cheshire Sheaf": Swift's lodging in Chester.' *N&Q*, CXC (1946), p. 18.

'Moor Park, Surrey, England: Stella's Cottage.' *Wilson Library Bulletin*, xx (1946), pp. 678–9.

Neumann, J. H. 'Eighteenth-century Linguistic Tastes as exhibited in Sheridan's Edition of Swift.' *American Speech*, XXI (1946), pp. 253–63.

Redinger, Ruby Virginia. 'Jonathan Swift, the Disenchanter.' *American Scholar*, XV (1946), pp. 221–6.

Scott-Thomas, Lois M. 'The Vocabulary of Jonathan Swift.' *Dalhousie Review*, XXV (1946), pp. 442–7.

Webb, D. A. 'Broadsides relating to Swift.' *Annual Bulletin, Friends of the Library of Trinity College, Dublin*, 1946, pp. 8–11.

Wiley, Autrey Nell. 'Jonathan Swift: a Bicentennial Exhibition.' *Library Chronicle of the University of Texas*, II (1946), pp. 17–20.

1947

Acworth, Bernard. *Swift.* Eyre and Spottiswoode, London, 1947, pp. xix + 250.

Davis, Herbert. *The Satire of Jonathan Swift.* Macmillan Co., New York, 1947, pp. 109.

Ehrenpreis, Irvin. 'Swift and Mr. John Temple.' *MLN*, LXII (1947), pp. 145–54.

—— 'Swift's Father.' *N&Q*, CXCII (1947), pp. 496–8.

Fink, Z. S. 'Political Theory in *Gulliver's Travels.*' *ELH*, XIV (1947), pp. 151–61.

Griffith, R. H. 'Swift's *Contests,* 1701: two editions.' *N&Q*, CXCII (1947), pp. 114–17.

Landa, Louis A. 'Jonathan Swift.' *English Institute Essays, 1946.* Columbia University Press, New York, 1947, pp. 20–40.

Teerink, H. 'Swift's Ordination, 1694–5.' *Dublin Magazine*, XXII, no. 2 (1947), pp. 7–9.

Ussher, Arland. 'Swift and Mankind.' *Dublin Magazine*, XXII, no. 4 (1947), pp. 7–11.

White, H. O. 'The Art of Swift.' *Hermathena*, LXIX (1947), pp. 1–8.

1948

Craig, Maurice James (ed.). *The Legacy of Swift. A Bi-Centenary Record of St. Patrick's Hospital, Dublin.* At the Sign of the Three Candles, Dublin, 1948, pp. xii + 70.

Ehrenpreis, Irvin. 'Swift's "Little Language" in the *Journal to Stella.*' *SP*, XLV (1948), pp. 80–88.

Honig, Edwin. 'Notes on Satire in Swift and Jonson.' *New Mexico Quarterly Review*, XVIII (1948), pp. 155–63.

Jacobs, M. *Jonathan Swift.* Wedding-Verlag, Berlin, 1948, pp. 239.

John Oldmixon, Reflections on Dr. Swift's Letter to Harley (1712); and Arthur Mainwaring, The British Academy (1712). With an Introduction by Louis A. Landa. (Ser. vi: *Poetry and Language,* no. 1) Augustan Reprint Society, September 1948.

Limouze, A. Sanford. 'A Note of Vergil and *The Battle of the Books.*' *PQ*, XXVII (1948), pp. 85–89.

McCullagh, R. *St. Patrick's Hospital, Dublin. Legacy of Swift.* St. Patrick's Hospital, James St., Dublin, W.5, 1948.

Mackenzie, Aline. 'Another Note on *Gulliver's Travels* (Part I, ch. iii).' *N&Q*, CXCIII (1948), pp. 533–8.

Moog, Florence. 'Gulliver was a Bad Biologist.' *Scientific American*, CLXXIX (1948), pp. 52–55.

Mundy, P. D. 'The Dryden-Swift Relationship.' *N&Q*, CXCIII (1948), pp. 470–4.

Quintana, Ricardo. 'Situational Satire: A Commentary on the Method of Swift.' *UTQ*, XVII (1948), pp. 130–6.

Sherburn, George. 'The Restoration and Eighteenth Century (1660–1789).' *A Literary History of England.* Ed. Albert C. Baugh. Appleton-Century-Crofts, New York, London, 1948, pp. 697–1108.

Swift, Jonathan. *Gulliver's Travels.* Ed. John F. Ross. Rinehart, New York, 1948, pp. xxiii + 295.

—— *Irish Tracts 1720–1723 and Sermons.* With an Introductory Essay and Notes on the Sermons by Louis A. Landa. (*The Prose Works of Jonathan Swift*, ed. Herbert Davis, vol. IX.) Blackwell, Oxford, 1948, pp. xxx + 386.

—— *Journal to Stella.* Ed. Harold Williams. Clarendon Press, Oxford, 1948, 2 vols., pp. lxii + 801.

—— *The Portable Swift.* Ed. Carl Van Doren. Viking Press, New York, 1948, pp. vi + 601.

Teerink, H. 'Swift's *Cadenus and Vanessa.*' *HLB*, II (1948), pp. 254–7.

Wiley, Autrey Nell. 'A Probable Source of the Text of Sheridan's "Inventory" as Printed in the *Cheltenham Journal.*' *N&Q*, CXCIII (1948), pp. 186–7.

[Wiley, Autrey Nell.] 'Unrecorded Printings of Thomas Sheridan's "Inventory" of Dean Swift's Goods at Laracor.' *N&Q*, CXCIII (1948), pp. 56–57.

Williams, Harold. 'Swift and Shakespeare.' *N&Q*, CXCIII (1948), pp. 194–5.

1949

Beckett, J. C. 'Swift as an Ecclesiastical Statesman.' *Essays in British and Irish History in honour of James Eadie Todd.* Ed. H. A. Cronne, T. W. Moody, and D. B. Quinn. Muller, London, 1949, pp. 135–52.

Bracher, Frederick. 'The Name "Lemuel Gulliver".' *HLQ*, XII (1949), pp. 409–13.

Case, Arthur E. 'Swift's Supposed Ingratitude toward his Uncle Godwin: a Surmise.' *Pope and his Contemporaries: essays presented to George Sherburn.* Ed. James L. Clifford and Louis A. Landa. Clarendon Press, Oxford, 1949, pp. 129–34.

Clifford, James L. 'Swift's *Mechanical Operation of the Spirit*.' Ibid. pp. 135–46.

Davis, Herbert. 'The Manuscript of Swift's Sermon on Brotherly Love.' Ibid. pp. 147–58.

Ehrenpreis, Irvin. 'Swift's *Enquiry*.' *N&Q*, CXCIV (1949), p. 360.

Elsoffer-Kamins, Louise. 'Une Imitateur original de Jonathan Swift: l'Abbé Coyer et ses *Bagatelles morales* (1745).' *Revue de littérature comparée*, XXIII (1949), pp. 469–81.

Hall, F. G. *History of the Bank of Ireland.* Hodges, Figgis, Dublin; Blackwell, Oxford, 1949. Ch. I, part iii, concerns Swift and the abortive project of 1719–21.

Hardy, Evelyn. *The Conjured Spirit — Swift.* Hogarth Press, London, 1949, pp. xii + 266.

Johnson, Maurice. 'The Ghost of Swift in "Four Quartets".' *MLN*, LXIV (1949), p. 273.

Landa, Louis A. 'Swift's Deanery Income: a new document.' *Pope and his Contemporaries: essays presented to George Sherburn.* Ed. James L. Clifford and Louis A. Landa. Clarendon Press, Oxford, 1949, pp. 159–70.

Stone, Edward. 'Swift and the Horses: Misanthropy or Comedy?' *MLQ*, X (1949), pp. 367–76.

Teerink, H. 'A Source-Book for *A Tale of a Tub* from Swift's own Library.' *Irish Book Lover*, Oct. 1949, pp. 59–62.

—— 'Swift's *Cadenus and Vanessa* again.' *HLB*, III (1949), pp. 435–6.

—— 'Swift's *Discourse ... contests ... Athens and Rome,* 1701.' *Library,* 5th ser., IV (1949), pp. 201–5.

Trevelyan, G. M. 'Jonathan Swift.' *An Autobiography and other essays.* Longmans, Green, London, 1949, pp. 206–10.

Williams, Harold. 'Swift's Early Biographers.' *Pope and his Contemporaries: essays presented to George Sherburn.* Ed. James L. Clifford and Louis A. Landa. Clarendon Press, Oxford, 1949, pp. 114–28.

1950

Ehrenpreis, Irvin. 'Lady Betty Butler to Swift.' Corr. in *TLS,* 15 Dec. 1950, p. 801.

—— 'Swift's Voyages.' *MLN,* LXV (1950), pp. 256–7.

Gogarty, Oliver St. John. 'Dean Swift as a Human Being.' *Atlantic Monthly,* Oct. 1950, pp. 54–56.

Green, David Bonnell. 'Keats, Swift, and Pliny the Elder.' *N&Q,* CXCV (1950), pp. 499–501.

Hone, Joseph M. 'The Story of the Damer Gold.' *Studies,* XXXIX (1950), pp. 419–26.

Jensen, Johannes V. *Swift og Oehlenschläger.* Gyldendal, Copenhagen, 1950, pp. 64.

Johnson, Maurice. 'A Love Song. In the Modern Taste.' *Johnsonian News Letter,* X, no. 1 (1950), pp. 4–5.

—— *The Sin of Wit: Jonathan Swift as a Poet.* Syracuse University Press, New York, 1950, pp. xvii + 145.

Joost, Nicholas. 'Gulliver and the *Free-thinker.*' *MLN,* LXV (1950), pp. 197–9.

Kermode, Frank. 'Yahoos and Houyhnhnms.' *N&Q,* CXCV (1950), pp. 317–18.

Leyburn, Ellen Douglass. 'Certain Problems of Allegorical Satire in *Gulliver's Travels.*' *HLQ,* XIII (1950), pp. 161–89.

Longe, Arthur. *The Old Night-Watchman, the Ghost of Spixworth Hall.* Cowell, Ipswich, 1950, pp. 44.

Maxwell, J. C. '*A Tale of a Tub*: a Correction.' *N&Q,* CXCV (1950), p. 249.

Memoirs of the Extraordinary Life, Works, and Discoveries of Mar-

tinus Scriblerus. Written in collaboration by the members of the Scriblerus Club: John Arbuthnot, Alexander Pope, Jonathan Swift, John Gay, Thomas Parnell, and Robert Harley, Earl of Oxford. Ed. Charles Kerby-Miller. Published for Wellesley College by Yale University Press, New Haven; Oxford University Press, London, 1950, pp. xi + 408.

Moore, John Robert. 'The Yahoos of the African Travellers.' *N&Q*, CXCV (1950), pp. 182–5.

Mundy, P. D. 'The Philpott Family: Ancestors of Jonathan Swift.' *N&Q*, CXCV (1950), pp. 314–17.

—— 'Thomas Swift, "Brother to Dean Swift".' *N & Q*, CXCV (1950), pp. 407, 481–2.

Orwell, George. 'Politics *vs.* Literature: an examination of *Gulliver's Travels.' Shooting an Elephant, and other essays*. Secker and Warburg, London, 1950, pp. 57–83.

Savage, D. S. 'Swift.' *Western Review*, XV (1950), pp. 25–36.

Starkman, Miriam Kosh. *Swift's Satire on Learning in 'A Tale of a Tub'*. Princeton University Press, 1950, pp. xix + 159.

Swift, Jonathan. *Gulliver's Travels*. Ed. George Sherburn. Harper & Brothers, New York, 1950, pp. xxx + 313.

—— *Selected Prose Works of Jonathan Swift*. Ed. John Hayward. Cresset Press, London, 1950, pp. 483.

Teerink, H. 'Swifte of Rotherham.' *N&Q*, CXCV (1950), pp. 41–42.

Tuveson, Ernest. 'Swift and the World-Makers.' *JHI*, XI (1950), pp. 54–74.

Wade, Ira O. *Voltaire's 'Micromégas': A Study in the Fusion of Science, Myth, and Art*. Princeton University Press, 1950, pp. xii + 190. Contains comparison between Voltaire and Swift.

1951

'A Book from Swift's Library.' *Bodleian Library Record*, III (1951), pp. 180–1.

Davis, Herbert. 'The Conversation of the Augustans.' *The Seventeenth Century: Studies in the History of English Thought and Literature from Bacon to Pope*, by Richard Foster Jones and others writing in his honour. Stanford University Press, 1951, pp. 181–97.

Elliott, Robert C. 'Swift's *Tale of a Tub*: an Essay in Problems of Structure.' *PMLA*, LXVI (1951), pp. 441–55.

French, David P. 'The Title of *A Tale of a Tub.*' *N&Q*, CXCVI (1951), pp. 473–4.

Hunting, Robert S. 'Gulliver among the Brobdingnagians: a Real-life Incident (?).' *N&Q*, CXCVI (1951), p. 413.

Jones, Richard Foster. 'The Background of *The Battle of the Books.*' *The Seventeenth Century: Studies in the History of English Thought and Literature from Bacon to Pope*, by Richard Foster Jones and others writing in his honour. Stanford University Press, 1951, pp. 10–40. Reprinted, abridged, from Washington University Studies, VII, Humanistic Series II (1920), pp. 99–162.

Kelling, H. D. 'Some Significant Names in *Gulliver's Travels.*' *SP*, XLVIII (1951), pp. 761–78.

Kulisheck, Clarence L. 'Hudibrastic Echoes in Swift.' *N&Q*, CXCVI (1951), p. 339.

Leyburn, Ellen Douglass. 'Swift's View of the Dutch.' *PMLA*, LXVI (1951), pp. 734–45.

Mundy, P. D. 'The Ancestry of Jonathan Swift.' *N&Q*, CXCVI (1951), pp. 381–7.

Ravesteyn, W. van. *Satyre als medicijn: Jonathan Swift*. Slaterus, Arnhem, 1951, pp. 46.

Rivers, Charles L. 'Swift and Ovid on Hypocrisy.' *N&Q*, CXCVI (1951), p. 496.

Sampson, Edward C. '*Gulliver's Travels*: Book III.' *N&Q*, CXCVI (1951), pp. 474–5.

Swift, Jonathan. *Political Tracts, 1711–1713*. (*The Prose Works of Jonathan Swift*, ed. Herbert Davis, vol. VI.) Blackwell, Oxford, 1951, pp. xxviii + 220.

—— *The History of the Four Last Years of the Queen*. With an Introduction by Harold Williams. (*The Prose Works of Jonathan Swift*, ed. Herbert Davis, vol. VII.) Blackwell, Oxford, 1951, pp. xxviii + 252.

Teerink, H. 'Swift's *Verses on the Death of Doctor Swift.*' *SB*, IV (1951), pp. 183–8.

Todd, William B. 'Another Attribution to Swift.' *PBSA*, XLV (1951), pp. 82–83.

Williams, Kathleen M. 'Gulliver's Voyage to the Houyhnhnms.' *ELH*, XVIII (1951), pp. 275–86.

Wilson, T. G. 'A Hitherto Undescribed Death-Mask of Dean Swift.' *Journal of the Royal Society of Antiquaries of Ireland*, LXXXI (1951), pp. 107–14.

1952

Boys, Richard C. (ed.). *Studies in the Literature of the Augustan Age: essays collected in honor of Arthur Ellicott Case*. Ann Arbor, Michigan. George Wahr Publishing Co., for the Augustan Reprint Society, 1952, pp. ix + 367. Reprints some essays on Swift.

Brain, Walter Russell. 'The Illness of Dean Swift.' *Irish Journal of Medical Science*, Aug.–Sept. 1952, pp. 337–46.

Burian, Orhan. 'Da Vinci and Swift.' *N&Q*, CXCVII (1952), pp. 451–2.

Calkins, Ernest Elmo. 'How Small is Lilliput?' *Atlantic Monthly*, July 1952, pp. 77–78.

Davie, Donald A. 'Irony and Conciseness in Berkeley and Swift.' *Dublin Magazine*, Oct.–Dec. 1952, pp. 20–29.

Davis, Herbert. 'Some Free Thoughts of a Tory Dean.' *Virginia Quarterly Review*, XXVIII (1952), pp. 258–72.

Ehrenpreis, Irvin. 'The Date of Swift's *Sentiments*.' *RES*, new ser., III (1952), pp. 272–4.

—— 'Swift and Satire.' *CE*, XIII (1952), pp. 309–12.

—— 'Swift on Liberty.' *JHI*, XIII (1952), pp. 131–46.

—— 'Swift's History of England.' *JEGP*, LI (1952), pp. 177–85.

Elliott, Robert C. 'Gulliver as Literary Artist.' *ELH*, XIX (1952), pp. 49–63.

Fitzgerald, Brian. *The Anglo-Irish, Three Representative Types: Cork, Ormonde, Swift*. Staples Press, London, 1952, pp. 369.

Johnson, Maurice. 'A Literary Chestnut: Dryden's "Cousin Swift".' *PMLA*, LXVII (1952), pp. 1024–34.

—— 'Swift's Renunciation of the Muse.' *N&Q*, CXCVII (1952), pp. 235–6.

Kelling, Harold D. *'Gulliver's Travels:* a Comedy of Humours.' *UTQ*, XXI (1952), pp. 362–75.

Leyburn, Ellen Douglass. 'Swift's Language Trifles.' *HLQ*, XV (1952), pp. 195–200.

Longhurst, John E. 'Fielding and Swift in Mexico.' *Modern Language Journal*, XXXVI (1952), pp. 186–7.

Moore, John Robert. 'Swift as Historian.' *SP*, XLIX (1952), pp. 583–604.

Olson, R. C. 'Swift's Use of the *Philosophical Transactions* in Section v of *A Tale of a Tub*.' *SP*, XLIX (1952), pp. 459–67.

Pons, Émile. 'Swift et Pascal: note complémentaire.' *EA*, IV (Nov. 1952), pp. 319–25.

Pope, Alexander. *The Art of Sinking in Poetry*. Ed. Edna Leake Steeves, with bibliographical notes on the last volume of the Swift–Pope *Miscellanies* by R. H. Griffith and E. L. Steeves. King's Crown Press, Columbia University, New York, 1952, pp. lxix + 6–207.

Rosenheim, Edward W., Jr. 'A "Source" for the Rope-dancing in *Gulliver's Travels*.' *PQ*, XXXI (1952), pp. 208–11.

Sherburn, George. 'The Swift–Pope *Miscellanies* of 1732.' *HLB*, VI (1952), pp. 387–90.

Stephens, John C., Jr. ' "7 Penny Papers of My Own".' *N&Q*, CXCVII (1952), pp. 139–40.

Williams, Harold. *The Text of 'Gulliver's Travels'*. (Sandars Lectures in Bibliography, 1950.) Cambridge University Press, 1952, pp. vii + 94.

1953

Block, Edward A. 'Lemuel Gulliver: Middle-class Englishman.' *MLN*, LXVIII (1953), pp. 474–7.

Bullitt, John M. *Jonathan Swift and the Anatomy of Satire: A Study of Satiric Technique*. Harvard University Press, 1953, pp. viii + 214.

Clark, Paul Odell. 'A *Gulliver* Dictionary.' *SP*, L (1953), pp. 592–624.

Davie, Donald. 'Academism and Jonathan Swift.' *Twentieth Century*, CLIV (1953), pp. 217–24.

Dearing, Vinton A. 'Jonathan Swift or William Wagstaffe?' *HLB*, VII (1953), pp. 121–30.

Ehrenpreis, Irvin. 'Swift's April Fool for a Bibliophile.' *Book Collector*, II (1953), pp. 205–8.

Ferguson, Oliver W. 'Swift, Tisdall, and *A Narrative*.' *N&Q*, CXCVIII (1953), pp. 485–6.

Johnson, Maurice. 'Swift and "the Greatest Epitaph in History".' *PMLA*, LXVIII (1953), pp. 814–27.

Landa, Louis A. ' "The Insolent Rudeness of Dr. Swift".' *MLN*, LXVIII (1953), pp. 223–6.

Moore, John R., and Johnson, Maurice. 'Dryden's "Cousin Swift".' *PMLA*, LXVIII (1953), pp. 1232–40.

O'Leary, J. J. 'Swift and Esther.' Corr. in *TLS*, 27 Nov., 1953, p. 761.

Preu, James. 'Jonathan Swift and the Common Man.' *Florida State University Studies*, XI (1953), pp. 19–24.

Price, Martin. *Swift's Rhetorical Art: A Study in Structure and Meaning. Yale Studies in English, 123.* Yale University Press, 1953, pp. viii + 117.

Quintana, Ricardo. *The Mind and Art of Jonathan Swift.* First published by the Oxford University Press in 1936. Reprinted by Methuen, with additional Notes and Bibliography, 1953, pp. xviii + 400.

Sherburn, George. 'Gibberish in 1730–1.' *N&Q*, CXCVIII (1953), pp. 160–1.

—— 'The Swift-Pope *Miscellanies* of 1732: Corrigendum.' *HLB*, VII (1953), p. 248.

Swift, Jonathan. *Political Tracts, 1713–1719.* Ed. Herbert Davis and Irvin Ehrenpreis. (*The Prose Works of Jonathan Swift*, ed. Herbert Davis, vol. VIII.) Blackwell, Oxford, 1953, pp. xl + 243.

—— *Swift on his Age: Selected Prose and Verse.* Ed. Colin J. Horne. Life, Literature, and Thought Library. Barnes and Noble, New York; Harrap, London, 1953, pp. 283.

'Thomas Tickell and Thersites.' *Bodleian Library Record*, IV (1953), p. 291.

Tuveson, Ernest. 'Swift: the Dean as Satirist.' *UTQ*, XXII (1953), pp. 368–75.

Williams, Harold. *'Gulliver's Travels.'* Corr. in *TLS*, 9 Jan., 1953, p. 25.

Yost, George, Jr. 'Well-filled Silences: the Case of Swift and Vanessa.' *Florida State University Studies*, XI (1953), pp. 25–55.

1954

Baker, Frank. 'Jonathan Swift and the Wesleys.' *London Quarterly and Holborn Review*, October 1954, pp. 290–300.

Brown, James. 'Swift as Moralist.' *PQ*, XXXIII (1954), pp. 368–87.

Clark, J. Kent. 'Swift and the Dutch.' *HLQ*, XVII (1954), pp. 345–56.

Davis, Herbert. 'The Manuscripts of Swift's *Directions to Servants.*' *Studies in Art and Literature for Belle da Costa Greene.* Ed. Dorothy Miner. Princeton University Press, 1954, pp. 433–44.

Ehrenpreis, Irvin. 'Swift and Esther.' Corr. in *TLS*, 8 Jan. 1954, p. 25.

—— 'Swift's First Poem.' *MLR*, XLIX (1954), pp. 210–11.

Elliott, Robert C. 'Swift and Dr. Eachard.' *PMLA*, LXIX (1954), pp. 1250–7.

Ewald, William Bragg, Jr. *The Masks of Jonathan Swift.* Blackwell, Oxford; Harvard University Press, 1954, pp. 203.

Frye, Roland Mushat. 'Swift's Yahoo and the Christian Symbols for Sin.' *JHI*, XV (1954), pp. 201–17.

Horne, Colin J. 'An Epitaph attributed to Swift.' *N&Q*, CXCIX (1954), pp. 525–7.

Jarrett, James L. 'A Yahoo *versus* Jonathan Swift.' *Western Humanities Review*, VIII (1954), pp. 195–200.

Johnson, Maurice. ' "Verses on the Death of Dr. Swift".' *N&Q*, CXCIX (1954), pp. 473–4.

Johnston, Denis. *The Dreaming Dust.* A play about Swift, in *The*

Golden Cuckoo and other Plays. Jonathan Cape, London, 1954, pp. 133–211. See also the Introduction, pp. 13–17.

Kelling, Harold D. 'Reason in Madness: *A Tale of a Tub*.' *PMLA*, LXIX (1954), pp. 198–222.

Kulisheck, Clarence L. 'Swift's Octosyllabics and the Hudibrastic Tradition.' *JEGP*, LIII (1954), pp. 361–8.

Landa, Louis A. *Swift and the Church of Ireland*. Clarendon Press, Oxford, 1954, pp. xvi + 206.

Leslie, Sir Shane. 'The Swift Manuscripts in the Morgan Library.' *Studies in Art and Literature for Belle da Costa Greene*. Princeton University Press, 1954, pp. 445–8.

Mayhew, George P. 'A Draft of Ten Lines from Swift's Poem to John Gay.' *Bulletin of the John Rylands Library*, XXXVII (1954), pp. 257–62.

—— 'Swift's Anglo-Latin Games and a Fragment of *Polite Conversation* in Manuscript.' *HLQ*, XVII (1954), pp. 133–59.

—— 'Swift's Games with Language in Rylands English MS. 659.' *Bulletin of the John Rylands Library*, XXXVII (1954), pp. 413–48.

—— 'Swift's Manuscript Version of *On his own Deafness*.' *HLQ*, XVIII (1954), pp. 85–87.

—— 'Two Burlesque Invitations by Swift.' *N&Q*, CXCIX (1954), pp. 55–57.

Moore, John Robert. 'A Possible Model for the Organization of *A Tale of a Tub*.' *N&Q*, CXCIX (1954), pp. 288–90.

—— 'Was Jonathan Swift a Moderate?' *South Atlantic Quarterly*, LIII (1954), pp. 260–7.

Mundy, P. D. 'Jonathan Swift's Chester Relatives.' *N&Q*, CXCIX (1954), pp. 248–9.

Murry, John Middleton. *Jonathan Swift: A Critical Biography*. Jonathan Cape, London, 1954, pp. 508.

Ong, Walter J. 'Swift on the Mind: The Myth of Asepsis.' *MLQ*, XV (1954), pp. 208–21.

Preu, James. 'Swift's Influence on Godwin's Doctrine of Anarchism.' *JHI*, XV (1954), pp. 371–83.

The Rothschild Library: A Catalogue of the Collection of Eighteenth-Century Printed Books and Manuscripts Formed by Lord Roths-

child. Privately printed at the University Press, Cambridge, 1954. 2 vols., pp. xx + 840. Includes a collection of Swift.

Smith, Roland M. 'Swift's Little Language and Nonsense Names.' *JEGP*, LIII (1954), pp. 178–96.

Swift, Jonathan. *A Letter to a Young Lady on her Marriage.* Caxton Press, Christchurch, 1954, pp. 24.

Teerink, H. ' "Verses on the Death of Doctor Swift" Again.' *SB*, VII (1954 for 1955), pp. 238–9.

Todd, W. B. 'The Text of *Gulliver's Travels.*' *Library*, 5th ser., IX (1954), pp. 135–6.

Welply, W. H. 'Jonathan Swift's Chester Relatives.' *N&Q*, CXCIX (1954), pp. 339–40.

Williams, Kathleen M. ' "Animal Rationis Capax.": A Study of Certain Aspects of Swift's Imagery.' *ELH*, XXI (1954), pp. 193–207.

1955

Aden, John M. 'Dryden and Swift.' *N&Q*, CC (1955), pp. 239–40.

Day, Robert A. 'An Anonymous Attack on Swift.' *N&Q*, CC (1955), pp. 530–2.

Ehrenpreis, Irvin. 'Four of Swift's Sources.' *MLN*, LXX (1955), pp. 95–100.

—— 'The Pattern of Swift's Women.' *PMLA*, LXX (1955), pp. 706–16.

—— and Clifford, James L. 'Swiftiana in Rylands English MS. 659 and Related Documents.' *Bulletin of the John Rylands Library*, XXXVIII (1955), pp. 368–92.

Elwood, John R. 'Swift's "Corinna".' *N&Q*, CC (1955), pp. 529–30.

Ferguson, Oliver W. 'The Authorship of "Apollo's Edict".' *PMLA*, LXX (1955), pp. 433–40.

Greenacre, Phyllis. *Swift and Carroll: A Psychoanalytic Study of Two Lives.* International Universities Press, New York, 1955, pp. 306.

Lawlor, John. 'Radical Satire and the Realistic Novel.' *E&S*, new ser., VIII (1955), pp. 58–75. Particular reference to *Gulliver's Travels.*

Mabbott, Thomas. ' "Bounce to Fop" by Swift and Pope.' *N&Q*, CC (1955), p. 433.

Maxwell, J. C. 'The Text of *A Tale of a Tub*.' *English Studies*, XXXVI (1955), p. 64.

Milic, Louis T. ' "Vive la Bagatelle!" ' *N&Q*, CC (1955), pp. 363–4.

Monk, Samuel H. 'The Pride of Lemuel Gulliver.' *Sewanee Review*, LXIII (1955), pp. 48–71.

Morris, Harry C. 'The *Dialogues of Hylas and Philonous* as a Source in *Gulliver's Travels*.' *MLN*, LXX (1955), pp. 175–7.

Murry, John Middleton. *Swift*. Longmans, Green, for the British Council and the National Book League, 1955, pp. 44.

Nemser, William. 'Linguistic Economy in Lagado.' *History of Ideas News Letter*, I, iv (1955), pp. 7–10.

Pettit, Henry. ' "The Pleasing Paths of Sense": The Subject-Matter of Augustan Literature.' *Literature and Science*. (International Federation for Modern Languages and Literatures: Proceedings of the Sixth Triennial Congress, Oxford, 1954.) Blackwell, Oxford, 1955, pp. 169–74. Contains a discussion of *A Tale of a Tub*.

Preu, James Arthur. 'Antimonarchism in Swift and Godwin.' *Writers and Their Critics: Studies in English and American Literature. Florida State University Studies*, XIX (1955), pp. 11–28.

Quintana, Ricardo. *Swift: An Introduction*. Oxford University Press, London, 1955, pp. viii + 204.

Swift, Jonathan. *Irish Tracts, 1728–1733*. (*The Prose Works of Jonathan Swift*, ed. Herbert Davis, vol. XII.) Blackwell, Oxford, 1955, pp. xlvii + 357.

Taylor, Aline Mackenzie. 'Cyrano de Bergerac and Gulliver's *Voyage to Brobdingnag*.' *Tulane Studies in English*, V (1955), pp. 83–102.

Wahlund, Per Erick. *En Gulliver kommentar*. Stockholm, 1955, pp. 60.

Wilson, T. G. 'The Death Masks of Dean Swift.' *Princeton University Library Chronicle*, XVI (1955), pp. 107–10.

1956

Allen, Robert J. 'Swift's *Contests and Dissensions* in Boston.' *New England Quarterly*, XIX (1956), pp. 73–82.

Baker, Sheridan. 'Swift, "Lilliputian", and Catullus.' *N&Q*, CCI (1956), pp. 477–9.

Colie, Rosalie L. 'Gulliver, the Locke-Stillingfleet Controversy, and the Nature of Man.' *History of Ideas News Letter*, II (1956), pp. 58–62.

Ferguson, Oliver W. 'Jonathan Swift, Freeman of Dublin.' *MLN*, LXXI (1956), pp. 405–9.

Holloway, John. 'The Well-Filled Dish: An Analysis of Swift's Satire.' *Hudson Review*, IX (1956), pp. 20–37.

Jarrell, Mackie L. 'The Proverbs in Swift's *Polite Conversation*.' *HLQ*, XX (1956), pp. 15–38.

Leyburn, Ellen Douglass. *Satiric Allegory: Mirror of Man*. Yale Studies in English, 130. Yale University Press, 1956, pp. ix + 142. Contains a chapter on *Gulliver's Travels*.

Loomis, C. Grant. 'Superstitions and Beliefs in Swift.' *Western Folklore*, XV (1956), pp. 126–8.

Nicolson, Marjorie, and Mohler, Nora M. 'The Scientific Background of Swift's "Voyage to Laputa".' First appeared in *Annals of Science*, 1937, reprinted in Marjorie Nicolson's *Science and Imagination*, Oxford University Press, London, 1956, pp. ix + 238. See also pp. 193–9 of 'The Microscope and English Imagination' in the same volume.

Quinlan, Maurice J. 'Swift's *Project for the Advancement of Religion and the Reformation of Manners*.' *PMLA*, LXII (1956), pp. 201–12.

Roberts, Donald R. 'A Freudian View of Jonathan Swift.' *Literature and Psychology*, VI (1956), pp. 8–17.

Ruoff, James E. 'Swift's *Gulliver's Travels*, Part IV, Chapter III.' *Explicator*, XV (1956), item 20.

Swift, Jonathan. *An Enquiry into the Behaviour of the Queen's Last Ministry*. Ed. Irvin Ehrenpreis. (Indiana University Publications, Humanities Series, no. 36.) Indiana University Press, 1956, pp. xliii + 109.

Taylor, Aline M. 'Swift's Use of the Term "Canary Bird".' *MLN*, LXXI (1956), pp. 175–7.

Watt, Ian. 'The Ironic Tradition in Augustan Prose from Swift to Johnson.' *Restoration and Augustan Prose: papers delivered by James R. Sutherland and Ian Watt at the third Clark Library Seminar, 14 July 1956*. Clark Memorial Library, Los Angeles, 1956, pp. 19–46.

Woodring, Carl R. 'The Aims, Audience, and Structure of the Drapier's Fourth Letter.' *MLQ*, XVII (1956), pp. 50–59.

Wyatt, Frederick; Bacon, Deborah; and Eastman, Arthur M. Review Article on Phyllis Greenacre, *Swift and Carroll: A Psychoanalytic Study of Two Lives* (1955). *Literature and Psychology*, VI (1956), pp. 18–27.

1957

Baker, Donald C. 'Tertullian and Swift's *A Modest Proposal*.' *Classical Journal*, LII (1957), pp. 219–20.

Barroll, J. Leeds. 'Gulliver in Luggnagg: A Possible Source.' *PQ*, XXXVI (1957), pp. 504–8.

Benjamin, Edwin B. 'The King of Brobdingnag and *Secrets of State*.' *JHI*, XVIII (1957), pp. 572–9.

Bennett, Hiram R. 'Jonathan Swift, Priest.' *Anglican Theological Review*, XXXIX (1957), pp. 131–8.

Clark, Paul Odell. 'Swift's Little Language and Nonsense Names.' Corr. in *JEGP*, LVI (1957), pp. 154–7. Also Roland M. Smith, ibid. pp. 157–62.

The 'Dignitas Decani' of St. Patrick's Cathedral, Dublin. Ed. Newport B. White with an Introduction by Aubrey S. Gwynn, S.J. (Irish Manuscripts Commission.) Stationery Office, Dublin, 1957, pp. xxviii + 205.

Ehrenpreis, Irvin. 'The Origins of *Gulliver's Travels*.' *PMLA*, LXXII (1957), pp. 880–99.

Foot, Michael. *The Pen & the Sword*. MacGibbon and Kee, London, 1957, pp. 387. On the journalistic war against Marlborough by Swift and others.

French, David P. 'Swift and Hobbes — A Neglected Parallel.' *Boston University Studies in English*, III (1957), pp. 243–55.

—— 'Swift, the Non-Jurors, and Jacobitism.' *MLN*, LXXII (1957), pp. 258–64.

Geering, R. G. 'Swift's Struldbruggs: The Critics Considered.' *Journal of the Australasian Universities Language and Literature Association*, VII (1957), pp. 5–15.

Greenberg, Robert A. 'Swift's *Gulliver's Travels*, Part IV, Chapter III.' *Explicator*, XVI (1957), item 2.

Jarrell, Mackie L. 'Joyce's Use of Swift's *Polite Conversation* in the "Circe" Episode of *Ulysses*.' *PMLA*, LXXII (1957), pp. 545–54.

Jefferson, D. W. 'An Approach to Swift.' *From Dryden to Johnson*. (Vol. IV of *The Pelican Guide to English Literature*. Ed. Boris Ford.) Penguin, Harmondsworth, 1957, pp. 230–50.

Kassner, Rudolf. *Der goldene Drachen*. Erlenbach, Zürich; Eugen Rentsch, Stuttgart, 1957, pp. 294. Includes an essay on Swift.

Main, C. F. 'Defoe, Swift, and Captain Tom.' *HLB*, XI (1957), pp. 71–79.

Miner, Earl Roy. 'A Poem by Swift and W. B. Yeats's *Words upon the Window-Pane*.' *MLN*, LXXII (1957), p. 273.

Osseton, N. E. 'Butter for Fish.' *English Studies*, XXXVIII (1957), pp. 266–7. Swift's use of this phrase in the *Complete Collection of Genteel and Ingenious Conversation* (1738).

Quinlan, Maurice J. 'Swift and the Prosecuted Nottingham Speech.' *HLB*, XI (1957), pp. 296–302.

Roch, Herbert. *Richter ihrer Zeit: Grimmelshausen, Swift, Gogol*. Gebrüder Weiss Verlag, Schöneberg, Berlin, 1957, pp. 227.

Scouten, Arthur H. 'Materials for the Study of Swift at the University of Pennsylvania.' *Library Chronicle*, University of Pennsylvania, XXIII (1957), pp. 47–52.

Seronsy, Cecil C. 'Some Proper Names in *Gulliver's Travels*.' *N&Q*, CCII (1957), pp. 470–1.

Stedmond, J. M. 'Another Possible Analogue for Swift's *Tale of a Tub*.' *MLN*, LXXII (1957), pp. 13–18.

Sutherland, John H. 'A Reconsideration of Gulliver's Third Voyage.' *SP*, LIV (1957), pp. 45–52.

Swift, Jonathan. *A Proposal for Correcting the English Tongue, Polite Conversation, Etc*. Ed. Herbert Davis with Louis Landa.

(*The Prose Works of Jonathan Swift*, ed. Herbert Davis, vol. IV.) Blackwell, Oxford, 1957, pp. xl + 309.

Taylor, Aline Mackenzie. 'Sights and Monsters and Gulliver's Voyage to Brobdingnag.' *Tulane Studies in English*, VII (1957), pp. 29–82.

Ure, Peter. 'Laputans and Eleutheri: Swift and the Vindicator of the Clergy.' *N&Q*, CCII (1957), pp. 164–7.

1958

Adams, Robert M. 'Swift and Kafka.' *Strains of Discord: Studies in Literary Openness*. Cornell University Press, Ithaca, 1958, pp. 146–79.

Baker, Donald C. 'Metaphors in Swift's *A Tale of a Tub* and Middleton's *The Family of Love*.' *N&Q*, CCIII (1958), pp. 107–8.

Barnds, William Joseph. 'Jonathan Swift, Preacher.' *Anglican Theological Review*, XL (1958), pp. 42–47.

Barroll, J. Leeds, III. 'Gulliver and the Struldbruggs.' *PMLA*, LXXIII (1958), pp. 43–50.

Bewley, Marius. 'The Poetry of Swift.' *Spectator*, 29 Aug. 1958, pp. 283–4.

Brandt, E. H. 'Some Proper Names in Gulliver's Travels.' *N&Q*, CCIII (1958), p. 44.

Byers, John R., Jr. 'Another Source for *Gulliver's Travels*.' *JEGP*, LVII (1958), pp. 14–20.

Clark, Paul Odell. 'Lapponia, Lapland, and Laputa.' *MLQ*, XIX (1958), pp. 343–51.

Danchin, Pierre. 'Le lecteur anglais d'aujourd'hui peut-il connaître *Gulliver's Travels?*' *EA*, XI (1958), pp. 97–111.

Dyson, A. E. 'Swift: The Metamorphosis of Irony.' *E&S*, new ser., XI (1958), pp. 53–67.

Ehrenpreis, Irvin. *The Personality of Jonathan Swift*. Methuen, London; Harvard University Press, 1958, pp. 158.

Greenberg, R. A. 'Gulliver a True Wit.' *N&Q*, CCIII (1958), p. 296.

Gros, Léon-Gabriel, and others. 'Langues imaginaires et langage secret chez Swift.' *Cahiers du Sud*, XLVI, no. 344 (1958), pp. 3–44.

Jarrell, Mackie L. 'The Handwriting of the Lilliputians.' *PQ*, XXXVII (1958), pp. 116–19.

Johnson, James William. 'Tertullian and *A Modest Proposal*.' *MLN*, LXXIII (1958), pp. 561–3.

Johnson, Maurice. 'The Structural Impact of *A Modest Proposal*.' *Bucknell Review*, VII (1958), pp. 234–40.

Jones, Myrddin. '*Further Thoughts on Religion*: Swift's Relationship to Filmer and Locke.' *RES*, new ser., IX (1958), pp. 284–6.

Long, Littleton. 'Swift's Arithmetic.' *N&Q*, CCIII (1958), p. 219.

Manley, Francis. 'Swift Marginalia in Howell's *Medulla Historiae Anglicanae*.' *PMLA*, LXXIII (1958), pp. 335–8.

Mayhew, George P. 'Swift's First Will and the First Use of the Provost's Negative at T.C.D.' *HLQ*, XXI (1958), pp. 295–322.

Mundy, P. D. 'A Note on Samuel Butler (1612–80) and Jonathan Swift.' *N&Q*, CCIII (1958), pp. 294–6.

—— 'The Mother of Jonathan Swift.' *N&Q*, CCIII (1958), pp. 444–5.

Raymond, John. 'The Excremental Vision.' *New Statesman*, LV (7 June 1958), pp. 735–6.

Sherburn, George. 'Errors concerning the Houyhnhnms.' *MP*, LVI (1958), pp. 92–97.

Spector, Robert Donald. 'Lagerkvist, Swift, and the Devices of Fantasy.' *Western Humanities Review*, XII (1958), pp. 75–79.

Sutherland, James. *English Satire*. Cambridge University Press, 1958, pp. x + 174.

Swift, Jonathan. '*A Tale of a Tub*.' *To Which Is Added 'The Battle of the Books' and the 'Mechanical Operation of the Spirit' by Jonathan Swift*. Ed. with an Introduction and Notes Historical and Explanatory by A. C. Guthkelch and D. Nichol Smith. 2nd ed. Clarendon Press, Oxford, 1958, pp. lxxviii + 374. 1st ed. 1920.

—— '*Gulliver's Travels*' and other *Writings*. Ed. Ricardo Quintana. Modern Library, New York, 1958, pp. xiv + 550.

—— *The Collected Poems of Jonathan Swift*. Ed. with an Introduction and Critical Comments by Joseph Horrell. The Muses' Library. Routledge and Kegan Paul, London; Harvard University Press, 1958. 2 vols., pp. lxvi + 402; xii + 403–818.

—— *The Poems*. Ed. Harold Williams. 2nd ed. Clarendon Press,

Oxford, 1958. 3 vols., pp. xliii + 356; xiii + 357–766; xii + 767–1242. 1st ed. 1937.

Wasiolek, Edward. 'Relativity in *Gulliver's Travels*.' *PQ*, XXXVII (1958), pp. 110–16.

Williams, Kathleen. *Jonathan Swift and the Age of Compromise*. University of Kansas Press, 1958, pp. xi + 238.

Wilson, James R. 'Swift, the Psalmist, and the Horse.' *Tennessee Studies in Literature*, III (1958), pp. 17–23.

—— 'Swift's Alazon.' *Studia Neophilologica*, XXX (1958), pp. 153–64.

Wilson, T. G. 'The Mental and Physical Health of Dean Swift.' *Medical History*, II (1958), pp. 175–90.

1959

Ball, Albert. 'Swift and the Animal Myth.' *Transactions of the Wisconsin Academy of Sciences, Arts, and Letters*, XLVIII (1959), pp. 239–48.

Barker, Elizabeth. 'Gelli's *Circe* and Jonathan Swift.' *Cesare Barbieri Courier*, II, i (1959), pp. 3–15.

Brown, Norman O. 'The Excremental Vision.' *Life against Death: The Psychoanalytical Meaning of History*. Routledge & Kegan Paul, London, 1959, pp. 179–201.

Clifford, James L. (ed.). *Eighteenth-Century English Literature: Modern Essays in Criticism*. Galaxy Books, 23. Oxford University Press, New York, 1959, pp. xi + 351. Reprints three essays on Swift.

Davis, Herbert. 'Recent Studies of Swift and Johnson.' *Sprache und Literatur Englands und Amerikas*. Dritter Band: *Die wissenschaftliche Erschliessung der Prosa*. (Lehrgangsvorträge der Akademie Comburg.) Niemeyer, Tubingen, 1959, pp. 11–25.

Dobrée, Bonamy. 'Swift, 1715–1745.' *English Literature in the Early Eighteenth Century 1700–1740*. (*The Oxford History of English Literature*, vol. VII.) Clarendon Press, Oxford, 1959, pp. 432–74.

Ehrenpreis, I. 'Swift's Grandfather.' Corr. in *TLS*, 12 June 1959, p. 353.

Ferguson, Oliver W. 'Swift's *Saeva Indignatio* and *A Modest Proposal*.' *PQ*, XXXVIII (1959), pp. 473–9.

Fussell, Paul, jr. 'Speaker and Style in *A Letter of Advice to a Young Poet* (1721), and the Problem of Attribution.' *RES*, new ser., x (1959), pp. 63–67.

Honig, Edwin. *Dark Conceit: The Making of Allegory.* Northwestern University Press, 1959, pp. xii + 210. Includes a discussion of Swift.

Huxley, Herbert H. '*Sanguis Equinus* (Virgil *Georg.* 3.463) and Dean Swift.' *Classical Philology*, LIV (1959), p. 122.

Jarrell, Mackie L. 'Swiftiana in *Finnegan's Wake*.' *ELH*, XXVI (1959), pp. 271–94.

Johnston, Denis. *In Search of Swift.* Hodges, Figgis, Dublin; Macmillan, London; Barnes & Noble, New York, 1959, pp. xii + 240.

McCue, Daniel L., jr. 'A Newly Discovered Broadsheet of Swift's *Last Speech and Dying Words of Ebenezor Elliston*.' *HLB*, XIII (1959), pp. 362–8.

Mayhew, George P. 'A Missing Leaf from Swift's *Holyhead Journal*.' *Bulletin of the John Rylands Library*, XLI (1959), pp. 388–413.

Merle, Robert. 'Les desseins de Gulliver.' *Revue de Paris*, April 1959, pp. 15–23.

Papajewski, Helmut. 'Swift and Berkeley.' *Anglia*, LXXVII (1959), pp. 29–53.

Pinkus, Philip. 'Swift and the Ancients-Moderns Controversy.' *UTQ*, XXIX (1959), pp. 46–58.

Powell, William S. 'A Swift Broadside from the Opposition.' *Virginia Magazine of History and Biography*, LXVII (1959), pp. 164–9.

Preu, James A. 'The Dean and the Anarchist.' *Florida State University Studies*, XXX (1959), pp. 124.

Ricks, Christopher. 'A Debt of Pope to Swift.' *N&Q*, CCIV (1959), pp. 398–9.

Rogers, Katherine M. ' "My Female Friends": the Mysogyny of Jonathan Swift.' *Texas Studies in Literature and Language*, I (1959), pp. 366–79.

Rossi, Matti M. 'Notes on the Eighteenth-Century German Translations of Swift's *Gulliver's Travels*.' *Library Chronicle*, University of Pennsylvania, XXV (1959), pp. 84–88.

Sams, Henry W. 'Swift's Satire of the Second Person.' *ELH*, XXVI (1959), pp. 36–44.

Spillane, James M. 'Herder's Estimate of Swift.' *Kentucky Foreign Language Quarterly*, VI (1959), pp. 140–9.

Starkman, Miriam K. 'Quakers, Phrenologists, and Jonathan Swift.' *JHI*, XX (1959), pp. 403–12.

Swift, Jonathan. *Directions to Servants, and Miscellaneous Pieces, 1733–1742.* (*The Prose Works of Jonathan Swift*, ed. Herbert Davis, vol. XIII.) Blackwell, Oxford, 1959, pp. xliv + 233.

—— *Selected Prose and Poetry*. Ed. Edward Rosenheim, jr. Rinehart, New York, 1959, pp. xxx + 412.

Tilton, John W. '*Gulliver's Travels* as a Work of Art.' *Bucknell Review*, VIII (1959), pp. 246–59.

Welply, W. H. 'Swift's Grandfather.' Corr. in *TLS*, 17 July 1959, p. 423.

1960

Atherton, James S. *The Books at the Wake. A Study of Literary Allusions in James Joyce's 'Finnegan's Wake'*. Viking Press, New York, 1960, pp. 308. Includes a section on Swift.

Beaumont, Charles Allen. 'Swift's Classical Rhetoric in *A Modest Proposal.*' *Georgia Review*, XIV (1960), pp, 307–17.

Brain, Russell. 'Jonathan Swift: l'Enfant Terrible.' *Some Reflections on Genius and other Essays*. Pitman Medical Publishing Co., London, 1960, pp. 23–33.

Danchin, Pierre. 'The Text of *Gulliver's Travels.*' *Texas Studies in Literature and Language*, II (1960), pp. 233–50.

Dircks, Richard J. 'Gulliver's Tragic Rationalism.' *Criticism*, II (1960), pp. 134–49.

Dustin, John E. 'The 1735 Dublin Edition of Swift's *Poems.*' *PBSA*, LIV (1960), pp. 57–60.

Elliott, Robert C. *The Power of Satire: Magic, Ritual, Art*. Princeton University Press, 1960, pp. xi + 300.

Fussell, Paul, jr. 'The Frailty of Lemuel Gulliver.' *Essays in Literary History Presented to J. Milton French*. Ed. Rudolf Kirk and C. F. Main. Rutgers University Press, 1960, pp. 113–25.

Gray, James. 'The Modernism of Jonathan Swift.' *QQ*, LXVII (1960), pp. 11–17.

Greenberg, Robert A. '*A Modest Proposal* and the Bible.' *MLR*, LV (1960), pp. 568–9.

Hart, Jeffrey. 'The Ideologue as Artist: Some Notes on *Gulliver's Travels*.' *Criticism*, II (1960), pp. 125–33.

Holloway, John. 'Analysis of Swift's Satire.' *The Charted Mirror: Literary and Critical Essays*. Routledge & Kegan Paul, London, 1960, pp. xi + 226.

Horne, Colin J., and Powell, Hugh. 'A German Analogue for *A Tale of a Tub*.' *MLR*, LV (1960), pp. 488–96.

Kallich, Martin. 'Three Ways of Looking at a Horse: Jonathan Swift's "Voyage to the Houyhnhnms" Again.' *Criticism*, II (1960), pp. 107–24.

Mayhew, George P. ' "Rage or Raillery": Swift's *Epistle to a Lady* and *On Poetry: A Rhapsody*.' *HLQ*, XXIII (1960), pp. 159–80.

Menon, P. B. K. 'Genius and Madness.' *Indian Review*, LX (1960), pp. 410–12. Swift and others.

Morrall, John B. 'Around and About Swift.' *Studies*, XLIX (1960), pp. 305–12.

O'Hehir, Brendan. 'Meaning of Swift's "Description of a City Shower".' *ELH*, XXVII (1960), pp. 194–207.

Paulson, Ronald. 'Swift, Stella, and Permanence.' *ELH*, XXVII (1960), pp. 298–314.

—— *Theme and Structure in Swift's 'Tale of a Tub'*. Yale Studies in English, 143. Yale University Press, 1960, pp. xiv + 259.

Peake, Charles. 'Swift and the Passions.' *MLR*, LV (1960), pp. 169–80.

Pinkus, Philip. '*A Tale of a Tub* and the Rosy Cross.' *JEGP*, LIX (1960), pp. 669–79.

Reiss, Edmund. 'The Importance of Swift's Glubbdubdrib Episode.' *JEGP*, LIX (1960), pp. 223–8.

Ricks, Christopher. 'Notes on Swift and Johnson.' *RES*, new ser., XI (1960), pp. 412–13.

Spillane, James M. 'Herder's Translations from Swift.' *Kentucky Foreign Language Quarterly*, VII (1960), pp. 156–64.

Stavrou, C. N. 'Gulliver's Voyage to the Land of Dubliners.' *South Atlantic Quarterly*, LIX (1960), pp. 490–9.

Swift, Jonathan. *'Gulliver's Travels' and Other Writings*. Ed. Louis A. Landa. Riverside Editions B25. Houghton Mifflin, Boston, 1960, pp. xxviii + 564.

Tague, Wilma L. 'Stephen Gosson and "Homer's Iliades in a Nutte Shell".' *N&Q*, CCV (1960), pp. 372–3.

Thorpe, Annette P. 'Jonathan Swift's Prescriptions concerning the English Language.' *CLA Journal*, III (1960), pp. 173–80.

Wilson, T. G. 'The Death-Masks of Swift.' *Medical History*, IV (1960), pp. 49–58.

Winton, Calhoun. 'Conversion on the Road to Houyhnhnmland.' *Sewanee Review*, LXVIII (1960), pp. 20–33.

1961

Beaumont, Charles Allen. *Swift's Classical Rhetoric*. University of Georgia Monographs, no. 8 (1961), pp. vii + 158.

Cook, Richard I. 'Dryden's *Absalom and Achitophel* and Swift's Political Tracts, 1710–1714.' *HLQ*, XXIV (1961), pp. 345–8.

Corder, Jim. 'Gulliver in England.' *CE*, XXIII (1961), pp. 98–103.

Crane, R. S. 'The Rationale of the Fourth Voyage.' *Gulliver's Travels*. Ed. Robert A. Greenberg. Norton, New York, 1961, pp. 300–7.

Duncan-Jones, E. E. 'Joseph's Party-Coloured Coat and *A Tale of a Tub*.' *N&Q*, CCVI (1961), p. 251.

Foster, Milton P. (ed.). *A Casebook on Gulliver among the Houyhnhnms*. Crowell, New York, 1961, pp. xiii + 319.

Frietzsche, Arthur H. 'The Impact of Applied Science upon the Utopian Ideal.' *Brigham Young University Studies*, III (1961), pp. 35–42.

Goldgar, Bertrand A. *The Curse of Party: Swift's Relations with Addison and Steele*. University of Nebraska Press, 1961, pp. ix + 198.

Harth, Phillip. *Swift and Anglican Rationalism: The Religious Background of 'A Tale of a Tub'*. University of Chicago Press, 1961, pp. 171.

Hughes, R. E. 'The Five Fools in *A Tale of a Tub*.' *Literature and Psychology*, XI (1961), pp. 20–22.

Johnson, Maurice. 'Remote Regions of Man's Mind: The Travels of Gulliver.' *University of Kansas City Review*, XXVII (1961), pp. 299–303.

Jones, Richard Foster. *Ancients and Moderns. A Study of the background of the 'Battle of the Books'*. 2nd ed. Washington University Studies, no. 6, St. Louis, 1961, pp. xii + 354. 1st ed. 1936.

McAleer, John J. 'Swift's Letcombe Admonition to Bolingbroke.' *CLA Journal*, IV (1961), pp. 188–95.

McDonald, W. U., jr. 'A Letter of Sir Walter Scott to William Scott on the Jeffrey-Swift Controversy.' *RES*, new ser., XII (1961), pp. 404–8.

Mayhew, George P. 'Swift's Notes for his *The History of the Last Four Years*, book IV.' *HLQ*, XXIV (1961), pp. 311–22.

—— 'The Early Life of John Partridge.' *SEL*, I (1961), pp. 31–42.

—— 'Two Entries of 1702–3 for Swift's *Polite Conversation, 1738*.' *N&Q*, CCVI (1961), pp. 49–50.

Pons, Émile, and Axelrad, José. 'Rénovation de la biographie swiftienne.' *EA*, XIV (1961), pp. 314–20.

Røstvig, Maren-Sofie. *The Background of English Neo-Classicism. With Some Comments on Swift and Pope*. Universitetsforl, Oslo, 1961, pp. 110.

Seelye, John D. 'Hobbes' *Leviathan* and the Giantism Complex in the First Book of *Gulliver's Travels*.' *JEGP*, LX (1961), pp. 228–239.

Sherburn, George. 'The "Copies of Verses" about *Gulliver*.' *Texas Studies in Literature and Language*, III (1961), pp. 3–7.

Swift, Jonathan. *Gulliver's Travels: an annotated text with critical essays*. Ed. Robert A. Greenberg. Norton, New York, 1961, pp. viii + 361.

Tallman, Warren. 'Swift's Fool: A Comment upon Satire in *Gulliver's Travels*.' *Dalhousie Review*, XL (1961), pp. 470–8.

Tracy, Clarence. 'The Unity of *Gulliver's Travels*.' *QQ*, LXVIII (1961–2), pp. 597–609.

Traugott, John. 'A Voyage to Nowhere with Thomas More and

Jonathan Swift: *Utopia* and *The Voyage to the Houyhnhnms.*' *Sewanee Review*, LXIX (1961), pp. 534–65.

Yunck, John A. 'The Skeptical Faith of Jonathan Swift.' *Personalist*, XLII (1961), pp. 533–54.

1962

Béranger, J. 'Swift en 1714: Position politique et sentiments personnels.' *EA*, xv (1962), pp. 233–47.

Calderwood, James L. 'Structural Parody in Swift's *Fragment.*' *MLQ*, XXIII (1962), pp. 243–53.

Chiasson, Elias J. 'Swift's Clothes Philosophy in the *Tale* and Hooker's Concept of Law.' *SP*, LIX (1962), pp. 64–82.

Cook, Richard I. 'The 'Several Ways . . . of Abusing One Another': Jonathan Swift's Political Journalism.' *Speech Monographs*, XXXIX (1962), pp. 260–73.

—— 'Swift as a Tory Rhetorician.' *Texas Studies in Literature and Language*, IV (1962), pp. 72–86.

—— 'The Uses of *Saeva Indignatio*: Swift's Political Tracts (1710–1714) and His Sense of Audience.' *SEL*, II (1962), pp. 287–307.

Crane, R. S. 'The Houyhnhnms, the Yahoos, the History of Ideas.' *Reason and the Imagination: Studies in the History of Ideas, 1600–1800*. Ed. J. A. Mazzeo. Columbia University Press, 1962, pp. 231–53.

Davis, Herbert. 'Alecto's Whip.' *REL*, III (1962), pp. 7–17.

Drozdowski, Eugene C. 'Jonathan Swift, Political Propagandist, 1710–13.' *Appalachian State Teachers College Faculty Publications*, 1962, pp. 3–34.

Eby, Cecil D. 'When Swift First Employed George Faulkner.' *PBSA*, LVI (1962), pp. 354–6.

Ehrenpreis, Irvin. *Swift: The Man, his Works, and the Age.* vol. I: *Mr. Swift and his Contemporaries.* Methuen, London; Harvard University Press, 1962, pp. xii + 294.

—— 'The Literary Side of a Satirist's Work.' *Minnesota Review*, II (1962), pp. 179–97.

—— 'The Meaning of Gulliver's Last Voyage.' *REL*, III (1962), pp. 18–38.

Ferguson, Oliver W. *Jonathan Swift and Ireland.* University of Illinois Press, 1962, pp. xii + 217.

Fletcher, John. 'Samuel Beckett et Jonathan Swift: vers une étude comparée.' *Annales publiées par la Faculté des Lettres de Toulouse,* 1962, pp. 81–117.

Harlow, Benjamin C. 'Houyhnhnmland: A Utopian Satire.' *McNeese Review,* XIII (1962), pp. 44–58.

Henrion, Pierre. *Jonathan Swift Avoue.* Lycée Hoche, Versailles, 1962, pp. 100.

Honore, Jean. 'Charles Gildon redacteur du *British Mercury* (1711–1712): les attaques contre Pope, Swift, et les wits.' *EA,* xv (1962), pp. 347–64.

Hitt, Ralph E. 'Antiperfectionism as a Unifying Theme in *Gulliver's Travels.*' *Mississippi Quarterly,* xv (1962), pp. 161–9.

Johnston, Oswald. 'Swift and the Common Reader.' *In Defense of Reading.* Ed. R. A. Brower and R. Poirier. Dutton, New York, 1962, pp. 174–90.

Kermode, Frank. 'Jonathan the First.' *New Statesman,* 14 Sept. 1962, pp. 321–2.

Killham, John. *Gulliver's Travels. Notes on English Literature.* Blackwell, Oxford, 1962, p. 64.

Le Brocquy, Sybil. *Cadenus: A Reassessment in the Light of New Evidence of the Relationships between Swift, Stella and Vanessa.* Dolmen Press, Dublin; Oxford University Press, 1962, pp. 160.

McCall, Raymond G. 'H. L. Mencken and the Glass of Satire.' *CE,* XXIII (1962), pp. 633–6. Contrasts Mencken with Swift.

Mayhew, George P. 'Jonathan Swift's Hoax of 1722 upon Ebenezor Elliston.' *Bulletin of the John Rylands Library,* XLIV (1962), pp. 360–80.

Mercier, Vivian. 'Swift and the Gaelic Tradition.' *REL,* III (1962), pp. 69–79. Also included in *The Irish Comic Tradition,* by Vivian Mercier, Clarendon Press, Oxford, 1962, pp. xx + 258.

Mortenson, Robert. 'A Note on the Revision of *Gulliver's Travels.*' *Library Chronicle,* University of Pennsylvania, XXVIII (1962) pp. 26–28.

Peake, Charles. 'Swift's "Satirical Elegy on a Late Famous General".' *REL,* III (1962), pp. 80–89.

Rawson, C. J. 'Swift's Certificate to Parnell's "Posthumous Works".' *MLR*, LVII (1962), pp. 179–82.

Rosenheim, Edward, jr. 'The Fifth Voyage of Lemuel Gulliver: A Footnote.' *MP*, LX (1962), pp. 103–19.

Scouten, A. H. 'The Earliest London Printings of "Verses on the Death of Doctor Swift".' *SB*, XV (1862), pp. 243–7.

Slepian, Barry. 'When Swift First Employed George Faulkner.' *PBSA*, LVI (1962), pp. 354–6.

Snethlage, Jacob L. *Jonathan Swift, De Engelse Voltaire*. Helden van de Geest, no. 17, Den Haag, pp. 157.

Subramanyam, N. S. *Jonathan Swift*. Masters of English Literature Series, no. 2. Kitab Mahal, Allahabad, 1962, pp. ii + 116.

Swift, Jonathan. *Miscellaneous and Autobiographical Pieces, Fragments, and Marginalia*. (*The Prose Works of Jonathan Swift*, ed. Herbert Davis, vol. v.) Blackwell, Oxford, 1962, pp. xl + 375.

Taylor, Dick, jr. 'Gulliver's Pleasing Visions: Self-Deception as a Major Theme in *Gulliver's Travels*.' *Tulane Studies in English*, XII (1962), pp. 7–61.

Tracy, Clarence. 'The Unity of *Gulliver's Travels*.' *QQ*, LXVIII (1962), pp. 597–609.

Traugott, J. (ed.). *Discussions of Jonathan Swift*. Heath, Boston, 1962, pp. xi + 130.

Voigt, Milton. 'Swift and Psychoanalytic Criticism.' *Western Humanities Review*, XVI (1962), pp. 361–7.

Wilson, T. G. 'Swift's Personality and Death-Masks.' *REL*, III (1962), pp. 39–68.

1963

Andreasen, N. J. C. 'Swift's Satire on the Occult in *A Tale of a Tub*.' *Texas Studies in Literature and Language*, V (1963), pp. 410–21.

Bond, Richmond P. 'Isaac Bickerstaff, Esq.' *Restoration and Eighteenth-Century Literature: Essays in honor of Alan Dugald McKillop*. Ed. Carroll Camden. For William Marsh Rice University by the University of Chicago Press, 1963, pp. 103–24.

—— 'John Partridge and the Company of Stationers.' *SB*, XVI (1963), pp. 61–80.

Bruckmann, Patricia. 'Gulliver, cum grano salis.' *Satire Newsletter*, I (1963), pp. 5–11.

Carnochan, W. B. 'The Complexity of Swift: Gulliver's Fourth Voyage.' *SP*, LX (1963), pp. 23–44.

Carroll, John. 'Richardson on Pope and Swift.' *UTQ*, XXXIII (1963), pp. 19–29.

Cook, Richard I. 'Swift's Polemical Characters.' *Discourse*, VI (1962–3), pp. 30–38, 43–48.

—— 'The Audience of Swift's Tory Tracts, 1710–14.' *MLQ*, XXIV (1963), pp. 31–41.

Davis, Herbert. 'A Modest Defence of "The Lady's Dressing Room".' *Restoration and Eighteenth-Century Literature: Essays in honor of Alan Dugald McKillop*. Ed. Carroll Camden. For William Marsh Rice University by the University of Chicago Press, 1963, pp. 39–48.

Dennis, Nigel. 'On Swift and Satire.' *Encounter*, XXI (1963), pp. 14–28.

Donoghue, Denis. 'A Note on Swift.' *New Statesman*, 13 Dec. 1963, pp. 877–8.

Ehrenpreis, Irvin. 'Personae.' *Restoration and Eighteenth-Century Literature: Essays in honor of Alan Dugald McKillop*. Ed. Carroll Camden. For William Marsh Rice University by the University of Chicago Press, 1963, pp. 25–37.

French, David P. 'Swift, Temple, and "A Digression on Madness".' *Texas Studies in Literature and Language*, V (1963), pp. 42–57.

Gilbert, Jack G. 'The Drapier's Initials.' *N&Q*, CCVIII (1963), pp. 217–18.

Jarrell, Mackie L. 'A New Swift Attribution: The Preface to Sheridan's Sermon on St. Cecilia's Day.' *PMLA*, LXXVIII (1963), pp. 511–15.

Klima, S. 'A Possible Source for Swift's Struldbrugs?' *PQ*, XLII (1963), pp. 566–9.

Pinkus, Philip. 'The Upside-down World of *A Tale of a Tub*.' *English Studies*, XLIV (1963), pp. 161–75.

Preu, James A. 'The Case of the Mysterious Manuscript.' *English Journal*, LII (1963), pp. 579–86.

Rosenheim, Edward W., jr. *Swift and the Satirist's Art.* University of Chicago Press, 1963, pp. xiii + 243.

Seronsy, Cecil C. 'Sir Politic Would-Be in Laputa.' *ELN*, I (1963), pp. 17–24.

Slepian, Barry. 'The Ironic Intention of Swift's Verses on His Own Death.' *RES*, new ser., XIV (1963), pp. 249–56.

—— 'The Publication History of Faulkner's Edition of *Gulliver's Travels.*' *PBSA*, LVII (1963), pp. 219–21.

Smith, T. Henry. 'Swift's "The Day of Judgement".' *Explicator*, XXII (1963), no. 6.

Steensma, Robert C. 'Swift on Standing Armies: A Possible Source.' *N&Q*, CCVIII (1963), pp. 215–16.

Stephens, Lamarr. ' "A Digression in Praise of Digressions" as a Classical Oration: Rhetorical Satire in Section VII of Swift's *A Tale of a Tub.*' *Tulane Studies in English*, XII (1963), pp. 41–49.

Swift, Jonathan. *Gulliver's Travels.* Ed. Martin Price. Bobbs-Merrill, New York, Indianapolis, 1963, pp. xlvi + 314.

—— *Swift's Polite Conversation.* Ed. with Introduction, Notes and Extensive Commentary by Eric Partridge. Deutsch, London; Oxford University Press, New York, 1963, pp. 182.

—— *The Correspondence of Jonathan Swift.* Ed. Harold Williams. Clarendon Press, Oxford, 1963. 3 vols., pp. lxx + 428; xx + 476; xviii + 512.

Teerink, H. *A Bibliography of the Writings of Jonathan Swift.* Ed. Arthur H. Scouten. 2nd ed. University of Pennsylvania Press, 1963, pp. xviii + 453. 1st ed. 1937.

Torchiana, Donald T. 'W. B. Yeats, Jonathan Swift, and Liberty.' *MP*, LXI (1963), pp. 26–39.

Traugott, John. 'Swift's Allegory: The Yahoo and the Man-of-Mode.' *UTQ*, XXXIII (1963), pp. 1–18.

West, Paul. 'Swift and Dry Religion.' *QQ*, LXX (1963), pp. 431–40.

Williams, Kathleen. 'Swift's Laputans and "Mathematica".' *N&Q*, CCVIII (1963), pp. 216–17.

1964

Bloom, Allan. 'An Outline of *Gulliver's Travels.' Ancients and*

Moderns: Essays on the Tradition of Political Philosophy in honor of Leo Strauss. Ed. Joseph Cropsey. Basic Books, New York, London, 1964, pp. 238–58.

Brown, William J. 'Gulliver's Passage on the Dutch *Amboyna.' ELN,* I (1964), pp. 262–4.

Carnochan, W. B. *'Gulliver's Travels*: An Essay on the Human Understanding?' *MLQ,* xxv (1964), pp. 5–21.

—— 'Some Roles of Lemuel Gulliver.' *Texas Studies in Literature and Language,* v (1964), pp. 520–9.

Davis, Herbert. *Jonathan Swift, Essays on his Satire and Other Studies.* Galaxy Books, 106. Oxford University Press, New York, 1964, pp. 292.

Dennis, Nigel. *Jonathan Swift: A Short Character.* Macmillan Co., New York, 1964, pp. 160.

French, David P. 'The Swift-Gulliver Litigation.' *N&Q,* ccix (1964), pp. 52–53.

Frédérix, Pierre. *Swift, le véritable Gulliver.* Hachette, Paris, 1964, pp. 378.

Galey, Matthieu. 'Une vie de "Yahoo".' *Revue de Paris,* Aug.–Sept. 1964, pp. 116–22.

Greene, Donald. 'The Sin of Pride: A Sketch for a Literary Exploration.' *New Mexico Quarterly,* xxxiv (1964), pp. 8–30.

Hopkins, Robert H. 'The Issue of Anonymity and the Beginning of the Steele–Swift Controversy of 1713–14: A New Interpretation.' *ELN,* II (1964), pp. 15–21.

Jarrell, Mackie L. ' "Jack and the Dane": Swift Traditions in Ireland.' *Journal of American Folklore,* LXXVII (1964), pp. 99–117.

Kendle, Burton S. 'D. H. Lawrence: The Man who Misunderstood Gulliver.' *ELN,* II (1964), pp. 42–46.

Leyburn, Ellen Douglass. 'Gulliver's Clothes.' *Satire Newsletter,* I (1964), pp. 35–40.

Mayhew, George P. 'Swift's Bickerstaff Hoax as an April Fools' Joke.' *MP,* LXI (1964), pp. 270–80.

Ohlin, Peter. ' "Cadenus and Vanessa": Reason and Passion.' *SEL,* IV (1964), pp. 485–96.

Passon, Richard H. 'Gay to Swift on Political Satire.' *American N&Q,* III (1964), p. 87.

Peterson, Leland D. 'On the Keen Appetite for Perpetuity of Life.' *ELN*, I (1964), pp. 265–7.

Sachs, Sheldon. *Fiction and the Shape of Belief: A Study of Henry Fielding with Glances at Swift, Johnson and Richardson.* University of California Press, 1964, pp. ix + 278.

Schuster, Sister M. Faith, O.S.B. 'Clothes Philosophy in *Gulliver's Travels.*' *American Benedictine Review*, XV (1964), pp. 316–26.

Slepian, Barry. 'Some Forgotten Anecdotes about Swift.' *Bulletin of the New York Public Library*, LXVIII (1964), pp. 33–44.

Smith, Curtis C. 'Metaphor Structure in Swift's *Tale of a Tub.*' *Thoth*, V (1964), pp. 22–41.

Stavrou, C. N. 'The Love Songs of J. Swift, G. Bernard Shaw and J. A. A. Joyce.' *Midwest Quarterly*, Pittsburg, Kansas, VI (1964), pp. 135–62.

Swift, Jonathan. *Directions to Servants.* With drawings by Joseph Low. Anthony Blond, London; Pantheon Books, New York, 1964, pp. 128.

—— *Jonathan Swift: Poetry & Prose.* With appreciations by Pope, Johnson, Scott, Hazlitt and others. Ed. Herbert Davis. Clarendon Press, Oxford, 1964, pp. xlviii + 160.

Traugott, John. 'The Refractory Swift.' Review article in *MLQ*, XXV (1964), pp. 205–11.

Tuveson, Ernest (ed.). *Swift: A Collection of Critical Essays.* Twentieth Century Views Series. Prentice Hall, Englewood Cliffs, N.J., 1964, pp. 176.

Voigt, Milton. *Swift and the Twentieth Century.* Wayne State University Press, Detroit, 1964, pp. 205.

Wilson, T. G. 'Swift and the Doctors.' *Medical History*, VIII (1964), pp. 199–216.

1965

Banks, Loy Otis. 'Moral Perspective in *Gulliver's Travels* and *Candide:* Broadsword and Rapier?' *Forum*, Houston, Texas, IV (1965), pp. 4–8.

Beaumont, Charles A. *Swift's Use of the Bible: A Documentation and a Study of Allusion.* University of Georgia Monographs, no. 14 (1965), pp. 68.

Bernard, F. V. 'Swift's Maxim on Populousness: A Possible Source.' *N&Q*, XII (1965), p. 18.

Clifford, James L. 'The Eighteenth Century.' *MLQ*, XXVI (1965), pp. 111–34. Includes an assessment of recent Swift scholarship.

Falle, George. 'Swift's Writings and a Variety of Commentators.' Review article in *UTQ*, XXXIV (1965), pp. 294–312.

Fussell, Paul. *The Rhetorical World of Augustan Humanism: Ethics and Imagery from Swift to Burke.* Clarendon Press, Oxford, 1965, pp. ix + 314.

Halewood, William H. 'Plutarch in Houyhnhnmland: a Neglected Source for Gulliver's Fourth Voyage.' *PQ*, XLIV (1965), pp. 185–94.

—— and Levich, Marvin. 'Houyhnhnm est Animal Rationale.' *JHI*, XXVI (1965), pp. 273–81.

Jarrell, Mackie L. ' "Ode to the King": Some Contests, Dissensions, and Exchanges among Jonathan Swift, John Dunton, and Henry Jones.' *Texas Studies in Literature and Language*, VII (1965), pp. 145–59.

Johnson, James W. 'Swift's Historical Outlook.' *JBS*, IV, no. 2 (1965), pp. 52–77.

Mayhew, George P. 'Some Dramatizations of Swift's *Polite Conversation* (1738).' *PQ*, XLIV (1965), pp. 51–72.

Meyers, Jeffrey. 'Swift, Johnson, and the Dublin M.A.' *American N&Q*, IV (1965), pp. 5–7.

Neumeyer, Peter F. 'Franz Kafka and Jonathan Swift: A Symbiosis.' *Dalhousie Review*, XLV (1965), pp. 60–65.

Pinkus, Philip. 'Sin and Satire in Swift.' *Bucknell Review*, XIII (1965), pp. 11–25.

Quintana, Ricardo. 'Émile Pons and the Modern Study of Swift's *Tale of a Tub.*' *EA*, XVIII (1965), pp. 5–17.

Rawson, C. J. 'A Phrase of John Gay in Swift's *Modest Defence of the Lady's Dressing Room?*' *RES*, new ser., XVI (1965), pp. 406–7.

—— ' "The Vanity of Human Wishes"? line 73: a Parallel from Swift.' *N&Q*, XII (1965), pp. 20–21.

Reichard, Hugo M. 'Gulliver the Pretender.' *Papers on English Language and Literature*, I (1965), pp. 316–26.

Roscelli, William John. '*A Tale of a Tub* and the "Cavils of the Sour".' *JEGP*, LXIV (1965), pp. 41–56.

San Juan, E., jr. 'The Anti-Poetry of Jonathan Swift.' *PQ*, XLIV (1965), pp. 387–96.

Slepian, Barry. 'George Faulkner's *Dublin Journal* and Jonathan Swift.' *Library Chronicle*, University of Pennsylvania, XXXI (1965), pp. 97–116.

Smith, Raymond, J., jr. 'The "Character" of Lemuel Gulliver.' *Tulane Studies in English*, X (1965), pp. 133–40.

Steensma, Robert C. 'Swift's Model for Lord Munodi.' *N&Q*, XII (1965), pp. 216–17.

Suits, Conrad. 'The Rôle of the Horses in "A Voyage to the Houyhnhnms".' *UTQ*, XXXIV (1965), pp. 118–32.

Swift, Jonathan. *A Selection of his Works*. Ed. Philip Pinkus. Macmillan, Toronto and London; St. Martin's, New York, 1965, pp. xxxix + 517.

—— *Œuvres*. Édition présentée, établie et annotée par Émile Pons, avec la collaboration de Jacques et Maurice Pons et Benedicte Lilamand. Bibliothèque de la Pléiade, 180. Gallimard, Sainte Catherine, Bruges, 1965, pp. xli + 1940.

—— *The Correspondence of Jonathan Swift*. Ed. Harold Williams. Oxford University Press, 1965, vol. IV, 1732–6, pp. xix + 560; vol. V, 1737–45, pp. xii + 404.

Tyne, James L., S.J. 'Gulliver's Maker and Gullibility.' *Criticism*, VII (1965), pp. 151–67.

Waingrow, Marshall. ' "Verses on the Death of Dr. Swift".' *SEL*, V (1965), pp. 513–18.

Williams, Kathleen. 'Restoration Themes in the Major Satires of Swift.' *RES*, new ser., XVI (1965), pp. 258–71.

Yeomans, W. E. 'The Houyhnhnm as Menippean Horse.' *CE*, XXVII (1966), pp. 449–54.

Zall, Paul M. 'Lolita and Gulliver.' *Satire Newsletter*, III (1965), pp. 33–37.

Zimansky, Curt A. 'Gulliver, Yahoos, and Critics.' *CE*, XXVII (1965), pp. 45–49.

Notes on Contributors

J. C. BECKETT was educated at the Royal Belfast Academical Institution and the Queen's University, Belfast. After being History Master at the Belfast Royal Academy (1934–45) he joined the staff of the Queen's University, Belfast, as Lecturer in History (1945–52). He was Reader in this subject (1952–8) and was appointed to his present post as Professor of Irish History in 1958. His publications include *Protestant Dissent in Ireland, 1687–1780* (1948); (with T. W. Moody) *Queen's, Belfast, 1845–1949* (1959); *Short History of Ireland* (3rd ed. 1966); and *The Naming of Modern Ireland* (1966).

MARJORIE W. BUCKLEY is a graduate of the University of Alberta and of Baylor University. She studied drama at the Frank Lloyd Wright Theater in Dallas, has received four awards in the Canadian Playwriting Competition, and published a book on costume for the amateur stage in 1960, her play on Emily Brontë being published by the Canada Council the following year. She is at present teaching drama and literature at Edmonton, Alberta, and is writing a play about Swift and Stella.

HERBERT DAVIS was a Professor of English in the universities of Toronto (1922–37) and Cornell (1938–40), then President of Smith College from 1940 to 1949. At the University of Oxford he was Reader in Textual Criticism (1949–53) and Professor until his retirement in 1960. He is the Editor of the *Prose Works of Jonathan Swift*, 14 vols. (1939–) and also edited *The Drapier's Letters* (1935; reprinted 1965). He has written various essays on Swift, some of which appeared in *Jonathan Swift: Essays on his Satire and other Studies* (1964); he has edited the *Complete Poems of Pope* in the Oxford Standard Authors (1966) and the *Complete Plays of William Congreve* (1966).

BONAMY DOBRÉE was educated at the Royal Military Academy, Woolwich, and the University of Cambridge. He was a lecturer at London University before becoming Professor of English at the Egyptian University, Cairo (1926–9); he was Professor of English Literature at the

University of Leeds from 1936 to 1955. His publications include *Restoration Comedy* (1924); *Essays in Biography* (1925); the Nonesuch *Vanbrugh* (1927); the World's Classics *Congreve* (1928); *Restoration Tragedy* (1929); *The London Book of English Prose*, with Herbert Read (1931); *The London Book of English Verse*, with Herbert Read (1949); *Alexander Pope* (1951); *The Early Eighteenth Century: The Oxford History of English Literature* (1959). He is at present completing a study of Kipling.

IRVIN EHRENPREIS was educated at the City College of New York (B.A., 1938) and Columbia University (Ph.D., 1944), and received an honorary degree (Docteur Honoris Causa) from the University of Besançon in 1965. Following a long career at Indiana University, he is now Professor of English at the University of Virginia. He has held research fellowships of the Guggenheim Foundation and the American Council of Learned Societies. Among his recent publications are *Fielding: Tom Jones* (1964) and an essay on Robert Lowell in *American Poetry* (1965), a collaborative volume of which he was an associate editor. The second volume of his life of Swift will appear in 1967.

MACKIE LANGHAM JARRELL is Professor of English at Connecticut College, New London, Connecticut, where she lectures on eighteenth-century English literature and Anglo-Irish literature. She received a doctoral degree from the University of Texas in 1954, and has taught at the University of Texas and at the Woman's College of the University of North Carolina. She is the author of six other articles on Swift and has recently completed a book entitled *W. B. Yeats: Irish Backgrounds and English Ways*, to be published as a Random House Study in Language and Literature.

A. NORMAN JEFFARES, who was educated in the universities of Dublin and Oxford, was Jury Professor of English in the University of Adelaide before becoming Professor of English Literature in the University of Leeds in 1957. He has lectured in various African, American, Canadian, European, and Indian Universities, edits the quarterly *A Review of English Literature*, is Chief Editor of the Writers and Critics series, Co-Editor of the Biography and Criticism series and General Editor of the New Oxford English Series. He has written biographical and critical studies of Yeats as well as editing his plays, poems, prose, and criticism in Pocket

Papermacs and his poetry in the Scholar's Library. He has written on American and Commonwealth Literature as well as Anglo-Irish, his main field of critical and editorial interest.

CLAIRE LAMONT is a graduate of the University of Edinburgh. From 1964 to 1966 she worked as Research Archivist in the School of English at the University of Leeds. At present she is working on a study of eighteenth-century Scottish literature at the University of Oxford.

F. R. LEAVIS, visiting Professor of English in the University of York since 1965, and Honorary Fellow of Downing College, Cambridge, since 1962, was educated at the Perse School and Emmanuel College, Cambridge. He was a Fellow of Downing College, Cambridge (1936–62) and University Reader in English (1959–62). He was one of the founders and the Editor of *Scrutiny* (1932–53). His publications include *D. H. Lawrence* (1930); *New Bearings in English Poetry* (1932); *Revaluation: Tradition and Development in English Poetry* (1936); *Education and the University* (1943); *The Great Tradition: George Eliot, James and Conrad* (1948); *The Common Pursuit* (1952); and *D. H. Lawrence: Novelist* (1955).

GEORGE P. MAYHEW, Harvard A.B. *magna cum laude*, M.A., Ph.D. From 1946 to 1954 he was a Teaching Fellow and Assistant Dean of Harvard College. In 1954 he moved to the California Institute of Technology, where he is now Associate Professor of English. He is the author of more than twenty articles on Swift, Yeats, and Joyce; a Fellow of the Henry Huntington Library (1962–3), publishers of his '*Rage or Raillery': The Swift Manuscripts at the Huntington Library*; co-author of a forthcoming work on Yeats, *The Shadowy Waters*, and author of *The Early Life and Art of Jonathan Swift*, also forthcoming.

VIVIAN MERCIER is Professor of English at the University of Colorado. Born in Dublin in 1919, he was educated at Portora Royal School and at Trinity College, Dublin. After obtaining a Ph.D., he went to the United States in 1946, and has taught at Bennington College, the City College of New York, and the University of California. Author of *The Irish Comic Tradition*, he has contributed to numerous periodicals and volumes of critical essays in Ireland, England, the United States, and France. He is now at work on a book about *le nouveau roman*.

NORA M. MOHLER, D.Sc., Ph.D., Professor Emeritus of Smith College, has — except for three years at the Radar Division of the National Research Commission (1944–6) — held academic positions in physics at Smith College from 1927 until 1962. She is the author of journal articles on ultraviolet spectroscopy, photography, nuclear physics, and the history of physics. She is a Fellow of the American Physical Society and the American Association for the Advancement of Science.

MARJORIE NICOLSON, Ph.D., D.Litt., L.H.D., has held distinguished academic posts, including professorships of English at Smith College (1929–41) and Columbia (1941–62) and the professorship of Renaissance Studies at Claremont Graduate School (1962–3). She is a member of the Institute for Advanced Study, Princeton. Her books include *The Art of Description, Newton Demands the Muse, Voyages to the Moon, The Breaking of the Circle, Mountain Gloom and Mountain Glory*, and *A Reader's Guide to Milton*.

GEORGE ORWELL (1903–50) was born in Bengal. He was educated at Eton, and served in the Indian Imperial Police from 1922 to 1927 before becoming a writer. His novels include *Burmese Days* (1934); *A Clergyman's Daughter* (1935); *Keep the Aspidistra Flying* (1936); *Coming up for Air* (1939); *Animal Farm* (1946); *Nineteen Eighty-Four* (1949). He also wrote *Down and Out in Paris and London* (1933); *The Road to Wigan Pier* (1937); *Homage to Catalonia* (1938); *Socialism and the English Genius* (1941); *Critical Essays* (1946); *Shooting an Elephant* (1950); *England, Your England* (1953); *Collected Essays* (1961).

RICARDO QUINTANA graduated with a B.A. from Harvard, where he also took his Ph.D. He is now a member of the English Department at the University of Wisconsin, having over the years served frequently as departmental chairman. His fields of interest are English literature of the seventeenth and eighteenth centuries, contemporary literature, and satire in general. His publications include many short items concerning Swift, and two books on Swift: *The Mind and Art of Jonathan Swift* (1936; reprinted with revisions, 1953), and *Swift: An Introduction* (1955). At the moment he is working on a critical study of Oliver Goldsmith.

A. L. ROWSE was a Scholar in English Literature at Christ Church, Oxford, but took the History school and was elected a Fellow of All

Souls College, in History. His work exemplifies his belief in the value of the historical approach to literature, and in history as equally a branch of literature. Major works: *The England of Elizabeth*, *The Expansion of Elizabethan England*, *William Shakespeare: A Biography*, a family history, *The Churchills*, studies of Sir Richard Grenville, Sir Walter Ralegh, Marlowe, and Southampton. Two volumes of autobiography and five volumes of verse attest his dual interest in literature and history. A Fellow of the British Academy. Work in progress: *The Cornish in America*, and *Poems of Cornwall and America*.

D. NICHOL SMITH (1875–1962) was the first graduate of Edinburgh University's new Honours School in English, in 1895. He spent a year at the Sorbonne, became an assistant in Glasgow University (1902), Professor at Armstrong College, Newcastle (1904), and then Goldsmiths' Reader at Oxford (1908). A Fellow of Merton College (1921), he was elected to the Merton Chair in 1929, an appointment he held until his retirement in 1946. He held the Jury Chair in the University of Adelaide in 1950–1 and had earlier visited the Huntington Library and Smith College. The bibliography in the volume of *Essays on the Eighteenth Century* demonstrates the range of his scholarship in the seventeenth- and eighteenth-century literature. He edited *A Tale of a Tub* with A. C. Guthkelch (1920; rev. ed. 1958) and *The Letters of Jonathan Swift to Charles Ford* (1935). He was general editor of the Clarendon Series of English Literature, edited *The Oxford Book of Eighteenth-Century Verse* (1926), and edited Johnson's *Poems* with Edward L. McAdam (1941). He was working on an edition of Swift's *Gulliver's Travels* at the time of his death.

KATHLEEN WILLIAMS was educated at Somerville College, Oxford, and was for some years in the English Department at the University College of South Wales and Monmouthshire as Lecturer and Senior Lecturer. She joined the University of California at Riverside in 1964, and is now a Professor of English at the Rice University, Houston, Texas. Her book *Jonathan Swift and the Age of Compromise* was published in America in 1958 and in England in 1959, and *Spenser's World of Glass*, a study of *The Faerie Queene*, appeared in 1966. She is currently working on contemporary criticism of Swift and on Renaissance poetry.

THOMAS G. WILSON is surgeon in charge of the Ear, Nose and Throat Department of the Royal City of Dublin Hospital, the National

Children's Hospital, and Dr. Steevens's Hospital, Dublin. He was President of the Royal College of Surgeons in Ireland from 1958 to 1961, is an Honorary Fellow of the Royal College of Surgeons of England and of Edinburgh. In 1942 he was awarded the Litt.D. of Trinity College, Dublin, for *Victorian Doctor*, his biography of Sir William Wilde, the father of Oscar Wilde. He has published a textbook on disease of the ear, nose, and throat and various medical and scientific papers. During the late war he received a suspensory sentence of twelve months imprisonment and was heavily fined for helping British and Allied airmen to escape from internment in Ireland.

His interest in both Swift and Wilde dates from shortly after he graduated from Trinity College, Dublin, when he was appointed to the staff of Dr. Steevens's Hospital with which both were closely connected.

VIRGINIA WOOLF (1882–1941) was a daughter of Sir Leslie Stephen, the scholar and critic who edited the English Men of Letters series. She was privately educated. In 1912 she married Leonard Woolf, with whom she founded the Hogarth Press in 1917. Her novels include *The Voyage Out* (1915); *Night and Day* (1919); *Jacob's Room* (1922); *Mrs. Dalloway* (1925); *To the Lighthouse* (1927); *Orlando* (1928); *The Years* (1937). Some of her critical work is included in *Mr. Bennett and Mrs. Brown* (1924); *The Common Reader* (1925); *A Room of One's Own* (1929); and *The Second Common Reader* (1932).

W. B. YEATS (1865–1939) was the son of an Irish artist. He wrote poetry from his teens to his seventy-third year. His critical writing appeared in newspapers and journals, in introductions, in volumes of essays, and in his autobiographical studies. Most of his published work is contained in the following volumes, which are in print: *Collected Poems*; *Collected Plays*; *Explorations*; *Essays and Introductions*; *A Vision: Mythologies*; and *Autobiographies*. The *Variorum Edition of the Poems* (ed. Peter Allt and Russell K. Alspach) gives an account of his numerous revisions and rewritings as does *The Variorum Edition of the Plays* (ed. Peter Alspach). *The Letters of W. B. Yeats* (ed. Allan Wade) also provide critical comments, and *A Bibliography of the Writings of W. B. Yeats* (ed. Allan Wade) provides a guide to the different editions of his works. This will be supplemented by *A Bibliography of Yeats Criticism* (ed. K. G. W. Cross and Ronald Dunlop) to be published by Macmillan.

Index

Note: Passing references to any item in this index on several consecutive pages are indicated by the first and last page number only. Pages where an item is discussed more fully are shown in italic type.

PRINTED IN GREAT BRITAIN BY ROBERT MACLEHOSE AND CO. LTD
THE UNIVERSITY PRESS, GLASGOW